D0309928

Metaphors of mind

Metaphors of mind

Conceptions of the nature of intelligence

Robert J. Sternberg
Yale University

CAMBRIDGE
UNIVERSITY PRESS

PUBLISHED BY THE PRESS SYNDICATE OF THE UNIVERSITY OF CAMBRIDGE
The Pitt Building, Trumpington Street, Cambridge CB2 1RP, United Kingdom

CAMBRIDGE UNIVERSITY PRESS
The Edinburgh Building, Cambridge CB2 2RU, United Kingdom
40 West 20th Street, New York, NY 10011-4211, USA
10 Stamford Road, Oakleigh, Melbourne 3166, Australia

© Cambridge University Press 1990

This book is in copyright. Subject to statutory exception and
to the provisions of relevant collective licensing agreements,
no reproduction of any part may take place without
the written permission of Cambridge University Press.

First published 1990
Reprinted 1990, 1992, 1993, 1995, 1997

Printed in the United States of America

Typeset in Times

A catalogue record for this book is available from the British Library

Library of Congress Cataloguing-in-Publication Data is available

ISBN 0-521-35579-6 hardback
ISBN 0-521-38633-0 paperback

This book is dedicated to the members of my research group at Yale, past and present, who have made possible the development of my thinking and research on the nature of intelligence:

Eric Amsel	Michael Barnes	Cynthia Berg
Kastoor Bhana	David Caruso	Holly Chen
Barbara Conway	Janet Davidson	Diane Dobson
Cathryn Downing	Peter Foltz	Louis Forster
Peter Frensch	Michael Gardner	Joyce Gastel
Susan Grajek	Martin Guyote	Jacky Hawkins
Alice Jackson	Daniel Kaye	Jerry Ketron
John Kolligian	Maria Lasaga	Man Liu
Todd Lubart	Diana Marr	Marie Martin
Timothy McNamara	Elizabeth Neuse	Georgia Nigro
Lynn Okagaki	Janet Powell	Bathsheva Rifkin
Robert Rist	Margarita Rodriguez	Brian Ross
Patricia Ruzgis	William Salter	Miriam Schustack
Julie Sincoff	Lawrence Soriano	Louise Spear
Judith Suben	Diane Svigals	Sheldon Tetewsky
Roger Tourangeau	Meg Turner	Richard Wagner
Evelyn Weil	Wendy Williams	Sandra Wright

Contents

Tables

Preface

Some books come quickly, others come slowly. This book came slowly. I first envisioned writing the book during my last year of graduate school at Stanford – in 1975. My plan was to write it during my first year as an assistant professor at Yale, when I signed on to teach an upper level undergraduate course, Theories of Intelligence. But like Tristram Shandy trying to write the story of his life, I found that I could not keep up in my book writing and, in my case, with my teaching. Eventually, I fell hopelessly behind in my writing and was left with rough drafts of four chapters.

The book sat still for a number of years. For a period during the late 1970s and early 1980s, the field seemed to be moving so rapidly forward that I thought any book such as this one that I might write would so quickly become out of date that there was no point to writing it then.

Three years ago, I received a Guggenheim Fellowship to write this book, but found myself not quite ready to write it. Instead I wrote an invited lead article for *Science,* "Human intelligence: The model is the message," which became the basis for the book. Indeed, it was not until after I wrote that article that I realized what form this book would take, a form completely different from what I originally envisioned.

Metaphors of mind: Conceptions of the nature of intelligence is a book about how people in various disciplines, but especially psychology, have viewed intelligence. The main theme is that theories of intelligence are guided by underlying metaphors of mind. To understand the theories and their interrelations properly, one has to understand the underlying metaphors. Moreover, in comparing theories, it is important to distinguish between comparisons that occur within versus across metaphors. Comparing theories across metaphors is much like comparing apples and oranges: Both are fruits, but fruits of a different kind. Similarly, theories guided by, or in some cases even generated by, different metaphors are all theories, but of different kinds. Typically, they deal with different aspects of intelligence, and comparisons are somewhat fruitless, much as would be comparing answers to different questions. Although the theories may appear to be answering the same question – What is intelligence? – it turns out that the question really is: What is intelligence as viewed from the standpoint of a particular metaphor? In order fully to understand intelligence, we need to understand that through a skillful blending, as opposed to a haphazard mixing, of the various metaphors, one can make sense of it. This book, therefore, is addressed to students of intelligence who seek to understand what may at times seem to be a bewildering variety of unintegrated and even unintegrable points of view.

There certainly exist many other volumes on the topic of intelligence, including some highly comprehensive ones (Sternberg, 1982a; Wolman, 1985). And there are certainly many accounts of how a model-based approach can be applied to the understanding of the human mind (Chapman & Jones, 1980; Gentner & Grudin, 1985; Roediger, 1980). But I believe that this volume is the first comprehensively to apply a metaphor-based approach to the study of different kinds of theories of intelligence, just as my 1985 *Science* article was the first article to approach this task. The idea of metaphors in conceptualizing intelligence is not new, however, going back at least to Spearman (1927) and, arguably, to Plato in his cave metaphor.

I have attempted to bring together into a systematic and comprehensive framework all of the major theories of human intelligence that have been proposed during the twentieth century and to include as well material on the nature of intelligence that dates back well before the beginning of the twentieth century. The book differs from many others on intelligence in that it attempts to deal solely with alternative conceptions of intelligence and with how they have been guided by metaphors and expressed as definitions and theories. No attempt has been made to deal with the many other issues that confront intelligence research – such as heritability, testing, and training of intelligence – except as these issues directly follow from the definitions and theories to be considered. Thus, these issues are considered as outgrowths of theory, rather than the other way around, as has been conventional in the field of human intelligence.

The book is divided into five main parts. These parts are Introduction, Definitions of intelligence, Theories of intelligence looking inward,

Theories of intelligence looking outward, and Theories of intelligence looking inward and outward.

In Part I, which consists of a single chapter, I deal with the idea of metaphors as providing the underlying foundations for theories of intelligence. I discuss the role metaphors play in science, and in the science of human intelligence in particular. I describe the alternative metaphors that have been used and how they have affected the way intelligence is perceived by various theoreticians and practitioners. I also argue that students of intelligence have often unwittingly fallen victim to their own synecdoches: They have constructed a theory of part of the phenomenon of intelligence and have mistakenly believed their theory to apply to the phenomenon as a whole. Yet any one metaphor cannot possibly serve as a complete basis for understanding any construct, certainly not one as complex as human intelligence.

Part II presents and discusses various pretheoretical ideas about the nature of intelligence. These take the form of definitions, or implicit theories. Definitions of intelligence are essentially ideas about the nature of intelligence that exist in the minds of those who create the definitions. They might be referred to as "implicit theories" because they are theories that exist, in some sense, in people's heads, without being explicitly formalized as scientific theories. People may or may not be aware that they have these implicit theories. But it is important to realize that all explicit theories of intelligence, of the kind discussed in the remainder of the book, originally arise from implicit theories. Even theories that are empirically derived, such as through factor analysis, have their bases in implicit theories, because the implicit theories are what generated the choice of tests, and hence the universe of possible factors, in the first place. Thus, in order fully to understand explicit scientific theories and the metaphors that underlie them, we need first to understand the implicit theories that gave rise to them.

In Chapter 2, I discuss historical views of intelligence, ranging from those of ancient philosophers to those of philosophers at the end of the nineteenth century. Obviously, such a wide-ranging treatment of ideas about intelligence cannot possibly be complete. But it does cover the views of many major thinkers. In some cases, these views may be idiosyncratic, but, for the most part, they are at the heart of Western thought. Often without our even realizing it, these ideas have heavily influenced twentieth-century thinking about intelligence. They are so much a part of our way of thinking and of our assumptions of how we should understand intelligence that we are hardly aware that these ideas even exist.

In Chapter 3, I discuss contemporary views of intelligence – that is, those of the twentieth century. There are many sources to which one could turn for an understanding of how people in this century have defined intelligence, but I have concentrated on three major sources of thought. The first two are symposia on the nature of intelligence, one of which appeared in the *Journal of Educational Psychology* in 1921 and the other of which appeared in a book edited by myself and Douglas Detterman in 1986. The other main source comes from studies explicitly addressing people's implicit theories of the nature of intelligence. There have been a number of such studies, looking at various groups of respondents and target populations, and these studies give a broad panorama of how people in various walks of life view intelligence as it applies to a variety of populations.

I devote an entire chapter, Chapter 4, to the views of just two early theorists, Galton and Binet, who might be viewed as the forefathers of most contemporary work on intelligence. Galton is most well known for his work at the end of the nineteenth century and Binet for his work at the beginning of the twentieth century, although the two overlapped somewhat in the time span of their work. In order to understand virtually all that has been done on intelligence in the twentieth century, one has to understand the thinking of Galton and Binet. The tension that existed between their contrasting points of view is one that has continued even to the present day in various attempts to understand the nature of intelligence. To a large extent, the conflict between them set the stage for the conflict that was to emerge among contemporary theorists.

Part III is about theories of intelligence that look inward. The four main metaphors looking inward are the geographic, computational, biological, and epistemological. These provide understanding of intelligence in terms of the internal world of the individual – in terms of what goes on inside the head when a person thinks or acts intelligently. To understand intelligence, theorists guided by these metaphors seek to understand mental processes, structures, representations, and content.

Chapter 5 deals with theories guided by a geographic metaphor of intelligence, in which intelligence is understood in terms of a map of the mind. To understand intelligence would be to understand the map that underlies our basic processes of thought, and theorists of intelligence adhering to a geographic metaphor could be viewed as cartographers, seeking tools to help them create maps that accurately locate and describe the various abilities that constitute human intelligence. These cartographers of the mind have not always been quick to realize that, similar to the physical world, there is no one map or set of coordinate systems that uniquely portrays a geographic structure. Rather, alternative mappings are possible, depending on the coordinate system and the particular phenomena upon which one chooses to concentrate.

Chapter 6 concerns the computational metaphor of mind. The theories dealt with here view the mind, roughly, in terms of the software of a computer or other computing device. Some of the theorists explicitly use computer simulation; others do not. But all share the notion that the mind, like the computer, is a computational device. Therefore, in theory at least, the mind could be simulated on a computer powerful enough to represent the mind's complexity. Computational theories were originally proposed in experimental psychology as an alternative to stimulus–response and other forms of behavioral theorizing. In the field of human intelligence, though, they quickly became perceived as an alternative to psychometric theorizing and, therefore, to what I have called the geographic metaphor. In their early work, computational theorists were sometimes disdainful of geographic ones, believing that what they did served as a replacement for geographic theorizing. In retrospect, many of these theorists realized that the computational metaphor is complementary to the geographic metaphor. Computational processes can be mapped onto geographic structures, and vice versa, so that the two approaches can be used in conjunction rather than in mutual exclusion.

The topic of Chapter 7 is the biological metaphor underlying some theories of intelligence. Some theorists of intelligence have felt that computational theories do not go far enough – that although they may tell us something about the workings of the human mind, they do so at so molar a level that little or no connection can be made with the organ of intelligence, namely, the brain. Biological theorists seek to make this connection and hence, in some sense, represent the ultimate in reductionism for the study of human intelligence. In much of the biological work, the connection between behavioral data and the biology of the brain proves to be somewhat speculative and is itself metaphorical. But in other work, direct mappings of functions to areas of the human brain are attempted, and some of these have generated quite a bit of excitement, seeming to isolate portions of the brain that are responsible for various cognitive and other functions observed in intelligent behavior. These theories are not really a replacement for computational or geographic ones. To understand the functioning of a car, one might seek a knowledge of molecular structures of the various parts of the car, but one might also seek to map out these various parts or to understand their molar functions. When a car does not start, one seeks to localize the source of the difficulty and the function that is not being performed correctly; one probably does not investigate at a molecular level. As with understanding of the car, understanding of the mind can be sought at multiple levels and in multiple ways, none of which is intrinsically any "better" than any other.

Chapter 8, unlike the other chapters in this book, deals with a metaphor that is largely, although not exclusively, attributable to just a single individual – the epistemological metaphor of Jean Piaget. Although Piaget's work was influenced by biology as well as philosophy, the philosophical underpinnings are stronger, I believe, and the metaphor is largely one that seeks to understand the mind in terms of the structure of knowledge. The obvious advantage of this approach is that the powerful machinery of the field of epistemology can be brought to bear on the study of the mind. The obvious danger is that the structure of knowledge will be confused with the structure of the mind. Indeed, many have argued that Piaget's theory is a theory of human competence rather than of human performance. But whatever may be the case, the epistemological metaphor has proved to be a powerful and influential one in studying thinking. Like the metaphors described above, it was generated largely in response to the geographic metaphor. Indeed, Piaget worked in Binet's laboratory, and his interest in intelligence grew partly as a result of his interest in the bases of wrong rather than right answers in children's responses to questions on the Binet–Simon Intelligence Scale. The epistemological metaphor, as used by Piaget, is the most interactive of the metaphors considered in this part of the book with respect to the relation between the internal and external worlds of the individual, and hence provides a natural bridge to the next part.

Part IV deals with theories of intelligence looking outward. These theories provide understanding of intelligence primarily in terms of the external world of the individual. The theories draw on two main metaphors, anthropological and sociological, although these are not always clearly distinguishable.

In Chapter 9, I discuss the anthropological metaphor for theories of intelligence. Theories guided by this metaphor seek to understand how culture affects or even determines the nature of intelligence. Those ad-hering to this metaphor believe that, at minimum, the nature of intelli-gence differs at least somewhat from culture to culture. At the extreme, theorists adhering to this metaphor believe that intelligence is essentially a different thing in one culture versus another. Thus, these theorists are characterized by the view that the nature of intelligence differs qualita-tively across cultures. Therefore, direct quantitative comparisons of levels of intelligence of people in different cultures are often meaning-less, because the comparisons are on different scales, and deceptive, because the numbers mean different things for different cultures. Thus, for these theorists, levels of intelligence can be compared much more easily within than between cultures. Sometimes even that is difficult, because individuals may come from different subcultures that stress different aspects of adaptive behavior as intelligent. Unsurprisingly, theorists guided by the anthropological metaphor have been highly critical of theorists who are guided by metaphors of intelligence that look inward to understand the nature of intelligence, because anthropo-logically oriented theorists believe that intelligence cannot be under-stood outside its cultural context. For them, any metaphor that seeks to understand intelligence simply in terms of the inner mechanisms of mind misses the critical point that intelligence is not just a set of processes or structures in the head. Rather, it is in large part a cultural invention.

Whereas the anthropological theorists described in Chapter 9 have been highly critical of metaphors that look inward, the sociological theorists discussed in Chapter 10 have been critical particularly of the epistemological metaphor as applied by Piaget. The most well known of these theorists, Lev Vygotsky, to some extent argued the opposite of Piaget's point of view. Whereas Piaget argued that intelligence moves from the inside outward – that we first learn what needs to be done by and for ourselves, and that we later externalize it – Vygotsky argued that we do the opposite – that we learn first from seeing what other people do, usually in social settings, and then internalize it. In other words, Vygotsky theorized from the outside inward, whereas Piaget theorized from the inside outward. Vygotsky emphasized the role of socialization processes in human intellectual development, as did Reuven Feuerstein after him, but the idea is that we cannot understand intelligence unless we understand the social forces that shape it.

Part V covers very recent theories of intelligence that seek simulta-neously to look both inward and outward. Chapter 11 deals primarily with the two most recent: Howard Gardner's theory of multiple intelligences and my own triarchic theory of human intelligence. Each of these theories tries in a different way to combine aspects of the various metaphors described above. In effect, they employ a systems metaphor in which the system consists of the different parts of intelligence as conceived by a number of various metaphors. Gardner, for example, draws heavily on the geographic metaphor but uses the biological one as well. I draw heavily on the computational metaphor but also draw on the anthropological and sociological ones. But whatever the combination may be, the paramount idea is not to be locked into one system, but rather to draw on many systems and thereby seek to obtain a more nearly full understanding of what intelligence is. In Chapter 12, I discuss the implications of the metaphorical approach and attempt to show why it is important to understand theories of intelligence in terms of the metaphors that guide them.

As is always true, a number of people have contributed to the formation of the ideas in the production of this book. Probably most important has been my research group at Yale, to whom the book is dedicated. My colleagues in this group have conversed with and supported me ever since I came to Yale, and I owe them an enormous debt. Of course, the thinking in this book represents an amalgamation of that of many theorists of intelligence, all of whom have contributed immensely to the ideas contained within. Sandra Wright typed the manuscript and did the name index. Susan Milmoe contracted the book, many years ago. She waited patiently for a manuscript to appear. To you all, I am grateful.

Part I

Introduction

1

Metaphors as the foundations for theories of intelligence

Upon her death bed, Gertrude Stein has been said to have inquired, "What is the answer?" Getting no answer, she said, "In that case, what is the question?" (Toklas, 1963)

Metaphors as a way of viewing the mind

In the study of human intelligence, perhaps no response is more apt. Once a question about intelligence is posed, one must go yet one step further back, and wonder, why that question? The root source of many of the questions asked about intelligence appears to be the model, or metaphor, that drives the theory and research. In order to understand the evolution and current state of theory and research on intelligence, one must first look at the metaphors that have motivated the theory and research and then at the questions that the metaphors have generated in the theories addressed. The study of human intelligence has been marked by noisy and often passionate debates, but debates that have seemingly been over answers have, as often as not, truly been debates over metaphors and the questions about intelligence they generate. If the debates have been unresolved, and usually they have been, it is perhaps because their true nature has so often gone unrecognized. People have as often talked past each other as to each other, without even recognizing that they are doing so.

The basic thesis of this book, following Kuhn (1970), is that research in the field of human intelligence, as in other scientific fields of endeavor, is guided by a somewhat motley collection of models or metaphors. Each metaphor generates a series of questions about intelligence, which the theories and research seek to address. Scientists are sometimes unaware of the exact nature of the metaphor underlying the research, and may even be unclear about the particular and limited set of questions that their metaphor generates. They may thus see their partial theories, which address only the questions generated by a single

Table 1.1. *Synopsis of major alternative metaphors of intelligence*

Metaphor	Major motivating (presupposed) question	Major motivating (derivative) question	Typical theories	Typical Theorists
Geographic	What is the relation of intelligence to the internal world of the individual?	What form does a map of the mind take?	Two-factor Primary mental abilities Structure-of-intellect Hierarchical	Spearman Thurstone Guilford Cattell–Vernon
Computational	What is the relation of intelligence to the internal world of the individual?	What are the information-processing routines (programs) underlying intelligent thought?	Verbal efficiency Componential	Hunt Sternberg
Biological	What is the relation of intelligence to the internal world of the individual?	How do the anatomy and physiology of the brain and the central nervous system account for intelligent thought?	Hemispheric localization Speed of neural transmission Accuracy of neural transmission	Levy Jensen Eysenck
Epistemological	What is the relation of intelligence to the internal world of the individual?	What are the structures of the mind through which knowledge and mental processes are organized?	Genetic epistemological	Piaget
Anthropological	What is the relation of intelligence to the external world of the individual?	What forms does intelligence take as a cultural invention?	Radical cultural relativism Conditional comparativism Ethological	Berry Cole Charlesworth
Sociological	What is the relation of intelligence to the external world of the individual?	How are social processes in development internalized?	Zone of proximal development Mediated learning experience	Vygotsky Feuerstein
Systems	What is the relation of intelligence to the internal and external worlds of the individual?	How can we understand the mind as a system in a way that crosscuts metaphors?	Multiple intelligences Triarchic	Gardner Sternberg

metaphor, as full theories of a phenomenon. Comparison of their theories with alternative ones derived from the same metaphor (within-metaphor comparison) can be fruitful, but comparisons with alternative theories derived from different metaphors (between-metaphor comparison) can be frustrating. The alternative partial theories are not really theories of the same thing, namely, that part of the phenomenon under investigation. Moreover, even the within-metaphor comparison may be less meaningful than the scientists believe, because experimental operations that they view as choosing the "correct" theory of intelligence may merely be serving to distinguish among alternative instantiations of a given metaphor. The theory may indeed be correct in some respects, but that correctness is predicated on the usefulness of the metaphor underlying it.

By becoming more aware of the metaphors underlying their theories and research, and of the specific questions that their metaphors generate, scientists should become more aware of both the range and boundaries of their theories with respect to the phenomenon they seek to investigate. In particular, scientists may have a better idea both of the questions that their theories can address and of those that they cannot address because of the limitations of the metaphors upon which they are predicated.

In this book, I will examine some of the principal metaphors that have underlain theories of intelligence and the particular theories that have been guided by these metaphors. In examining these metaphors and theories, I will be particularly concerned with how they address either or both of two questions:

1. What is the relation of intelligence to the internal world of the individual?
2. What is the relation of intelligence to the external world of the individual?

A better appreciation of the questions and their answers, and of the latent metaphors guiding theory and research on intelligence, can help move the field forward and assist us in recognizing properly the role of past contributions in shaping future ones. I believe it is difficult to understand the history of theoretical work on intelligence and how the different approaches to intelligence interrelate unless one understands past and present theories in terms of their underlying metaphors.

Table 1.1 lists the various metaphors that have underlain intelligence research and some theories guided by these metaphors, as well as the principal question about human intelligence that each of the theories has addressed. Today, as in the past, there seem to be as many definitions of intelligence as there are investigators of it, with each definition depending, to some extent, on both the metaphor and the theory used. Two chapters – Chapters 2 and 3 – will be devoted to definitions of intelligence. But in order to make clear my biases up front, I should say that I define intelligence as consisting of those mental functions purposively employed for purposes of adaptation to, and shaping and selection of, real-world environments.

Table 1.1 provides a synopsis of the various metaphors considered in Parts III, IV, and V of this book. Part II deals with implicit theories, including definitions, and hence does not fall under the metaphorical rubric. Six metaphors are considered.

The geographic metaphor

The geographic metaphor is based on the notion that a theory of intelligence should provide a map of the mind. The use of the map as a metaphor almost automatically generates certain questions, but not others. Geographic theories will specialize in answering questions such as the following:

1. What are the latent sources of individual differences, or factors, along which people differ that generate observed individual differences in psychometric test scores?
2. How do people differ with respect to their scores on each of these factors?
3. How does the map of the mind evolve as an individual grows older? For example, do the factors of intelligence become more differentiated with age?
4. How predictive is each of the factors of intelligence of performance criteria, such as grades in school?

Various factorial theories compete to answer these questions. The competition often seems no more sensible than would a competition between a map using Cartesian coordinates and a map using polar coordinates, or between a geographical map and a topographical map. A given geographical entity or set of entities can be mapped in many different ways, and often the alternative theories correspond to different ways of mapping the same regions. In fact, there are an infinite number of possible maps that could be correct for a given geographical region, and which map is best turns out to be a question of usefulness rather than of veridicality. Each map may be useful, but for its own particular purposes. The major difference among the geographic theories is in the way in which they orient axes within a factorial space, and mathematically, any orientation of axes is correct. The argument among theorists often therefore becomes one of what the correct psychological orientation of axes is, but of course, there is no one correct orientation. If one wishes simply to predict overall performance, a theory that emphasizes a general factor may be most useful. If one wishes differential prediction, a theory that emphasizes various group factors may be more useful.

Because geographic theories are structural, they tend to address questions about structure but not about other aspects of intelligence. For example, most of the geographically based theories have little or nothing to say about process, although there are exceptions to this generalization (e.g., Guilford, 1967). Moreover, they have nothing to say about how the geographic regions that are isolated map into the brain. Although geographic theorists can deal with development by showing maps of the mind at different points in a child's developmental course, geographic theories do not tend to deal with the transition mechanisms that lead individuals from one map to another. Because the theories are static, they simply do not deal with dynamic development, the way, say, a biological or sociological theory can. Geographically based theories also tend to be derived on the basis of individual-difference data, so that their depiction of intelligence is in terms of sources of individual differences. To the extent that intellectual abilities exist that are common in both the nature and level of ability across people, geographical theories tend not to represent them.

A difficult issue for all of the geographic theorists is how fine a mapping one wishes of the mind. A major source of disagreement among geographic theorists has been in terms of how many factors of intelligence there are, but if one appreciates the metaphor underlying these theories, one realizes that this debate is a fruitless one. Just as different kinds of mappings are possible, so are different degrees of differentiation within regions. For example, a map of a state or province will go into much greater detail with regard to cities and communities within the state or province than will a map of an entire country. Just as it is possible to split geographic subdivisions essentially endlessly, so is it possible to split factors of the mind by including within the battery of tests narrower and narrower portions of the spectrum of human abilities.

The point to be realized here is that when one views geographic theories in terms of the metaphor that underlies them, one better appreciates both the strengths and the weaknesses of the theories. Questions that have been paramount in the minds of the theorists and have been major sources of debate seem to be fruitless in terms of yielding a unique answer. There is no correct orientation of axes or number of factors in a factorial theory, any more than there is any one correct orientation of axes or degree of localization in a map of a geographic region. Moreover, just as maps can answer some questions about a region but not others, so can geographically based theories answer some questions about intelligence but not others. Appreciating the metaphor leads one to a better sense of what questions can and cannot be answered by any theory that subscribes to a given metaphor.

The computational metaphor

The computational metaphor envisions the mind as a computing device and analogizes the processes of the mind to the operations (software) of a computer. The metaphor has proven enormously productive of both theory and research. Perhaps because the computational metaphor was generated largely in response to the geographic one, its strengths and weaknesses tend to be complementary. For example, whereas the geographic metaphor, because of its static nature, tends to be weak in addressing questions of process, the computational metaphor tends to be very strong in addressing questions of process. But in the computational metaphor, inferences about structure are much more indirect than they are in the geographic metaphor, in which the results of a factor analysis directly provide a structural model. Moreover, whereas data from experiments generated by geographically based theories primarily make use of individual-differences data, data from experiments generated by computationally based theories tend to focus on commonalities across people and processing. Normally, the main source of variation observed is across stimulus conditions rather than across subjects, with the result that the computational metaphor tends to be strong in pointing out commonalities in processing rather than individual differences. Indeed, many information-processing studies do not consider individual differences at all, whereas psychometric studies virtually always do.

The computational metaphor seemed, when it was first used, to be an answer to the ever proliferating number of factors being posited by geographic theorists. But in fact, it provides no answer, because just as factors can be subdivided endlessly, so can processes be endlessly subdivided. For example, one can speak of "encoding" stimuli, but certainly there are many subprocesses involved in figuring out what a stimulus is. Again, there is no one correct level of analysis: It depends upon what one wishes to do with the theory. But it is important to realize that arguments over how finely processes should be split will tend to be fruitless, because there is no one right answer. For example, in a computer program, one would wish to pay more attention to the details of how stimuli are perceived in a program that is designed to simulate visual perception than in a program that uses visual perception only in the service of, say, inductive reasoning.

Because of the insensitivity of many computational theorists to individual differences, these theorists have not always been quick to realize that often there is no one correct information-processing model, either of performance on a given task or of performance on classes of tasks. Rather, there may well be individual differences in the processes and strategies different people use to solve a given problem or class of problems. Indeed, the particular processes or strategies that an individual chooses may depend in part on the structure of his or her abilities as revealed by a geographically based theory. In early work (e.g., Sternberg, 1977), there was a tendency to view elementary information processes as underlying factors. In other words, the idea was that by isolating the processes of intelligence, we could identify for each geographic factor what the underlying computational mechanisms were. But it has become clear that there is no real way of knowing whether it is the processes that underlie the factors or the factors that underlie the processes. It could just as well be that certain structural entities in the brain generate the various processes isolated by information-processing analyses. Hence, arguments over which level of analysis is more basic, say, geographic or computational, are likely to go nowhere. In general, it will be shown throughout the book that questions as to what metaphor is "most basic" are fruitless: Metaphors are not right or wrong; they are more or less useful for various purposes.

Computational theorists have argued among themselves as to exactly what constitutes an information-processing theory. Some theorists, such as Newell and Simon (1972), have viewed their computer programs as the theories themselves. Other investigators, such as Schank (1972), view computer programs as operationalizations, and imperfect ones at that, of theories. My own thinking tends to be in accord with

Schank, but again, I doubt that there is a right or wrong answer regarding what, exactly, is the underlying theory.

Perhaps the biggest danger with computational metaphors is that they will fail to distinguish the forest from the trees. Because they tend to deal with information processing at a nitty-gritty level, it is easy for computational theorists to get wrapped up in the details of information processing and at times to lose sight of why they are studying a particular task or even of where performance on that task fits into the grander scheme of things. Certainly, not all information-processing theorists are guilty of tunnel vision, or of losing the forest, but there are many information-processing theories in studies of task performance that, while elegant, at the same time seem to tell us relatively little about fundamental and generalizable principles of intelligence.

The biological metaphor

Biologically based theories seek to understand intelligence in terms of the functioning of the brain. Because our understanding of the brain is still quite rudimentary, biological theories often have a highly speculative tinge associated with them. Data that have been collected, for the most part, are of three kinds.

The first kind results from studies that seek to localize specific abilities in the brain. Most commonly, subjects are patients who have had damage of one kind or another that has resulted in the destruction of a portion of the brain. This portion of the brain is considered no longer to be functional, and neuropsychologists study the effects of the lesion on information processing. In other words, they seek to find out what functions are lost as a result of the damage to the brain. Most of the neuropsychologists who do this kind of work are not interested just in intelligence, but in cognitive functioning more generally. However, their findings often have important implications for intelligence research. The biggest problem in interpreting this research is that the data from different laboratories often seem to be contradictory. These contradictions could well result from differences in the patients studied or in the exact methods used to study the patients. But the picture that emerges from this research is not always crystal clear. Nevertheless, this kind of research has been very informative with regard to localization of certain intellectual functions.

My worry in interpreting these studies is that data from patients with severe lesions may not generalize to or be representative of the population at large. In other words, the patients used in these studies are obviously highly nonrepresentative of a typical population that would be studied by other psychologists, and it is possible that because of this nonrepresentativeness, false generalizations could be made. However, it is obviously not possible to create lesions in humans just for the purpose of studying intelligence, so the data we get are about as good as can possibly be hoped for. Of course, lesions are sometimes purposely created in animals, but we still end up with a generalization problem, in this case, the generalization from other species to the human one.

A second kind of data is electrophysiological. Electrodes are generally taped to a person's skull, and evoked potentials or EEGs are measured either while subjects are at rest or while they are performing some task. The idea here is usually to look at patterns in the electrophysiological data or to combine the data into one or more scores and then relate the patterns or scores to measures that are believed to assess intelligence, such as the Wechsler Adult Intelligence Scale. The data obtained from users of electrophysiological paradigms have been highly variable, but so have been the locations at which recordings have been made as well as the measures used to summarize the electrophysiological data. In a number of instances, moderate or even fairly high correlations have been obtained between scores on electrophysiological indices and scores on conventional intelligence tests. Enough positive data have been obtained to suggest that there is some relationship, although the exact nature of the relationship is not yet clear.

As I read the data, there are two major problems in the electrophysiological approach as it pertains to intelligence. These problems need to be taken into account in interpreting electrophysiological data.

First, the astonishingly large number of recording sites available as well as ways of scoring and summarizing the data from electrophysiological studies leaves a fairly wide margin for capitalization on chance. We need to be at least somewhat concerned with the replicability of results, in particular, replicability outside the laboratory in which a certain data set was initially collected, and even replicability outside the sphere of influence of the researchers who collected those data. This concern seems especially important, as in at least one instance, the reported correlation between an electrophysiological index and measured IQ was roughly at the level of the reliabilities of the measures, a result that is likely to arouse suspicion in at least some readers of the original report.

Second, although it is tempting to leap to causal explanations of significant correlations, especially when electrophysiological data are involved, one must be cautious in interpreting the correlations, in some cases, more cautious than the investigators themselves. Many electrophysiological measures are composite hash recordings. A tremendous number of different variables go into any one index. As a result, it is hazardous to ascribe causal status to the number expressing the electrophysiological performance, because it is almost never clear what this number represents. At best, it is often some hashlike index so that we replace one unknown general factor with another unknown, a "general hash index." There is often a very substantial gap between the operationalization and the conceptual conclusion drawn from it. It seems as likely that cognitive variables influence electrophysiological ones, as the other way around. For example, changes in attention have been shown to influence the P300 evoked potential, so that in studies of P300, attention can be viewed as the causal variable, rather than P300. Of course, it is also possible that both the electrophysiological recording and the cognitive process are dependent on some third, higher order variable, the nature of which may not be immediately clear. All of this is to say that whereas it is tempting to draw reductionist conclusions from electrophysiological data, at the present time it is probably a mistake. The correlations are interesting and even tantalizing, but we need to go a long way before they are explained.

The third kind of paradigm, and, to my mind, certainly the most fruitful in terms of the conclusions that can be drawn from it, involves measurement of blood flow in the brain during cognitive processing. Some investigators have monitored blood flow as revealed by the distribution of a radioactive isotope during cognitive processing, and the monitoring of blood flow is probably the most direct way we presently have of localizing in what parts of the brain different forms of cognitive processing take place. Blood flow studies do not fall prey to some of the criticisms that would apply to hemispheric-specialization and evoked-potential studies and therefore seem especially useful as a way of mapping intellectual functions onto the brain.

The epistemological metaphor

The epistemological metaphor is due primarily to Jean Piaget, although Piaget was influenced by others, such as James Mark Baldwin. Piaget referred to his own brand of theorizing as "genetic epistemological," reflecting its joint influence by biology as well as philosophy. Although Piaget's theory is multifaceted, his theory as it applies to intelligence has two main parts. One part is the theory of equilibration, according to which the absorption of new information is accomplished by a dynamic equilibrium between two complementary processes, assimilation and accommodation. The other part of the theory is the account of periods of development, beginning with the sensorimotor period and ending with the formal-operational period. Piaget's theory has been enormously influential in developmental psychology and in psychology in general. Indeed, it is arguable that the theory is second only to Freud's in the influence it has had on psychology. At the present time, however, it seems that its influence may not be as long lasting, as many aspects of the theory now seem not to be correct. (Perhaps Freud was at the advantage in that his theory is somewhat harder to falsify!)

Piaget's theory is not only formal itself, but draws heavily on formal logic and other aspects of the philosophy of knowledge in its development. As a result, it has sometimes been viewed as a theory of competence rather than of performance, describing the formal structures that underlie development rather than the way these structures are put into practice. Piaget's insights about development were profound, perhaps more so than those of any other cognitive developmental psychologist. Nevertheless, the theory has been battered heavily in the last decade.

First, the theory is much more successful and nearly complete in accounting for the development of formal and logical thought than it is in accounting for the development of intuitive and aesthetic thought. It is what might colloquially be called a "left-brain" theory. But much of intelligence is not understandable in terms of the scientific modes of thought that Piaget has investigated, and hence the theory almost certainly needs supplementation by other theories that deal more with the intuitive and less rational modes of thinking that are nevertheless, according to many people, important parts of intelligence.

Second, there seem to be real problems with stagelike theories, whether Piaget's or anyone else's. Several critiques have been written of stage theories, but the biggest problem is that intellectual development just does not seem to show the strictly stagelike properties that it is supposed to show, according to Piaget's theory. Piaget himself was aware of the problem and introduced the concept of "horizontal decalage" to account for the fact that not all operations within a given period seem to develop at the same time. But giving a name to a problem does not in itself solve or dispense with the problem.

Third, it now appears that children can accomplish many tasks at earlier ages than Piaget thought possible. In some cases, children defined problems differently from the way Piaget and his co-workers defined them, resulting in their performance looking poorer than it might have if they had better understood what the examiner intended to convey. In other cases, the sources of difficulty that Piaget and his co-workers attributed as critical to the problems now seem not to be quite correct. In some cases, memory rather than logical operations has proven to be the key to understanding children's difficulty. In other cases, knowledge rather than thought processes has proven to be the key. Indeed, Piaget's theory seems severely to underestimate the role of knowledge in intellectual development. In many instances, children cannot solve a problem not because of a lack of logical operations, but because they did not know enough to solve the problem successfully.

Fourth, many theorists now believe that formal operations, as Piaget called the last period, which begins roughly at the age of 11 or 12, no longer seem to be the end of the line with respect to intellectual development. A variety of research efforts have suggested periods of intellectual development that go beyond formal operations. At the same time, it has become clear that not everyone reaches these post-formal-operational periods, and indeed, the best indications are that not everyone even reaches full formal operations.

Piaget was not much interested in individual differences, which he tended to view as an "American problem." Nevertheless, all our indications are that there exist fairly substantial individual differences in people's abilities to perform a variety of intellectual tasks, and the problem is not one limited to any one country or social or cultural group. Rather, individual differences constitute a problem that every theory needs to address, and to address in a way that goes beyond merely positing differences in rate of development. Piaget's theory, then, has been one of the most important in psychology and certainly in developmental psychology, but at the present time, it is problematical in a number of respects.

The anthropological metaphor

Exponents of the anthropological metaphor view intelligence as a cultural invention. On their view, intelligence is a different thing from one culture to another, because what it takes to adapt in one culture will be quite different from what it takes to adapt in another. Thus, we can learn little or nothing about the intelligence in one culture from studying intelligence in another culture, and indeed, our attempts to transfer knowledge may actually be harmful, because we will make generalizations that are likely not to be correct. From an anthropological point of view, the best example of this is IQ testing, in which a test that is developed in one culture is often brought directly into another culture, with at best a translation that often does not even adequately convey the meanings of the items to the individuals in the new culture. Not all adherents of the anthropological view are radical cultural relativists who believe that there is nothing common across cultures, but all of them believe that in order fully to understand intelligence within a culture, one needs to study that culture in its own right and not assume that generalization can be made from one culture to another.

The anthropological metaphor provides a needed counterbalance to the metaphors considered above, because it views intelligence in terms of the external rather than the internal world of the individual. The metaphors considered up to now have all assumed that intelligence is something that is solely inside the head, and there is now a broad array of evidence suggesting that context has enormous effects on behavior as well as on what is considered adaptive. At the same time, there are several potential criticisms of the anthropological view.

First, a problem with some of this work is that it goes from one extreme to another. Whereas adherents of other metaphors often fail to consider context at all, or at least in a meaningful way, adherents of the anthropological metaphor have not been at the forefront of helping us understand the part of intelligence that is in the head. In fact, some of them seem to believe that what is in the head is irrelevant to understanding intelligence, and this view seems to be a mistake. In psychology, there is often a tendency to go from one extreme to another, and in the study of intelligence, this gyration is probably not what will most advance the field.

Second, although anthropologically oriented psychologists have been quick to point out the importance of context, often the word begins to acquire a hollow undertone. Anthropologically oriented psychologists have not gone far in elucidating exactly how context works or in making clear just what it is. We need a theory of context as much as we need a theory of intelligence as an internal construct, but what theories of context have been proposed have been rather vaguely specified. Hence, we need to go beyond talking about context and be more explicit as to exactly what it comprises.

Finally, whereas adherents of some of the other metaphors might be accused of doing precise and elegant experimental research that nevertheless deals with small problems, adherents of the anthropological approach have, in some cases, indulged in research that could euphemistically be called less than definitive. It is certainly understandable why lack of definitiveness would be a problem: It is much more difficult to do research in the field than it is to do it under the controlled conditions of a laboratory. Nevertheless, it has often been difficult to draw strong conclusions from the research that has been done under the anthropological metaphor, with the result that the data sometimes seem to have the characteristic of a Rorschach: One can read into the research almost whatever one wishes.

In sum, I view the anthropological approach as an important one, certainly if one is going to understand the role of context in defining and guiding the development of intelligence. But the anthropological metaphor, like the others, is best when it does not stand alone. All of the metaphors need to be complemented by others in order to achieve a more nearly complete grasp of what intelligence is all about.

The sociological metaphor

The sociological metaphor owes as much to Lev Vygotsky as the epistemological metaphor does to Jean Piaget. Whereas Piaget tended to view intelligence as moving from the inside outward, Vygotsky viewed it as moving from the outside inward. As children grow up, they internalize and make a part of themselves the social processes they observe in the environment. The sociological metaphor, therefore, zeroes in on how socialization processes affect the development of intelligence. There can be no doubt that socialization processes are important: In Chapter 3, it is shown that different social groups have different conceptions of intelligence, and children will generally be at an advantage in school if the conception of the household in which they grow up matches the conception held by the teachers in their classrooms.

The sociological metaphor is a popular one today in developmental psychology, perhaps partly as a reaction to Piaget. However, its being in vogue is probably also partly because socialization factors are truly so important in all aspects of development, including intellectual ones. It is difficult at this point in time to critique work based on the sociological metaphor because the amount of work is not yet that great, and the theories are not particularly well specified. It just is not clear yet how far the metaphor can be pushed. But there exists nothing even resembling a complete theory of intelligence that is based on the sociological metaphor. Rather, the sociological metaphor is useful in pointing out how socialization affects conceptions of intelligence, and also how it affects the development of intelligence. It may be that within the next few years, proponents of this metaphor will find a way to push it far enough to yield something resembling a reasonably complete theory of intelligence. Indeed, Reuven Feuerstein, an Israeli psychologist, has been moving in this direction. But as of the present time, the claims that have been made for the sociological metaphor have generally been modest and reasonable in showing the effects of society on intelligence.

The systems metaphor

The systems metaphor is perhaps the vaguest of all that have been considered, because almost anything can be called a "system" in some respect. I have grouped under the systems metaphor those recent theories that seek to understand intelligence in terms of the interaction of multiple systems of intelligence or even multiple intelligences. These theories are more complex than theories of the past generally have been in that they not only distinguish among different aspects of intelligence, but among different kinds of intelligences. One goal of these theories seems to be to understand intelligence in a way that transcends a single metaphor and that combines aspects of at least several of the metaphors that have been considered above. This combination seems to be a salutary direction for future theory and research, because if there has been one point that I have been attempting to drive home, it is that any single metaphor cannot provide a complete understanding of intelligence. We will understand intelligence fully only when we find a way of integrating metaphors without callously mixing them.

The dangers inherent in systems theories are not easily dismissed. The theories usually become complex and, as a result, difficult to falsify. At times, metatheory mixes with theory in a way that makes it difficult to distinguish the two. Moreover, there are many ways in which the various metaphors can be integrated, and because of the size and scope of the theories, it becomes difficult to choose among these different ways which is best or, at least, heuristically most useful. Theories can begin to crumble from their own weight, and there is always the danger that systems theories will do precisely that. At the same time, I believe that the systems theories are the closest we have come toward a complete understanding of intelligence, although even with them, we have a long way to go. Whatever form future theorizing about intelligence takes, it will almost certainly need to take into account the various systems that operate and interact in forming, and in some cases controlling, our intelligent thought. I believe the future of intelligence theory and research to be in systems thinking, but as noted above, systems thinking can encompass so many different ideas that it is not clear how constraining the metaphor is. The advantage of a relatively unconstrained metaphor is that it leaves many possibilities open and forecloses relatively few possibilities. A disadvantage is that the metaphor can become so broad that it becomes meaningless as a metaphor, permitting within its bounds almost any kind of theory at all. The challenge of future theorizing will be to provide theories that are broad but at the same time at least somewhat constrained, so that the theories do not become a hodgepodge of ideas sewn together from different metaphors. Kalmar and Sternberg (1988) discuss how the technique of "theory knitting" can be used to form theories that knit together ideas from a variety of past theories in a unified and sensible way.

Conclusion

Intelligence can be viewed from many vantage points. These vantage points, characterized in the present book as metaphors, guide the kinds of questions that theorists of intelligence ask about intelligence as a construct. It is important to understand the metaphor or metaphors underlying one's theory so as to understand the questions one is likely to ask and why one is likely to ask them. At the same time, an understanding of the base metaphor helps one appreciate the questions that are not being asked and how the failure to ask them constrains and narrows the understanding of intelligence that is possible through a particular metaphor. Without an understanding of the metaphors that generate or at least guide various theories of intelligence, it is often hard to know which theories can be compared and which cannot, and to what extent two particular theories even address the same questions about intelligence when the theorists claim to have constructed "theories of intelligence." An understanding of the base metaphors provides a certain unity and coherence to the field of intelligence theory and research that otherwise would be lacking. The metaphors show that the theories are not just a motley assortment of alternative views, but rather a fairly systematic collection of points of view based on differing higher order conceptions of how the concept of intelligence should be viewed.

The bulk of this book will elucidate metaphors and the theories guided by them. But first, it is important to examine the implicit (as opposed to explicit) theories that people have in their heads regarding what intelligence is. These implicit theories provide the bases for the formal explicit theories that are considered in Part III. Part II of the book, then, which follows immediately, considers the antecedents of the various theories to be considered later.

Part II

Definitions of intelligence

2

Historical views of intelligence

At least some concept of intelligence goes back to the ancient Greeks, and the concept probably goes back further, although in this chapter on historical views of intelligence, I will start with ancient Greece. For convenience and uniformity, as well as a reflection of the way I did my research, I shall refer to writers through citations to *Great Books of the Western World* (1987). All references, then, will be in terms of volume (in italics) and page numbers (in roman script).

Homer

Even Homer, one of the most ancient of the Greek writers, recognized intelligence as an entity and distinguished it from other skills. Homer is believed to have lived in about the sixth century B.C., although this dating is open to dispute. In the *Odyssey*, Ulysses chastises Euryalus, who has accused Ulysses of being unskilled in any sports:

You are an insolent fellow – so true is it that the Gods do not grace all men alike in speech, person, and understanding. One man may be of weak presence, but heaven has adorned this with such a good conversation that he charms every one who sees him; his honeyed moderation carries his hearers with him so that he is leader in all assemblies of his fellows, and where ever he goes he is looked up to. Another may be as handsome as a God, but his good looks are not crowned with discretion. This is your case. No God could make a finer looking fellow than you are, but you are a fool. (*4*, 223)

Plato

Plato made his major contributions in the fourth century B.C., although he was born in the fifth century B.C.. Plato had a great deal to say about intelligence, and it would be impossible to review it all here. One aspect of intelligence, according to Plato, is the ability to learn. In the *Republic* Book 5, Socrates asks Glaucon:

When you spoke of a nature gifted or not gifted in any respect, did you mean to say that one man will acquire a thing easily, another with difficulty; a little learning will lead the one to discover a great deal; whereas the other, after much study and application, no sooner learns than he forgets; or again, did you mean, that the one has a body which is a good servant to his mind, while the body of the other is a hindrance to him? – Would not these be the sort of differences which distinguish the man gifted by nature from the one who is ungifted? (7, 359)

Glaucon agrees with Socrates that his observations are correct.

As is well known by many, Plato believed in the rule of philosopher-kings. He believed philosophers to be most qualified to govern the state because of their unique intellectual gifts. In Book 6 of the *Republic,* Socrates elicits from Glaucon some of the characteristics that separate philosophers from others. Socrates demonstrates to Glaucon that part of human intelligence is the love of learning and knowledge; truthfulness and unwillingness to accept falsehoods, and indeed, love of the truth; and having naturally well proportioned and gracious minds, which Socrates believes spontaneously would move them toward the truth.

Plato suggests an interesting metaphor of a block of wax in the mind of man in order to elaborate his views on intelligence. Socrates asks Theaetetus, in the dialogue *Theaetetus,* to imagine that there exists in the mind of man a block of wax, which is of different sizes in different men. The block of wax can also differ in hardness, moistness, and purity. Socrates, citing Homer, suggests that when the wax is pure and clear and sufficiently deep, the mind will easily learn and retain and will not be subject to confusion. It will only think things that are true, and because the impressions in the wax are clear, they will be quickly distributed into their proper places on the block of wax. But when the wax is muddy or impure or very soft or very hard, there will be defects of the intellect. People whose wax is soft will be good at learning but be apt to forget. People whose wax is hard will be slow to learn, but will retain what they learn. People whose wax is shaggy or rugged or gritty, or whose wax has an admixture of earth or dung, will have only indistinct impressions. Those with hard wax will have the same, because there will be no depth to the thoughts. If the wax is too soft, the impressions will be indistinct, because they can be easily confused or remolded (see 7, 540).

Aristotle

Aristotle, the second giant of Greek philosophy, also had some well-formed views on the nature of intelligence. Aristotle lived in the fourth century B.C. In the *Posterior Analytics Book 1* he conceived of intelligence in terms of "quick wit":

Quick wit is a faculty of hitting upon the middle term instantaneously. It would be exemplified by a man who saw that the moon has a bright side always turned towards the sun, and quickly grasped the cause of this, namely that she borrows her light from him; or observes somebody in conversation with a man of wealth and defined that he was borrowing money, or that the friendship of these people sprang from a common enmity. In all these instances he has seen the major and minor terms and then grasped the causes, the middle terms.

Let *a* represent "bright side turned sunward," *b* "lighted from the sun," *c* "the moon." Then *b*, "lighted from the sun," is predicable of *c*, "the moon," and *a*, "having a bright side towards the source of her light," is predicable of *b*. So *a* is predicable of *c* through *b*. (*8*, 122)

Augustine

Augustine lived from the fourth to the fifth century A.D. In the writings of both Plato and Aristotle, and of the large majority of their successors, intelligence is seen as a good. Indeed, in the writings of some of the twentieth-century psychologists to be considered later, it can become difficult to distinguish intelligence from some kind of overall judgment of a person's quality or value. But this view is not universal, and it is useful to see the other side, if only for balance. In Book 4 of the *Confessions*, Saint Augustine both describes his conception of intelligence and questions its value:

Whatever was written, either on rhetoric, or logic, geometry, music, and arithmetic, by myself without much difficulty or any instructor, I understood, Thou knowst, O Lord my God; because both quickness of understanding, and acuteness in discerning, is Thy gift: yet did I not thence sacrifice to Thee. So then it served not to my use, but rather to my perdition, since I went about to get so good a portion of my substance into my own keeping; and I kept not my strength for Thee, but wandered from Thee into a far country, to spend it upon harlotries. For what profited me good abilities, not employed to good uses? (*18*, 26)

Augustine goes on to question whether those who are less intelligent might not be better off, in that they would be less susceptible to departing from the will of God and the "nest" of the Church. Some have argued that there are at least hints of anti-intellectualism in certain religious writings, and some might see such hints in Augustine's *Confessions* here.

Aquinas

Saint Thomas Aquinas lived in the thirteenth century. Aquinas, in the first part of the *Summa Theologica,* discusses his views on the intellect. He argues that God understands all things, whereas man does not. People of superior intellect have understanding that is more universal and deeper, whereas inferior intellects have less universal understanding and lesser comprehension. However, if

the inferior substances received forms in the same degree of universality as the superior substances, since they are not so strong in understanding, the knowledge which they would derive through them would be imperfect and of a general and confused nature. We can see this to a certain extent in man, for those who are of weaker intellect fail to acquire perfect knowledge through the universal conceptions of those who have a better understanding, unless things are explained to them singly and in detail. (*19,* 474)

Thus, for Aquinas, the less intelligent not only have less universal and incomplete comprehension, but are not well able to profit from the better understanding of their superiors. What they can ascertain is both general and confused, and even this is only the result of fastidious teaching.

Montaigne

Montaigne lived in the sixteenth century. In *Essays I,* Montaigne suggests that intelligent people are those who seek out knowledge and truth. Unintelligent people, in contrast, are people

who by reverence and obedience simply believe and are constant in their belief. In the average understandings and the middle sort of capacities, the error of opinion is begotten; they follow the appearance of the first impression, and have some color of reason on their side to impute our walking on in the old beaten path to simplicity and stupidity, meaning us who have not informed ourselves by study. The higher and nobler souls, more solid and clear-sighted, make up another sort of true believers, who by a long and religious investigation of truth, have obtained a clear and more penetrating light into the Scriptures. (*25,* 150)

Montaigne suggested that whereas we readily attribute to others superiority and courage, strength, experience, activity, beauty, and the like, we virtually never attribute to them superior intelligence. And the reason for this is that we believe that if we had only decided to turn our thoughts the way they have, we could have learned or figured out everything that they have learned or figured out. For Montaigne, part of being intelligent is to know one's own weaknesses as well as one's strengths.

Hobbes

Thomas Hobbes published the *Leviathan* in 1651. In *Leviathan*, Hobbes expresses some of his views regarding the nature of intelligence. Hobbes distinguishes between natural and acquired "wit." But Hobbes does not mean by the distinction between natural and acquired that which is innate versus that which is learned. Rather, by *natural*, he means intellectual skills that are acquired by use and experience rather than through direct instruction, whereas by *acquired*, he refers to that which is instilled by culture and instruction. He believes that natural wit consists principally of two skills: "celerity of imagining," or the swiftness with which one moves from one thought to another; and "steady direction," or one's ability to move toward some approved end. He views unintelligent people as ones who are slow in thought and who cannot easily move toward an approved end (see *23, 66*).

Hobbes also believed that intelligent people are those who can see similarities in things that others do not observe. The intelligent can also observe differences that others might not see. With respect to acquired "wit," Hobbes believed that there is only one skill, namely, reason. Intelligence is largely motivational in origins, and hence differences in intelligence are due largely to differences in motivation, or what he referred to as "passions":

The causes of this difference of wits are in the passions, and the difference of passions proceedeth partly from the different constitution of the body, and partly from different education. For if the difference proceedeth from the temper of the brain, and the organs of sense, either exterior or interior, there would be no less difference of men in their sight, hearing, or other senses than in their fancies and discretions. (*23, 68*)

Hobbes believed that men differ very little in the intelligence with which they are born. Whereas he acknowledged that one person might be better in one skill than another, when all was said and done, the other person would be better than the first in some other skill. Thus, men are born basically equal in ability (*23, 24*).

Pascal

Blaise Pascal lived in the seventeenth century. In *Pensées*, Pascal offered some thoughts on the structure of intelligence. For one thing, he believed that there are two kinds of intellect:

> the one able to penetrate acutely and deeply into the conclusions of given premises, and this is the precise intellect; the other able to comprehend a great number of premises without confusing them, and this is the mathematical intellect. The one has force and exactness, the other comprehension. Now the one quality can exist without the other; the intellect can be strong and narrow, and can also be comprehensive and weak. (*33*, 172)

Pascal further believed that some people are intelligent within a broad array of fields, whereas others show their intelligence only within a narrow band of fields.

Today it is fashionable to distinguish between "left-brained" and "right-brained" people, the former being more logical and sequential and the latter being more intuitive and random or nonsequential in their thought. But Pascal made a very similar distinction back in the seventeenth century. He suggested that bright people can have either a mathematical or an intuitive mind. Mathematically oriented people will not start reasoning until they have carefully inspected and arranged the principles upon which they are to reason. They like to begin with definitions and then axioms, and to proceed to reason deductively upon them. Intuitive types, in contrast, judge quickly and at a single glance, and have little use for or comprehension of using definitions and axioms to achieve a deductive conclusion. They see things with little effort and tend to be impatient and holistic in their thinking. However, Pascal comments that unintelligent people are neither intuitive nor mathematical. They do not have any set way of grasping information.

Locke

John Locke was an empiricist philosopher of the seventeenth century. Locke, in *An Essay Concerning Human Understanding*, like Pascal, believed in two kinds of intelligence. But this seventeenth-century philosopher had a rather different conception of what the two kinds of intelligence are. He distinguished between *wit* and *judgment*. He suggested that people who have a great deal of the one do not necessarily have a great deal of the other.

For *wit* lying most in the assemblage of ideas, and putting those together with quickness and variety, wherein can be found any resemblance or congruity, thereby to make up pleasant pictures and agreeable visions in the fancies; *judgment,* on the contrary, lies quite on the other side, and separating carefully, one from another, ideas wherein can be found the least difference, thereby to avoid being misled by similitude, and by affinity to take one thing for another. (35, 144)

Locke also foreshadowed later ideas about the importance of mental speed and intelligence. He suggested that bright people are those who have their ideas in memory quickly ready at hand. He also suggested that bright people keep their ideas unconfused, and that they are well able to distinguish one thing or idea from another. Where there is the least difference, brighter people can see it, whereas duller ones cannot. Locke, of course, is perhaps most well known for his idea of the tabula rasa, the notion that people are born with a blank slate that they proceed to fill up.

Smith

Up to now, the modal view has been that there are different kinds or at least aspects of intelligence, and that people differ in their degrees of these various kinds or aspects of intelligence. At the very least, all of the philosophical thinkers considered up to this point have believed that intelligence is an important natural disposition to be reckoned with. Adam Smith, in *The Wealth of Nations,* expressed a different view. Smith, an economic philosopher of the nineteenth century, suggested that the differences we see are not truly of intelligence or of natural talents, but rather of the work people do.

The difference of natural talents in different men is, in reality, much less than we are aware of; and the very different genius which appears to distinguish men of different professions, when grown up to maturity, is not upon many occasions so much the cause as the effect of the division of labor. The difference between the most dissimilar characters, between a philosopher and a common street porter, for example, seems to arise not so much from nature as from habit, custom, and education. When they came into the world, and for the first six or eight years of their existence, they were perhaps very much alike, and neither their parents nor playfellows could perceive any remarkable difference. About that age, or soon after, they come to be employed in very different occupations. The difference of talents comes then to be taken notice of, and widens by degrees, till at last the vanity of the philosopher is willing to acknowledge scarce any resemblance. (*39*, 7–8)

Smith suggests that were it not for the natural disposition of people to barter and exchange economic goods, they would all do the same work, and would all be essentially the same in their abilities. Thus, for Smith, differences in talents have an economic origin, and reside not so much in the individual as in the experience to which economics leads them.

Kant

Immanuel Kant, perhaps the most famous philosopher of the eighteenth century, believed that intelligence, or what he referred to as "the higher faculties of cognition," comprises three parts: understanding, judgment, and reason. Kant's *Critique of Pure Reason* is, in part, an elaboration of this point of view. Kant suggests that the structure of logic mirrors the structure of the mind, and hence Kant may be viewed as a forerunner of the epistemological theorists considered later in the book.

Kant further distinguishes between creative and imitative intelligence, which he refers to as *genius* in opposition to the spirit of *imitation*.

Genius (1) is a *talent* for producing that for which no definite rule can be given, and not an aptitude in the way of cleverness for what can be learned according to some rule; and that consequently *originality* must be its primary property. (2) Since there may also be original nonsense, its products must at the same time be models, i.e., be *exemplary;* and, consequently, though not themselves derived from imitation, they must serve that purpose for others, i.e., as a standard or rule of estimating. . . . Everyone is agreed on the point of the complete opposition between genius and the *spirit of imitation*. Now since learning is nothing but imitation, the greatest ability, or aptness as a pupil (capacity), is still, as such, not equivalent to genius. (*42*, 525–6)

Mill

John Stuart Mill, writing in the nineteenth century, had a dim view of the capabilities of ordinary men. He was particularly interested in one facet of the intellect – originality:

Originality is the one thing which unoriginal minds cannot feel the use of. . . . In sober truth, whatever homage may be professed, or even paid, to real or supposed mental superiority, the general tendency of things throughout the world is to render mediocrity the ascendant power among mankind. . . . Those whose opinions go by the name of public opinion are not always the same sort of public. . . . But they are always a mass, that is to say, collective mediocrity. And what is a still greater novelty, the mass do not now take their opinions from dignitaries in Church or State, from ostensible leaders, or from books. Their thinking is done for them by men much like themselves, addressing them or speaking in their name. . . . I am not complaining of all this. I do not assert that anything better is compatible, as a general rule, with the present low state of the human mind. But that does not hinder the government of mediocrity from being mediocre government. (*43, 298*)

Mill believed that persons of genius are more individual than other people. As a result, they are less able to fit themselves into the small number of molds that society provides. Society attempts to reduce them to the commonplace, and in order truly to be people of genius, they need to resist the pressure that they experience. Although people in general profess to admire originality, at heart, they think it is something that they could do nicely without.

James

It is appropriate to conclude our discussion of historical views of intelligence with the views of William James, because James was both a philosopher and a psychologist, and hence provides a bridge between the philosophical views of this chapter and the psychological views of the next one. Writing primarily in the latter part of the nineteenth century, James is sometimes viewed as the forerunner of modern thinking in experimental psychology.

James suggested in his *Principles of Psychology* that the most basic difference between humans and nonhumans is in the difference in their ability to associate ideas by similarity: "But, now, since nature never makes a jump, it is evident that we should find the lowest men occupying in this respect an intermediate position between the brutes and the highest men. And so we do" (*53, 686*).

James extended this difference to an understanding of genius, suggesting that genius is the possession of associative ability to an extreme degree. He cites, for example, Newton's realization of the similarity between an apple and the moon, or Darwin's recognition of the similarity between the rivalry for food in nature and the rivalry for man's selection, as examples of remote associations that could be perceived only by a genius.

James, like Pascal before him, suggests a difference between analytical and intuitive intelligence. He suggests that

> *minds of genius may be divided into two main sorts, those who notice the bond* *[of identity] and those who merely obey it.* The first are the abstract reasoners, properly so called, the men of science, and philosophers – the analysts, in a word; the latter are the poets, the critics – the artists, in a word, the men of intuitions. These judge rightly, classify cases, characterize them by the most striking analogic epithets, but go no further. (*53*, 687)

James believed analytical thinking to represent a higher stage of thought than intuitive thinking. For example, he remarked that although it has been suggested that Shakespeare possessed more intellectual power than anyone who had ever lived, in fact, his intellectual power was intuitive rather than analytic. For example, Shakespeare could render the death of Othello in a way that would stir the spectator's blood, but, according to James, he probably could not have said why his techniques were so effective.

Conclusion

In this chapter, I have briefly reviewed the thoughts of some of the major philosophers on the nature of intelligence. These thoughts provide a backdrop and foundation for modern thinking, and indeed, many of the views I have expressed could as well have been expressed in the twentieth century. Many of the key elements of contemporary views of intelligence – understanding, judgment, knowledge, direction, and so on – have their origins in views of intelligence that date back many centuries. If there is a lack of agreement among the philosophers, one cannot attribute it to the "philosophical method": There is little more agreement today among psychologists than there has been among philosophers over the past three thousand years. In the next chapter, I consider what some of the contemporary views are, looking not only at the definitions of psychologists, but of other groups of individuals as well, including laypeople.

3

Contemporary views of intelligence

There may be as many different definitions of intelligence as there are people who are asked to define it, and so my goal in this chapter is not to list every definition that anyone in the twentieth century has ever given, but rather to report some of the major and representative definitions and then to seek some common trends, as well as differences among them. Thus, I will start in this chapter with definitions of two groups of experts, one group from the 1920s and another group from the 1980s, and proceed to a broader sample of definitions, namely, those of nonexperts as well as experts in the field of intelligence. But before turning to the definitions from these various samples of individuals, it is first necessary to deal with perhaps the most famous, or maybe, infamous, definition of them all, that of E. G. Boring.

Expert definitions of intelligence

The operational definition

Boring (1923), in an article in the *New Republic,* proposed that "intelligence is what the tests test." Boring was not so foolish as to believe that this operational definition was the end of the line for understanding intelligence. To the contrary, he saw it as a "narrow definition, but a point of departure for a rigorous discussion . . . until further scientific discussion allows us to extend [it]" (p. 35). This definition was adopted by Arthur Jensen in a 1969 article in the *Harvard Educational Review,* in which he argued that we really cannot do much to teach intelligence, and to the extent that there are racial differences, they are pretty much here to stay. And the definition has been adopted, explicitly or implicitly, by many others. Perhaps there are not that many people who would admit to believing in Boring's definition, but many nevertheless act as though it were true. For example, I have met many an individual in the gifted-education business who, although believing that there is more to intelligence than IQ, uses IQ as the exclusive or almost exclusive basis for selecting children for programs for the gifted. Thus, trivial or even frivolous as the definition may seem, it is one with which we have to deal. And because tests of intelligence tend, for the most part, to be positively intercorrelated with each other – the so-called positive manifold – one might view this definition as converging on whatever it is that the tests measure in common.

For whatever convenience the definition may hold out, it is a seriously flawed definition from both scientific and educational points of view. First, it defines away rather than defines intelligence. To this day, people are not sure of just what it is that conventional intelligence tests measure, so defining intelligence as what it is that the tests measure substitutes one unknown for another. It does little to elucidate the construct of intelligence. Second, we know that although the tests intercorrelate, they do not intercorrelate perfectly and that the differences are not due only to reliability or sampling variation. Therefore, the definition does not make clear even what the universe of intelligence is, nor does it make clear what tests to count as measuring intelligence. Anyone can say that they have a test measuring intelligence, and some criterion is needed for deciding whether or not to include a given test within the range of the operational definition. Third, the definition is an extremely conservative one, in that it assumes that whatever it is that we measure by intelligence tests today is truly what intelligence is. But if we take the standpoint, as I do, that we are continually attempting to progress toward a better understanding and assessment of intelligence, then we probably do not want to get stuck defining intelligence with whatever testing procedures we have now, as we very likely in the future can do better than we are presently doing. Fourth, the definition educationally legitimates a view of intelligence that may not be the best one for making decisions regarding selection, diagnosis, and placement in educational decision making. And it is a weak scientific legitimation indeed, because it need be based on no scientific theory or research at all. It simply accepts, pro forma, what we already have. And finally, as has been pointed out many times before, the definition is circular. Originally, the idea of testing was that it would be based on some definition, no matter how vague, of what intelligence is. We now find ourselves, however, defining intelligence in terms of the tests, rather than the other way around. So the operational definition is not likely to move us far forward in seeking an understanding of the nature of intelligence.

The 1921 symposium

The most famous study of experts' definitions of the scope of intelligent behavior is probably that done by the editors of the *Journal of Educational Psychology* ("Intelligence and its measurement," 1921) roughly 70 years ago. Contributors to the symposium were asked to address two issues:

1. What do I conceive "intelligence" to be, and by what means can it best be measured by group tests?
2. What are the most crucial "next steps" in research?

Fourteen experts gave their views on the nature of intelligence, with such definitions as the following:

1. the power of good responses from the point of view of truth or facts (E. L. Thorndike);
2. the ability to carry on abstract thinking (L. M. Terman);
3. sensory capacity, capacity for perceptual recognition, quickness, range or flexibility of association, facility and imagination, span of attention, quickness or alertness in response (F. N. Freeman);
4. having learned or ability to learn to adjust oneself to the environment (S. S. Colvin);
5. ability to adapt oneself adequately to relatively new situations in life (R. Pintner);
6. the capacity for knowledge and knowledge possessed (B. A. C. Henmon);
7. a biological mechanism by which the effects of a complexity of stimuli are brought together and given a somewhat unified effect in behavior (J. Peterson);
8. the capacity to inhibit an instinctive adjustment, the capacity to redefine the inhibited instinctive adjustment in the light of imaginally experienced trial and error, and the capacity to realize the modified instinctive adjustment in overt behavior to the advantage of the individual as a social animal (L. L. Thurstone);
9. the capacity to acquire capacity (H. Woodrow);
10. the capacity to learn or to profit by experience (W. F. Dearborn); and
11. sensation, perception, association, memory, imagination, discrimination, judgment, and reasoning (N. E. Haggerty).

Others of the contributors to this symposium did not provide clear definitions of intelligence, but rather, concentrated on how to test it. Of course, there have been many definitions of intelligence since those represented in the journal symposium, and an essay has been written on the nature of definitions of intelligence (Miles, 1957). But a subsequent symposium was designed specifically to update the views of the 1921 contributors.

Why didn't all of the contributors to the 1921 symposium provide definitions of intelligence? B. Ruml refused to present a definition of intelligence, arguing that not enough was known about the concept of intelligence adequately to define it at that time. S. L. Pressey similarly refused to present a definition of intelligence, describing himself as not very interested in the question, despite the fact that he spent a large proportion of his time devising tests of intelligence!

The 1986 symposium

Douglas Detterman and I sought to update the 1921 symposium, addressing the issues it raised in a way that might reflect any progress that had been made from the beginning to the ending years of the twentieth century (Sternberg & Detterman, 1986). We solicited two dozen brief essays by experts in the field of intelligence, who were asked to respond to the very same questions that were posed to the experts in the 1921 symposium. The two dozen responses were diverse.

In an introductory essay, I suggested that the responses could be classified in terms of a general framework for understanding loci of intelligence. This framework views intelligence in its relation both to the internal world of the individual and to the external world of the individual – the environment. The proposed framework for understanding the various definitions of intelligence is shown in Table 3.1.

The theorists in this symposium identify three main loci of intelligence – intelligence within the individual, intelligence within the environment, and intelligence within the interaction between the individual and the environment. Within these three main loci, however, there are a number of more specific loci for intelligence.

Theorists identifying intelligence as within the individual seem to be dealing with three main levels of analysis: a biological level, a molar level, and a behavioral level. The biological level can be established either across or within organisms. Consider in turn each of these viewpoints.

Across organisms, one can view intelligence within the context of the evolution of species, within the context of the genetics of a single species, or within the interaction between interspecies evolution and intraspecies genetics. For example, one might consider how insects

Table 3.1. *Loci of intelligence*

I. In individual
  A. Biological level
    1. Across organisms
      a. Between species (evolution)
      b. Within species (genetics)
      c. Between–within interaction
    2. Within organisms
      a. Structure
      b. Process
      c. Structure–process interaction
    3. Across–within interaction
  B. Molar level
    1. Cognitive
      a. Metacognition
        i. Processes
        ii. Knowledge
        iii. Process–knowledge interaction
      b. Cognition
        i. Processes
          (a) Selective attention
          (b) Learning
          (c) Reasoning
          (d) Problem solving
          (e) Decision making
        ii. Knowledge
        iii. Process–knowledge interaction
      c. Metacognition–cognition interaction
    2. Motivational
      a. Level (magnitude) of energy
      b. Direction (disposition) of energy
      c. Level–direction interaction
  C. Behavioral level
    1. Academic
      a. Domain general
      b. Domain specific
      c. General–specific interaction
    2. Social
      a. Within person
      b. Between persons
      c. Within–between interaction

Table 3.1. *(cont.)*

---

      3. Practical
        a. Occupational
        b. Everyday living
        c. Occupational–everyday living interaction
    D. Biological–molar–behavioral interaction

II. In environment
    A. Level of culture/society
      1. Demands
      2. Values
      3. Demands–values interaction
    B. Level of niche within culture/society
      1. Demands
      2. Values
      3. Demands–values interaction
    C. Level x sublevel interactions

III. Individual–environment interaction

Source: Reproduced with permission from Table 1 in Chapter 1 of Sternberg and Detterman (1986).

differ from rats in their intelligence and how rats differ from humans. Or one might consider variability within any one of these species – say, humans – from one generation to the next. Or one might consider genetic transmission in both its constancies and its variabilities across generations of different species.

Within organisms, one can view intelligence in terms of structural aspects of the organism (e.g., hemispheres of the brain), or in terms of process aspects (e.g., the neuronal processes that give rise to evoked potentials). Furthermore, it is possible to look at the interaction between structure and process, considering, for example, how certain regions of the brain generate particular evoked potentials.

An integrated biological viewpoint would take into account the interaction of biological factors across and within organisms. For example, one might seek to understand the evolution of the brain and its aspects or the genetic bases for brain development. An integrated biological approach to intelligence appears to be the ultimate goal of biologically oriented theorists.

The molar level of theorizing seems to emphasize two principal aspects of mental functioning: the cognitive and the motivational. Cognitive theorists of intelligence deal with two main kinds of cognition – metacognition and ordinary cognition – although not all of these theorists would accept this distinction between the two kinds of cognition. Metacognition refers to knowledge about and the control of one's cognition. Ordinary cognition refers to what is known and controlled by metacognition. Note that both metacognition and cognition can be divided into process and knowledge aspects. An example of metacognition as knowledge would be the awareness of what one does and does not know, whereas cognition as knowledge would be the knowledge itself. An example of metacognition as control processes would be the formation of a strategy to solve a problem, whereas an example of cognition as cognitive processes would be the mental steps that are actually used to solve the problem.

The processes of cognition are manifold. Theorists of intelligence seem especially to emphasize sets of processes involved in selective attention, learning, reasoning, problem solving, and decision making. Processes and knowledge interact, of course, and this interaction takes place through learning, which requires processes that bring old knowledge to bear on new knowledge. It is important to add that, just as processes and knowledge interact, so do metacognition and cognition: In order to function intelligently, one must change one's metacognition to accommodate one's cognition, and vice versa. As one learns new things, for example, one must take account of this new learning in one's understanding of what one can do. For another example, when one sets up a strategy for solving a problem, one must then choose just those cognitive processes that will make the strategy a success. Whether or not one accepts the distinction proposed here and elsewhere between metacognition and ordinary cognition, both aspects of functioning would seem to be needed, regardless of what they are called or how they are classified.

Motivational theorists of intelligence argue that there is more to intelligence than cognition – that one should look to motivation as well. Indeed, much cognition is motivated (some might argue that it all is), and one's motivation to cognize may determine both the quality and the quantity of cognition. Motivational theorists focus on two principal properties of motivation – the level or magnitude of the motivation and its direction or disposition. For example, there is, within a given individual, a motivation to learn. But this motivation is not equally directed to all kinds of learning, and hence it is necessary to take direction into account. One's intelligence is affected not only by the amount of learning that takes place, but also by the kinds of learning that take place, and both amount and kind are affected, in turn, by motivation. Level and direction of motivation interact with each other, of course, in that one may have high motivational levels in some directions but low levels in others.

The behavioral level of analysis looks not "inside" the head, but outside it – at what the person does rather than at what he or she thinks. The argument of the behavioral theorists (who need not be behaviorists!) is that intelligence resides in one's behavior rather than in (or in addition to) the mental functioning that leads to this behavior. The behaviorally oriented theorists seem to concentrate on three main domains of behavior – academic, social, and practical.

The academic domain includes the behavior exhibited in school work, including subjects such as language, mathematics, natural science, social science, and the arts. Two major controversies in theorizing about behavior need to be considered. The first concerns the breadth of behavior that falls within the domain of intelligence – for example, is artistic behavior or dancing behavior "intelligent" in the ordinary sense, or does it fall within some other domain? The second controversy concerns the domain specificity of intelligence: Are the processes and structures underlying intelligent behavior relatively domain general or relatively domain specific? For example, are the mental processes used to solve mathematics problems the same as those used to solve social scientific problems, and if they are not the same, just how much overlap is there? Although the argument over domain generality is not limited to academic contents, it seems to generate the greatest controversy for these kinds of contents. Most theorists would agree that there is some domain generality as well as some domain specificity of functioning and would see as their goal the determination of just which mental structures and processes fall within which class.

The social domain includes the behavior exhibited in between- as well as within-person interactions. How does a person use intelligence to facilitate interactions with other people, but also, how does a person use intelligence to facilitate interaction with (or understanding of) himself or herself? Although not all theorists would distinguish within- from between-person interactions, the distinction seems to be a viable one. People know that their understanding of themselves often seems not to match their understanding of others. The two kinds of understanding may, of course, interact: Getting to know oneself better may help one understand others better, and vice versa.

The practical domain includes the behavior exhibited in one's occupation and in one's daily living. Occupational aspects might include knowing how to perform one's job effectively, how to get ahead in one's job, and how to make the most of the job one has. Everyday living aspects might include knowing how to balance a checkbook, how to cook for oneself, and how to shop intelligently. Theorists do not agree as to just how much the everyday domain should be considered in understanding and assessing intelligence: On the one hand, some theorists would look at cooking or shopping as mundane and as uninteresting bases for theories about individual differences in intelligence; on the other hand, some theorists would argue that it is in behaviors such as these that true understanding of intelligence is to be found. Occupational and everyday behaviors are not independent, but interactive: For example, some of us find that our preoccupation with our occupations prevents us from accomplishing or even learning how to accomplish some of the things that we need to do to make a go of our lives outside our occupations.

Although theorists often think and write as though the biological, molar, and behavioral domains are independent, it is doubtful that anyone believes this. Certainly, the three work together in ways that are not yet totally understood. Our lack of understanding sometimes leads to theoretical disagreement. For example, most molar theorists would agree that molar structures and processes are capable, ultimately, of being understood at the biological level. But they might not agree that such understanding is the most desirable at this time or for all purposes. An analogy often used is that of the automobile: One does not best understand the malfunctions of an automobile at the level of the atoms or molecules that contribute to the parts of that automobile. But one need not rely on analogy: Many molar theorists would argue, for example, that the evoked-potential patterns measured by some biologically oriented psychologists are a function of cognitive processes, rather than the cognitive processes being a function of the evoked potentials. Of course, basic biological processes underlie both cognitive processing and evoked potentials – which are, after all, only a dependent variable – but theorists differ considerably in the emphasis they place on the most fruitful level of analysis at which to pursue understanding of evoked potentials and other dependent variables used in the measurement of intelligence.

Not all theorists view intelligence as residing within the individual: Some view it as residing within the environment, either as a function of one's culture and society or as a function of one's niche within the culture and society, or both. For example, some would argue that intelligence is wholly relativistic with respect to culture and hence that it is impossible to understand intelligence without understanding the culture: In essence, the culture determines the very nature of intelligence and determines who has what levels of it through labeling or attributional processes. What the culture, society, or niche within culture and society deems to be intelligent will generally be a function of the demands of the environment in which people live, the values that are held by the people within that environment, and the interaction between demands and values. For example, societal functions that are in high demand but that are not easily filled may come to be valued highly.

Many theorists of intelligence would define the locus of intelligence as occurring neither wholly within the individual nor wholly within the environment, but rather within the interaction between the two: How does the individual function – mentally and/or behaviorally – within various environmental milieus? People do not think or behave intelligently within a vacuum, nor can culture or society set standards for what constitutes intelligence without reference to the functions people perform in that culture or society. Thus it may be difficult to understand intelligence fully without first considering the interaction of the person with one or more environments and recognizing the possibility that a person may be differentially intelligent in different environments, depending upon the demands of these various environments.

In sum, I have proposed here a framework for understanding definitions of intelligence. Now consider a precis of each of the definitions proposed in this symposium and how they fit into this framework.

Anne Anastasi conceives of intelligence as a quality of behavior (I.C in Table 3.1). However, she emphasizes that intelligent behavior is behavior that is adaptive, representing effective ways of meeting the demands of the environment as they change (III). What constitutes adaptive behavior varies across species (I.A.1.a) and with the context in which the organism lives (II), so that intelligence is a pluralistic concept.

Paul Baltes expresses a preference for speaking not in terms of intelligence per se, but rather in terms of the specific constructs that constitute what we ordinarily think of as intelligence – constructs such as innate intellectual capacity (I.A.1.b), intellectual reserve capacity, learning capacity (I.B.1.b.i.(b)), problem solving ability (I.B.1.b.i.(d)), and knowledge systems (I.B.1.b.ii). He believes that by building theories in terms that permit theoretical specificity and precision, we will achieve a better understanding of intelligence than if we attempt to build a macrotheory that fails to do justice to intelligence in all of its aspects.

Jonathan Baron defines intelligence as the set of abilities involved in the achievement of rationally chosen goals (I.B.1.b.i(e)), whatever these goals might happen to be. He distinguishes between two types of abilities: capacities (I.B), which are things like mental speed (I.B.1) and mental energy (I.B.2.a); and dispositions, which include, for example, the disposition to be self-critical (I.B.2.b). Baron emphasizes that in order to be considered as components of intelligence, these capacities and dispositions must be domain general (I.C.1.a) rather than domain specific.

John Berry views intelligence as the end product of individual development in the cognitive psychological domain (I.B.1), as distinguished from the affective or motivational domains. Berry includes sensory and perceptual functioning but not motor, motivational, emotional, and social functioning. He believes that intelligence is adaptive for a given cultural group in permitting members of the group, as well as the group as a whole, to operate effectively in a given ecological context (II, III).

In their definition of intelligence, Ann Brown and Joseph Campione emphasize especially the processes and products of learning (I.B.1.b.i.(b), I.B.1.b.ii), as well as the interaction between these processes and products (I.B.1.b.iii). These authors note that their view of the relationship of learning and knowledge to intelligence differs from earlier views, such as that of Woodrow, in terms of their emphasis not only on speed of learning, but on the metacognitive processes and knowledge that interact with learning (I.B.1.a, I.B.1.c). Brown and Campione's view also differs from earlier views, which did not prove very fruitful, in terms of its emphasis upon learning as it operates in the everyday environment (II), as opposed merely to learning in the laboratory. Brown and Campione have collected an impressive array of data showing how their emphasis on the metacognitive bases of learning and upon learning as it occurs in the real world results in a much more productive approach to the understanding of the relationship between learning and intelligence than have earlier approaches.

Earl Butterfield emphasizes four bases of individual differences in intelligence that emerge from the literature of cognitive psychology.

Like Brown and Campione, he emphasizes the centrality of learning in intelligence (I.B.1.b.i.(b)). The four aspects of Butterfield's definition are that less intelligent people have smaller and less elaborately organized knowledge bases (I.B.1.b.ii); use fewer, simpler, and more passive information-processing strategies (I.B.1.b.i); have less metacognitive understanding of their own cognitive systems and of how the functioning of these systems depends upon the environment (I.B.1.a.ii, I.B.1.a.iii); and use less complete and flexible executive processes for controlling their thinking (I.B.1.a.i). Butterfield is especially concerned with how these four aspects of cognition interact (I.B.1.c).

John Carroll argues that the domains to which intelligence is applied are basically threefold: academic and technical (I.C.1), practical (I.C.3), and social (I.C.2). He argues that first and foremost, intelligence must be understood as a concept in the mind of a society at large and that the exact nature of this concept may depend upon the society (II.A). However, he concentrates in his definition upon our own society. He limits his definition to cognitive capacities (I.B.1), purposefully excluding motivational tendencies (I.B.2) and physical capacities. He notes that a major goal of scientific research on intelligence is to bring to us greater understanding of the societal concept of intelligence, both as it applies in laboratory settings and in the real world. Although the greatest success of scientific research so far has been in studying intelligence in laboratories in academic settings (I.C.1), he notes the importance of studying intelligence in social and practical settings as well (I.C.2, I.C.3).

J. P. Das views intelligence as the sum total of all cognitive processes (I.B.1), including planning (I.B.1.a.i), coding of information (I.B.1.b), and arousal of attention (I.B.1.b.i.(a)). He believes that the cognitive processes required for planning have the highest status, or most central role, in intelligence (I.B.1.a.i). Das defines planning broadly, including within it the generation of plans and strategies, selection from among available plans, and the execution of these plans. He also includes decision making within the purview of intelligence (I.B.1.b.i.(e)). Das believes that it is important to understand these elements of intelligence not only in isolation, but in interaction (I.B.1.c).

Douglas Detterman views intelligence as a complex system composed of numerous independent cognitive processes (I.B.1). These processes contribute to the appearance of a general factor. He draws an analogy between an intelligence test score and a global rating of a university. One can evaluate the overall quality of a university, but this overall quality is a function of many interrelated elements, working singly and together. As with intelligence, the functioning of the university can be evaluated at multiple levels.

William Estes suggests that the most promising path to increasing our understanding of human intelligence may be through borrowing upon recent research that has been done in artificial intelligence. He suggests that three central capacities that have been isolated in artificial-intelligence research are critical for human intelligence as well: the capacity to manipulate symbols (I.B.1.b.i), the capacity to evaluate the consequences of alternative choices (I.B.1.b.i.(b), I.B.1.b.i.(e)), and the capacity to search through sequences of symbols (I.B.1.b.i.(a)). Estes also notes a critical distinction between human and animal intelligence, namely, that animals seem to concentrate on learning information that is relevant to problems that they face immediately, whereas humans tend to concentrate on learning of information whose consequences may be long term rather than merely short term.

Hans Eysenck clearly concentrates on the biological (I.A) rather than the molar (I.B) bases of intelligence. Indeed, he believes that a scientific understanding of intelligence requires understanding at the biological level. He views intelligence as deriving from the error-free transmission of information through the cortex (I.A.2.b). He suggests that the use of evoked potentials measured from the cortex provides a particularly apt way of assessing accuracy of transmission.

Howard Gardner suggests the need to understand intelligence in terms of variations in types of naturally occurring cognition in the everyday environment (II), and especially to concentrate upon the cognitive contents of intelligence (I.C.1.b). He believes that there is no one intelligence, but rather multiple, independent intelligences. He further believes that our understanding of these intelligences will increase only if we move away from laboratory studies toward understanding of the interaction of the individual with the everyday environment (III). His approach to identifying the intelligences has drawn not upon conventional intelligence tests, but upon the end states that can be attained by a variety of individuals both within and between cultures (II.A, II.B). Gardner suggests that, at least for the present, we can identify seven different intelligences: linguistic, logical-mathematical, musical, spatial, bodily-kinesthetic, interpersonal, and intrapersonal (I.B.1, I.C).

Robert Glaser defines intelligence as proficiency (or competence) and intellectual cognitive performance (I.B.1), using the term *intellectual* to separate out emotional cognition from intelligence. Glaser distinguishes between knowledge in artifactual domains, such as most of the academic ones (I.C), and intelligence in natural domains (II). Whereas intelligence in artifactual domains is usually acquired primarily through formal schooling (I.C.1), intelligence in natural domains is usually acquired more informally and spontaneously through interactions with the everyday world (III). Glaser develops his notion of cognitive proficiency as a basis for intelligence through an analogy to athletic proficiency.

Jacqueline Goodnow views intelligence as a judgment or attribution, comparable to the judgments we make about people being physically attractive or friendly, rather than as a quality residing in the individual (III). In order to understand intelligence, therefore, we should not look to intelligence tests, cognitive tasks, or physiologically based measures, but rather to the attributions people make about themselves and each other with respect to intelligence. Goodnow is explicit in emphasizing that intelligence should be viewed as encompassing situations in which people interact with one another or solve problems together (I.C.2), not merely situations in which people work on their own or interact with objects or abstract concepts. She notes that conventional views of intelligence are based upon inadequate knowledge of the nature of the attributions people make and, moreover, that the tests that are based upon these conventional notions usually reflect and perpetuate the existing social order.

John Horn is critical of our use of the concept of intelligence, because he believes it represents the reification of a functional unity that does not in fact exist. He argues that what we refer to as intelligence represents a hodgepodge of cognitive capacities and that our goal should be to try to understand these cognitive capacities rather than to understand an illusory unified capacity that we call intelligence. Horn does believe, however, that there are certain broad abilities that need to be understood in order to comprehend various kinds of intellectual performances, namely, visual thinking, auditory thinking, short-term acquisition-retrieval, long-term retrieval-storage, speediness in reading, correct decisions, attentive speediness, structured knowledge of the culture, and flexibility of reasoning under novel conditions (I.B.1).

Lloyd Humphreys defines intelligence as the repertoire of intellectual knowledge and skills available to a person at a particular point of time (I.B.1). He believes that the term *intellectual* can be defined only by a consensus of experts. He suggests that it is necessary to understand both the content and the processes of intelligence and that we should understand that intelligence is so complex that any one attempt to describe it or its aspects will be inadequate. He compares us to the proverbial blind men stationed at different parts of an elephant's anatomy who sought fully to describe the elephant. We, like they, cannot attain such a complete description.

Earl Hunt views intelligence as a shorthand term for the variation in competence on cognitive tasks that is statistically associated with personal variables, either as main effects or as interaction terms (I.B.1). Thus, Hunt defines intelligence in terms of demonstrated individual differences in mental competence. He notes that because variation (individual differences) is a population concept, an individual cannot have "intelligence," although an individual can have specific competencies. Hunt's approach to understanding individual-difference variations is computational. He draws an analogy between the functional architecture and computing of a computer and that of a human. In particular, he believes that intelligence should be understood in terms of the manipulation of symbol systems by the individual. We need to understand both the conscious strategies that people use in manipulating symbols and the elementary information-processing operations that combine into these strategies (I.C.1.b). Hunt notes that a full understanding of intelligence would require a theory of three levels of performance and their interactions: the level of biology (I.A), the level of elementary information processes (I.B.1.b.i), and the level of both general and specific information-processing strategies (I.B.1.c).

Arthur Jensen defines intelligence in terms of the general factor obtained from factoring an intercorrelation matrix of a large number of diverse mental tests. He notes that the tests that load most highly on the general factor usually involve some forms of relation induction or relatively complex mental transformations or manipulations of stimulus input in order to achieve the correct response (I.B.1.b.i.(c), I.B.1.b.i.(d)). He argues that although the general factor that will be obtained differs somewhat from one collection of tests to another, one's goal ought to be to obtain that general factor from a set of tests that is most highly correlated with the general factors obtained from other sets of tests. Jensen notes that he emphasizes the general factor, rather than group or specific ones, because it is the general factor that proves to be the largest single source of individual differences in all cognitive activities involving some degree of mental complexity that eventuate in behavior that can be measured in terms of some objective standard of performance. He also notes that the general factor carries far more

weight than any other single factor or combination of factors in predicting performance in a variety of settings, including both academic
(I.C.1) and occupational (I.C.3.a) ones. Jensen believes that intelligence has a biological substrate (I.A) but that it is usefully studied both
in the context of laboratory cognitive tasks (I.B.1) and of the everyday
environment (II).

James Pellegrino argues that in order to understand intelligence, we
need to understand the nature of human cognition (I.B.1) as well as the
nature of the value system within which that cognition functions (II).
He argues that intelligence is implicitly determined by the interaction
of the individual's cognitive machinery with that individual's social-
cultural environment (III). In terms of cognition, Pellegrino emphasizes the special importance of metacognitive aspects of mental
functioning (I.B.1.a), but these metacognitive processes and contents
cannot be understood outside the context of the cognitive processes and
contents upon which they act (I.B.1.c).

Sandra Scarr notes that the question "What is intelligence?" is actually several questions. A first question pertains to the structure of
intelligence, a second to the cognitive processes of intelligence, a third
to the neurological processes of intelligence, a fourth to the evolution
of intelligence, and a fifth to the sources of individual variability of
intelligence (I). Scarr clearly takes a broad rather than narrow view
of intelligence, arguing that it is time to conceive of it in terms of the
functioning, adaptation, and considerations of how people live their
everyday lives (III). Intelligence requires broad forms of personal
adaptation in formulating strategies for solving both the small and the
large problems that confront us in our everyday lives.

Roger Schank views intelligence largely in terms of understanding.
He suggests that there are three levels of understanding. The lowest
level, making sense, involves finding out the events that took place and
relating them to a perception of the world. For example, reading a newspaper article generally involves what Schank refers to as making sense.
Cognitive understanding involves building an accurate model of the
thought processes of a given person. For example, in reading a set of
stories about airplane crashes, one might try to understand the thoughts
that went through the heads of the people who were in the plane.
Complete empathy involves emotional as well as cognitive understanding. One comprehends not only the thoughts of another, but the person's feelings (I.B.1, I.C.2, I.C.3, III). How can one distinguish
between a system that can produce the appearance of understanding

and one that truly understands? According to Schank, the key is the ability of a system to explain its own actions. Without such explanations, it is possible that a set of response outputs merely mimics understanding.

Richard Snow's definition of intelligence has six aspects: the incorporation of concisely organized knowledge into purposive thinking (I.B.1.b.iii), apprehension of experience (I.B.1.a, I.B.1.b), adaptive purposeful striving (III), fluid-analytical reasoning (I.B.1.b.i.(c)), mental playfulness (I.B.2.b), and idiosyncratic learning (I.B.1.b.i.(b)). Snow notes that these six aspects of intelligence are interactive, working together to produce observable behavior. He does not believe that these six aspects of intelligence constitute necessary or sufficient conditions for intelligence. Rather, he views intelligence as a family resemblance concept, or prototype, which is organized around aspects such as the ones described here.

Robert Sternberg suggests that intelligence should be viewed as mental self-government. He seeks this understanding by elaborating an analogy between intelligence, on the one hand, and government, on the other. He views intelligence as providing a means to govern ourselves so that our thoughts and actions are organized, coherent, and responsive to both our internally driven needs and to the needs of the environment (I.B, I.C, II, III). In elaborating this analogy, Sternberg attempts to show parallels between intelligence and the functions of government, levels of government, forms of government, scope of government, political spectrum of government, and efficacy of government.

Edward Zigler emphasizes the arbitrary nature of definitions and the fact that definitions cannot be right or wrong, but only useful or not useful. He views intelligence as a hypothetical construct that has its ultimate reference in the cognitive processes of the individual (I.B.1), but he supports this definition in terms of its usefulness, not in terms of any arbitrary standard of correctness. Zigler also believes that intelligence has a motivational component (I.B.2). As a developmental psychologist, Zigler is particularly interested in the developmental interaction between the individual and the environment (III) and presents a model of the form this interaction takes over time.

Comparison of the 1921 and 1986 symposia

In order to understand how definitions of intelligence have evolved, Cynthia Berg and I attempted to trace the evolution of the concept of

Table 3.2. *Frequencies of attributes that contributors used to define intelligence in 1986 and 1921*

	1986		1921	
	No.	%	No.	%
1. Adaptation, in order to meet the demands of the environment effectively	3	13	4	29
2. Elementary processes (perception, sensation, attention)	5	21	3	21
3. Metacognition (knowledge about cognition)	4	17	1	7
4. Executive processes	6	25	1	7
5. Interaction of processes and knowledge	4	17	0	0
6. Higher level components (abstract reasoning, representation, problem solving, decision making)	12	50	8	57
7. Knowledge	5	21	1	7
8. Ability to learn	4	17	4	29
9. Physiological mechanisms	2	8	4	29
10. Discrete set of abilities (e.g., spatial, verbal, auditory)	4	17	1	7
11. Speed of mental processing	3	13	2	14
12. Automated performance	3	13	0	0
13. g	4	17	2	14
14. Real-world manifestations (social, practical, tacit)	2	8	0	0
15. That which is valued by culture	7	29	0	0
16. Not easily definable, not one construct	4	17	2	14
17. A field of scholarship	1	4	0	0
18. Capacities prewired at birth	3	13	1	7
19. Emotional, motivational constructs	1	4	1	7
20. Restricted to academic/cognitive abilities	2	8	2	14
21. Individual differences in mental competence	1	4	0	0
22. Generation of environment based on genetic programming	1	4	0	0
23. Ability to deal with novelty	1	4	1	7
24. Mental playfulness	1	4	0	0
25. Only important in its predictive value	0	0	1	7
26. Inhibitive capacity	0	0	1	7
27. Overt behavioral manifestation (effective/successful responses)	5	21	3	21

Source: Reproduced with permission from Table 1 in Chapter 26 of Sternberg and Detterman (1986).

intelligence from the 1921 to the 1986 symposium. Table 3.2 lists twenty-seven attributes that appeared in the present and past definitions of intelligence and their frequencies in each of the two symposia. The small number of listings for each attribute would render formal statistical analysis hazardous. But some generalizations can nevertheless be made.

First, at least some general agreement exists across the two symposia regarding the nature of intelligence. The correlation between the two sets of frequencies is .50, indicating moderate overlap in present and past conceptions. Attributes such as adaptation to the environment, basic mental processes, and higher order thinking (e.g., reasoning, problem solving, decision making) were prominent in both listings.

Second, certain themes recur in both symposia. The issue of the one versus the many – Is intelligence one thing or is it manifold? – continues to be of concern, although no consensus exists upon this matter. The issue of breadth of definition also continues to be of concern. As in the earlier symposium, some panelists define intelligence quite narrowly in terms of biological or, especially, cognitive elements, whereas others include a broader array of elements, including motivation and personality. The issue of breadth, like that of the one versus the many, remains unresolved. Investigators still disagree as to the relative emphases that should be placed in theory and research upon physiological versus behavioral manifestations of intelligence, and the respective roles of process and product in defining intelligence also remain unresolved.

Third, despite the similarities in views over the 65 years, some salient differences in the two listings can also be found. Metacognition – conceived of as both knowledge about and control of cognition – plays a prominent role in the 1986 symposium but virtually no role at all in the 1921 symposium. The salience of metacognition and executive processes can undoubtedly be attributed to the predominance of the computer metaphor in the current study of cognition and in information-processing approaches to intelligence. In the present symposium, a greater emphasis has been placed on the role of knowledge and the interaction between this knowledge and mental processes. The change in emphasis is not entirely with respect to functions that occur within the organism. The present panelists show considerable emphasis on the role of context, and particularly of culture, in defining intelligence, whereas such emphasis was absent in the earlier symposium.

Table 3.3 lists the contributors to the two symposia and the behaviors from the list in Table 3.2 mentioned by each.

Table 3.3. *Behaviors mentioned by contributors for definition of intelligence*

1986 symposium	1921 symposium
Anastasi	Buckingham
1 5 14 15 16	3 13 16 27
Baltes	Colvin
16 17	1 8
Baron	Dearborn
3 6 18 27	8
Berry	Freeman
1 16	2 4 6 11
Brown & Campione	Haggerty
3 4 8	2 6 16 18 20
Butterfield	Henmon
3 4 6 7 8	7 8 9
Carroll	Peterson
6 10 11 13 14 15 20 27	1 6 9 10
Das	Pintner
2 4 6	1 9 11 20 23
Detterman	Pressey
2 10 13	13 25
Estes	Ruml
2 4 5	2 6
Eysenck	Terman
2 9 11 13	6
Gardner	Thorndike
6 10 15 27	6 27
Glaser	Thurstone
6 7 12 15 18	6 19 26 27
Goodnow	Woodrow
15	1 6 8 9
Horn	
6 10 11 12 16	
Humphreys	
5	
Hunt	
2 6 9	
Jensen	
13 20	
Pellegrino	
4 5 15 27	
Scarr	
18 22	
Schank	
3 6 7	
Sternberg	
1 6 12 15 23 27	
Snow	
4 6 7 8 21 24	
Zigler	
6 7 8 19	

Source: Reproduced with permission from Table 2 in Chapter 26 of Sternberg and Detterman (1986).

To summarize, the field of intelligence has evolved from one that concentrated primarily on psychometric issues in 1921 to one that concentrates primarily on information processing, cultural context, and their interrelationships in 1986. Prediction of behavior now seems to be somewhat less important than the understanding of that behavior, which needs to precede prediction. On the one hand, few if any issues about the nature of intelligence have been truly resolved. On the other hand, investigators of intelligence seem to have come a rather long way toward understanding the cognitive and cultural bases for the test scores since 1921.

Other definitions

Although I have concentrated on the 1921 and 1986 symposia on the nature of intelligence, as well as on the operational definition of intelligence, of course there have been other definitions. For example, Burt (1955) defined intelligence as "innate, general, cognitive ability" (p. 162). Heim (1970) defined intelligent activity as "grasping the essentials in a given situation and responding appropriately to them" (p. 29). Heim purposefully used the term "intelligent activity" rather than "intelligence" in order to avoid suggesting the existence of a trait that everyone possesses in greater or lesser degree. Cleary, Humphreys, Kendrick, and Wesman (1975) defined intelligence as "the entire repertoire of acquired skills, knowledge, learning sets, and generalization tendencies considered intellectual in nature that are available at any one period in time" (p. 19). Of course, these definitions represent only a smattering of all the ones that could be produced. However, they are reasonably representative of the range of ways in which intelligence has been defined by experts in the field.

Implicit theories

Definitions are just one form of implicit theory of intelligence. But implicit theories can be presented in forms other than the definitional one, because there are many ways of expressing ideas about intelligence that people have "in their heads." In general, theories of intelligence can be classified as being of two kinds: explicit and implicit. Explicit theories of intelligence are constructions of psychologists or other scientists that are based, or at least tested, on data collected from people performing tasks presumed to measure intellectual functioning. For example, a battery of intellectual tests might be administered to a large group of people and the data from these tests analyzed to isolate the proposed sources of intellectual functioning in test performance.

Implicit theories of intelligence are constructions of people (psychologists or laypersons or others) that reside in the minds of these individuals, whether as definitions or otherwise. Such theories need to be discovered rather than invented because they already exist, in some form, in people's heads. The goal of research on implicit theories is to find out the form and content of people's informal theories of intelligence. Thus, one attempts to reconstruct already existing theories rather than to construct new ones. The data of interest are people's communications regarding their notions about the nature of intelligence or its aspects. One might ask people simply to define intelligence, or one might ask them to perform other tasks. For example, a survey of questions regarding the nature of intelligence might be administered to a large group of people and the data from the survey analyzed in order to reconstruct people's belief systems.

The role of implicit theories in scientific understanding

Why even bother to seek to understand people's implicit theories of intelligence or any other construct? What difference do such theories make, given that they are not formal scientific theories but rather merely people's conceptions of a given phenomenon? Under what kinds of circumstances might one seek such understanding?

Understanding behavior motivated by implicit theories. Implicit theories of intelligence drive the way in which people perceive and evaluate both their own intelligence and that of others. To understand better the judgments people make about their own and others' intelligence, it is useful to learn about their implicit theories. For example, parents' implicit theories of their children's language development will determine at what ages they will be willing to make various corrections in their children's speech. More generally, parents' implicit theories of children's cognitive development will determine at what ages they believe their children are ready to perform various intellectual tasks. In sum, knowledge about implicit theories is important because it is so heavily used by people in making judgments in their everyday lives.

Defining the scope of an as yet poorly understood phenomenon. Certain kinds of methodology can be particularly useful at different stages of research into various phenomena. For example, rigorous mathematical modeling of variation in experimental stimuli requires that one have an explicit model of task performance and hence tends to be useful in the middle or later stages of research. In contrast, exploratory factor analysis and protocol analysis can be useful for gleaning an idea of just how individuals approach a task that is poorly understood. Because of its exploratory nature, implicit-theoretical analysis probably has some of its greatest uses during the early stages of research into a given phenomenon.

Because implicit theories of scientific investigators ultimately give rise to their explicit theories, it is useful to find out what these implicit theories are, perhaps even before the explicit theories have been proposed. Implicit theories essentially provide a framework, or a lay of the land, that can be useful in defining the general scope of a new phenomenon to be investigated. Sometimes, the phenomenon is not itself newly discovered, but there is a need for a new approach to an old phenomenon. Again, understanding implicit theories can suggest what aspects of the phenomenon have been more or less attended to in previous investigations. Finally, studying implicit theories can be useful when an investigator suspects that existing explicit theories are wrong or misleading. If an investigation of implicit theories reveals little correspondence with the explicit theories, the implicit theories may be wrong. The possibility also has to be taken into account, however, that the explicit theories are wrong and in need of correction or supplementation. For example, the implicit theories of intelligence to be described suggest the need for broader rather than more narrow views of the construct.

Understanding developmental and cross-cultural differences. Many, if not most, psychological investigators have a tendency to extrapolate the validity of the results beyond the population from which their sample(s) can reasonably be construed as having been drawn. Consider, for example, the field of intelligence. Investigators were drawing universal conclusions about the nature of intelligence before they had ever systematically investigated the intelligence of people in other cultures. They continue to do so to this day, using tests on single or multiple homogeneous populations and drawing conclusions about others as well (see, e.g., chapters in Eysenck, 1982).

Similarly, investigators make unwarranted extrapolations about developmental phenomena. For many years, the standard operating procedure in the study of intelligence across the life span was to administer various kinds of standard psychometric tests and to draw conclusions about the growth or decline of levels of intelligence with age. More recently, investigators have come to realize the importance of defining exactly what intelligence is at various ages. For example, we do not measure the intelligence of infants or even young children in the early school years in the same way that we measure the intelligence of adults. Analogously, it may be necessary to measure the intelligence of older adults in ways that are different from those we use to measure the intelligence of younger adults. For example, tests such as the Scholastic Aptitude Test and the Graduate Record Examination require fairly extensive knowledge of algebraic and geometric concepts in their mathematical sections. Such knowledge may or may not be fairly common among high school and college students, but it is not likely to be common knowledge among older adults, many of whom will not have used algebraic formulas and geometric principles for as much as half a century or more. The point, quite simply, is that we cannot blindly assume that intelligence or any other aspect of mental functioning is necessarily the same across populations, especially if the construct is, at least in part, a social construction. Analysis of implicit theories can provide a useful means for suggesting similarities and differences in psychological constructs across populations.

I should add that whereas I view implicit theories as helping roughly to define the scope of a theory of intelligence, others view implicit theories as telling us something more. Neisser (1979), for example, views intelligence solely as a stipulative concept. He believes that intelligence does not exist except as a resemblance to a prototype, that is, as a degree of similarity between actual persons and some ideally intelligent person. According to Neisser, then, we are intelligent to the extent that our abilities correspond to the abilities of some person we view as ideally intelligent, however we may decide that intelligence ideally should be defined. Neisser notes that this view can be traced back at least to Thorndike (1924), who suggested that

> for a first approximation, let intellect be defined as that quality of mind (or brain or behavior if one prefers) in respect to which Aristotle, Plato, Thucydides, and the like, differed most from Athenian idiots of their day, or in respect to which the lawyers, physicians, scientists, scholars, and editors of reputed greatest ability at constant age, say a dozen of each, differ most from idiots of that age in asylums. (p. 241)

Neisser (1979) collected informal data from Cornell undergraduates about their concepts of intelligence. More formal studies have been conducted by Cantor (1978), who asked adult subjects to list attributes of a bright person, and by Bruner, Shapiro, and Tagiuri (1958), who asked people how often intelligent persons display various personality traits. Bruner et al. found, for example, that intelligent people are likely to be characterized as clever, deliberate, efficient, and energetic and not as apathetic, unreliable, dishonest, or dependent.

I am not as pessimistic as is Neisser regarding the possibilities for attaining a scientifically valid and heuristically useful explicit theory of intelligence. I believe that implicit theories play an important role in understanding intelligence, but not an exclusive role. We need to understand what people think intelligence is, but also to separate these implicit theories from what intelligence actually may be. After all, I believe that it is possible that people are wrong. For example, the fact that some people believe that intelligence is nothing more than what conventional intelligence tests measure does not, in my view, render intelligence tests thereby the ultimate arbiters of what intelligence is. People's implicit theories will affect their actions, but if anything, we need to improve their implicit theories by constructing better explicit theories that inform laypeople as well as experts of what any construct, including intelligence, is according to our best understanding at a given time.

Implicit theories of mainland U.S. adults

Some of the principal studies of implicit theories of intelligence among mainland U.S. adults have been conducted by my collaborators and myself. We have been involved in three major sets of studies. The first was on implicit theories of intelligence, academic intelligence, and everyday intelligence in laypersons and experts (Sternberg, Conway, Ketron, & Bernstein, 1981). The second set was done on implicit theories of intelligence across the adult life span (Berg & Sternberg, 1985). A third set of studies was on implicit theories of intelligence, wisdom, and creativity in adults who were either laypersons or experts in various fields of endeavor (Sternberg, 1985b).

*Implicit theories of intelligence, academic intelligence,
and everyday intelligence*

In the first set of studies (Sternberg et al., 1981), we sought to ascertain how people view intelligence, academic intelligence, and everyday intelligence. Our 186 subjects were divided into 61 people studying in a college library, 63 people waiting for trains in a railroad station during morning and afternoon rush hours, and 62 people entering a local supermarket. Students predominated among the library sample, commuters among the railroad sample, and homemakers among the supermarket sample. In a first study involving behavioral listings for intelligence, academic intelligence, and everyday intelligence, we found that frequencies for listed behaviors could tell us something about similarities and differences in the viewpoints of the various subject groups.

Intelligence and academic intelligence were significantly correlated for the library group, but not for either the railroad group or the supermarket group. In contrast, intelligence and everyday intelligence were significantly correlated for the railroad and supermarket groups, but not for the library group. In other words, subjects in the library (students) viewed intelligence as closer to academic intelligence, whereas the other subjects saw intelligence as closer to everyday intelligence. When we analyze people's self-ratings of their own intelligence in the library group, self-ratings of intelligence and academic intelligence were much more highly correlated than self-ratings of intelligence and everyday intelligence. Thus, intelligence was perceived as much closer to academic than to everyday intelligence. In contrast, in the railroad group, the commuters viewed their academic intelligence and their everyday intelligence as equally related to their intelligence. The supermarket group came out in-between. Thus, people were shown to have differing views as a function of their walk in life.

In a second study, we tested 120 laypersons who responded to newspaper advertisements and 140 experts in the field of intelligence who responded to a mailed questionnaire. All experts were psychologists with doctoral degrees doing research on intelligence in major university research centers around the country. Material consisted of a list of 250 behaviors compiled from the first study. A page on which laypersons could rate themselves by using a percentile scale on intelligence, academic intelligence, and everyday intelligence was also included. Laypersons received the Henmon–Nelson Test of Mental Abilities.

Four different questionnaires were prepared. All four questionnaires were distributed to laypersons; only the first two questionnaires were distributed to experts. No individual received more than one questionnaire. All items required ratings on a scale of 1 (low) to 9 (high). The first questionnaire required ratings of how *important* each of 170 behaviors associated with intelligence (as opposed to unintelligence, the content of the other 80 behaviors) was in defining their concept of an ideally (a) intelligent person, (b) academically intelligent person, and (c) everyday intelligent person. The second questionnaire required ratings of how *characteristic* each of the behaviors was of an ideally (a) intelligent person, (b) academically intelligent person, and (c) everyday intelligent person. The third questionnaire required the same ratings, except for the ideal concept rather than for the ideal person. And the fourth questionnaire required ratings of how *characteristic* each of 250 behaviors was of (a) the person filling out the questionnaire, and (b) the adult whom that person knew best.

Several major points of interest emerged from the data. First, experts view intelligence as very closely related behaviorally to both academic and everyday intelligence. Laypersons view academic and everyday intelligence as less closely related to intelligence. Experts see academic and everyday intelligence as less closely related than they see intelligence as related to each of academic and everyday intelligence, but again, the laypersons see an even weaker relationship. Clearly, though, both experts and laypersons distinguish between behaviors associated with academic and with everyday intelligence. Second, ratings of importance and of characteristicness showed generally similar trends and were, in fact, highly correlated. Third, ratings of experts and laypersons for comparable kinds of intelligence were quite highly correlated. Experts and laypersons seem to have similar, but not identical, perceptions of the nature of intelligence.

The data from the second questionnaire were subjected to principal-component analysis, followed by varimax rotation of the factorial axis. Because of the unwieldiness of the original set of 170 intelligent behaviors as input into the final analysis, preliminary factor analyses were done to reduce the original set to a more tractable set of 98 behaviors.

Three interpretable factors emerged from the analysis of ratings of the ideally intelligent person as supplied by the laypersons. The factors were labeled Practical Problem Solving Ability, Verbal Ability, and Social Competence. The first factor includes behaviors such as *reasons logically and well, identifies connections among ideas,* and *sees all aspects of a problem.* The second factor includes behaviors such as *speaks clearly and articulately, is verbally fluent,* and *converses well.* The third factor includes behaviors such as *accepts others for what they are, admits mistakes,* and *displays interest in the world at large.*

Factor analyses were also conducted on the ratings of academic intelligence and everyday intelligence. For academic intelligence, three interpretable factors emerged: Verbal Ability, Problem Solving Ability, and Social Competence. For everyday intelligence, four interpretable factors emerged: Practical Problem Solving Ability, Social Competence, Character, and Interest in Learning and Culture.

Several points are worth noting. First, the factors for the three kinds of intelligence are highly overlapping. Second, Problem Solving Ability and Social Competence crosscut all three kinds of intelligence. Third, the cognitive factors that constitute people's belief systems for intelligence seem closely to resemble the two principal factors in Cattell and Horn's theory of fluid and crystallized intelligence (R. B. Cattell, 1971; Horn, 1968). Fluid intelligence emphasizes reasoning and problem solving skills, whereas crystallized intelligence emphasizes verbal-comprehension skills.

Comparable factor analyses were conducted for the ratings of experts. Three interpretable factors emerged in the experts' ratings of characteristicness of behaviors for intelligence: Verbal Intelligence, Problem Solving Ability, and Practical Intelligence. The first factor included behaviors such as *displays a good vocabulary, reads with high comprehension,* and *displays curiosity.* The second factor included behaviors such as *is able to apply knowledge to problems at hand, makes good decisions,* and *poses problems in an optimal way.* The third factor included behaviors such as *sizes up situations well, determines how to achieve goals,* and *displays awareness to world around him or her.* Comparable factor analyses were conducted for academic and everyday intelligence. For academic intelligence three factors were obtained: Problem Solving Ability, Verbal Ability, and Motivation. For everyday intelligence the three factors were Practical Problem Solving Ability, Practical Adaptive Behavior, and Social Competence.

Four main points emerged from these analyses. First, as was the case for laypersons, Problem Solving Ability is perceived as playing a major role in all three kinds of intelligence. Second, Practical Intelligence sometimes emerged in the factors for intelligence and everyday intelligence. Third, a Motivation factor emerged in the analysis of data for ratings regarding academic intelligence. Finally, the first two cognitive factors in the experts' conceptions of intelligence, like those in the laypersons' conceptions, seemed to correspond closely to fluid and crystallized abilities, whereas the third factor again seemed to represent some kind of practical or social adaptation.

We also computed a prototypicality measure by correlating each layperson's pattern of self-ratings with the pattern of ideal-subject ratings of characteristicness of behaviors from the data set described earlier. The mean prototypicality index (i.e., mean correlation between self-described actual and ideal behaviors) was .40 for intelligence, .31 for academic intelligence, and .41 for everyday intelligence. Correlations of the prototypicality measure with IQ were .52 for the intelligence measure, .56 for the academic intelligence measure, and .45 for the everyday intelligence measure. Thus, the prototypicality measure actually serves as a relatively good predictor of IQ, especially for academic intelligence.

In a third study, we sought to ascertain the extent to which people actually use behaviors associated with intelligence and unintelligence in their evaluations of other people's intelligence, particularly when they are presented with written behavioral descriptions of the others. A questionnaire was sent to 168 persons selected at random from a local telephone book. Of these persons, 65 responded in time for their data to be used in the study.

The principal experimental material was a 90-item questionnaire. Each item consisted of a verbal description of behaviors characterizing some particular person. People were told that they would "find a brief description of different people, listing various characteristics they had. Assume that the list for each person is made of characteristics that teachers have supplied to describe that person as accurately as possible." The subject's task was to "read the characteristics for each person and then to rate each person on how intelligent" the subject considered the person to be. Ratings were made on a scale from 1 to 9, where 1 was labeled *not at all intelligent,* 5 was labeled *average intelligent,* and 9 was labeled *extremely intelligent.* Half of the items on the questionnaire presented unquantified behavioral descriptions (e.g., "She converses well"), and half presented a mixture of quantified (e.g., "She often converses well") and unquantified descriptions. Moreover, half of the descriptions were paired with male names and half with female names: A given description was paired half the time with a name of each sex.

The following is an example of a problem from this study:

Susan:
She keeps an open mind.
She is knowledgeable about a particular field of knowledge.
She converses well.
She shows a lack of independence.
She is on time for appointments.

All subjects received the same questionnaire items, except that half of the subjects received quantified items presented before unquantified ones and the other half received the reverse ordering; different names were paired with different descriptions so that those descriptions that were male for half the subjects were female for the other half, and vice versa.

The mean rating of intelligence over the 45 unquantified descriptions was 5.1; the mean rating over the 45 quantified descriptions was 4.5. The difference between ratings was significant, indicating the quantification generally lowered ratings of intelligence. The correlation between the unquantified statements and their paired quantified versions was .87, indicating that although quantification lowered ratings, it changed their pattern only slightly. It made no difference in means whether a given description was matched with a male or female name. The means for the male and female names were practically indistinguishable (within .01 on the rating scale), and the correlation between identical descriptions paired for male versus female names was .99 in the unquantified condition and .98 in the quantified condition.

Two basic kinds of modeling were done for the unquantified descriptions. In the first, we took means and sums of characteristicness ratings from experts from Study 2 and computed means on the basis of those behaviors listed in each description given in the present experiment. The correlation between ratings of intelligence and the mean characteristicness rating for each fictitious person was .96; the correlation between ratings of intelligence and the summed characteristicness ratings for each fictitious person was .97. Comparable correlations were obtained if laypersons' rather than experts' prototypes were used. Hence, the prototype ratings from the earlier experiment provided excellent predictions of the ratings in the present experiment.

In the second kind of modeling, multiple regression was used to predict the overall rating of the intelligence of the fictitious person from counts of numbers of behaviors in each of the factors of intelligence (and the behavior characterizing unintelligence) found in each description. The multiple correlation between the ratings of the intelligence of the fictitious person, on one hand, and the aspects of perceived intelligence and unintelligence, on the other, was .97. Regression weights were .32 for practical problem solving ability, .33 for verbal ability, .19 for social competence, and −.48 for unintelligence. All weights were significant and in the predicted directions. The same kinds of analyses were performed on the data for quantified descriptions, with very similar results. Thus, we can conclude that people use their implicit theories of intelligence in evaluating the intelligence of others as well as themselves. As in the self-ratings, people seem to weigh cognitive factors more heavily than noncognitive ones and to take into account negative as well as positive information.

The studies described above concern different conceptions of intelligence held by experts and nonexperts. In a second set of studies, Berg and Sternberg (1985) investigated the development of implicit theories of intelligence over the life span. Their subjects ranged in age from 20 to 83 and were divided into three groups averaging 30, 50, and 70 years of age. Without going into all of the details of method and results, the main finding was that, in general, older individuals view everyday competence as more important in characterizing the difference between individuals of average and exceptional intelligence than do younger individuals. Moreover, middle-aged and older individuals tend to combine crystallized intelligence with problem-solving abilities for most age-specific prototypes. Thus, the distinction between fluid and crystallized abilities seems less important to the older individuals than to the younger ones. For all subjects, the older the age of the hypothetical individual being rated, the more important everyday competence was to intelligence. Hence, everyday competence increases in its importance to intelligence both as a function of the age of the rater and of the ratee.

In a final set of studies, I examined views on intelligence of experts, but not experts in the field of intelligence. Rather, the experts in this study were 65 individuals in the field of art, 70 in the field of business, 65 in the field of philosophy, 85 in the field of physics, as well as 30 laypersons. The results for the laypersons were similar to those in past studies. But there were some interesting differences among experts in the various fields.

Whereas professors of art emphasized knowledge and the ability to use that knowledge in weighing alternative possibilities and in seeing analogies, business professors emphasized the ability to think logically, to focus on essential aspects of a problem, and both to follow others' arguments easily and to see where these arguments lead. The emphasis on assessment of argumentation in business professors' implicit theories is far weaker in art professors' implicit theories. Philosophy professors emphasize critical and logical abilities very heavily, especially the ability to follow complex arguments, to find subtle mistakes in these arguments, and to generate counterexamples to invalid arguments. The philosophers' view very clearly emphasizes those aspects of logic and rationality that are essential in analyzing and creating philosophical arguments. Physicists, in contrast, place more emphasis on precise mathematical thinking, on the ability to relate physical phenomena to the concepts of physics, and on the ability to grasp quickly the laws of nature. Thus, experts tended, sometimes subtly, to emphasize the skills important in their profession when queried as to their implicit theories of intelligence.

Implicit theories of and about children

Some of the most interesting work on implicit theories of intelligence has been done by investigators seeking an understanding of the nature of intelligence in children. Siegler and Richards (1982) asked college students what they thought intelligence was at different ages. In particular, subjects were asked to describe the nature of intelligence in 6-month-olds, 2-year-olds, 10-year-olds, and adults. The authors reported the five traits (in the order of the frequency with which they were mentioned) that most often were mentioned as characterizing intelligence at different ages. At 6 months old, these traits were recognition of people and objects, motor coordination, alertness, awareness of environment, and verbalization. At 2 years old, they were verbal ability, learning ability, awareness of people and environment, motor coordination, and curiosity. At 10 years old, they were verbal ability, followed by learning ability, problem solving ability, reasoning ability – all tied for second place in frequency of mention – and creativity. At the adult level, the traits were reasoning ability, verbal ability, problem solving ability, learning ability, and creativity. Clearly, there is the trend toward conceiving of intelligence as less perceptual-motor and as more cognitive with increasing age.

One of the most interesting studies of implicit theories regarding children's intelligence was done with teachers rather than college students as subjects. Fry (1984) asked teachers at the primary, secondary, and tertiary levels about their conceptions of intelligence. Several studies converged upon an interesting set of results. Elementary school teachers tended to emphasize social variables such as popularity, friendliness, respect for law and order, and interest in the environment in their conceptions of intelligence. Secondary teachers, in contrast, tended to stress verbal variables, such as verbal fluency and energy, in their conceptions. The tertiary teachers tended to regard cognitive variables such as reasoning ability, broad knowledge, logical thinking, and dealing maturely with problems as most important to intelligence. Thus, the teachers at the three levels in effect recapitulated the three factors obtained by Sternberg et al. (1981) in their study of implicit theories, but the emphasis was on different factors applying at different ages. Problem Solving Ability applied most to teachers' conceptions of college students' intelligence, Verbal Ability to their conceptions of secondary school students' intelligence, and Social Competence to their conceptions of elementary students' intelligence. My own experience is consistent with the results obtained by Fry, suggesting that teachers of elementary school students tend very heavily to emphasize social-competence skills in their assessment of the intelligence of children.

Yussen and Kane (1985) studied conceptions of intelligence, but they used as their subjects children rather than adults. They interviewed students in the first, third, and sixth grades. Children were asked questions concerning such issues as visible signs of intelligence, qualities associated with intelligence, the constancy or malleability of intelligence, and the definition of intelligence. The authors found that older children's conceptions were more differentiated than those of younger children and that with increasing age children increasingly characterized intelligence as an internalized quality. But older children are less likely than younger ones to think that overt signs signal intelligence: They are less global in the qualities they associate with intelligence than are younger children. There is also a tendency for younger children to think of intelligence largely in terms of social skills but for older children to think of it largely in terms of academic skills.

Dweck and Elliott (1983) have also investigated concepts of intelligence among children and found that children tend to have one of two kinds of concepts regarding the plasticity of intelligence. "Entity theorists" believe that intelligence is something you are born with and that its level remains constant across the life span. Because these children believe there is not much they can do to increase their intelligence, they tend to be oriented toward showing their intelligence through their performance. They are often afraid to make mistakes, particularly if they will be observed by others, and attempt to "look good" to others in their work. "Incremental theorists," on the other hand, believe that intelligence is something that increases throughout the life span and that the method of increase is through learning. They tend, therefore, to be learning rather than performance oriented and to seek out new challenges that will help them improve their intelligence.

Cross-cultural investigations

The studies described up to now have all utilized North American subjects in their studies of implicit theories of intelligence. Indeed, with the exception of Fry's study, which was done in Canada, all of the studies have looked at conceptions of intelligence in the United States. Some cross-cultural work has been done, however.

Wober (1974) investigated concepts of intelligence among members of different tribes in Uganda as well as within different subgroups of the tribes. Wober found differences in concepts of intelligence both within and between tribes. The Bagandans, for example, tended to associate intelligence with mental order, whereas the Batoro tribespeople associated it with some degree of mental turmoil. On semantic-differential scales, Baganda tribespeople thought of intelligence as persistent, hard, and obdurate, whereas the Batoro thought of it as soft, obedient, and yielding.

Serpell (1974, 1976) asked Chewa adults in rural eastern Zambia to rate village children on how well they could perform tasks requiring adaptation to the everyday world. He found that the ratings did not correlate with children's cognitive test scores, even when the tests that were used were adapted to seem culturally appropriate. Serpell concluded that the rural Chewian criteria for judgments of intelligence were not related to Western notions of intelligence.

Super (1983) analyzed concepts of intelligence among the Kokwet of western Kenya. He found that intelligence in children seemed to be conceived differently from intelligence in adults. The word *ngom* was applied to children and seemed to note responsibility, highly verbal cognitive quickness, the ability to comprehend complex matters quickly, and good management of interpersonal relations. The word *utat* was applied to adults and suggested inventiveness, cleverness, and sometimes, wisdom and unselfishness. A separate word, *keelat,* was used to signify smartness or sharpness.

Some of the earliest work done by anyone on implicit theories of intelligence was done by Irvine (1966, 1969, 1970). Irvine studied implicit theories of intelligence by examining proverbs in common use among the Mashona people of Zimbabwe. He started by collecting a hundred sayings and beliefs, and his analysis led him to the conclusion that the Mashona word for intelligence, *ngware,* refers to the tendency to be cautious and prudent, particularly in social relationships. According to Irvine, "intelligent acts are then of a conforming kind having primary reference to the affective climate of one's own relationships with the spiritual force of the living and ancestral spirits of the kin group" (Irvine, 1969, p. 98).

Keats (Gill & Keats, 1980; Keats, 1982) has compared Australian conceptions of intelligence with those of Malian and Chinese people. She has found that the Malian and Australians agreed, within the domain of mental abilities, that understanding and thinking were critical aspects of intelligence. Among various skills, however, Australians rated reading, speaking, and writing as the three most important skills, whereas the Malians rated symbolic and social skills as coming in importance right below speaking. In her comparison of Australians with Chinese, both groups mentioned the importance of creativity, originality, problem solving, and a large knowledge base to intelligence. The Chinese frequently mentioned imitation, observation, carefulness, and correctness in thinking, whereas the Australians did not mention these attributes at all. Conversely, Australians believed that communicational language skills were important, but these were not mentioned by the Chinese.

Other studies have been done as well that compare conceptions of intelligence across cultures. However, not all of these studies can be reviewed here. For an excellent review of the various studies, see Berry (1984).

Conclusion

Implicit theories of intelligence, whether expressed as definitions, factors, or whatever, provide a valuable means for gaining insight regarding how various groups of people – the observers – view intelligence in various groups of people – the targets. It is possible, as has been shown, to ask people to characterize the intelligence of their own group, of another group, or of themselves. Understanding people's implicit theories is important because it is these theories that motivate people in their everyday judgments of the intelligence of others, and it is also these theories that give rise to explicit theories. Implicit theories also help us understand something of the scope of phenomena, such as intelligence, that are not yet well understood, and they are particularly helpful in elucidating conceptions of intelligence across the life span and across various cultures and subcultures. Implicit theories can help us realize how incomplete our current explicit theories are. Although, strictly speaking, they tell us not about the phenomenon under investigation – in this case, intelligence – but rather about people's conceptions of this phenomenon, people often act as though their conceptions of a phenomenon are veridical with respect to understanding the phenomenon itself, and so it is particularly important to understand what people's implicit theories are.

Two of the best examples of how implicit theories can give rise to important bodies of work are in the work of the two main forefathers of contemporary thought about intelligence, Francis Galton and Alfred Binet. Each had a very different conception of intelligence, which led him in a completely different direction with regard to thinking about and measuring the construct. The views of Galton and Binet are considered in the next chapter.

4

The seminal views of Galton and Binet

If current thinking about the nature of intelligence owes a debt to any scholars, the debt is to Sir Francis Galton and to Alfred Binet. These two investigators – Galton at the end of the nineteenth century and Binet at the beginning of the twentieth century – have had a profound impact on thinking about intelligence, an impact that carries down to the present day. Many present conflicts regarding the nature of intelligence can be traced to conflicts between Galton and Binet. To understand contemporary thinking about intelligence, one needs to know how Galton and Binet thought about the subject. Therefore, one whole chapter is devoted to the thinking of these two men, whose views will be considered in succession.

Sir Francis Galton's view of intelligence

Galton links intelligence to energy and sensitivity

The publication of Darwin's (1859) *Origin of Species* had a profound impact on many lines of scientific endeavor. One of these lines of endeavor was the investigation of human intelligence. The book suggested that the capabilities of humans were in some sense continuous with those of lower animals, and hence could be understood through scientific investigation.

One scholar who followed up the suggestion was Darwin's cousin, Francis Galton. Galton (1883) proposed a theory of the "human faculty and its development." Because Galton also proposed techniques for measuring the "human faculty," his theory could be applied directly to human behavior. The combination of theory and measurement techniques opened a door to the understanding of human intelligence.

Galton proposed two general qualities that distinguished the more from the less intellectually able. The first was energy, or the capacity for labor. Galton believed that intellectually gifted individuals in a variety of fields were characterized by remarkable levels of energy. The second general quality was sensitivity. Galton observed that the only information that can reach us concerning external events passes through the senses and the more perceptive the senses are of differences in luminescence, pitch, odor, or whatever, the larger would be the range of information on which intelligence could act. Galton did not mince words when speaking of the lower range of the intellectual spectrum. In his 1883 book, he observed:

The discriminative facility of idiots is curiously low; they hardly distinguish between heat and cold, and their sense of pain is so obtuse that some of the more idiotic seem hardly to know what it is. In their dull lives, such pain as can be excited in them may literally be accepted with a welcome surprise. (p. 28)

For seven years (1884–90), Galton maintained an anthropometric laboratory at the South Kensington Museum in London where, for a small fee, visitors could have themselves measured on a variety of psychophysical tests. Consider some examples of the tests Galton used.

One such test was weight discrimination. The apparatus consisted of a number of cases of gun cartridges, filled with alternative layers of shot, wool, and wadding. The cases were all identical in appearance and differed only in their weights. Subjects were tested by a sequencing task. They were given three cases and, with their eyes closed, had to arrange them in proper order of weight. The weights formed a geometric series of heaviness, and the examiner recorded the finest interval that an examinee could discriminate. Galton suggested that similar geometric sequences could be used for testing other senses, such as touch and taste. With touch, Galton proposed the use of wirework of various degrees of fineness, whereas for taste, he proposed the use of stock bottles of solutions of salt of various strength. For olfaction, he suggested the use of bottles of attar of rose in various degrees of dilution.

Galton also contrived a whistle for ascertaining the highest pitch that different individuals could perceive. Tests with the whistle enabled him to discover that people's ability to hear high notes declines considerably as age advances. He also discovered that people are inferior to cats in their ability to perceive tones of high pitch. This finding presents a problem for any psychophysically based theory of intelligence that subscribes to a notion of evolutionary continuity. It suggests that, in at least this one respect, cats are superior in intelligence to humans. Although one may grant this superiority to cats, one will then be obliged to grant superiority to various animals in many other psychophysical characteristics, leaving people in a mediocre position to which they are not accustomed, especially if they believe that they represent the pinnacle of evolutionary development up to now.

Cattell proposes a battery of psychophysical tests

James McKean Cattell brought many of Galton's ideas across continents to the United States. As head of the psychological laboratory at Columbia University, he was in a good position to publicize the psychophysical approach to the theory and measurement of intelligence. J. M. Cattell (1890) believed that psychology could not attain the certainty and exactness of the physical sciences unless it rested on a foundation of experiment and measurement. A step in this direction was to be obtained through the devising of mental tests based on Galton's notions.

J. M. Cattell (1890) proposed a series of 50 psychophysical tests, 10 of which he described in detail:

1. *Dynamometer pressure*. The dynamometer measures the pressure resulting from the greatest possible squeeze of one's hand.
2. *Rate of movement*. This test is a measure of the quickest possible movement of the right hand and arm from rest through a distance of 50 cm. Cattell measured the rate of movement by using an apparatus that started an electric current when the hand was first moved and stopped the current when the hand came to rest.
3. *Sensation areas*. This test measures the distance on the skin by which two points must be separated in order for them to be felt as separate points. Cattell suggested that the back of the closed right hand between the first and second fingers be used as the basis for measurement.
4. *Pressure causing pain*. Cattell suggested that the point at which pressure first causes pain may be an important constant. He used the tip of hard rubber five mm in radius as his pain-producing instrument and recommended the center of the forehead as the place at which to apply the instrument.
5. *Least noticeable difference in weight*. Cattell believed that both the just noticeable sensation and the least noticeable difference in sensation are psychological constants of great interest to theorists of intelligence. Cattell measured least noticeable differences in weight with

small wooden boxes. Subjects were handed two such boxes and asked to indicate which was heavier.

6. *Reaction time for sound.* For this test, Cattell used what he called a "Hipp Chronoscope" to measure the time elapsing before an auditory stimulus called forth a reaction in the subjects being tested.

7. *Time for naming colors.* Cattell pasted ten 2-cm square pieces of paper on a strip of black paste board. The squares were arranged vertically, separated from each other by a distance of 1 cm. Cattell measured the time it took a subject to name all 10 colors and then computed the average time per color. Data from two separate trials were collected, but only the faster time was counted.

8. *Bisection of a 50-cm line.* In this test, subjects were required to divide a strip of wood into two equal parts by means of a movable line.

9. *Judgment of 10-sec duration.* This test required the examiner to strike a table with the end of a pencil at the beginning and at the end of a 10-sec interval. Subjects were then asked to repeat the procedure, taking care to strike the pencil for the second time after an equal interval of time had elapsed.

10. *Number of letters repeated after a single exposure.* This test began with the examiner's reciting names of six letters at the rate of two letters per second. If the examinee succeeded in repeating the letter names back, the examiner went up to seven letters, eight letters, and so on, until the examinee failed. If the examinee failed on six letters, he received two more trials with different letters. If each trial was failed, the examiner went backward to five, four, and three letters, continuing backward until the examinee succeeded in repeating back the sequence.

Wissler blows the whistle on psychophysical tests

Psychophysical tasks find little or no place in modern-day tests of intelligence as administered in schools and in industry. Indeed, such tests ceased to play an important role in practical mental measurement by the turn of the century, although, as will be discussed later, they are coming back into vogue among certain theoreticians. The tests were abandoned because they were found to show a chance pattern of correlations both with each other and with external criteria used to validate the tests.

The coup de grace was administered by a student in Cattell's own laboratory, Clark Wissler. Wissler (1901) proposed that Cattell's tests should correlate both with each other and with external criteria of academic success, such as grades in the undergraduate program at Columbia

University. Wissler based his study on Cattell's tests. He used 21 of Cattell's tests: perception of size, size of head, strength of hand, fatigue, eyesight, color vision, hearing, perception of pitch, perception of weight or force of movement, sensation areas, sensitivity to pain, color preference, reaction time, rate of perception, naming colors, rate of movement, accuracy of movements, rhythm and perception of time, association, imagery, and memory. While an examinee was being tested, an observer noted a number of physical characteristics of the examinee: straight versus sloping forehead, color of hair, darkness and clearness of complexion, color of eyes, straightness of hair, convexity and elevation of nose, size and projection of ears, size of mouth, thickness of lips, size of hands in relation to size of body, size of fingers in relation to width of hand, and malformation of face and head. During the testing session, examinees were asked to supply information about their family background, so that the relationship between test perfor-mance and family situations could be assessed.

Wissler's results were disappointing, at least to Cattell. Wissler found the tests to correlate with each other only at the level that would be expected as a result of a distribution corresponding to the laws of chance. Moreover, he found that whereas students' grades in college correlated with each other at a very high level, they showed only trivial correlations with the mental tests of Cattell, as based on the work of Galton.

Wissler realized that there was an apparent contradiction between his research results and certain of people's common preconceptions:

It is often claimed that quickness, for example, will show itself in all our acts, and that therefore there must be a correlation in tests of quickness. . . . But this comes from a misconception. A chance correlation does not mean that no one will manifest such efficiency, but that the number of individuals excelling in all can be closely approximated according to the laws of chance. In this instance one exception does not break the rule. (p. 52)

Wissler concluded that his tests told us nothing about the general ability of college students, and indeed, he interpreted his results as casting doubt on the notion that there even exists such a thing as general ability.

It is ironic, in retrospect, that a study as influential as Wissler's was as inconclusive as the study actually turned out to be. Wissler used as his subjects undergraduates at Columbia University, who were rather restricted in their range of mental abilities toward the upper end of almost any mental ability scale. Hence, correlations obtained with these subjects would tend to be lower than would be those obtained with a broader range of subjects. Nevertheless, the results obtained with these subjects are not so different from those obtained with a wider range of subjects, although with enough range, more substantial and in many cases significant correlations begin to emerge between psychophysical tests and other measures of mental abilities. Nevertheless, the Wissler study seriously undermined the approach of Galton and his successor, Cattell, for many years to come.

Alfred Binet's view of intelligence

The importance of judgment

In 1904, the minister of public instruction in Paris named a commission charged with studying or creating tests that would insure that mentally defective children received an adequate education. The commission decided that no child suspected of retardation should be placed in a special class for the retarded without first being given an examination "from which it could be certified that because of the state of his intelligence, he was unable to profit, in an average measure, from the instruction given in the ordinary schools" (Binet & Simon, 1916a, p. 9). Binet and Simon devised tests to meet this placement need. Thus, whereas theory and research in the tradition of Galton grew out of pure scientific concerns, theory and research in the tradition of Binet grew out of practical educational concerns.

At the time, definitions for various degrees of subnormal intelligence lacked both precision and standardization. Personality and intellectual deficits were seen as being of the same ilk. Binet and Simon noted a case of one institutionalized child who seemed to be a victim of the state of confusion that existed: "One child, called imbecile in the first certificate, is marked idiot in the second, feebleminded (debile) in the third, and degenerate in the fourth" (Binet & Simon, 1916a, p. 11).

Binet and Simon's conception of intelligence and of how to measure it differed substantially from that of Galton and Cattell, whose tests they referred to as "wasted time." To Binet and Simon, the core of intelligence is

judgment, otherwise called good sense, practical sense, initiative, the faculty of adapting one's self to circumstances. To judge well, to comprehend well, to reason well, these are the essential activities of intelligence. A person may be a moron or an imbecile if he is lacking in judgment; but with good judgment he can never be either. Indeed the rest of the intellectual faculties seem of little importance in comparison with judgment. (1916a, pp. 42–3)

Binet cited the example of Helen Keller as someone of known extraordinary intelligence whose scores on psychophysical tests would be notably inferior and, yet, who could be expected to perform at a very high level on tests of judgment.

Binet and Simon's (1916a) theory of intelligent thinking in many ways foreshadowed the research being done today on the development of metacognition (see, e.g., Brown & DeLoache, 1978; Flavell & Wellman, 1977). According to Binet and Simon (1916b), intelligent thought is composed of three distinct elements: direction, adaptation, and control.

Direction consists in knowing what has to be done and how it is to be accomplished. When we are required to add two numbers, for example, we give ourselves a series of instructions on how to proceed, and these instructions form the direction of thought. These instructions need not always be conscious:

In the beginning, when we commence an art not yet learned, we have the full consciousness of the directions we are to follow; but little by little, the influence of the directing state becomes weaker on the movement of the thought and of the hand. One no longer needs to make an express appeal to the verbal formula of the instructions; it falls into the vague state of an intellectual feeling, or even completely disappears. (Binet & Simon, 1916b, p. 137)

In many respects, these ideas about the development of direction over time foreshadow current theorizing regarding automaticity of information processing (see, e.g., Schneider & Shiffrin, 1977; Shiffrin & Schneider, 1977). According to Binet and Simon (1916b), retarded individuals show an absence or weakness of direction that manifests itself in two different forms: "Either the direction, once commenced, does not continue, or it has not even been commenced because it has not been understood" (p. 138).

Adaptation refers to one's selection and monitoring of one's strategy during the course of task performance:

There is not only a direction in the movement of thought, there is also a progress; this progress manifests itself in the nature of the successive states through which one passes; they are not equivalent, the first is not of the same value as the last. One arrives at the last state only because he has already passed the first state. (Binet & Simon, 1916b, pp. 139–40)

Thought consists of a series of selections: "It consists in constantly choosing between many states, many ideas, many means, which present themselves before it like routes which diverge from a crossroad. . . . To think is constantly to choose in view of the end to be pursued" (Binet & Simon, 1916b, p. 140). Retarded children, according to Binet and Simon (1916b), show a lack of adaptive ability, which manifests itself in part in terms of what these authors call *n'importequisme* ("no-matter-whatism"). No-matter-whatism derives from a lack of critical sense, a lack of differentiation in thinking, and an absence of persistence of intellectual effort. Suppose, for example, an individual is presented with a puzzle in which a whole pattern can be reconstructed by joining pieces of the cards to reconstruct the whole, as in a jigsaw puzzle. The normal person tries many different solutions. When one combination does not succeed, the person tries other combinations and either maintains successful parts of previous constructions or abandons previous ideas and visualizes new schemes. However, "not only does the imbecile content himself with something nearly true, owing to the absence of critical sense, but moreover the number of attempts which he makes is extremely small, two or three for example, where a normal would make ten" (Binet & Simon, 1916b, p. 145).

Control is the ability to criticize one's own thoughts and actions. Binet and Simon (1916b) believed much of this ability to be exercised beneath the conscious level. Defectives show a lack of control. Their actions are frequently inappropriate to the task at hand. For example, a retarded individual "told to copy an 'a' scribbles a formless mass at which he smiles in a satisfied manner" (p. 149).

Binet and Simon (1916b) distinguished between two types of intelligence, ideational intelligence and instinctive intelligence. Ideational intelligence operates by means of words and ideas. It uses logical analysis and verbal reasoning. Instinctive intelligence operates by means of feeling. It refers not to the instinct attributed to animals and to simple forms of human behavior, but to the "lack of a logical perception, of a verbal reasoning, which would permit of explaining and of demonstrating a succession of truths" (Binet & Simon, 1916b, p. 316). It seems to be very similar to what we might refer to as an intuitive sense. Retardates are seen as deficient in both, to greater or lesser extents.

The above formulation should make clear that, contrary to the contemporary conventional wisdom, Binet was not atheoretical in his approach to intelligence and its development. To the contrary, he and Simon conceived of intelligence in ways that were theoretically sophisticated – more so than most of the work that followed theirs – and that resembled in content much of the most recent thinking regarding metacognitive information processing. Whatever may be the distinction between the thinking of Binet and that of Galton, it was not (as some would have it) that Galton was theoretically motivated and Binet atheoretically motivated (cf., Hunt, Frost, & Lunneborg, 1973). If anything, Binet had a more well developed theory of the nature of intelligence. Instead, the distinction was in the way these scientists selected items for the tests that they proposed to measure intelligence.

Galton's test items had construct validity in terms of his theory that intelligence is closely related to physical abilities, but Galton did not empirically validate his test items. Binet's test items had construct validity in terms of his theory of intelligence, in that these test items measured the kinds of judgmental abilities that Binet theorized constituted intelligence, but they were also chosen so that they would differentiate between the performance of children of different ages or mental capacities as well as be intercorrelated with each other at a reasonable level. What were the kinds of items Binet and his successors (e.g., Terman & Merrill, 1973) used to measure intelligence at various age levels?

The Binet tradition for testing intelligence

The Stanford–Binet scale in its contemporary form (Terman & Merrill, 1973) starts with tests for children of age 2. Examples of tests at this level are a three-hole form board, which requires children to put circular, square, and triangular pieces into holes on a board of appropriate shape; identification of parts of the body, which requires children to identify body parts on a paper doll; block building, which requires children to build a four-block tower; and picture vocabulary, which requires children to identify pictures of common objects.

Six years later, by age 8, the character of the tests changes considerably, although the tests are still measuring the kinds of higher cognitive processes that the tests for age 2 attempt to tap. At age 8, the tests include vocabulary, which requires children to define words; verbal absurdities, which requires recognition of why each of a set of statements is foolish; similarities and differences, which requires children to say how each of two objects is the same as and different from the other; comprehension, which requires children to solve practical problems of the sort encountered in everyday life; and naming the days of the week.

After six more years, when subjects are age 14, there is some overlap in tests, although, on the average, the tests are still more difficult. They include vocabulary; induction, in which the experimenter makes a notch in an edge of some folded paper and asks subjects how many holes the paper will have when it is unfolded (the test seems to be more spatial than inductive in character); reasoning, which requires solution of an arithmetic word problem; ingenuity, which requires individuals to indicate the series of steps that could be used to pour a given amount of water from one container to another; orientation, requiring reasoning about spatial directions; and reconciliation of opposites, which requires individuals to say in what ways two opposites are alike. The most difficult level, "Superior Adult III," includes measures of vocabulary, interpretation of proverbs, orientation, reasoning, repetition of main ideas in a story, and solution of analogies.

The early Binet tests, like the early Galton tests (as modified and expanded by J. M. Cattell), were subjected to empirical test rather early on. Sharp (1899) undertook a large-scale experiment to discover the usefulness of the Binet–Simon tests in applied settings. Sharp "provisionally accepted [the notion] that the complex mental processes, rather than the elementary processes, are those the variations of which give most important information in regard to the mental characteristics whereby individuals are commonly classed" (p. 348). Sharp used a curious sample of tests, however. She included five memory tests, a mental imagery test, a test of imagination, a test of attention, a test of discrimination, and a test of taste and tendencies. The heavy emphasis upon memory tests was peculiar, especially in view of Binet and Simon's (1916a) belief that memory is not an important aspect of intelligence: "At first glance, memory being a psychological phenomenon of capital importance, one would be tempted to give it a very conspicuous part in an examination of intelligence. But memory is distinct from and independent of judgment. One may have good sense and lack memory. The reverse is also common" (p. 43). Unfortunately, Binet and Simon's point was lost not only on Sharp but on many of her successors. A review of the fairly extensive post-Binet literature on the relationship between memory and intelligence reveals the truth of what Binet recognized many years ago – that memory is not a particularly integral part of intelligence (see Estes, 1982). It should come as no surprise that Sharp's (1899) results were only slightly more encouraging than Wissler's (1901). But the fact that Sharp's data had much less impact than did Wissler's is probably due not to the questionable aspects of her selection of materials but to the fact that Binet, like Galton, had a popularizer in this country – one who was much more successful than Cattell in marketing new ideas about how to measure intelligence.

The contribution of Lewis Terman

Lewis M. Terman, a professor of psychology at Stanford University, constructed the earliest versions of what have come to be called the Stanford–Binet Intelligence Scales (Terman & Merrill, 1937, 1973). The tests already described are from Terman's versions of the Binet scales. Terman is well known for his applied rather than his theoretical work. One example of such work, of course, is the set of Stanford–Binet scales. A second example of equal renown is the longitudinal study of the gifted conducted by Terman and his successors (e.g., Terman, 1925; Terman & Oden, 1959). In his sample of the gifted, Terman included California children under age 11 with IQs over 140 as well as children in the 11–14 age bracket with slightly lower IQs (to allow for the lower ceiling at this age in test scores). The mean IQ of the 643 subjects selected was 151; only 22 of these subjects had IQs of under 140. The accomplishments in later life of the selected group were extraordinary by any criterion. By 1959, there were 70 listings among the group in *American Men of Science* and 3 memberships in the highly prestigious National Academy of Science. In addition, 31 men were listed in *Who's Who in America* and 10 appeared in the *Directory of American Scholars*. There were numerous highly successful business-men as well as individuals who were succeeding unusually well in all of the professions. The sex bias in these references is obvious. Because most of the women became housewives, it is impossible to make any meaningful comparison between the men, on the one hand (none of whom were reported to be househusbands), and the women, on the other hand.

Terman's other major accomplishment, the Stanford–Binet Intelligence Scale, is still one of the two most widely used individual tests of intelligence. In earlier versions of the scale and in much of the literature on the development of intelligence, three interrelated concepts have played a critical role. The first concept, chronological age, refers simply to a person's physical age. The second concept, mental age, refers to a person's level of intelligence in comparison to the "average" person of a given age. If, for example, a person performs at a level comparable to that of an average 12-year-old, the person's mental age will be 12, regardless of the person's chronological age. The third concept, intelligence quotient (IQ), traditionally refers to the ratio between mental age and chronological age multiplied by 100. A score of 100 signifies that mental age is equivalent to chronological age. Scores above 100 indicate above-average intelligence; scores below 100 indicate below-average intelligence.

For a variety of reasons, the concept of mental age has proven to be something of a weak link in the psychometric analysis of intelligence. First, increases in mental age seem to slow at about the age of 16. The interpretation of the mental age concept above this age, thus, becomes equivocal. Second, increases in mental age vary nonlinearly with chronological age, even up to the age of 16. The interpretation of mental ages and of IQs computed from them may, therefore, vary for different chronological ages. Third, the unidimensionality of the mental age scale seems to imply a certain sameness over age levels in the concept of intelligence – a sameness that the contents of the tests do not bear out. For these and other reasons, IQs have tended in recent years to be computed on the basis of relative performance within a given age group (see, e.g., Terman & Merrill, 1973) – one's performance is evaluated relative only to the performance of others of the same age. Commonly, scores have been standardized to have a mean of 100 and a standard deviation of 15 or 16. These deviation IQs (as they are called) have been used in much the same way as the original ratio IQs, although in spirit they are quite different. In fact, the deviation IQs are not quotients at all!

The contributions of David Wechsler

Deviation IQs are used in the second major individual intelligence scale applied in contemporary assessment. This scale is the Wechsler Adult Intelligence Scale (Wechsler, 1958) and its companion scale for children, the Wechsler Intelligence Scale for Children (Wechsler, 1974). These two scales are known as the WAIS and the WISC, respectively.

These scales are based on Wechsler's notion of intelligence as "the overall capacity of an individual to understand and cope with the world around him" (1974, p. 5). Intelligence is conceived of as a global entity in which no one particular ability is of crucial or overwhelming importance:

Ultimately, intelligence is not a kind of ability at all, certainly not in the same sense that reasoning, memory, verbal fluency, etc., are so regarded. Rather it's something that is inferred from the way these abilities are manifested under different conditions and circumstances. . . . General intelligence, however viewed, is a multifaceted construct. Most definitions differ not so much by what they include as by what they omit. They cover only a modest range of the many abilities and aptitudes that may enter into or determine intelligent behavior, and these pertain primarily to cognitive skills or processes (e.g., ability to reason, ability to learn, ability to solve problems, etc.). Intelligent behavior, however, may also call for one or more of a host of aptitudes (factors) which are more in the nature of conative and personality traits than cognitive capabilities. These involve not so much skills and know-how as drives and attitudes, and often what may be described as sensitivity to social, moral, or aesthetic values. They include such traits as persistence, zest, impulse control, and goal awareness – traits which, for the most part, are independent of any particular intellectual ability. (pp. 5–6)

The Wechsler intelligence scales, like the Stanford–Binet scales, are wide ranging in their content. However, these scales do not do full justice to the breadth of their originator's conception of the nature of intelligence. Indeed, it is unlikely, even today, that any scale could be constructed that would do full justice to the broad conceptions of Binet and Wechsler.

The most recent version of the WISC, the WISC-R (Wechsler, 1974), is appropriate for children in the age range from 6 to 16. The test contains 12 subtests, 10 of which are considered mandatory and 2 of which are considered optional. The content of the test is almost identical to that of the adult scale, except that items are easier, as befits their lower targeted age range. The tests are equally divided into two parts, verbal tests and performance tests. Each part yields a separate deviation IQ, and it is possible as well to obtain a deviation IQ for the full scale. Like the Stanford–Binet, the test must be individually administered. In both tests, one administers only items appropriate to the age and ability of the subject. Subjects begin with items easier than appropriate for their age and end with items difficult enough to result in repeated failure of solution on the part of the child.

The verbal part of the test includes as subtests the following: information, which requires the demonstration of knowledge about the world; similarities, which requires an indication of a way in which two different objects are alike; arithmetic, which requires the solution of arithmetic word problems; vocabulary, which requires definition of common English words; comprehension, which requires understanding of societal customs; and, optionally, digit span, which requires recall of strings of digits presented forward in one section of the subtest and backward in another. The performance part of the tests includes as subtests the following: picture completion, which requires recognition of a missing part in a picture of an object; picture arrangement, which requires rearrangement of a scrambled set of pictures into an order that tells a coherent story from beginning to end; block design, which requires children to reproduce a picture of a design, constructed from a set of red, white, and half-red/half-white blocks, by actually building the design with physical blocks; object assembly, which requires children to manipulate jigsaw puzzle pieces to form a picture of a common object in the real world; coding (the analogue of digit symbol at the adult level), which requires rapid copying of symbols that are paired with pictures of objects according to a prespecified key that links the pictures with the objects; and, optionally, mazes, which requires tracing of a route through each of a set of mazes from beginning to end.

Several studies have been conducted of just what it is that the Stanford–Binet and Wechsler tests measure at different age levels. Most of these studies have been conducted by using a methodology that grew not out of the tradition of Alfred Binet, but out of the tradition of another key psychologist in the history of research on intelligence, Charles Spearman. To understand these results, it is necessary first to understand something about this methodology, so I defer a presentation of these results until I describe the methodology Charles Spearman invented – factor analysis. The contributions of Spearman and other psychometrically oriented theorists of intelligence are discussed in Chapter 5.

Part III

Theories of intelligence looking inward

5

The geographic metaphor

The geographic metaphor views a theory of intelligence as a map of the mind. This view extends back at least to Gall (see Boring, 1950), perhaps the most famous of phrenologists. Gall implemented the metaphor of a map in a literal way: He investigated the topography of the head, looking (and feeling) for the hills and valleys in each specific region of the head that would tell him a person's pattern of abilities. The measure of intelligence, according to Gall, resides in a person's pattern of cranial bumps.

During the first half of the twentieth century, the metaphor of intelligence as something to be mapped dominated theory and research. However, the metaphor of the map became more abstract, and less literal, than it had been for Gall. The psychologist studying intelligence was both an explorer and a cartographer, seeking to chart the innermost regions of the mind. Visual inspection and touching just would not do. The psychologist needed tools, and in the case of research on intelligence, the indispensable tool appeared to be the statistical method of factor analysis. Factor analysis was invented by Charles Spearman, and so to understand its origins we need to go back to an understanding of Spearman's work.

Charles Spearman and the two-factor theory

The father of psychometric theorizing about intelligence, Charles Spearman, was nothing if he was not contentious. Unfortunately, his contentiousness marked the beginning of a mutual antipathy between psychometrically oriented and experimentally oriented psychologists that has continued through much of the twentieth century and that led to the publication of Lee Cronbach's (1957) article in which he pled for the unification of the so-called "two disciplines of scientific psychology." Ironically, Spearman himself did cognitive theorizing and published a whole book on the topic (Spearman, 1923), considered in the next chapter. But in his initial major article on intelligence, Spearman (1904) made it clear how he felt about experimental work.

Spearman criticized the work of Wundt and other experimental psychologists of the late nineteenth century on two grounds. First, he argued that the methods of experimental psychology were insignificant and trivial. Spearman did not mince words: He noted that he and other critics "regarded as an infatuation to pass life in measuring the exact average time required to press a button or in ascertaining the precise distance apart where two simultaneous pin pricks cannot anymore be distinguished from one another" (1923, p. 203). Spearman's second criticism was that experimental psychology does not deal with substantive issues of real interest. He believed that there had come to be a "yawning gulf" between science and reality and that this gulf was the result of experimental psychology's use of trivial methods to solve trivial problems. Spearman proposed a new, "correlational" psychology, which he believed would better do justice to the complexity of human behavior.

By this time, the approach of Galton was in decline because of the work of Wissler, and the approach of Binet had not yet gained momentum. But Spearman shrugged off the work of Galton and his disciples. He criticized much of the work showing no interrelationships among tests as lacking precise quantitative expression, not taking into account error of measurement in the tests, not clearly defining the problem that it is addressing, and not taking into account errors of observation. Spearman thereby paved the work for his own correlational psychology, the fullest expression of which was in his 1927 book, *The Abilities of Man*.

Spearman's (1927) book represents the major statement of his "two-factor" theory of intelligence. The book opens with a critical review of what Spearman believes to be the major competing doctrines in understanding intelligence. The first of these is the "monarchic doctrine," according to which intelligence is a single entity that rules supreme. The monarchic view, according to Spearman, is the one widely accepted by laymen, as illustrated by their use of adjectives such as "clever," "bright," "sharp," and "brainy." The second doctrine, an oligarchic one, suggests a small number of faculties that collectively constitute intelligence. Examples of such faculties are sensory perception, intellect, memory, imagination, attention, and language. The third doctrine, the anarchic, views intelligence as a bundle of separate, independent abilities, each one correlated with all the others. This is the

Table 5.1. *Hypothetical correlation matrix for ability tests*

	1	2	3	4	5
1. Opposites	1.00	.80	.60	.30	.30
2. Completion		1.00	.48	.24	.24
3. Memory			1.00	.18	.18
4. Discrimination				1.00	.09
5. Cancellation					1.00

point of view adopted by Wissler on the basis of his study of the Cattell tests. But Spearman accepted none of these doctrines.

Spearman proposed instead what he refers to as a two-factor theory of intelligence. The theory posits a general factor common to all tasks requiring intelligence, and one specific factor unique to each different type of task. Note that the name of the theory is something of a misnomer. Spearman is not claiming that there are two factors of intelligence, but rather two kinds of factors: general and specific. The general factor is indeed a single one, but there are as many different specific factors as there are tests to measure mental abilities, and each specific factor is uncorrelated with every other.

Where, exactly, did Spearman get the idea that a general factor underlies all tests of human intelligence? The idea derived from his noticing what is sometimes called the "positive manifold,"' namely, the tendency for different tests of intellectual abilities to correlate positively with each other. Spearman noticed an interesting fact about correlation matrices with a positive manifold.

Spearman noted a pattern in correlation matrices for intellectual abilities tests of the kind shown in Table 5.1. The pattern is one of vanishing "tetrad differences." Consider the equation

$$(r_{ap} \cdot r_{bq}) - (r_{aq} \cdot r_{bp}).$$

Spearman called a group of four correlations a "tetrad," and a tetrad difference was the difference between subsets of the four. (The tetrad difference is today known as a determinant.) Often, in correlation matrices, the tetrad difference vanishes (indicating a singular matrix) or is very small (see Table 5.1).

In actual correlation matrices, the tetrad difference will usually not be precisely equal to 0. However, it will often come quite close. What does this pattern suggest? To Spearman, it suggested that the rank of the correlation matrix is 1 – that one underlying variable can account for the entire pattern of correlations. Actually, it suggests that only the rank of the matrix is less than its order, in other words, that at least one of the variables in the matrix is linearly dependent on the others.

Spearman recognized that the tetrad differences will not always be exactly equal to 0. What was left over, he believed, could be accounted for by a specific factor for each test. Thus, if all tetrad differences are 0, the general factor (g) can account for all the data, according to Spearman. If the differences are not all 0, then a general factor plus specific factors for each test can account for the data.

What is g, the general factor? We know from the pattern of correlations that it is roughly what is measured by intelligence tests. But this is not much of an explanation. Spearman considered a number of alternative explanations, such as attention, will, plasticity of the nervous system, and the state of the blood. His preferred explanation, however, was that of "mental energy."

According to Spearman, the concept of mental energy originated with Aristotle. But the concept had a different meaning for Aristotle from the one it had for Spearman. For Aristotle, energy signaled any actual manifestation of change. For Spearman, one's total output and the mental energy from which it derives is a constant. Constancy in mental energy and hence in output is achieved by universal mental competition: The commencement of one mental activity causes some other activity to cease, whereas conversely, the cessation of that other activity would allow the first one to commence. In other words, we have a fixed amount of mental energy, which we can assign at will at different times to different tasks.

Godfrey Thomson and the theory of bonds

Spearman's theory instigated criticism from a number of quarters. One of Spearman's chief critics was another British psychologist, Sir Godfrey Thomson, who accepted Spearman's statistics but not his interpretation of them. Thomson (1939) argued that it was possible to have a general factor in the absence of a general ability in the head. To Thomson, g was not a statistical reality but a psychological artifact, with the artifact stemming from the fallacious view that a single factor necessarily means that there is a single ability corresponding to it.

Thomson suggested that the general factor might result from the workings of an extremely large number of what he called "bonds," all of which are sampled simultaneously in intellectual tasks. Imagine, for example, that each of the intellectual tasks found in Spearman and others' test batteries requires certain mental skills. Thomson never specified what these mental skills or bonds might be, other than to link them to the functioning of the neurons in the brain. But suppose that we were to say such skills would include encoding of the stimulus material, deciding exactly what the problem is that needs to be solved, drawing on past knowledge in order to solve that problem, setting up a strategy that would lead to a solution, responding to the problem, and so on. (These processes, I emphasize, are ones I suggest, not Thomson. Thomson was not clear as to exactly what the bonds were.) Now if each test samples all of these processes, then a factor analysis will lump the processes together into a general factor, because the processes are inextricably confounded with each other. Each process appears in every test, so collectively, they give the appearance of a general factor. But they are not one thing, other than in the statistical analysis. Rather, the statistical analysis is unable to separate the various processes or bonds, so they appear to be one thing.

Not all bonds would occur in all tests. Some might be specific to each given test, resulting in the appearance of specific factors. Others might appear in only some tests but not others, resulting in what have been called "group factors." But the point Thomson made was that one need not have accepted Spearman's two-factor theory on the basis of his statistical analyses. A theory of bonds could just as well account for the data and yet would have very different implications psychologically from the theory that Spearman proposed.

Thorndike and the theory of connections

A theory similar in some respects to that of Thomson was proposed by Edward Thorndike, who is much better known for his work in learning theory than for his work in intelligence. Thorndike, Bregman, Cobb, and Woodyard (1926) suggested that

in their deeper nature the higher forms of intellectual operations are identical with mere association or connection forming, depending upon the same sort of physiological connections but requiring *many more of them*. By the same argument the person whose intellect is greater or higher or better than that of another person differs from him in the last analysis in having, not a new sort of physiological process, but simply a larger number of connections of the ordinary sort. (p. 415)

Thorndike and his colleagues actually proposed a measure, c, the number of connections a person has, which they suggested is a measure of intelligence. Scores on intelligence tests were hypothesized to be indirect measures of c. The link between Thorndike's and Thomson's theories is shown by the fact that Thorndike referred to these connections in some instances as "bonds." Thorndike, then, suggested that no qualitative difference need be assumed to account for differences in people's levels of intelligence. Rather, people differ simply in the number of connections they have.

Although Thorndike proposed a learning-theory conception of intelligence, which makes sense because Thorndike was in fact a learning theorist, he went beyond just suggesting that intelligence is in the number of associative connections one has. He suggested that the measures of intelligence available at the time basically amounted to human judgments of value. When all is said and done,

we shall then accept for the present the status of measurements of intellect as measures of different products produced by human beings or of different ways taken by them to produce the same product, each of these products and ways having value attached to it as an indication of intellect by a somewhat vague body of opinion whether popular or scientific. (p. 20)

In other words, Thorndike saw intelligence testing as being in the vein of the implicit theories of intelligence discussed in Chapter 3. Basically, the tests measure products that society considers to be of value.

Thorndike suggested several principles that further clarify his notions about intelligence. The first principle is that, other things being equal, the harder the task a person can master, the greater that person's intelligence. A second principle is that, other things being equal, the greater the number of tasks of equal difficulty that a person masters, the greater is his or her intelligence. A third principle is that, other things being equal, the more quickly a person produces the correct response, the greater is his or her intelligence.

Thorndike distinguished among level, extent, and speed of performance. For practical purposes, these three aspects of performance will usually be combined in measurement, but they are separate conceptually. Thorndike proposed theorems relating to each of these aspects of performance. For example, a first theorem was that, all other things being equal, if a first person can do correctly all the tasks that a second person can do except for one, and in place of that one, can do one that is harder, then the first person is more intelligent than the second person. Other theorems were in a similar vein.

Thorndike considered many kinds of tests for assessing intelligence and came to the conclusion that four particular tests work best. His view on testing is sometimes referred to as "CAVD theory." CAVD is an acronym for Completions, Arithmetic problems, Vocabulary, and Directions. Completions involve supplying words so as to make a statement true and sensible. Arithmetic problems simply require solution of quantitative word problems. Vocabulary is the measurement of knowledge of single words in isolation. Directions provide an assessment of the person's ability to understand connected discourse, as in oral directions or paragraph reading.

Perhaps because Thorndike's main body of work was in the learning-theory tradition rather than in the psychometric tradition, his contributions to the theory and measurement of intelligence never caught on, as did the contributions of some other psychometricians. Many books about intelligence today do not even cite his work. However, it is of interest that he came to some of the same conclusions as Thomson, starting with a completely different perspective: a learning-theory perspective rather than a psychometric one.

Thurstone and the primary mental abilities

Intelligence as inhibition

Thurstone is most well known for his theory of primary mental abilities, considered below, but some of his most interesting thinking was expressed in an earlier and much less well known work, *The Nature of Intelligence* (Thurstone, 1924). The book was published before Thurstone settled down at the University of Chicago, where he taught for most of his career, and while he was still at the Carnegie Institute of Technology in Pittsburgh.

Thurstone begins by contrasting the viewpoints of psychoanalysis and experimental psychology. In experimental psychology, he argues, normal people are described as though they were nothing more than responding machines. Examiners are interested primarily in stimuli and responses instead of in the person. Thurstone saw the viewpoint of psychoanalysis as being quite different. He believed that psychoanalysis held as a fundamental truth that action originates in the actor himself. Thus, experimental psychology sees action as beginning in the environment, whereas abnormal psychology views action as beginning in the actor.

Thurstone's sympathies lay with psychoanalysis rather than with experimental psychology. Thurstone (1924) defined intelligence as "the capacity to make impulses focal at their early, unfinished stage of formation" (p. 159), which means that intelligence is the ability to inhibit an instinctive response. In the intelligent moment, an impulse is inhibited while it is still only partially specified and loosely organized. Thurstone believed the biological function of intelligence was to protect the organism from bodily risk and to satisfy its wants with the least possible chance of failing. These goals were accomplished by deflecting impulses headed toward failure before the failure was realized (p. 163). Thus, intelligent people are ones who, when they are about to respond instinctively in a certain way, can inhibit the impulse and reflect on whether their instinctive response is the optimal one.

Primary mental abilities

Thurstone, like Spearman, was an ardent advocate of factor analysis. However, despite his advocacy and eager use of the technique, he realized its limitations:

The exploratory nature of factor analysis is often not understood. Factor analysis has its principal usefulness at the borderline of intelligence. It is naturally superseded by rational formulations in terms of the science involved. Factor analysis is useful, especially in those domains where basic and fruitful concepts are essentially lacking and where crucial experiments have been difficult to conceive. The new methods have a humble role. They enable us to make only the crudest first mapping of a new domain. But if we have scientific intuition and sufficient ingenuity, the rough factorial map of a new domain will enable us to proceed beyond the exploratory factorial stage to the more direct forms of psychological experimentation in the laboratory. (Thurstone, 1947, p. 56)

Thurstone's (1938) investigation was based on 56 tests given to 240 subjects. The tests were chosen so as to represent a wide variety of different kinds of mental tasks. Combining the results of the 1938 study with those of Thurstone and Thurstone (1941), the theory of primary mental abilities comprises seven factors:

1. *Verbal comprehension.* This factor involves a person's ability to understand verbal material. It is measured by tests such as vocabulary and reading comprehension.
2. *Verbal fluency.* This ability is involved in rapidly producing words, sentences, and other verbal material. It is measured by tests such as one that requires the examinee to produce as many words as possible in a short amount of time beginning with a particular letter, such as *M*.

3. *Number*. This ability is involved in rapid arithmetic computation and in solving simple arithmetic word problems.
4. *Memory*. This ability is involved in remembering strings of words, letters, or numbers, or in remembering people's faces.
5. *Perceptual speed*. This ability is involved in proofreading and in rapid recognition of letters and numbers. It is measured by tests such as ones requiring the crossing out of *A's* in long strings of letters or in tests requiring recognition of which of several pictures at the right is identical to a picture at the left.
6. *Inductive reasoning*. This ability requires generalization – reasoning from the specific to the general. It is measured by tests, such as letter series, number series, and word classifications, in which the examinee must indicate which of several words does not belong with the others.
7. *Spatial visualization*. This ability is involved in visualizing shapes, rotations of objects, and how pieces of a puzzle would fit together. An example of a test would be the presentation of a geometric form followed by several other geometric forms. Each of the forms that follows the first one is either the same form rotated by some rigid transformation or it is the mirror image of the first form in rotation. The examinee has to indicate which of the forms at the right is a rotated version of the form at the left, rather than a mirror image.

In general, Thurstone was antagonistic to Spearman's theory of *g*. He believed that Spearman's general factor was obtained only because Spearman failed to rotate his factorial axes upon obtaining an initial solution. Thurstone was a major contributor to the literature of factor analysis and proposed a form of rotation, simple structure, that is still widely used today. The idea of simple structure is to "clean up" the columns of a factor pattern matrix so that factors display either relatively high or low loadings for given tests, rather than large numbers of moderate ones. Simple-structure rotations tend to eliminate or at least to weaken the general factor. Because Thurstone believed that simple-structure rotation is in some sense psychologically natural, he believed his theory to be more valid than Spearman's.

However, the argument between Spearman and Thurstone was not soluble in the terms they presented it. Mathematically, either rotation is correct, and it is of course arguable which is psychologically more valid. Historically, British theorists have been more inclined to leave factorial axes unrotated, whereas American theorists have been more inclined to rotate axes, often to simple structure. There exist today mathematical algorithms for rotations that approximate simple structure and that yield orthogonal factorial axes. However, a true simple structure often yields axes that are oblique. Indeed, factor scores on the seven primary mental abilities are almost invariably intercorrelated, and not simply due to error of estimation of the factor scores. There is a natural correlation between various abilities. The result, of course, is that if one factor analyzes the factor scores, one can end up with a general second-order factor. Thus, g reappears in another form. The fact that g reappears when the factors are themselves analyzed led to the formation by some theorists of hierarchical theories.

Holzinger and bifactor theory

Holzinger (1938) proposed a bifactor theory, which retained the general and specific factors of Spearman, but also permitted group factors, relevant to some tests but not others, as would be found in Thurstone's theory. The theory thus expanded upon the foundation of Spearman's theory, integrating some ideas of Thurstone, and Holzinger and Spearman actually collaborated in developing the bifactor theory. The theory never gained widespread support, however, perhaps because the work of Thurstone generated more enthusiasm.

Hierarchical theories

A number of hierarchical theories of intelligence have been proposed. Burt (1940) distinguished four kinds of factors likely to be found in the measurement of a given set of traits: general, group, specific, and error. General factors are common to all traits. Group factors are common to some of the traits. Specific factors are limited to each trait whenever it is measured. Error factors are limited to each trait on each particular occasion when it is measured.

Burt (1949) proposed a five-level hierarchical model. At the top of the hierarchy is "the human mind." At the second level, the "relations level," are g (the general factor) and a practical factor. At the third level are associations, at the fourth level is perception, and at the fifth level is sensation.

Probably more sophisticated is the hierarchical model proposed by Vernon (1971). At the top of the hierarchy is g. At the second level are two major group factors, $v{:}ed$ and $k{:}m$. The former refers to verbal-educational abilities of the kind measured by conventional tests of scholastic aptitude. The latter refers to spatial-mechanical abilities. At the third level of the hierarchy are minor group factors, and at the fourth level are specific factors.

R. B. Cattell (1971) proposed a theory similar to Vernon's, although the theory is much more detailed. For present purposes, we will concentrate on the two major abilities in the theory, which Cattell believed to be nested under *g*. Crystallized ability is similar to Vernon's *v:ed* factor. It is measured by tests such as vocabulary, reading comprehension, and general information. Crystallized ability is essentially the accumulation of knowledge and skills through the life course. Fluid ability, similar although not identical to Vernon's *k:m,* is a measure of flexibility of thought and the ability to reason abstractly. It is measured by tests such as number series, abstract analogies, matrix problems, and the like. Gustafsson (1984) has used confirmatory factor analysis to study the model of Cattell and has come to the conclusion that the general factor is essentially identical to Cattell's fluid ability. In other words, the strict hierarchy seems to break down, in that Gustafsson, at least, was unable to distinguish general ability from fluid ability.

R. B. Cattell's (1971) theory went beyond postulating just fluid and crystallized abilities. Another aspect of it was what he referred to as the "triadic theory." The basic idea is that intellectual abilities are of three basic types. *Capacities* are abilities reflecting limits to brain action as a whole. *Provincial powers* are kinds of local organizations relevant to different sensory and motor modalities. *Agencies* are abilities to perform in different areas of cultural contents. The agencies are acquired through the investment of fluid abilities in learning.

Another hierarchical model was proposed by Arthur Jensen (1970). The model appears to be rather loosely based on factor analysis. According to Jensen, there are two broad classes of abilities. Level I abilities involve simple encoding, storage, and retrieval of sensory inputs. These abilities are involved in rote learning tasks, such as memorizing a string of unrelated words. Level II abilities are involved in reasoning tasks and seem to be similar to what Spearman referred to as *g*.

Guilford and the structure-of-intellect model

The structure-of-intellect (SI) model of J. P. Guilford (Guilford, 1967; Guilford & Hoepfner, 1971) is one of the most ambitious theories of intelligence ever proposed. It posits 120 distinct abilities (increased to 150 by Guilford, 1982), organized along three dimensions. These dimensions are operations, products, and contents. There are five operations, six products, and four contents. Because these dimensions are completely crossed with each other, there are a total of $5 \times 6 \times 4 = 120$ abilities.

Operations are of five types: cognition, memory, divergent production, convergent production, and evaluation. Cognition is defined as awareness, immediate discovery, or recognition of information in various forms. Memory is the ability to recall information. Divergent production is the solution of a problem that requires, or at least allows, multiple responses. Convergent production is the solution of a problem that requires just a single, uniquely correct response. For example, inductive reasoning can be divergent, but deductive reasoning is generally convergent. Evaluation is the comparing of something new to something known according to logical criteria and making a decision on the bases of those criteria. It comes close to what we ordinarily refer to as judgment.

The six types of products are units, classes, relations, systems, transformations, and implications. Units are single and usually circumscribed items of information. Examples would be numbers or letters. Classes are recognized sets of items grouped by virtue of their common properties, such as odd numbers or vowels. Relations are recognized connections between two items of information, such as the relation that seven is greater than six or that *a* precedes *b*. Systems are organized or structured aggregates of items of information, such as letter series. Transformations are changes of various kinds of existing or known information in their attributes, meaning, role, or use. Common transformations include changes in sensory qualities, in location, or in arrangement of parts. Finally, implications emphasize expectancies, anticipations, and predictions. An example of an implication is the logical statement "If *A*, then *B*."

The four kinds of content are figural, symbolic, semantic, and behavioral. Figural content is basically pictorial. Symbolic content is from a symbol system, such as the systems of numbers and letters. Semantic content is generally verbal, and behavior content refers to behavioral acts.

The set of abilities is commonly represented as a cube. The three dimensions of the cube are content, product, and operation, and within the cube are little cubes corresponding to each of the 120 ways in which the contents, products, and operations can be crossed. For each ability, Guilford has devised a number of tests purported to measure that ability.

Consider, for example, the ability *cognition of figural relations*. A test of this ability is the matrix problem, in which several elements of a figural matrix are presented and the subject must fill in the missing element or elements. Figural analogies can also provide a measure of this ability, if the difficulty of the item is in inferring the relation between the first two figures rather than in applying that relation (which is a different ability).

Cognition of semantic units is often measured by a vocabulary test. Vocabulary can be measured in many forms: synonyms, antonyms, completions, and so on. Many tests that are supposed to measure other things end up being measures of cognition of semantic units.

Divergent production of symbolic units is what Thurstone called word fluency. An example of a test of this ability would be to write as many words as one can ending with a certain suffix or beginning with a certain first letter.

Guilford's theory has come under attack from many different sources. One of the most telling attacks was that of Horn and Knapp (1973). They used the form of rotation that Guilford used – Procrustean rotation – to test randomly generated theories applied to Guilford's data. They found that

the support provided for such arbitrary theories is quite comparable to that put forth as providing support for SI theory. This pseudo-support for a theory can be obtained (a) with variables that are not random, (b) under a requirement that factors remain orthogonal, (c) when factor coefficients remain generally positive, (d) with a requirement that loadings be .30 or larger to be regarded as "significant," and (e) in samples as large as are customarily used in psychological research. (p. 42)

Guttman and the radex model

One of the most interesting and innovative models of intelligence has been proposed by Louis Guttman (1954). The model is what Guttman calls a radex, or a radial representation of complexity. The radex consists of two parts.

The first part is what Guttman refers to as a simplex. If one imagines a circle, then the simplex refers to the distance of a given point (ability) from the center of the circle. The closer an ability is to the center of the circle, the more central it is to human intelligence. Thus, g could be viewed as being at the center of the circle, whereas the more peripheral abilities such as perceptual speed would be nearer to the periphery of the circle. Abilities nearer to the periphery of the circle are viewed as being constituents of abilities nearer the center of the circle. A simplex relation is one in which success of elements in a sequence completely contain earlier elements in a sequence. Thus, the abilities nearer the periphery of the circle are completely contained by those nearer the center.

The second part of the radex is called a circumplex. It refers to the angular orientation of a given ability with respect to the circle. Thus, abilities are viewed as being arranged around the circle with abilities that are more highly related (correlated) nearer to each other in the circle. Thus, the radex functions through a system of polar coordinates. Snow, Kyllonen, and Marshalek (1984) have used nonmetric multidimensional scaling on Thurstone's (1938; Thurstone & Thurstone, 1941) data in order to demonstrate that the Thurstonian primary mental abilities can actually be mapped into a radex. Thus, the reanalysis of Snow and his colleagues suggests that the radex may be a particularly suitable psychometric representation of ability-test data.

Carroll's theory

Without doubt, the most comprehensive psychometric work on intelligence to be conducted is that of John Carroll (1988), who has reanalyzed via factor analysis practically every major data set, and many minor ones, that has ever been reported in the psychometric literature. Carroll's exhaustive analysis of psychometric data sets has tentatively revealed 20 separate factors.

Carroll's factors are a synthesis of what is in the literature. These factors are (a) general abilities, (b) reasoning abilities, (c) abilities in the domain of language behavior, (d) memory abilities, (e) visual perception abilities, (f) auditory perception abilities, (g) number facility, (h) mental-speed abilities, (i) abilities in producing and retrieving words, ideas, and figural creation, (j) sensory abilities (thresholds, acuity), (k) attention and concentration abilities, (l) abilities pertaining to interpersonal behavior, (m) factors pertaining to knowledge of different subject matters, (n) factors pertaining to school achievement, (o) factors whose interpretation was doubtful or postponed, (p) psychomotor and physical ability factors, (q) interest and motivation factors, (r) personality and affective factors, (s) administrative behavior factors, and (t) educational and social status background factors.

Carroll is not providing a list of what are necessarily factors of a single model of intelligence, but rather a synthesis of the factors in the literature that have emerged in his reanalyses. The list of factors that he believes to be confirmed as factors of intelligence include General Intelligence, Fluid Intelligence, Crystallized Intelligence, General Visual Perception Ability, General Auditory Perception Ability, General Mental Speed, General Idea Production or Fluency, and General Memory Capacity.

Psychometric conceptions and intellectual development

The psychometric approach has been used to address a large number of issues, such as the nature of development, group differences, heritability, prediction of performance, and the like. It would be impossible within the scope of this book to cover all of these issues, because complete coverage of this kind would itself become a book. Instead, I will cover just one central issue in psychometric theory, namely, the nature of intellectual development as viewed from the factorial standpoint.

Substantial literatures exist regarding the nature of intelligence and the development of intelligence as perceived from a psychometric point of view. Yet the two literatures are surprisingly autonomous: On the one hand, few of the major factor theorists of intelligence have given serious and detailed consideration to the place of intellectual development in their theories. On the other hand, few of the major developmental students of intelligence have given serious and detailed consideration to the place of theories of the nature of intelligence in their research. Despite notable exceptions (e.g., Horn, 1970; Stott & Ball, 1965), the literature on the development of intelligence has been very largely empirical in its orientation (see, e.g., Bayley's 1970 review of the literature on the development of mental abilities), and some of the work has been almost entirely atheoretical (see, e.g., Broman, Nichols, & Kennedy, 1975). I do not wish to overstate the separation between theory and data in the developmental literature, but merely to point out that the integration between them has often not been as nearly complete as one might have hoped. I attempt here to provide a framework for interrelating more closely work on the nature of intelligence with work on the development of intelligence. The basis for this integration is an enumeration of some of the possible loci of intellectual development in the factorial theories. The various loci are not mutually exclusive: To the contrary, it seems highly likely that multiple loci exist.

Changes in number of factors with age

One possible locus of intellectual development is in the number of abilities and, hence, of factors that constitute measured intelligence at different ages. Arguments in favor of change in number of factors as a locus of intellectual development usually take the form of differentiation theories. Although it is conceivable that intelligence could become either more or less differentiated with advancing age, the former position has been by far the more popular, and certainly the more plausible one. Perhaps the most noted proponent of this point of view has been Henry E. Garrett (1938, 1946). Garrett (1946) defined intelligence as comprising the abilities demanded in the solution of problems that require the comprehension and use of symbols. According to his developmental theory of intelligence, "abstract or symbol intelligence changes in its organization as age increases from a fairly unified and general ability to a loosely organized group of abilities or factors" (Garrett, 1946, p. 373). This theory has obvious implications for how various psychometric theories of intelligence might be interrelated:

It seems to effect a rapprochement between the Spearman General Factor and the Group Factor theories [e.g., that of Thurstone, 1938]. Over the elementary school years we find a functional generality among tests at the symbol level. Later on this general factor of "g" breaks down into the quasi-independent factors reported by many investigators. (Garrett, 1946, p. 376)

Several sources of evidence provide at least tentative support for the differentiation theory. Garrett, Bryan, and Perl (1935), for example, administered 10 tests of memory, verbal ability, and number ability to children of ages 9, 12, and 15. With one exception, intercorrelations among the three kinds of tests showed a monotone decrease between the ages of 9 and 12 and 12 and 15, suggesting increasing independence of the abilities with age. A factor analysis of the correlations showed a decrease in the proportion of variance accounted for by a general factor with increasing age. Similar results were obtained by Asch (1936), who found a decrease in the correlation between verbal and numerical test from ages 9 to 12. M. P. Clark (1944) administered an early version of the Primary Mental Abilities Test to boys of ages 11, 13, and 15 and found that scores on tests of verbal, number, spatial, memory, and reasoning abilities showed decreasing correlations with increasing age.

Other studies considered together (e.g., Schiller, 1934, for third and fourth graders; Schneck, 1929, for college students) also tend to support the hypothesis of a decrease in correlations with age. Reviewing the literature on changes in the organization of mental abilities with age, Bayley (1955) concluded that there was fairly substantial support for the differentiation notion.

In summary, then, one possible reconciliation among the various theories of the nature of intelligence is in terms of increasing differentiation of abilities with age. (See also Werner's, 1948, views of increasing differentiation of thought as cultures and individuals develop.) Theories postulating small numbers of interesting factors, such as Spearman's, may be relevant for younger children. Theories postulating large numbers of interesting factors, such as Thurstone's or conceivably Guilford's, may be relevant for older children and adults.

Changes in the relevance or weights of factors with age

Another possible locus of intellectual development is in the relevance or weights of factors as contributors to individual-differences variance in intelligence at different age levels. For example, a Perceptual-Motor factor may decrease in weight with age. Thus, it is not total number of factors, but importance of individual factors that changes with age. In this view, what makes one person more intelligent than another can be quite different across ages, because the abilities that constitute intelligence can shift dramatically in their importance. Variants of this viewpoint have been very popular in the literature on the development of intelligence (e.g., Hofstaetter, 1954). Despite their differences, these variants have virtually all been consistent with the notion that abilities of the kind proposed by Galton and successors in his tradition to constitute intelligence seem most relevant for infants and very young children; abilities of the kind proposed by Binet and successors in his tradition seem most relevant for older children and adults. These views, then, like the differentiation views, seem to point the way toward a developmental reconciliation of the theoretical positions. An interesting ramification of these views is that developmental theorizing becomes essential rather than adjunct to understanding theories of intelligence originally proposed for adults.

One of the most well known data sets supporting the notion that factors change in relevance with age is that of Hofstaetter (1954). Hofstaetter factor-analyzed data from Bayley's (1933, 1943, 1949,

1951) Berkeley Growth Study, which assessed intellectual performance from infancy through adulthood. Hofstaetter found that up to 20 months of age, a first factor, which he named Sensorimotor Alertness, accounted for most of the individual-differences variance in children's performance on intelligence tests. From the age of 40 months onward, this factor accounted for practically none of the variance in mental age scores. Between 20 and 40 months, the dominant source of individual-differences variance was in a second factor that Hofstaetter tentatively labeled Persistence. From 48 months onward, almost all of the individual-differences variance could be accounted for by a third factor that seemed appropriately labeled Manipulation of symbols or simply Abstract behavior. Hofstaetter suggested that this factor corresponds to Spearman's (1927) *g*, but he further noted that it was only because of limitations in the data that the factor appeared to be unitary in nature. Hofstaetter concluded from his data that

the term "an intelligent child" seems to refer to a lively (alert) infant at first and to a rather stubborn child at an age of three before it acquires the connotations which predominate all through the school-age. In talking about the development of "intelligence" we actually refer to the switches from one connotational pattern to another rather than to unidirectional growth. To the extent that test batteries truly reflect the meaning of the term "intelligence" as applied to infants and children, the changing composition of such batteries indicates also the connotational changes which the term itself undergoes when used with regard to children of differing age-level. (p. 163)

Semantic use of the term *intelligence* thus reflects the factors that show the highest weights at a given age level. In his concern with the changing nature of intelligence as a reflection of changes in the use of the term *intelligence,* Hofstaetter foreshadows Siegler (1976) in his later concern with changes in people's conceptions of intelligence as applied to children of differing ages.

Bayley's (1955) own view of her data is very similar to that of Hofstaetter (1954). Like Piaget (1972), however, Bayley has emphasized how the abilities of greater importance in later life build upon the abilities of greater importance in earlier life: "Intelligence appears to me. . . . to be a dynamic succession of developing functions, with the more advanced and complex functions in the hierarchy depending on the prior maturing of earlier simpler ones (given, of course, normal conditions of care)" (1955, p. 807). For example, verbal tasks require perceptual processing for their completion.

Bayley (1933) identifies six factors in the correlational data from her First-Year Scale and six factors in the data from her Preschool Scale. Like Hofstaetter (1954), she found that the factors that contributed substantially to individual differences in measured intelligence varied with age (see, especially, Bayley, 1970, Fig. 4). Up to 10 months, the factors with the highest weights were Visual Following, Social Responsivity, Perceptual Interest, and Manual Dexterity. Vocal Communications came to be of some importance at the very end of this time period. In the range from 10 to 30 months, factors with highest weights were Perceptual Interest (a carryover from the earlier period), Vocal Communications, Meaningful Object Relations (dexterity), Memory for Forms, and Verbal Knowledge. In the range from 30 to 50 months, the most important factors were Object Relations (a carryover), Memory for Forms, and Verbal Knowledge. In the period of time from 50 to 70 months, Memory for Forms and Verbal Knowledge (carryovers) were important, as were Complex Spatial Relations and Vocabulary. By the last period assessed in this particular analysis, 70 to 90 months, the important factors were Verbal Knowledge, Complex Spatial Relations, and Vocabulary. The factor of Memory for Forms, important in the immediately preceding period, had dropped out. Thus, we see a general tendency for the more complex factors to become of greater importance to individual differences in intelligence with increasing age.

Stott and Ball (1965) factor-analyzed data from intelligence tests administered to children in the age range from 3 to 60 months. They used Guilford's (1956, 1957) structure-of-intellect model as the theoretical framework within which to interpret their results. Although they found significant loadings for 31 of Guilford's factors at one age or another, and, although many factors appeared at multiple age levels, results for the younger age levels (especially below 1 year) included important other factors, such as Gross Psychomotor Skills, Locomotor Skills, and Hand Dexterity, which did not fit into the Guilford model and which did not apply at the upper age levels. Thus, the Guilford factors appeared not to be relevant at all ages.

Changes in the content (names) of factors within a given factor structure

Whereas the point of view discussed above suggests that the structure of mental abilities (or at least the factor structure important for generating individual differences) changes with age, the point of view considered here suggests that for a given theory, structure stays essentially the same across age groups but that the content that fills in this structure changes. For example, *g*, or general ability, might be conceived as perceptual-motor in nature at the infant level but as cognitive in nature later on. In each case, the factorial structure could be the same, that is, presence of a single general factor, but the content of that factor might differ across ages. The difference between structure and content is not always a clear-cut one, and we doubt that theorists propounding each of these two positions actually intended to be placed in separate camps. Nevertheless, the empirical claims of the two positions differ. Support for the preceding position requires a different factor structure at each age level. Support for the present position requires a different content filling in the structure at each level. Historically, proponents of this present position have tended to be most interested in the changing composition of Spearman's *g* over ages. They extract a general factor at each level but find that what is general changes with age.

McCall, Hogarty, and Hurlburt (1972) factor-analyzed data from the Gesell Developmental Schedule administered to children participating in the Fels Longitudinal Study. Children were studied at 6, 12, 18, and 24 months of age. The authors were interested primarily in the first principal component (general factor) at each age level. At 6 months, they found that items loading on this factor tended to measure visually guided exploration of perceptual contingencies. At 12 months, the factor reflected a mixture of sensorimotor and social imitations as well as rudimentary vocal-verbal behavior. The joint presence of sensorimotor and social imitation was interpreted as consistent with Piaget's (1977) notion that imitation mediates the transition between egocentric sensorimotor behaviors, on the one hand, and more decentered verbal and social behaviors, on the other hand. At 18 months, items loading on the first principal component reflected verbal and motor imitation, verbal production, and verbal comprehension. By 24 months, highly loading items measured verbal labeling, comprehension, fluency, and grammatical maturity. Again, we see transition between the types of behaviors studied by Galton (1883) at the lower levels and the types of behaviors studied by Binet and Simon (1916a, 1916b) at the upper levels.

It is important to note that the items loading on the first principal component are factorial but not behaviorally unitary: Multiple behaviors are general across the tests that McCall et al. (1972) studied at each age level. Thus, they load on a single general factor. The authors interpreted their data as supporting what they and Kagan (1971) before them had called a heterotypic model of mental development. In such a model, there is a discontinuity in the overt developmental function (i.e., the behaviors responsible for individual differences in intelligence), but there is stability in patterns of individual differences across these behaviors (i.e., in people's rank orders at different ages, despite the differences in the behaviors of consequence). This model was contrasted with five other models that were not as well supported. One such model, for example, was a homotypic model in which individual differences are purported to remain stable, as are the behaviors that generate the individual differences.

McCall, Eichorn, and Hogarty (1977) studied "transitions in early mental development" in much the same ways as had McCall and his colleagues in an earlier study (1972). In this study, however, the investigators used the developmental data from the Berkeley Growth Study, as had Hofstaetter before them. Whereas Hofstaetter factor-analyzed data across age levels, McCall et al. (1977) factor-analyzed data within age levels. The investigators interpreted their data (for infants) as supporting a five-stage model of intellectual development. During Stage 1 (1 to 2 months), the infant is responsive primarily to selected stimulus dimensions that in some sense match the structural predispositions of the infant's sensory-perceptual systems. Stage 2 (3 to 7 months) is characterized by more active exploration of the environment, although the infant's view of the world is alleged still to be completely subjective. At Stage 3 (8 to 13 months), means for doing things begin to be differentiated from ends. The separation is complete by Stage 4 (14 to 18 months), by which time the child is able to associate two objects in the environment without acting on either of them. Symbolic relationships emerge during Stage 5 (21+ months).

The emphasis on change in the composition of the first principal component or factor that characterizes the work described above does not emerge in all factor-analytic studies, although the difference in emphasis may reflect primarily differences in ages studied. McNemar (1942) reported factor analyses of the Stanford–Binet for children of ages 2 to 18 years. He found that a general factor did pervade the subtests at each of the age levels and that, at most age levels, the single factor was sufficient to account for the intercorrelations between subtests. At the age levels for which a single factor was insufficient (2, $2^{1}/_{2}$, 6, and 18 years), there was evidence of additional specific factors (in line with the Spearman, 1927, model), but the study was not sufficiently powerful (by McNemar's 1942, own admission) to identify group factors if they occurred. Finally, the content of the tests loading most highly on the first factor were approximately the same across age levels. McNemar concluded (perhaps a bit too strongly), "There is just one common factor at each level and also that the various levels are identical or nearly so, [so] that the IQ's for individuals of differing mental-maturity levels or for the same individual at different stages of development are comparable quantitatively and qualitatively" (1942, p. 123). Although McNemar did not find evidence of group factors in the Stanford–Binet, there is at least some evidence that such factors can indeed appear (Jones, 1954).

Changes in factor scores of fixed factors with age

The views expressed in the above discussions are all ones of qualitative changes in the nature of intelligence with age. However, most of the voluminous literature reflecting the psychometric approach to the development of intelligence has dealt with quantitative changes and how to account for them. The preponderance of studies has been atheoretical, although our emphasis here will be upon the more theoretically motivated research.

Two basic findings in the literature that have needed to be accounted for are, first, that absolute level of intelligence (as measured, say, by mental age or a comparable construct) increases with age and, second, that correlations between measurements of intelligence decrease with increasing intervals of time between measurements (see, e.g., Bayley, 1933, 1970; Dearborn & Rothney, 1941; Honzik, 1938; Sontag, Baker, & Nelson, 1958). An elegant attempt to account for these findings was made by J. E. Anderson (1940), who proposed that correlations of IQ at various ages with terminal IQ (say, at about the age of 16) increase because "the prediction of final status is based upon a larger proportion of that which is included in the total; that is, scores at 10 years include more of that which is present at age 16 years than do scores at 3 years" (p. 388). Anderson suggested that the increase in overlap between final scores and successively later scores would be predicted by a model in which increments to intelligence are additive over the age span and uncorrelated (or only modestly correlated) with each other and with the current level of intelligence. Anderson tested this simple model by reanalyzing data from the Harvard Growth Study (Dearborn, Rothney, & Shuttleworth, 1938) and the Honzik (1938) study. He compared mental growth curves from these data to Monte Carlo curves generated by cumulating the first to the sixteenth random number (for which each number represented a "year" of mental growth) in a table of random numbers of 300 artificial subjects. In the random-number table, of course, successive increments in the accumulated sum will be uncorrelated both with each other and with the current value of the sum. According to Anderson's model, the closer in time two measurements are, the less time there has been for intervening changes to take place and, hence, the more highly related those two measurements will be. Fits of the data to the model were quite good, providing at least tentative support for the model.

Most of the research that has been done on quantitative development of intelligence has assumed, as did Anderson, that intelligence increases in absolute amount over age and that one's goal should be to plot the form of this function and to account in some way for why the function takes this form. Bayley (1966, 1968), for example, plotted mental growth curves from infancy to 36 years on the basis of her data from the Berkeley Growth Study. Her findings were typical of this literature: Absolute level of intelligence increased fairly rapidly until early adolescence, showed some decrease in the rate of increase from early to middle adolescence, and then pretty much leveled off in middle to late adolescence. However, the assumption of a monotonic growth curve throughout the life span has been challenged as representing a composite of two different component functions, each of which is purported to show a different pattern of growth throughout the life span. The two component functions, in this view, represent what R. B. Cattell (1971; Cattell & Cattell, 1963) and Horn (1968) have referred to as fluid and crystallized intelligence.

Fluid and crystallized intelligence are proposed by R. B. Cattell (1971; Cattell & Cattell, 1963) and Horn (1968) to be subfactors of general intelligence (g). Fluid ability is best measured by tests that require mental manipulation of abstract symbols, for example, figural analogies, series completions, and classifications. Crystallized ability is best measured by tests that require knowledge of the cultural milieu in which one lives, for example, vocabulary, general information, and reading comprehension. Horn and Cattell (1966) reported that although the mean level of fluid intelligence was systematically higher for younger adults than for older adults, the mean level of crystallized intelligence was systematically higher for older adults than for younger adults. In general, crystallized ability seemed to increase throughout the life span, whereas fluid intelligence seemed to increase up until the 20s and slowly to decrease thereafter.

Schaie (1974) questioned what he called the myth of intellectual decline, namely, that some or all intellectual functions decline after some point in adulthood. Schaie noted that the evidence on the question of decline has been mixed. Cross-sectional studies have tended to support the notion of a decline (e.g., Jones & Conrad, 1933; Wechsler, 1939), whereas longitudinal studies have not (e.g., Bayley & Oden, 1955; Owens, 1953). Studies of both kinds have been subject to reasonable criticism. Cross-sectional studies are susceptible to cohort (age group) differences: Differences in scores may reflect differences in measured intelligence across different subjects of different cohorts rather than differences in measured intelligence across the same individuals within a given cohort. Longitudinal studies are susceptible to sampling bias as a result of differential dropout: Those who remain in a study over a large number of years are unlikely to be representative samples of the total group that started the study. Schaie (1965, 1973) suggested what he believed to be a way out of this apparent dilemma, and he has summarized the results that are obtained when this way out is followed:

Two approaches are needed: The first requires the replication of cross-sectional studies over several points in time. The second involves the carrying of several cohorts over the age ranges of interest. In our own work we have now done both and the results are indeed revealing. They show with great clarity that a much larger proportion of the variance associated with age can be attributed to generation differences than to ontogenetic change and that both peak levels and slopes of change in ability are changing in a positive direction. (Schaie, 1974, p. 804)

Schaie further suggested that the actual declines in test scores within a given individual that did occur in some cases might be attributable to increased cautiousness or reduced risk taking on the part of older subjects (Birkhill & Schaie, 1975; Botwinick, 1977; Wallach & Kogan, 1961) or to the fact that test items might be biased in their construction toward younger adults.

Horn and Donaldson (1976) attempted to refute the view advanced by Schaie (1974) and also the view that what has appeared to be a gradual intellectual decline in adulthood is in fact a decline appearing only just before death (Jarvik, Eisdorfer, & Blum, 1973; Riegel & Riegel, 1972). They argued, in the first place, that none of the sampling designs, including the ones advocated by Schaie (1974), were free of sampling bias, but that even the data obtained through these biased designs tend to support the notion of a decline in later life. The thrust of their argument was that the major evidence arguing against intellectual decline in many (if not all) individuals was based upon sampling bias and wishful thinking in the interpretation of research.

A final reply (for our purposes) by Schaie and Baltes (1977) seems to me to defuse the debate and to call into question whether there was much substantive basis for the debate in the first place. These authors argued that Horn and Donaldson (1976) had misrepresented the earlier positions taken by Baltes and Schaie (Baltes & Schaie, 1976; Schaie, 1974):

Schaie and Baltes do not reject the notion of intellectual decline *in toto*. Within the framework of a dialectical interpretation of intelligence in adulthood and old age, Schaie and Baltes emphasize plasticity as evidence of large interindividual differences, multidimensionality, multidirectionality, modifiability, and the joint import of age- and cohort-related determinants. (Baltes & Schaie, 1976, p. 720)

I doubt there are any substantive points in the above statement with which Horn and Donaldson would disagree. Both sets of authors seem to agree that, at the level of individual cases, later decline may or may not occur. There may be some disagreement as to trends in group means. But when group means camouflage multiple systematic patterns in data rather than reflect a single systematic pattern, their interpretability is doubtful in the first place. All parties seem to agree that *some* decline *sometimes* occurs. The substantive question that no one has yet resolved is: What circumstances lead to declines and why do they do so? If a debate is to continue, it will have to take a new form.

Current status of the geographical metaphor

The model of mental maps, and the factor-analytic methods used to create the maps have become increasingly less popular in some circles in the second half of the twentieth century. There have been three main reasons for the increasing skepticism.

First, the model of maps and the factor-analytic methods used to instantiate it had little, if anything, to say about mental processes. Yet two individuals could receive the same score on a mental ability test through very different processes, and indeed, by getting completely different items correct (Horn, & Knapp, 1973: Sternberg, 1977). By the 1960s, psychologists in all aspects of cognitive study were becoming especially concerned with information processing, and research on intelligence, like so much other research in the field, got caught up in this new wave of interest.

Second, it proved to be extremely difficult to test factor-analytic models against each other, or even to falsify them at all (Sternberg, 1977). This difficulty stemmed in large part from the problem of rotation of factorial axes. Although the points obtained from typical factor analyses are fixed in an n-dimensional Euclidean space, the orientation of the axes used to interpret the points is not fixed. Indeed, any of an infinite number of either orthogonal or oblique orientations may be used to characterize the locations of the points in space (just as lines of longitude and latitude, or polar coordinates, represent only two of an infinite number of possible descriptions for locations on the globe): The mathematical fit of the model to the data does not change as a function of orientation of axes, and each orientation is equally acceptable mathematically. But different factorial theories proved to differ as much in terms of the orientations of factorial axes for a given solution as in terms of anything else, so that model fitting did not prove to be useful in distinguishing among theories (Sternberg, 1977).

Psychometricians (psychologists specializing in measurement) resorted to arguing about the psychological plausibility of the various rotations, but such arguments proved to be inconclusive, because theorists in each camp thought their rotations to be most psychologically plausible. Modern, confirmatory methods of factor analysis do not yield solutions with arbitrary axes (Jöreskog & Sörbom, 1978), and such methods are now gaining widespread use among those wedded to a psychometric approach to intelligence and other psychological constructs (Whitely, 1979).

Third, the whole notion of trying to understand intelligence primarily on the basis of individual-differences data came under attack. NcNemar (1964) queried whether two identical twins, stranded on a desert island and growing up together, would ever generate the notion of intelligence if they never encountered individual differences in their mental abilities. Psychologists were coming to answer this question affirmatively and to believe that they should not be dependent upon the existence of substantial individual differences for isolating abilities. Yet factor analysis, as it was typically used, critically depended upon such differences.

Psychologists either had to find a new model, find a new method, or both. Most psychologists opted for both, and in recent years, most research on intelligence has followed neither the map model nor the method of factor analysis.

6

The computational metaphor

During the past decade, the predominant metaphor for studying intelligence has probably been that of the computer program. Researchers have sought to understand intelligence in terms of the information processing that people do when they think intelligently. Information-processing investigators have varied primarily in terms of the complexity of the processes they have sought to study. They have taken rather widely differing approaches.

Computational theorists tend to be highly critical of geographic approaches and especially of the individual who is seen as the originator of the geographic approach, Charles Spearman. It is therefore ironic, as few computational theorists realize, that the computational approach to intelligence, like the geographic one, dates back to none other than Charles Spearman.

The origins of the computational approach in Spearman's principles of cognition

Today, computational investigators seek to anchor a conception of intelligence within the framework of an entire psychology of cognition. The first individual to do this was Charles Spearman, who sought an integration between cognitive psychology and psychometrics almost a half-century before Cronbach's (1957) plea for an integration of these two areas.

Qualitative principles of cognition

Spearman (1923) proposed what he believed to be three fundamental qualitative principles of cognition.

> 1. *Apprehension of experience*. According to the first principle of cognition, the apprehension of experience, *"any lived experience tends*

to evoke immediately a knowing of its characters and experiencer" (p. 48).

The apprehension of experience is what today might be called the encoding of stimuli. What is the range of mental experience to which Spearman believed the first principle to be applicable? Spearman suggested three types of relevant experience: affect, cognition, and conation (motivation).

    2. *Eduction of relations.* According to the second principle, *"the mentally presenting of any two or more characters (* simple or complex*) tends to evoke immediately a knowing of relation between them"* (p. 63).

The eduction of relations is what today might be labeled an inference. Spearman recognized that inferences or eductions of relations are normally between two elements, which he called fundaments. But he also recognized, even back then, that it was possible to infer higher order relations between relations, with relations of successively higher orders continuing, in principle, up to infinity.

Spearman proposed that relations could be of two types: real and ideal. According to Spearman, there are seven real relations: attribution, identity, time, space, cause, objectivity, and constitution. The last two of these relations are not obvious in terms of their character. Objectivity refers to one fundament's being the object of another. For example, the thing seen would be the object of the sense of seeing. Constitution refers to the relation between the elements that constitute an entity and the entity itself. Spearman further proposed three ideal relations: likeness, evidence, and conjunction. He also believed it was possible to have an intermixture of these relations with each other, as well as with the real relations.

    3. *Eduction of correlates.* According to the third principle, *"the presenting of any character together with any relation tends to evoke immediately a knowing of the correlative character"* (p. 91).

Eduction of correlates refers to what today might be referred to as application of relations. Spearman gives several examples of eduction of correlates. The most straightforward is in analogy items. Consider the analogy, white : black :: good : ?. Eduction of a correlate occurs in solving the analogy for the correct answer. Actually, all three principles must be invoked in analogy items, making the solution of analogies a prototype for the application of the three qualitative principles of cognition. Apprehension of experience is involved in perceiving each term or fundament of the analogy. Eduction of relations is involved in inferring the relation between white and black. Finally, eduction of correlates is involved in applying the relation from good to its opposite, bad.

The quantitative principles of cognition

The three qualitative principles described above are supplemented by five quantitative principles. Spearman believed the quantitative principles to be subordinate to the qualitative ones, and hence less important. He was also less certain as to the ultimate validity of the quantitative principles. The five quantitative principles are as follows:

1. *Mental energy.* "Every mind tends to keep its total simultaneous cognitive output constant in quantity, however varying in quality" (p. 131).
2. *Retentivity.* "The occurrence of any cognitive event produces a tendency for it to occur afterwards" (p. 132).
3. *Fatigue.* "The occurrence of any cognitive event produces a tendency opposed to its occurring afterwards" (p. 134).
4. *Conative control.* "The intensity of cognition can be controlled by conation" (p. 135).
5. *Primordial potencies.* "Every manifestation of the preceding four quantitative principles is superposed upon, as its ultimate basis, certain primordial but variable individual potencies" (pp. 136–7).

Spearman's theory is little used and little cited today, and yet it is clear that the theory could appropriately be labeled as the first of the computational theories. For whatever one may think of his ideas, Spearman deserves tremendous credit as the first major theorist guided by two of the major metaphors of understanding intelligence.

Cognitive psychology approaches to intelligence

Cognitive psychologists have pursued a number of different approaches to understanding mental abilities. Expanding on a categorization scheme proposed earlier by Pellegrino and Glaser (1979), I have loosely classified these different approaches into four different categories, but it should be understood that these categories are neither mutually exclusive nor exhaustive with respect to current research approaches in cognitive psychology. I will briefly describe what each approach is, what its goals are, what kinds of research it has generated, and what my evaluation of it is.

Cognitive correlates

In the cognitive correlates approach to understanding mental abilities, subjects are tested in their ability to perform tasks that contemporary cognitive psychologists believe measure basic human information-processing abilities. (Information processing is generally defined as the sequence of mental operations and their products involved in performing a cognitive task.) Such tasks include, among others, the Posner and Mitchell (1967) letter-matching task, in which subjects are asked to state as quickly as possible whether the letters in a pair such as "A a" constitute a physical match (which they don't) or (in another condition) a name match (which they do); and the S. Sternberg (1969) memory-scanning task, in which subjects are asked to state as quickly as possible whether a target digit or letter, such as 5, appeared in a previously memorized set of digits or letters, such as 3 6 5 2. Individuals are usually tested either via tachistoscope (a machine that provides rapid stimulus exposures) or a computer terminal, and the principal dependent measure of interest is response time.

The proximal goal in this research is to estimate parameters (characteristic quantities) representing the durations of performance for the information-processing components constituting each task and then to investigate the extent to which these components correlate across subjects with each other and with scores on measures commonly believed to assess intelligence (e.g., Raven's Progressive Matrices test). Most commonly, correlations between parameter estimates and measured intelligence are statistically significant, but moderately low – usually around .3 (see, e.g., Hunt et al., 1973; Hunt, Lunneborg, & Lewis, 1975). The distal goal of cognitive correlates research is to integrate individual-differences research and mainstream cognitive psychological research – in particular, by providing a theoretical grounding from cognitive psychology for differential research (Hunt et al., 1973). Thus, instead of trying to draw theoretical conclusions from correlating scores on one empirically derived test (e.g., reasoning) with scores on another empirically derived test (e.g., vocabulary) as differential researchers have done, the cognitive correlates researcher draws theoretical conclusions from correlating scores on an empirically de-rived test with parameters generated by a cognitive model of some aspect of mental functioning (e.g., memory scanning).

On the one hand, cognitive correlates researchers like Hunt (1978), Jensen (1979), Keating and Bobbitt (1978), and Jackson and McClel-land (1979) must be given credit for providing a cognitive theoretical base for individual-differences research to supplement the psychomet-ric (and usually factorial) theoretical base that had existed earlier. On the other hand, one might question whether these researchers are pro-viding the optimal cognitive theoretical base. The relatively low corre-lations attained between task parameters and psychometric test scores might be due to the psychometric test performance's drawing on lower level perceptual and memory abilities of the kinds studied by cognitive correlates researchers, but only in a peripheral way. It is not clear that the rather simple kinds of information processing required by many of the perceptual and memory tasks cognitive psychologists have studied in their laboratories do justice to the rather complex kinds of informa-tion processing required by many psychometric tests of intelligence – at least to the extent that the reason for studying the relationships between the two kinds of tasks is to use the first to provide a theoretical grounding for the second. Nor do the simple tasks seem to measure constructs resembling what most people mean by "intelligence" (see Neisser, 1979; Sternberg et al., 1981).

Other explanations for the moderately low correlations between the cognitive task parameters and psychometric tests have been proposed as well. For example, Carroll (1981) has suggested that the cognitive tasks and psychometric tests may be related because they share a com-mon speed factor; Sternberg (1981b) has proposed that the relationship may be due to a degree of shared novelty, or nonentrenchment, between the two kinds of tasks (see also Hogaboam & Pellegrino, 1978).

A final evaluation of the cognitive correlates approach will almost certainly have to await our better understanding of the .3-level correla-tions between task parameters and test scores. In the meantime, cogni-tive correlates researchers deserve considerable credit for reawakening interest among cognitive psychologists in individual differences and for bringing individual-differences research closer to mainstream cognitive psychological research. Although I do not believe that the cognitive correlates approach will provide the keys to unlock the mysteries of intelligence, if only because the tasks these researchers have studied do not seem fundamental to intelligence (as opposed to, say, perception or memory), I do believe that the early contributions of Hunt and others will be remembered for having opened an area of research that for years had been all but ignored by cognitive psychologists.

Cognitive components

The nature of the approach. In the cognitive components approach to understanding mental abilities, subjects are tested in their ability to perform tasks of the kinds actually found on standard psychometric tests of mental abilities – for example, analogies, series completions, mental rotations, and syllogisms. Subjects are usually tested via a tachistoscope or a computer terminal, and response time is usually the principal dependent variable, but error rate and pattern-of-response choices can be secondary dependent variables. These latter dependent variables are of more interest in this approach than in the cognitive correlates approach because the tasks tend to be more difficult and thus more susceptible to erroneous responses.

The proximal goal in this research is first to formulate a model of information processing in performance on IQ-test types of tasks; second, to test the model at the same time as parameters for the model are estimated; and finally, to investigate the extent to which these components correlate across subjects with each other and with scores on standard psychometric tests. Because the tasks that are analyzed are usually taken directly from IQ tests, or else are very similar to tasks found on IQ tests, the major issue in this kind of research is not whether there is any correlation at all between cognitive task and psychometric test scores. Rather, the issue is one of isolating the locus or loci of the correlation that is obtained. One seeks to discover what components of information processing in task performance are the critical ones from the standpoint of the theory of intelligence.

The distinction between cognitive correlates and cognitive components research is not entirely clear-cut. There appear to be at least two major differences in emphasis in the two approaches, however. First, if one were willing to accept a continuum of levels of information processing extending from perception, to learning and memory, to reasoning and complex problem solving, cognitive correlates researchers would tend to study tasks measuring skills at the lower end of the continuum, whereas cognitive components researchers would tend to study tasks measuring skills at the higher end of the continuum. Thus, whereas cognitive correlates researchers tend to study perception, learning, and memory tasks, cognitive components researchers tend to study reasoning and problem solving tasks. Second, cognitive components research seems to place more emphasis on the formulation, fitting, and testing of formal information-processing models, which are usually operationalized either as sets of linear equations (e.g., Mulholland, Pellegrino, & Glaser, 1980; Sternberg, 1977, 1980a) or as computer simulations (e.g., Atwood & Polson, 1976; Simon & Kotovsky, 1963).

The differences between the two approaches are almost certainly more in emphasis than in kind. First, the theory and research of some investigators is quite difficult to classify (e.g., Carroll, 1976, 1981), as it seems to straddle the fence between the two approaches. Second, the research of some investigators who are usually seen as being in one camp or the other is sometimes on the borderline between the two approaches (e.g., MacLeod, Hunt, & Mathews, 1978).

In early cognitive components research (e.g., Royer, 1971; Sternberg, 1977), investigators generally isolated a single kind of information-processing component. There seems to have been some evolution of cognitive components research, however, such that investigators seem more apt these days to speak of multiple kinds of information-processing components (e.g., Snow, 1979; Sternberg, 1980b), such as metacomponents (or executive processes – higher order processes that serve to organize, plan, and monitor performance) and performance components. On the one hand, the differentiation among kinds of components seems to do better justice to the variety of kinds of information processing people are required to do in their daily lives. On the other hand, it is not clear how theories regarding taxonomies of kinds of component processes can be tested, nor is it clear how one could place constraints on the kinds of components such theories could generate (and thereby avoid an endless proliferation of kinds of components). The problem is not one of proliferation per se, which may or may not be desirable, but of the absence of logical or empirical constraints on proliferation.

As in many kinds of research, there have been surprises in cognitive components research. One of the more pleasant surprises has been the ability of formal componential models to account for large amounts of both task and person variation in response times and response choices (see, e.g., Frederiksen, 1980; Guyote & Sternberg, 1981; Mulholland et al., 1980; Pellegrino & Glaser, 1980; Schustack & Sternberg, 1981; Shepard & Metzler, 1971; Sternberg, 1977, 1980a). One of the less pleasant surprises has been that the magnitudes of correlations between information-processing latencies and psychometric test scores have been only moderate (often in the .4 to .6 range). More disturbing, the identified loci of these correlations have sometimes been ones that seem theoretically questionable (e.g., when most of the identified correlation between task and test scores turns out to be isolated to the response constant – Egan, 1976; Sternberg, 1977). Recent efforts have attempted to remedy this situation by studying metacomponential or executive functioning and by studying performance in nonentrenched, or novel, tasks (e.g., Sternberg, 1981b). Studies of these kinds have yielded higher correlations (often in the .6 to .8 range) and explanations for these correlations seem consistent with people's intuitions.

It is sometimes difficult to know where the cognitive components approach stops and other approaches that are more than mere variants of this approach begin. The research of some investigators (e.g., Frederiksen, 1980; Whitely, 1980), although "componential" in many respects, draws on psychometric techniques such as analysis of covariance structures (in the case of Frederiksen) or latent trait analysis (in the case of Whitely) that are not usually associated with the cognitive components approach. Consider four theories of how the information-processing components of intelligence might be organized: Carroll's, Brown's, Sternberg's, and Baron's:

Carroll's theory. According to Carroll (1976, 1981), performance on mental tests can be understood in terms of a relatively small number of basic underlying information-processing components. Carroll has investigated the major tests used in both psychometric and cognitive research. Based on a "logical and partly intuitive analysis of the task" (Carroll, 1981, p. 14), Carroll has identified a tentative list of ten types of cognitive components.

1. *Monitor* (MONITR). This process is a cognitive set or "determining tendency" that drives the operation of other processes during the course of task performance.
2. *Attention* (ATFTIM). This process evolves from an individual's expectations regarding the type and number of stimuli that are to be presented during task performance.
3. *Apprehension* (APSTIM). This process is used in the registering of a stimulus in a sensory buffer.
4. *Perceptual integration* (CLOZR). This process is used in the perception of the stimulus, or the attainment of perceptual closure of a stimulus, and its matching with any previously formed memory representation.

5. *Encoding* (REPFRM). This process is used in forming a mental representation of the stimulus and in its interpretation in terms of its attributes, associations, or meaning, depending on the requirements of a particular task.
6. *Comparison* (TSTFIF). This process is used to determine whether two stimuli are the same, or at least of the same class.
7. *Co-representation formation* (FOCORT). This process is used to establish a new representation in memory in association with a representation that is already there.
8. *Co-representation Retrieval* (FICORP). This process is used in finding in memory a particular representation in association with another representation on the basis of some rule or other basis for the association.
9. *Transformation* (TRAREP). This process is used to transform or change a mental representation on some prespecified basis.
10. *Response Execution* (XECUTR). This process is used to operate on some mental representation to produce either an overt or a covert response.

Carroll (1981) emphasizes that this list is tentative in that it may not exhaustively cover all the processes that might eventually be identified in the analysis of elementary cognitive tasks. He claims, however, that this list does cover all the processes that he has been able to identify in the long list of elementary cognitive tasks that he has considered. Although he is not certain that the processes are all mutually distinct from one another, they seem to be different enough to serve as the basis for an information-processing analysis of intelligent task performance.

In his 1981 article, Carroll analyzes a choice reaction-time task in terms of this set of processes. In the choice reaction-time task, an individual is presented with two or more stimuli: for example, bulbs that can be lit. The subject's task is to make one of several responses as a function of what happens to a given stimulus. Thus, for example, there might be two light bulbs, one on the left and one on the right. The subject's task might be to press a button with his left hand if the bulb on the left lights up and to press a button with his right hand if the bulb on the right lights up (see also Jensen, 1980). Carroll's task analysis shows that even this simple task requires quite a long and complicated set of information-processing components for its successful execution.

Brown's theory. Brown (1978; Brown & Campione, 1978; Campione & Brown, 1978) has divided processes of cognition into two kinds:

metacognitive processes, which are executive skills used to control one's information processing; and cognitive processes, which are non-executive skills used to implement task strategies. An essentially identical distinction has been proposed by a number of other investigators, for example, Butterfield and Belmont (1977), Flavell (1981), Markman (1981), and Reitman (1965). In Brown's particular version of this process dichotomy, five metacognitive processes are of particular importance: (1) *planning* one's next move in executing a strategy, (2) *monitoring* the effectiveness of individual steps in a strategy, (3) *testing* one's strategy as one performs it, (4) *revising* one's strategy as the need arises, and (5) *evaluating* one's strategy in order to determine its effectiveness. Metacognitive processes such as these would be used to decide on the cognitive processes appropriate for task solution. For example, these processes might be used to decide that in a learning task, the cognitive processes involved in rehearsal of material provide an appropriate way of memorizing a list of words.

Sternberg's theory. Sternberg (1980b, 1985a) distinguishes among three kinds of information-processing components.

Metacomponents are higher order control processes used for executive planning, monitoring, and evaluation of one's performance in a task. Metacomponents are comparable to what Brown refers to as meta-cognitive processes. Collectively, these processes are sometimes referred to by psychologists as the "executive" or the "homunculus." The 10 metacomponents believed to be most important in intelligent functioning are (1) recognition that a problem of some kind exists, (2) definition of just what the nature of the problem is, (3) selection of a set of lower order, nonexecutive components for performance on a task, (4) selection of a strategy for task performance, combining the lower order components, (5) selection of one or more mental representations for information, (6) decision on how to allocate attentional resources, (7) monitoring of or keeping track of one's place in task performance and of what has been done and needs to be done, (8) understanding of internal and external feedback concerning the quality of task performance, (9) knowledge of how to act on the feedback that is received, and (10) implementation of action as a result of the feedback. Note that this last metacomponent in effect assigns a crucial role to action in the theory of intelligent performance. According to this view, one cannot have an adequate theory of intelligence without considering both thought and the actions that emanate from it.

Performance components are lower order processes used in the execution of various strategies for task performance. Three examples of such components are (1) *encoding* the nature of a stimulus, (2) *inferring* the relations between two stimulus terms that are similar in some ways and different in others, and (3) *applying* a previously inferred relation to a new situation.

Knowledge acquisition components are processes involved in learning new information and storing it in memory. The three knowledge acquisition components believed to be most important in intelligent functioning are (1) *selective encoding,* by which relevant new information is sifted out from irrelevant new information (for the specific purpose for which the learning is taking place), (2) *selective combination,* by which the selectively encoded information is combined in a particular way that maximizes its internal coherence, or connectedness, and (3) *selective comparison,* by which the selectively encoded and combined information is related to information already stored in memory to maximize the connectedness of the newly formed knowledge structure to previously formed knowledge structures.

These three kinds of components are applied in task performance for reaching a solution or other goal. Components can vary widely in the range of tasks to which they apply. Some components, and especially the metacomponents, appear to be broadly applicable over a wide range of tasks. Other components apply to less broad ranges of tasks, and some apply only to a narrow range of tasks. Such components are of little theoretical interest, and generally of little practical interest as well.

Sternberg (1980b) has described four ways in which the various kinds of components can interact with each other: (1) direct activation of one kind of component by another, (2) indirect activation of one kind of component by another via the mediation of a third kind of component, (3) direct feedback from one kind of component to another, (4) indirect feedback from one kind of component to another via a third kind. In the proposed system, only metacomponents can directly activate and receive feedback from each other. Thus, all control passes directly from the metacomponents to the system, and all information passes directly from the system to the metacomponents. The other kinds of components can activate each other only indirectly and receive feedback from each other only indirectly; in every case, mediation must be supplied by the metacomponents. For example, the activation of information affects the retrieval of information and the various kinds of performances that can be done on that information, but only via the link of the two lower order kinds of components to the higher order metacomponents. Information from the knowledge acquisition components is filtered to the performance components through the metacomponents. Metacomponents are also unique among the three kinds of components in that they can directly activate and receive feedback from each other.

Consider a simplified example of how the proposed system might function in the solution of a word puzzle, such as an anagram (where the letters of a word are presented in scrambled fashion). As soon as one decides metacomponentially on a certain tentative strategy for unscrambling the letters of the word, activation of that strategy can pass directly from the metacomponents responsible for deciding on a strategy to the performance components responsible for executing the first step of the strategy; subsequently, activation can pass to the successive performance components needed to execute the strategy. Feedback will return from the performance components, indicating the strategy's level of success. The individual must decide how to act on this feedback and then must actually perform the required action. As a given strategy is being executed, new information is being acquired about how to solve anagrams in general. This information is also fed back to the metacomponents, which may act on or ignore this information. New information that seems useful is more likely to be transmitted indirectly from the relevant knowledge acquisition components to the relevant performance components for use in solving new problems, whether anagrams or otherwise.

The metacomponents are able to process only a limited amount of information at a given time. In a difficult task, the amount of information being fed back to the metacomponents may exceed their capacity to act on that information. In this case, the metacomponents become overloaded, and valuable information that cannot be processed may simply be wasted. The total information-handling capacity of the metacomponents of a given system will thus be an important limiting aspect of the system. This capacity can effectively be increased by automatization of componential execution. Automatic processing of information is theorized to require far less in the way of attentional resources than is required by controlled processing.

Baron's theory. Jonathan Baron (1985) has proposed a theory that rational thinking is the cornerstone of intelligence. Baron defines intelligence as "the set of properties within a psychological theory that make for effectiveness, regardless of the environment a person is in" (p. 15). A component of intelligence is then any property within this set. Although intelligence is based on rational thinking, it goes beyond it in including personal endowments such as capacities and knowledge that can lead to success.

Baron divides the general components of intelligence into capacities and dispositions. Capacities can be either inborn or environmentally developed. Dispositions are ways of approaching problems and dealing with the world. Baron's theory suggests that to teach intelligence, one would wish to develop people's rational thinking skills, as well as dispositions that lead to good problem solving.

A final evaluation of the cognitive components approach, like one of the cognitive correlates approach, will have to await further developments. The approach is still being used, and sufficient time has not elapsed to show everything it can or cannot do. I believe that a major contribution of this approach will be its demonstration that IQ test tasks can be understood, and understood well, in information-processing terms. Componential analyses have shown that cognitive components provide a view of mental abilities that is complementary (rather than contradictory) to that provided by the factors (Carroll, 1981; Sternberg, 1981c) characterizing differential theories of mental abilities. If the approach comes to be judged harshly, it may be because in the initial enthusiasm that accompanies new approaches to studying intelligence (or anything else), investigators following the cognitive components approach probably claimed more for their new approach than it could yield.

During the 1970s, cognitive correlates and cognitive components researchers were busy establishing their respective turfs, each trying to win converts to their new views on how intelligence should be studied. As investigators began to realize the fuzziness of the distinction between the two approaches and that each approach had something to contribute to the other (just as each approach had more to learn from the factor-analytic approach than had originally seemed to be the case), the competition between investigators following each of the two approaches started to wane. This outcome, which I believe represents the current state of affairs, may represent a new era of eclectic and integrative research approaches, or it may signal the need for a new paradigm that will use the cognitive correlates and cognitive components approaches as scapegoats in much the same way as these approaches once used the factor-analytic approach. The "dialectical" evolution of research on intelligence goes on (see Sternberg, 1981a, for a theory of this evolutionary dialectic).

Cognitive training

The cognitive training approach to understanding mental abilities can be used in conjunction with either the cognitive correlates approach or the cognitive components approach, or in conjunction with some other approach. The essence of this approach is aptly described by Campione, Brown, and Ferrara (1982). According to these authors, one starts with a theoretical analysis of a task and an hypothesis about a source of individual differences within that task. It might be assumed, for example, that components A, B, and C are required to carry out Task X and that less able children do poorly because of a weakness in component A. To test this assertion, one might train less able subjects in the use of A and then retest them on X. If performance improves, the task analysis is supported. If it does not, then either A was not an important component of the task or subjects were originally efficient with regard to A and did not need training.

The cognitive-training approach has been widely used in a variety of domains. For example, Belmont and Butterfield (1971), Borkowski and Wanschura (1974), and Campione and Brown (1978) have used the approach in learning and memory; and Feuerstein (1979), Holzman, Glaser, and Pellegrino (1976), and Linn (1973) have used it in reasoning and problem solving. One conclusion has emerged with striking regularity in many studies by many different investigators: To attain both durability and generalizability of training, it seems to be necessary to train both at the level of metacomponents (or executive processes) and at the level of performance components (or lower order processes used to carry out the orders of the executive processes – see, e.g., Belmont, Butterfield, & Ferretti, 1982; Feuerstein, 1979, 1980).

At a practical level, the cognitive training approach can be helpful in telling us what aspects of cognitive functioning are and are not trainable with reasonable amounts of effort and in actually effecting improvement in individuals' cognitive functioning. I am more impressed with the practical utility of the approach than with its theoretical utility for testing models of task performance because of interpretive problems I see in drawing theoretical conclusions about task performance from the results of training studies. I believe there are several such problems.

First, whereas successful training of a cognitive strategy for performing a particular task does imply that individuals might use that strategy in their spontaneous performance of the task, it does not imply that individuals necessarily use that strategy, or even that they are likely to use it. For example, we have found it easy to train a strategy for solving linear syllogisms that subjects only rarely use spontaneously (Sternberg & Weil, 1980).

Second, training in one or more components may change the strategy subjects use. An improvement in performance as a result of training certain components may indicate improved execution of the original strategy, or instead, it may indicate the adoption of a new, more successful strategy. The training approach, in itself, does not indicate which outcome has transpired.

Third, if training fails, it is not clear what conclusions one can draw from the failure. There seem to be at least four plausible interpretations. The first is that the component is simply not a component of natural intelligence – one cannot train it because it is not a natural part of a functioning cognitive system. A second interpretation is that the component is an aspect of intelligence but that it is essentially impervious to training. Not all intelligent acts need to be accessible or even available to consciousness, and the component may be an automatic one to which the individual has no access. A third interpretation is that the component is an aspect of intelligence and is trainable, but not by the methods used by the particular investigator. A fourth interpretation is that the component is an aspect of intelligence and that it is trainable, but not in the population being investigated. Many of the cognitive training studies have been conducted on retarded populations, who scarcely provide a representative basis for drawing conclusions about trainability of cognitive processes in the population at large (Sternberg, 1981c).

On the whole, I view the cognitive training approach as a significant and worthwhile one, but not for testing theories of intelligence. Rather, I see it as a desirable culmination of research on the nature of mental abilities that is originally undertaken following some other approach. First, one uses a set of methods such as those provided by cognitive correlates or cognitive components analysis to validate a particular subtheory of intelligence. If the validation is reasonably successful, then the practical utility of the theory can be tested through the cognitive training approach at the same time that one makes a potentially valuable contribution to people in need of intellectual improvement (which includes pretty much everyone).

A given theory may be internally valid, in the sense that it can account for task and subject variance, and externally valid, in the sense that parameters of the theory are highly correlated with measures commonly regarded as able to provide sound measurement of mental abilities. But theoretical utility of a theory does not imply practical utility: The level of analysis may be too microscopic or macroscopic to provide useful implications for training, or the theory may deal with processes that are too automatized to be trainable. The converse is also true: Practical utility of a theory does not imply theoretical utility. Successful training outcomes can be and have been attained in the absence of any theory at all. For example, although it is quite likely that taking mathematics courses improves mathematical abilities or that taking language courses improves linguistic abilities, there is, at least at present, no satisfactory theory to account for why this should be so.

To conclude, I believe the cognitive training approach provides a needed complement to other approaches for understanding mental abilities. It answers, or at least addresses, questions that other approaches do not and cannot answer or address. But the approach is not interchangeable with other approaches. It does not provide a good means for testing theories about the nature of mental abilities.

Cognitive contents

Recently, there has emerged on the cognitive psychological scene a new approach to research that has yet to be applied directly to the study of mental abilities but that seems to provide a good entree into such research. The approach, which might be referred to as a cognitive contents approach, seeks to compare the performances of experts and novices in complex tasks such as the solution of physics problems (Chi, Feltovich, & Glaser, 1981; Chi, Glaser, & Rees, 1982; Larkin, McDermott, Simon, & Simon, 1980a, 1980b), the selection of moves and strategies in chess and other games (Chase & Simon, 1973; DeGroot, 1965; Reitman, 1976), and the acquisition of domain-related information by groups of people at different levels of expertise (Chiesi, Spilich, & Voss, 1979). Research on expert–novice differences in a variety of task domains suggests that the way information is stored in and retrieved from long-term memory can largely account for the substantial differences in performance between experts and novices. This view would suggest that a possible locus of differences between more and less mentally able people is in their ability to organize information in long-term memory in a way that makes it readily accessible for a variety of purposes (see, e.g., Egan & Greeno, 1973). Presumably, information stored in such a flexible way is maximally available for transfer from old to new problem situations.

Because the cognitive contents approach has not yet been directly applied to the investigation of differences in mental abilities, it would be impossible to evaluate its utility for purposes of such investigation. But the approach seems to supply a valuable new inroad for mental abilities research, and I expect it will be a matter of only a short time before it is used for this purpose.

Conclusions

The cognitive approaches to the study of intelligence gave investigators in the field of intelligence a new lease on life at a time when their work was trapped in a prison of their own making. Exploratory factor analysis had pretty much run its course, at least for a while, and new methods were sorely needed. The cognitive psychologists came armed and freed the prisoner. The cognitive work gave intelligence researchers a new sense of purpose and unity, particularly in the face of their archenemy and straw man, the psychometrician. We refer to the so-called archenemy and straw man, because in retrospect, it is clear that psychometricians were investigating many of the same problems as the cognitive psychologists, except for differences in methodology. And there were about as many differences in methodology within the cognitive group as there were between the cognitive and psychometric groups. To the extent that there was any critical difference at all, it was probably in the greater emphasis of the cognitivists on stimulus variance and of psychometricians on subject variance. Even here, though, there was overlap, because factor analysis can be and has been applied to stimulus variance, and the cognitivists certainly did study individual differences.

But by the early 1980s, the sense of coherence and unity of purpose among cognitivists was beginning to be lost. Cognitivists were beginning to do what factor analysts had been doing for some time – applying the same techniques to task after task, ability after ability, filling in little holes, but essentially trapping the maiden in a new prison.

Something new was needed that went beyond task analysis after task analysis. Whereas the factor analysts had disagreed about rotations and had kept themselves going for years arguing about the appropriate rotation, cognitive analysts were arguing about levels of tasks and differences in cognitive methodology, and the arguments were going nowhere.

Some people began to think the field was stagnating because of a fundamental problem, pointed out by Neisser (1979), that sooner or later would have to be addressed. The problem was that, although the cognitivists scoffed at the psychometricians, the former were, in fact, using the intelligence tests of the latter as the criteria against which to test their new cognitive measures. In effect, the cognitivists were trying to "have it both ways." On the one hand, they derided psychometric tests; on the other hand, they correlated their response-time and error-rate measures against these tests and rejoiced when they got higher, rather than lower correlations. There was a need for broader, larger-scale theories that would address the relationship between intelligence and cognition more broadly and that would remove from cognitive theorists their dependence on psychometric tests.

A response to the challenge has sought a deeper analysis of the relationship between intelligence and cognition, but has, in fact, remained within the realm of cognition under the new, multidisciplinary banner of "cognitive science." The cognitive science approach has involved construction of macrotheories of human cognition that contain within them implications for understanding intelligence. Much of this work has been allied with, rather than integrated with, the study of human intelligence. The cognitive science researchers have studied some of the same problems as intelligence researchers but have seen their concerns as those of cognition, in general, rather than as those of intelligence, in particular. The cognitive science approach has involved the construction of painstakingly detailed, explicit models of cognition that nevertheless address very global issues of intelligence and cognition.

Cognitive science approaches to intelligence*

Cognitive science is not a term that is defined easily. Schank (1980), for instance, refers to cognitive science as a subfield of artificial

---

* This section was written in collaboration with Peter Frensch.

intelligence. Others would rather view it as a multidisciplinary approach to the study of cognition, subsuming and integrating various fields including artificial intelligence, cognitive psychology, philosophy, linguistics, and neuropsychology. For our purposes, it is sufficient to state that cognitive scientists are interested in cognition, be it machine or human cognition. Unlike the cognitive approaches described earlier in this chapter, however, cognitive science is concerned with constructing macrotheories of intelligent – human or nonhuman – systems at a very detailed level, that is, at a level where theories can be implemented and run on computers.

From the very beginning, the goals of scientists involved in cognitive science have been quite different from those of psychometric scientists concerned with the nature of human intelligence. Whereas the study of human intelligence has traditionally been a study of individual differences in abilities, cognitive science research on intelligence has generally focused on how intelligence works, that is, on how one would go about constructing a machine that would deal with a wide variety of tasks as intelligently as humans do.

Because of these basic differences in research goals, the fields of cognitive science research and of conventional human intelligence research have had, so far, only a small history of interaction (Schank, 1980). In this section of the chapter, I argue that progress in cognitive science can, in principle, lead to progress in the understanding of human intelligence and describe how and where it has done so already. Because the two fields have so rarely been connected in the past, my discussion is primarily aimed at opening new avenues for research on human intelligence. I will not be concerned with every single issue that has been dealt with in the field of cognitive science. Instead, I will limit the discussion to a few, basic issues that I believe have relevance to the understanding of human intelligence. More specifically, I will discuss what cognitive scientists think the major components and mechanisms of any intelligent system, human or nonhuman, are and how the interaction of these components and mechanisms might give rise to different degrees of intelligence.

Processes

Algorithms. Early work in cognitive science focused almost exclusively on process as the basic and sole component of intelligent systems.

With the introduction of computers, processes were thought of in terms of steps of a program, that is, as steps of algorithms. Algorithms specify the exact processes involved in solving a particular problem. They are guaranteed to arrive at the right solution, if there is one. Implemented on computers, algorithms could perform arithmetic operations and logical decisions much faster and more reliably than could humans. Very soon, however, it became clear that the superiority of algorithms was limited to only a very small subset of problems that intelligent systems, such as humans, encounter. When facing certain problems that humans would find only moderately complex, algorithms, even implemented at the speed of computers, could not compete with human problems solvers: They simply needed too much time. Samuel (1959), for instance, has calculated that an algorithm-based, exhaustive-search approach to playing the game of checkers would involve about 10^{40} possible moves, "which at 3 choices per millimicrosecond would still take 10^{21} centuries to consider" (p. 212). He estimated the possible number of moves in chess at about 10^{120}. Intelligent problem solvers, it appears, often do not rely on algorithms; instead they use heuristic strategies.

Domain-general heuristics. Like algorithms, heuristic strategies are rules that result in sequences of operations for solving a given problem. Unlike algorithms, however, they do not guarantee generation of the correct solution to a problem. One of the major advantages of heuristics is that they can be formulated generally enough to be used in a wide variety of problems. The Logic Theorist (Newell, Shaw, & Simon, 1958) and the General Problem Solver (Newell & Simon, 1961), for example, were early problem solving models that embodied the heuristics of working backward and of means–ends analysis.

The Logic Theorist (LT) proves theorems in plane geometry using symbolic logic. The LT is an axiomatic system with strict rules of inference, designed to work backward from the theorem to the axioms. The heuristic of working backward is successful because the number of solution paths leading from a theorem back to the axioms is relatively small, whereas the number of potential solution paths leading away from the axioms can be very large. Working backward is a commonly used heuristic in many formal systems, such as mathematics (Polya, 1957). More recently, research on expertise has demonstrated that novices are inclined to use the working-backward heuristic, whereas experts tend to use working-forward strategies (e.g., Simon & Simon, 1978).

The General Problem Solver employed the heuristic of means–ends analysis. Newell and Simon (1972) describe how means–ends analysis works:

I want to take my son to nursery school. What's the difference between what I have and what I want? One of distance. What changes distance? My automobile. My automobile won't work. What is needed to make it work? A new battery. What has new batteries? An auto repair shop. I want the repair shop to put in a new battery; but the shop does not know I need one. What is the difficulty? One of communication. What allows communication? A telephone . . . , and so on. (p. 416)

Intelligent systems, it appears, generally do not rely on exactly specified algorithms to solve complex problems. Rather, they use heuristic strategies. A major source of individual differences in abilities thus appears to be the availability and generality of heuristics. Any intelligent system must rely on heuristics to some extent; how well specified and how easily accessible they are, however, might differ among problem solvers.

Domain-general learning mechanisms. A somewhat different approach to constructing intelligent systems that was a major topic of early cognitive science research, also focusing on general processes as the primary source of intelligence, was the study of domain-general learning mechanisms. The basic assumptions underlying this approach were that cognitive systems start out with no or little initial knowledge and that learning is the major source of final intelligence. Examples of this early line of research on self-organizing systems were the Perceptron (Rosenblatt, 1958) and Pandemonium (Selfridge & Neisser, 1960). Both systems were intended to model the basic cognitive mechanisms underlying the perceptual recognition of two-dimensional patterns and words. Learning was thought to be equivalent to the modification of connection strengths between independent, neuronlike elements, resulting in incremental changes in the probabilities with which elements would transmit a signal. In their influential book, Minsky and Papert (1969) revealed strong theoretical limitations of knowledge-free, perceptronlike learning systems that, subsequently, led many researchers to abandon their efforts rather quickly. Self-organizing systems have recently reemerged in the context of research on models of parallel distributed processing and will be discussed later in this section.

Knowledge

Most of the early work in cognitive science almost totally neglected the issue of knowledge. It was thought that domain-general, problem solving heuristics or rules of learning were the most important ingredients of any intelligent system. Of course, this was not to say that intelligent systems did not have any knowledge. Heuristics and learning procedures had to operate on at least a limited amount of knowledge. It was to say, however, that knowledge was not a factor that would distinguish more intelligent from less intelligent systems.

More recently, the role of knowledge in intelligence has increasingly been acknowledged. Early failures to write programs that could compete with humans in the area of chess, for instance, have contributed significantly toward this trend. Despite their speed and reliability advantages, machines using solely domain-general heuristics were very slow and tended to get lost when trying to find the best move for each game constellation. Research on expert–novice differences in chess revealed some of the reasons why this was the case. For example, in their classic study on expert chess players, Chase and Simon (1973), replicating DeGroot's (1965) earlier findings, reported that experts spent less time, made fewer errors, needed fewer glances, and took in more information per glance than did novices when their task consisted of memorizing or reproducing briefly presented, meaningful chess patterns. However, experts' encoding ability dropped to the level of novices when they were forced to deal with meaningless chess patterns. Examining the recall clusters of their players, Chase and Simon found that the better players' clusters frequently were based upon attack or defense configurations, implying some sort of an abstract knowledge representation. It appeared, thus, that intelligent systems rely to a great extent on stored problem patterns when they face a familiar task. Instead of creating solutions from scratch for every problem situation, they make use of previously stored information in such a way that it facilitates their coping with the current problem.

The usefulness of prior knowledge is not restricted to the somewhat artificial domain of game playing, of course. It is at least equally important in more natural domains, such as language processing, for instance. Consider an example sentence that has been used repeatedly by Roger Schank and his colleagues (e.g., Dehn & Schank, 1982; Schank, 1980).

I was out until 2 A.M. yesterday.
Boy, did my wife give it to me.

Schank (1980) points out that a complete understanding of even a very simple sentence pair, such as the one given above, requires a memory structure that includes beliefs and expectations of people's normal behavior in the world. Knowledge, thus, is a necessary ingredient of any intelligent system.

Expert systems. Beginning in the mid-sixties, cognitive science researchers became increasingly involved in creating expert-level, knowledge-based systems that could perform intelligently in complex task domains. Expert systems, such as DENDRAL (Feigenbaum, Buchanan, & Lederberg, 1971), MYCIN (Shortliffe, 1976), and PROSPECTOR (Duda, Gaschnig, & Hart, 1979), for the domains of chemistry, medicine, and minerology, respectively, were constructed for a number of different task domains, each system limited strictly to a single domain and each based on the skillful (intelligent) application of a large data base containing domain-specific knowledge.

Expert systems can vary considerably from one another in terms of design and capabilities. In practice, most systems have many common features. Hayes-Roth, Waterman, and Lenat (1983) identify seven components of an ideal expert system. They are (a) a language processor facilitating communication between user and system, (b) a blackboard storing intermediate results, (c) a knowledge base, subdivided into knowledge of facts and of rules, including inference mechanisms, (d) an interpreter applying these rules, (e) a scheduler controlling the sequence of rule application, (f) a consistency enforcer modifying previous conclusions when new data are inconsistent, and (g) a justifier explaining the system's "line of reasoning."

Knowledge base. From a knowledge-engineering perspective, two aspects of a knowledge base are important. First, in which way is knowledge to be represented, and second, how is it to be organized so that it can be used to facilitate problem solving? We would argue that the representation of psychological constructs is of relatively little importance to understanding intelligence in machines and humans. Thus, in what follows we will be more concerned with the issue of the organization of knowledge than with the many different ways in which knowledge can be represented in expert systems.

Knowledge organization. The issue of knowledge organization comprises two distinct problems. First, how does any complex storage system find and access relevant prior knowledge, and second, how does it structure its knowledge in such a way that it guides its problem solving behavior? The first issue is one of multiple indexing; the second, one of high-level memory structures. Let us turn first to multiple indexing, the problem of finding relevant information.

Consider a system that has indexed the information "Bob is considering buying a new car" exclusively under "car." Such a system would be able to access the information only in the context of "car." Questions like "What did Bob do recently?" would not result in finding that information. According to Schank (1980), the ability to index information at many different places is crucial for any intelligent system. Poor indexing can result in a lack of understanding, especially when new information has to be related to previously acquired knowledge. Thus, "poor memory" can be due to not having processed incoming information appropriately.

The question of how high-level knowledge structures in memory are constructed and used has become increasingly important to cognitive scientists in recent years. A variety of different knowledge structures have been proposed, including, for instance, frames (Goldstein & Papert, 1976; Minsky, 1975) and scripts (Schank & Abelson, 1977). Common to all high-level knowledge structures is that they seek to organize the information that is stored in memory in such a way that it can be accessed easily and be used to understand new information.

Consider the now classic Burger King script (Schank & Abelson, 1977). Somebody who has never had any experience with a Burger King before might, upon entering the first time, be reminded of a McDonald's restaurant. In addition to being reminded of McDonald's, a person's McDonald's script might guide her expectations about what she is likely to encounter in a Burger King, what kind of food she will find, when she has to pay, and so on. Thus, the new situation will be interpreted in terms of previously acquired knowledge. In addition, Burger King might be stored in memory in terms of its deviations from the McDonald's script (Schank & Abelson, 1977). One important aspect of intelligent systems, then, is the ability to create high-level knowledge structures, such as scripts, and to view newly encountered situations as instances of such structures. Of course, not all features of existing knowledge structures are equally important with regard to the interpretation of new information, especially when existing knowledge structures cover only small portions of the new situation. Also, the new episode can be viewed as deviating from the old script in terms of a variety of features. The number of features that can be used to separate knowledge structure and new instance depends most heavily on the abstractness of the script. Thus, intelligence might be thought of, in part, as the ability to anticipate the most useful level of abstraction at the time a high-order knowledge structure is first constructed (Schank, 1980). Any intelligent system must, to some extent, be able to differentiate between relevant and irrelevant features of newly encountered situations, that is, it must anticipate what features will have predictive value in the future and what features will not.

Beliefs. On a general level, we can say that high-level knowledge structures partly determine what intelligent systems understand. Beliefs can be viewed as very high-level knowledge structures that can have profound impact on the ability to comprehend. The power of beliefs might be most obvious in the domain of politics. Carbonell (1979) examined the role of beliefs in comprehension through a program called POLITICS. POLITICS simulated the beliefs of either an American conservative or a liberal about the goals of the United States, the Soviet Union, and third-world nations. The following is an excerpt of the system's interpretations of the same input, first for a conservative and then for a liberal. Note that only the beliefs differed for the two "conversations"; all other mechanisms were identical.

Input text: Russia massed troops on the Czech border.
Dialogue with conservative:

> Q: Why did Russia do this?
> A: Because Russia thought it could take political control of Czechoslovakia by sending troops.
> Q: What should the United States do?
> A: The United States should intervene militarily. (p. 67)

Dialogue with liberal:

> Q: Why did Russia do this?
> A: Because Russia wanted to increase its political influence over Czechoslovakia.
> Q: What should the United States do?
> A: The United States should denounce the Russian action in the United Nations. (p. 72)

The example demonstrates convincingly how beliefs can affect the comprehension and interpretation of information. This is not to say that intelligent systems should subscribe to any particular belief, of course. It is to say, however, that a system's intelligence can only be viewed relative to its belief system.

Inferences. A large data base that is structured intelligently is, as we have shown, certainly a necessity for any intelligent system. In itself, however, the clever storage of a vast amount of information is not sufficient for intelligent performance on a complex task. Intelligent systems also have to be capable of drawing inferences, that is to say, they have to be capable of linking information in their knowledge bases in a meaningful way. One way of accomplishing this, as we have seen, is to create high-level knowledge structures that can aid in the processing of familiar information. When dealing with novel information, however, the system has to link parts of its knowledge structure that have not been linked before. In order to do this appropriately and not get lost in a seemingly endless number of possibilities, an intelligent system has to rely on some sort of guidance. Roger Schank and his colleagues (e.g., Cullingford, 1978; Schank, 1975, 1978; Schank, Lebowitz, & Birnbaum, 1978) have identified several mechanisms that control the inference process. Some of these mechanisms are partial parsing of input and reliance on high-order knowledge structures, plans, and goals. Most important of all is the notion of "interestingness." In Schank's own words, "Simply stated, the idea behind interestingness is that since people cannot pay attention to all possible inferences, they must attempt to predetermine what inference paths will turn out to be relevant and then pursue those paths that are found to be interesting" (1980, p. 8).

How do people know which inference paths are interesting? Schank (1978) claims that higher order knowledge structures contain some information about what normally to expect in any given situation. This "normality information" can be discovered through partial parsing of input and determines the interestingness of an inference path. In general, interestingness is directly proportional to abnormality. Thus, the more features of a given situation deviate from normally expected features in that situation, the more interesting the situation becomes.

Schank argues that the inference control mechanisms relate to different modes of processing new inputs and to different degrees of intelligence. For example, a system that does not limit its inferences at all will tend to become lost in all but the simplest situations. In contrast, a system that tends to rely only on scripts will be very successful when dealing with familiar situations but will completely fail in novel situations. According to Schank, the most intelligent system will make use of all inference control mechanisms guided by the concept of interestingness.

Architecture

So far, we have discussed some of the most important components and mechanisms of intelligent systems in isolation. Although there are only a few basic components to an intelligent system, as we have seen, these components can vary considerably in their implementation and in the ways they interact with each other. Creators of expert systems have come to acknowledge that the architectures of their systems are primarily determined by the types of problem the systems are expected to solve.

Stefik et al. (1983) categorize classes of problems according to a variety of dimensions, including the reliability of the data the systems are to work with, the time consistency of these data, and the characteristics of the search space. A brief comparison of the MYCIN (Shortliffe, 1976) and HEARSAY-II (Erman, Hayes-Roth, Lesser, & Reddy, 1980) systems demonstrates that intelligent problem solving in one domain is not necessarily intelligent problem solving in another domain.

MYCIN is an expert system that diagnoses blood and meningitis infections and recommends drug treatment on the basis of an interactive dialogue with a physician. The system typically copes with problems characterized by a small search space and by reliable and static data. Its problem solving behavior can be described as an exhaustive, backward-chaining search augmented by a heuristic that ranks competing hypotheses. MYCIN considers only one hypothesis at a time.

HEARSAY-II is a speech-understanding system that was developed at Carnegie-Mellon University. Its design represents one of the first attempts to deal with very complex problem solving tasks that are characterized by unreliable data that change over time, a large search space of possible solutions, and the need to integrate different subdomains of knowledge. Consequently, HEARSAY-II relies on an architecture that differs greatly from MYCIN's. The principal features of HEARSAY-II include a collection of independent, cooperating specialists, reasoning on different levels of abstraction, and the development of partial solutions based on particularly important data.

The conclusion that the type of problem that has to be solved very much determines the architecture of intelligent problem solving systems is, of course, reminiscent of theories of human intelligence, in which many theorists have proposed that some types of tasks are better suited for the purpose of measuring intelligent performance than are others. For example, R. B. Cattell (1971), Horn (1968), Raaheim (1974), and Sternberg (1985a), among others, have claimed that the ability to reason with novel and, particularly, partially novel information is an integral aspect of human intelligence.

We will now turn to how systems display intelligence on higher levels of processing. We will consider two higher order aspects of intelligent performance, understanding and learning.

Levels of understanding

One of the sine qua nons of intelligence is understanding. Without understanding, systems cannot perform intelligently. According to Schank (1984), any system's understanding could be tested by how it explains its own actions. Many expert systems (most notably MYCIN) provide an explanation (justification) facility that enables users to ask for explanations of the system's "line of reasoning." An expert system's justifier answers questions about why and how some conclusions were reached and why others were rejected.

Schank (1984) proposes a continuum of understanding. According to Schank, understanding on the most basic level can be circumscribed as "making sense." Operating on the level of making sense would mean that the system is able to explain its actions with a causal sequence of actions. To display higher levels of understanding, systems would have to include goals, alternative hypotheses, and previous knowledge in their explanations. To achieve the highest level of understanding, "complete empathy," a system's explanation of its own actions would have to include feelings and emotions. Schank argues that levels of intelligence are related to levels of understanding. The more complete a system's understanding, that is, the more appropriate its explanations of its own actions, the more intelligence it displays. Thus, intelligence might be tested in terms of understanding.

Learning

Any intelligent, human or nonhuman, system has to have the ability to learn. In fact, the ability to learn under partial instruction has been used to measure human intelligence (e.g., Feuerstein, 1979). The link between learning and intelligence is most obvious in the absence of any learning capabilities. A system that repeatedly makes the same errors can hardly be classified as intelligent.

Consider now the mechanisms of learning as they have been discussed in cognitive science during the past three decades and how these mechanisms might be related to intelligent behavior. Langley and Simon (1981) have described some of the loci of learning in information-processing systems. Their taxonomy includes additions to and reorganization of an existing knowledge base, augmentation of recognition mechanisms, and creation and modification of search and evaluation heuristics. In general, learning can occur in each of the basic components of intelligent systems that we described in some detail above. Which parts of a system's architecture are to be modified is determined primarily by the exact type of learning required. Early self-organizing systems in cognitive science, for instance, focusing on mainly rote learning, strived to develop general-purpose learning mechanisms that included no or little initial knowledge. In these systems, learning was basically equivalent to the modification of recognition mechanisms. Such systems typically consisted of a network of interconnected, neuronlike elements. Learning was modeled by the continuous modification of the connection strengths between the individual elements. Learning systems that were based on this discriminant function logic included Rosenblatt's Perceptron (1958) and Selfridge's Pandemonium (Selfridge & Neisser, 1960).

The modification of connection strengths between independent elements is only one of numerous possible ways of describing learning phenomena. Other types of learning systems that have been developed in cognitive science in the past focus, for instance, on symbolic concept-oriented learning through the analysis of examples and counterexamples (e.g., Quinlan, 1979; Winston, 1975) or on decision-theoretic techniques (e.g., Samuel, 1959, 1963).

With the increasing emphasis on knowledge-based expert systems in cognitive science, researchers have come to regard learning as a much more domain-dependent phenomenon that is characterized by the interaction of specific learning heuristics operating on specifically arranged knowledge structures. Consider, for example, John Anderson's (1986) theory of knowledge acquisition that is based on his ACT* theory of cognition (J. R. Anderson, 1983) and has been developed and implemented in the form of a production system.

Learning in production systems. In its most fundamental form, a production system consists of two data structures, a long-term declarative memory of facts and a production memory, that are connected through a processing cycle. The production memory can be described as a collection of if–then, condition–action rules (productions). When an *if* part in the production memory matches some active part of the declarative memory (often referred to as short-term memory or working memory), the *then* part of the rule is executed, resulting in either the activation, modification, or execution of an existing memory structure. Consider the following example: A production dealing with the grammar of the English language that has been formed by most English-speaking people by the age of 5 might be "If the goal is to form the plural of woman, then say women." Whenever a person's generated flow of language hits the goal of forming the plural of "woman," the appropriate rule will be activated in the production memory and will be executed.

Neches, Langley, and Klahr (1987) identify the three stages of the processing cycle. The *match* process finds productions whose conditions match some subset of the current (active) content of working memory, the *conflict resolution* process determines which of several matching productions is executed, and the *act* process applies the then part of the selected production.

According to Neches et al. (1987), "A system has 'learned' if, as a result of experience, it comes to apply a different production in some situation than it would have applied in the equivalent situation at an earlier point in its life time" (p. 47). Thus, learning in a production system is equivalent to creating either a new production or to modifying an existing one.

J. R. Anderson (1986) argues that two learning mechanisms are sufficient to explain learning at all stages of skill acquisition. His first mechanism, proceduralization, operates by building declarative knowledge into productions and is mainly responsible for speedup effects and automatization. Anderson's second learning mechanism, composition, originally proposed by Lewis (1978), combines two or more existing rules into a new rule. For instance, the two rules (X-Y) and (V-W) would result in (XV-YW). Some theories that consider composition a basic mechanism of learning hold that composition occurs whenever two rules are applied in sequence (e.g., Lewis, 1978), whereas others argue that composition occurs only in the presence of goals (e.g., J. R. Anderson, 1986).

J. R. Anderson (1986) claims that the two mechanisms of composition and proceduralization can reproduce effects that have been previously attributed to the additional, inductive, learning mechanisms of discrimination and generalization.

The general framework of production systems together with Anderson's learning mechanisms bears heavily on the issue of intelligence. According to the production-system view of cognition, any intelligent system solves problems in a match, conflict resolution, and act-processing cycle and learns through composition and proceduralization. A system that is unable to determine which of several matching productions to fire at any moment, for instance, is demonstrating a chance approach to problem solving. Also, a system that does not modify existing rules is unable to learn at all. It will repeatedly make the same errors. Different degrees of intelligence might be related to differences in the speed and efficiency with which basic production-system processes are executed or to qualitative differences in the application of the learning mechanisms. Thus, less intelligent systems might, for example, proceduralize the "wrong" declarative facts into rules or might compose two productions that co-occurred only by chance without having any internal connection.

As mentioned earlier, learning can be described at different loci in an information-processing system (Langley & Simon, 1981), with production-system-based theories concentrating primarily on modifications of the knowledge base. In a very different approach to modeling learning phenomena, one that was originally proposed in the late fifties (e.g., Rosenblatt, 1958; Selfridge & Neisser, 1960), systems learn by self-modifying connection strengths between neuronlike elements. This type of learning system has recently regained widespread prominence under the new label of "parallel distributed processing" (PDP) (e.g., McClelland, Rumelhart, & the PDP Research Group, 1986; Rumelhart, McClelland, & the PDP Research Group, 1986).

We now turn to a brief discussion of the general characteristics of parallel distributed processing models and their learning mechanisms. We will then discuss how these mechanisms might be related to intelligence.

Learning in PDP models. The terms *parallel distributed processing* or *connectionist* models, as they are sometimes called (e.g., Feldman & Ballard, 1982), refer to a whole class of neuron-based microtheories of cognition whose individual members share some basic characteristics but which can be quite different with regard to their particular implementations of those common characteristics. Rumelhart, Hinton, and McClelland (1986) list some of the major aspects of PDP models. These models generally consist of a set of independent, neuronlike processing units. Each unit can take on an activation level that is either discrete or analog. The activation level of a unit partly determines the output value of that particular unit that gets distributed to other units in the network through a set of unidirectional connections in a parallel fashion. Associated with each connection is a connection strength that determines the amount of effect the sending unit has on the receiving unit at the other end of the connection. An activation rule, considering all inputs on a particular receiving unit together with the current activation state of the unit, determines the new activation level of the unit.

PDP models are extremely flexible in that the connection strengths among the individual units are not fixed but rather are modifiable with experience. Although PDP models are constructed at a very basic neuronlike level of cognition and thus lend themselves most easily to the description of lower, perceptual levels of cognition, like vision and audition, most researchers in this area believe that their systems are capable of modeling higher level phenomena as well. Rumelhart, Smolensky, McClelland, and Hinton (1987), for example, have demonstrated that schemata and sequential thought processes can be modeled by PDP models. McClelland and Rumelhart (1986) have presented a PDP-based model of human learning and memory.

For PDP researchers, all knowledge is in the connections. Thus, learning involves modifying the patterns of interconnectivity among units. Rumelhart, Hinton, and McClelland (1986) describe three kinds of modifications that can occur in PDP models: (1) the development of new connections, (2) the loss of existing ones, and (3) the modification of existing connection strengths. These researchers claim that the first two modifications can be viewed, at least to a first approximation, as special cases of the modification of connection strengths that already exist.

Virtually all types of PDP models employ some variation of the Hebbian learning rule (Hebb, 1949) as the function for connection-strength modification. In general terms, Hebb claimed that if both a sending unit and a receiving unit are highly active during the course of transmitting a signal, then the connection strength between the units should be strengthened. The most commonly used modification of the Hebbian rule in current PDP models is the Widrow–Hoff or Delta rule (Sutton & Barto, 1981), which relates the amount of learning (change in an existing connection strength) to the difference between the actual activation achieved in the receiving unit and the target activation provided by the sending unit.

In PDP models, two distinct types of learning can occur, associative learning and regularity discovery (Rumelhart, Hinton, & McClelland, 1986). In associative learning, one pattern of activation of a set of units is learned to produce another pattern of activation, either within the same set of units (autoassociation) or in a different one (pattern association). In regularity discovery, a unit extracts some regular, "interesting" pattern on the basis of an internal teaching function.

How is learning in PDP models related to our discussion of the mechanisms of intelligence? Learning in PDP models is generally affected by three global parameters: (1) the environment, (2) structural constraints in the system's architecture, and (3) the learning rules employed. As Rumelhart and McClelland (1986) point out, "People are smarter than rats" (p. 143) because of fundamentally different system architectures and because the human environment offers specific devices that help to organize their cognitive system in intelligent ways. Because learning is a product of both the current state of the organism and the current pattern of input, systems that continually act in similar environments will respond very similarly to the same problems, and thus will demonstrate similar degrees of observable intelligence. Furthermore, the more experience a system has gained in a particular domain, the more dependent it will become on the environmental structure.

Although PDP theorists generally aim at constructing a few basic, powerful learning mechanisms applicable to all systems in the same fashion, it is conceivable that differences in the environmental input or in (maybe prewired) architectural constraints could lead to differences in the preferred learning mechanisms of organisms. In addition to the basic, Hebbian-based learning rule proposed in most PDP models that determines the degree to which a connection strength will be modified, a system has to decide which weights to change to begin with and at which rate. Norman (1986), in a general evaluation of PDP models, suggests that, in addition to PDP mechanisms, a more conscious control mechanism is needed to evaluate and monitor the setting of the connection strengths. In his hybrid model, a symbolic processing control system is coupled with a PDP net or set of nets. (A similar proposal has been made by Schneider, 1985.) A higher level evaluation structure could be an additional source for different degrees of intelligence.

In summary, intelligent systems, described at the microlevel of cognition at which PDP models aim, learn by applying very simple, general learning mechanisms to connections between independent, neuronlike units. The degree of intelligence displayed by a system is determined by the environment, the internal architecture of the system, and the exact learning rule employed.

PDP models are still in their infancy. Thus, although they already offer some interesting insights into the functioning of cognitive systems, it is much too early to offer a concluding statement on the (potentially enormous) impact they might have on our understanding of intelligence in the future.

Hardware and software

Finally, consider the issue of hardware versus software. So far, we have been dealing mainly with software issues, that is, no reference has been made as to why knowledge and processes are implemented in any particular intelligent machine. Although hardware has some importance, the exact nature of a mechanism's hardware implementation does not tell us very much about intelligence.

The position advocated here is one of functionalism. Functionalism holds that mental states are to be understood in terms of their functional relationship, not in terms of any particular material instantiation. Therefore, the same mental states that occur in humans can also occur in other living beings, or even in machines. Only when functionalism is assumed can findings in nonhuman intelligence be related directly to human intelligence. With the increasing popularity of PDP models (e.g., McClelland, Rumelhart, & the PDP Research Group, 1986; Rumelhart, McClelland, & the PDP Research Group, 1986) as models of human cognition, functionalists' claim that hardware and software are independent might soon have to be modified. It may be that parallel models allow for types of processing that serial models cannot deal with. Thagard (1986) already argues that parallel processing differs not only quantitatively but also qualitatively from serial processing, leading to both faster execution of programs and to different styles of programming, such as less rigid reliance on hierarchically structured programs. Systems that operate in parallel allow for the simultaneous and independent consideration of competing, and even contradicting, hypotheses without necessarily getting bogged down (see Thagard, 1984).

Whereas it is much too early to predict all of the effects that models of parallel processing will have on our understanding of human and nonhuman cognition in the future, it seems that their major area of impact will be limited to relatively low-level aspects of human processing. We would thus argue that the contribution of cognitive science to our understanding of intelligence will not be strongly affected by the changing conceptions of hardware.

Conclusions

In this section of the chapter, we have tried to show how research in cognitive science can enhance our understanding of human intelligence. We have argued that cognitive science touches upon issues in intelligence in two different ways. First, by examining how an artificial, intelligent system can be constructed, cognitive science reveals the basic underlying components and mechanisms of intelligence. Second, findings in cognitive science can be taken as suggestions as to where individual differences in intelligence might arise. Cognitive science has demonstrated that intelligent systems need to apply domain-general heuristics to an appropriately structured knowledge base. It also has demonstrated that raw reasoning power cannot be the source of intelligence. Considering all aspects of an even moderately complex problem simply takes too much time. Instead, intelligent systems know what aspects to consider and what aspects not to consider. In other words, intelligent systems know where to focus attention. With regard to individual differences, cognitive science suggest a variety of components and mechanisms where different degrees of intelligence might arise. We have discussed multiple indexing, high-order knowledge structures, beliefs, drawing inferences, levels of understanding, and finally, learning mechanisms.

Understanding human abilities from a computational viewpoint

Many computationally based theories, unlike most of the geographically based ones, are not of intelligence as a whole, but rather of particular aspects of intelligence. These aspects would be at the level, roughly, of the group factors in Thurstone's theory of primary mental abilities. In order to understand the computational metaphor and the theory and research it has generated, it would be helpful to understand something of the kinds of theory and research that have been proposed within each of these different aspects of human abilities. It is not possible here to review the wide range of research on all of these different aspects. For such reviews, see Sternberg (1984a). In order to give some sense of what this research is like, however, I will review work on two abilities: verbal ability and quantitative ability, the two most often measured by conventional tests of scholastic aptitude constructed on the basis of psychometric theorizing.

Verbal ability

Verbal ability is sometimes divided into two separate kinds of skills: verbal comprehension abilities and verbal fluency abilities (Thurstone, 1938). *Verbal comprehension* refers to a person's ability to understand linguistic material such as newspapers, magazines, textbooks, lectures, and the like. *Verbal fluency* refers to a person's ability to generate words and strings of words easily and rapidly. Verbal comprehension is typically measured by tests such as reading comprehension and vocabulary. Verbal fluency is typically measured by tests such as word generation. For example, an individual might be asked to think of as many words as he or she can think of beginning with the letter *b* in the, say, 5 minutes allotted for the test. In this section, only verbal comprehension abilities will be considered, because they have received much more attention in psychological research (but see Sincoff & Sternberg, 1987, for a discussion of verbal fluency abilities).

Verbal comprehension abilities have been recognized as an integral part of intelligence in both psychometric theories (e.g., Guilford, 1967; Thurstone, 1938; Vernon, 1971) and information-processing theories (e.g., Carroll, 1976; Heim, 1970; Sternberg, 1980b), and have, under a variety of aliases, been a major topic of research in differential and experimental psychology for many years.

Three major information-processing approaches to understanding the nature of verbal comprehension are a knowledge-based approach, a bottom-up approach, and a top-down approach. The knowledge-based approach deals with the role of prior information in the acquisition of new information. The bottom-up approach deals with speed of execution of certain very basic mechanistic cognitive processes. The top-down approach deals with higher order utilization of cues in understanding complex verbal material. The three approaches are complementary rather than contradictory.

The knowledge-based approach. The knowledge-based approach assigns a central role to old knowledge in the acquisition of new knowledge.

Although "knowledge" is often referred to in the sense of domain-specific knowledge, the knowledge-based approach can also encompass research focusing on general world knowledge, knowledge of structures or classes of text (as in story grammars), and knowledge about strategies for knowledge acquisition and application (see, e.g., Bisanz & Voss, 1981). Proponents of this approach differ in the respective roles that they assign to knowledge and process in the acquisition of new knowledge. Proponents of this approach usually cite instances of differences between expert and novice performance – in verbal and other domains – that seem to derive more from knowledge differences than from processing differences. For example, Keil (1984) suggests that development in the use of metaphor and in the use of defining features of words seems to be due more to differential knowledge states than to differential use of processes or speed of process execution. Chi (1978) has shown that whether children's or adults' recall performance is better depends on the knowledge domain in which the recall takes place and, particularly, the relative expertise of the children and the adults in the respective domains. Finally, Chase and Simon (1973) found that differences between expert and novice performance in chess seemed largely to be due to differential knowledge structures rather than processes.

The bottom-up approach. Bottom-up research has emerged from the tradition of investigation initiated by Earl Hunt (e.g., Hunt, 1978; Hunt et al., 1975) and followed up by a number of other investigators (e.g., Jackson & McClelland, 1979; Keating & Bobbitt, 1978; see also Perfetti & Lesgold, 1977, for a related approach). According to Hunt (1978), two types of processes underlie verbal comprehension ability – knowledge-based processes and mechanistic (information-free) processes. Hunt's approach has emphasized the latter kind of process. Hunt et al. (1975) studied three aspects of what they called "current information processing" that they believed to be key determinants of individual differences in developed verbal ability. These were (1) sensitivity of overlearned codes to arousal by incoming stimulus information, (2) the accuracy with which temporal tags can be assigned and hence order information can be processed, and (3) the speed with which the internal representations in STM and intermediate term memory (ITM, memory for events occurring over minutes) can be created and altered (p. 197).

   Their basic hypothesis was that individuals varying in verbal ability differ even in these low-level mechanistic skills – skills that are free from any contribution of disparate knowledge or experience. Intelligence tests are hypothesized to measure indirectly these basic information-processing skills by measuring directly the products of these skills, both in terms of their past contribution to the acquisition and storage of knowledge (such as vocabulary) and their present contribution in the current processing of information.

The top-down approach. Top-down processing refers to expectation- or inference-driven processing, or to knowledge-based processing, to use Hunt's (1978) terminology. Top-down processing has been an extremely popular focus for research in the past decade, with many researchers attempting to identify and predict the sorts of inferences a person is likely to draw from a text and how these inferences (or lack thereof) will affect text comprehension (see, e.g., Kintsch & van Dijk, 1978; Rieger, 1975; Rumelhart, 1980; Schank & Abelson, 1977; Thorndyke, 1976). Usually, top-down researchers look at how people combine information actually present in the text with their own store of world knowledge to create a new whole representing the meaning of the text (e.g., Bransford, Barclay, & Franks, 1972). To my knowledge, however, the top-down approach, although often used in models of text processing in general, has been only minimally applied to understanding individual differences in verbal ability or to understanding vocabulary acquisition as a special subset of knowledge acquisition in general.

The first of a small handful of investigators who looked at the use of inference in the acquisition of word meanings from context were Werner and Kaplan (1952), who proposed that the child acquires the meanings of words principally in two ways. One is by explicit reference either verbal or objective; he learns to understand verbal symbols through the adult's direct naming of objects or through verbal definition. The second way is through implicit or contextual reference; the meaning of a word is grasped in the course of conversation, that is, it is inferred from the cues of the verbal context (p. 3).

Jensen (1980) has suggested that vocabulary is such a good measure of intelligence "because the acquisition of word meanings is highly dependent on the *eduction* of meaning from the contexts in which the words are encountered" (p. 146). Marshalek (1981) has tested this hypothesis by using a faceted vocabulary test, although he did not directly measure learning from context. The vocabulary test was administered with a battery of standard reasoning and other tests. Marshalek found that (1) subjects sometimes could give correct examples of how a given word is used in sentences, despite their having inferred incorrect defining features of the word; (2) subjects with low reasoning ability had major difficulties in inferring word meanings; and (3) reasoning was related to vocabulary measures at the lower end of the vocabulary difficulty distribution but not at the higher end. Together, these findings suggested that a certain level of reasoning ability may be prerequisite for extraction of word meanings. Above this level, the importance of reasoning begins to decrease rapidly.

It has been assumed in the above review that the ability to learn from external context leads to higher vocabulary. It should be pointed out, however, that the relationship between learning from context and level of vocabulary is probably bidirectional (Anderson & Freebody, 1979; Sternberg, 1980b): Learning from context can facilitate vocabulary level at the same time that a higher vocabulary level can facilitate learning from context.

Sternberg and Powell (1983a) have presented a theory of verbal comprehension ability based upon learning from context. The theory has three parts: contextual cues, mediating variables, and component processes of verbal learning. Context cues are hints contained in a passage that facilitate (or, in theory and sometimes in practice, impede) deciphering the meaning of an unknown word. An example of the use of some of these cues in textual analysis might help concretize this descriptive framework. Consider the sentence "At dawn, the *blen* arose on the horizon and shone brightly." This sentence contains several external contextual cues that could facilitate one's inferring that *blen* probably means *sun*. "At dawn" provides a temporal cue, describing when the arising of the *blen* occurred: "arose" provides a functional descriptive cue, describing an action that a *blen* could perform; "on the horizon" provides a spatial cue, describing where the arising of the *blen* took place; "shone" provides another functional descriptive cue, describing a second action a *blen* could do; finally, "brightly" provides a stative descriptive cue, describing a property (brightness) of the shining of the *blen*. With all of these different cues, it is no wonder that most people would find it very easy to figure out that the neologism *blen* is a synonym for the familiar word *sun*.

Whereas the contextual cues describe the types of information that might be used to infer the meaning of a word from a given verbal context, they do not at all address the problems of recognition of the applicability of a description to a given concept, weeding out irrelevant information, or integration of the information gleaned into a coherent model of the word's meaning. For this reason, a set of mediating variables is also proposed that specifies relations between a previously unknown word and the passage in which it occurs and that mediates the usefulness of the contextual cues. Thus, whereas the contextual cues specify the particular kinds of information that might be available for an individual to use to figure out the meanings of unfamiliar words, the mediating variables specify those variables that can affect, either positively or negatively, the application of the contextual cues present in a given situation.

Consider, for example, how the variable "variability of contexts in which multiple occurrences of the unknown word appear" can mediate utilization of contextual cues. Different types of contexts, for example, different kinds of subject matter or different writing styles, and even just different contexts of a given type, such as two different illustrations within a given text of how a word can be used, are likely to supply different types of information about the unknown word. Variability of contexts increases the likelihood that a wide range of types of cues will be supplied about a given word and thus increases the probability that a reader will get a full picture of the scope of a given word's meaning. In contrast, mere repetition of a given unknown word in essentially the same context as that in which it previously appeared is unlikely to be helpful as a variable context repetition because few or no really new cues are provided regarding the word's meaning. Variability can also present a problem in some situations and for some individuals: If the information is presented in a way that makes it difficult to integrate across appearances of the word or if a given individual has difficulties in making such integrations, then the variable repetitions may actually obfuscate rather than clarify the word's meaning. In some situations and for some individuals, variable contexts may cause a stimulus overload to occur, resulting in reduced rather than increased understanding. The other mediating variables for external context can similarly facilitate or inhibit the acquisition of a word's meaning from a given text.

Three components of knowledge acquisition are critical in the acquisition of word meanings and of verbal concepts in general: (1) selective encoding, (2) selective combination, and (3) selective comparison. Selective encoding involves sifting out relevant information from irrelevant information. When new information is presented in natural contexts, relevant information for one's given purposes is embedded in the midst of large amounts of purpose-irrelevant information. A critical task facing the individual is that of sifting the wheat from the chaff, recognizing just what information among all the pieces of information presented is relevant for one's purposes. Selective combination involves combining selectively encoded information in such a way as to form an integrated, plausible whole. Simply sifting out relevant from irrelevant information is not enough to generate a new knowledge structure; one must know how to combine the pieces of information into an internally connected whole (see Mayer & Greeno, 1972). Selective comparison involves relating newly acquired information to information acquired in the past. Deciding what information to encode and how to combine it does not occur in a vacuum. Rather, encoding and combination of new knowledge are guided by retrieval of old information. New information will be all but useless if it cannot somehow be related to old knowledge to form an externally connected whole (Mayer & Greeno, 1972).

To conclude, three major approaches have been proposed to studying verbal comprehension: knowledge-based, bottom-up, and top-down. Each deals with a somewhat different aspect of verbal comprehension. Ultimately, a complete theory will integrate aspects of all three theories.

Quantitative ability

Whereas models of verbal comprehension have been cast in the role of general models of the whole verbal comprehension domain, models of quantitative ability have generally been cast in the role of models of more limited subdomains of knowledge and information processing. It is not clear that the models of verbal ability actually are more general; it seems as likely that the major difference in generality with respect to models of quantitative ability is in the generality of claims rather than in coverage. In this chapter, I will deal with two domains: computational and problem solving abilities.

Computational abilities. The most salient ability for children in the primary grades is probably computational ability. At the very least, primary school children need to demonstrate facility in addition and subtraction. The component skills involved in addition and subtraction have been studied by cognitive psychologists.

Groen and Parkman (1972) proposed three alternative models of how children (as well as adults) might add pairs of numbers. These models are predicated upon the assumption that addition processes can be understood as a set of discrete, serial operations. A "counter" is set to some initial value. Subsequently, an iterative process is executed whereby the value of the counter is incremented until it reaches the sum of two numbers. Consider how the three proposed models differ from each other. In order to illustrate these differences, I will show how they apply to the simple addition problem 4 + 2 = 6.

In one model, Model A, the counter is initially set to zero. Then, it is incremented by the value of the first of the two addends. Finally, it is incremented by the value of the second of the two addends. The final value of the counter is the sum of the two numbers. In the example, the counter is initially set to 0; then it is incremented by 4, the value of the first addend; finally, it is incremented by 2, the value of the second addend. The sum is thus found to be equal to 6. Note that in this model, the counter is incremented six times. More generally, if M is the first addend and N the second addend, the counter is incremented $M + N$ times. The number of increments made to the counter is important in the prediction of reaction time for the computation of sums. The model predicts that reaction time will vary linearly as a function of $M + N$.

In the second model, Model B, the counter is initialized not as 0, but rather as a value corresponding to the first addend. After this initialization, the counter is incremented by a number of times corresponding to the value of the second addend. In the example, the counter is initially set at 4. It is then incremented by 2, so that the final value of the sum is 6. Note that in this model, it was necessary to increment the counter only two, rather than six, times. In general, the number of times the counter needs to be incremented is equal to N, where N is the value of the second addend. Note that this model makes quite different predictions about reaction time from those predictions made by the first model. Whereas in the first model, reaction time is a linear function of $M + N$, in this model, reaction time is a linear function simply of N.

In a third model, Model C, the counter is initially set to the value of whichever of the two addends is greater. The incrementing procedure is then applied to the other of the two addends. In the example, the counter would initially be set to 4 and then incremented by 2. Thus, for this problem, the predictions of Models B and C are identical. However, for the example, 2 + 4 = 6, the predictions of the models would be different. In Model B, the counter would initially be set to 2, and then incremented by 4; in Model C, the counter would initially be set to 4, and then incremented by 2. In Model C, therefore, reaction time is a linear function of either M or N, depending upon whichever of these two values is smaller.

Woods, Resnick, and Groen (1975) extended this kind of information-processing modeling to subtraction, with good results. But the linear-modeling approach that characterizes the above research is not the only approach that has been taken to understanding arithmetic computation.

Brown and Burton (1978) and Ginsburg (1977) have sought to understand the sources of error in children's algorithms for computation. Brown and Burton even developed a computer program, BUGGY, that analyzes students' algorithms for three-column subtraction. The program analyzes students' answers to a large number of three-column subtractions, for example, $436 - 281 = 155$. If the student answers all items correctly, BUGGY categorizes students as using the correct algorithm for subtraction. If there are errors, however, BUGGY attempts to find the one or more "bugs" that best account for the source of the errors in subtraction. Some examples of bugs are (1) not knowing how to borrow from zero, (2) not knowing how to subtract a larger digit from a smaller digit, and (3) not knowing how to subtract a digit from zero.

It is interesting to note that although the BUGGY program was able to identify hundreds of bugs or combinations of bugs in students' performance, it was by no means totally successful in diagnosing all of the sources of students' errors. In fact, the program was able to find algorithms that either totally or partially produced the answers given by only 43 percent of the students. The remaining errors were either random or were at least in part inconsistent in the kinds of bugs involved. Thus, although the approach used by Brown and Burton enabled one to identify quite precisely the kinds of knowledge about computations students lack, it could do so only for some problems and for some people.

To conclude, then, at least two approaches have yielded some success in understanding how people solve arithmetic computation problems. A first approach is based upon information-processing modeling of the components individuals use in solving problems such as addition and subtraction. The approach is used to predict *reaction time* in solving computation problems. The second approach is used to predict *errors* in solving computation problems. The idea in this approach is to use a computer program to analyze the kinds of errors students make in order to understand what facts about computation they lack. Clearly, the two approaches are complementary rather than mutually exclusive. It would be useful to use them in combination in order to understand both the speed and accuracy with which people solve arithmetic computation problems.

Problem solving ability. Mathematical problem solving is often broken down into two basic steps (Bobrow, 1968; Hayes, 1981; Mayer, 1983): problem representation and problem solution. In problem representation, a problem is converted from a series of words and numbers into an internal mental representation of the terms of the problem. In problem solution, operations are performed so as to deduce a solution to the problem from the internal mental representation. Each of these stages in problem solving is a source of individual differences in overall problem solving ability.

A striking example of how difficult problem representation can be, even for college students, was provided by Soloway, Lochhead, and Clement (1982). These investigators asked college students to represent statements such as "There are six times as many students as professors at this university" in terms of an equation. Roughly one-third of the college students represented problems such as this one incorrectly. In this example, they would have represented it by the incorrect equation $6S = P$, where S refers to student and P to professor. An interesting sideline to this experiment showed the powerful effect of mental representation upon students' ability to represent the problems correctly. Consider the following problem: "At the last company cocktail party, for every 6 people who drank hard liquor, there were 11 people who drank beer." Some students were asked to translate this statement into a mathematical equation; other students were asked to translate this statement into a little program in the BASIC computer language. The error rate for students translating the problem into an equation was 55 percent, whereas the error rate for students translating the problem into the computer language was only 31 percent.

Mayer (1982) has also studied the abilities of college students to represent mathematical problems. Two sets of data analyses are of particular interest in this research. In order to illustrate these analyses, I will consider the following algebra problem: "A river steamer travels 36 miles downstream in the same time that it travels 24 miles upstream. The steamer's engine drives in still water at a rate of 12 miles per hour more than the rate of the current. Find the rate of the current." The students were asked to recall problems such as these as best they could.

In the first set of data analyses, Mayer looked at which kinds of content students most tended to forget. He divided problem content into three kinds: *assignments,* which assigned a value to a variable, for example, "A river steamer travels 36 miles downstream"; *relations,* which express a quantitative relation between two variables, for example, "The steamer's engines drive in still water at a rate of 12 miles per hour more than the rate of the current"; and *questions,* which ask for a solution to the problem, for example, "Find the rate of the current."

Mayer found that students made about three times as many errors in recalling relational propositions (error rate: 29 percent) as in recalling assignment propositions (error rate: 9 percent). This result is consistent with that of Soloway et al. (1982) and others in suggesting students' greatest difficulty is in representing relational information about mathematical problems.

In the second data analysis, Mayer examined the kinds of errors students make in recalling propositions: *omission errors*, in which the proposition is not recalled; *specification errors*, in which a variable in the original proposition is somehow changed to a different variable in recall, for example, "A river steamer travels 36 miles downstream" is recalled as "A boat travels 36 miles downstream"; and *conversion errors*, in which the form of the proposition is changed from an assignment to a relation, or vice versa, for example, "The steamer's engine drives in still water at 12 miles per hour more than the rate of the current" is translated into "The steamer's engine drives in still water at 12 miles per hour." By far, the largest proportion of errors made was in errors of omission. The smallest number of errors made was in errors of conversion. This pattern held true for assignment relations and questions. It is of interest to note that there was a systematic bias in the form taken by conversion errors. Of 21 cases of conversion, 20 involved changing a relation into an assignment, whereas only 1 involved changing an assignment into a relation. Thus, one can begin to see that students' greatest difficulty appears to be in representing relational information.

Davidson and Sternberg (1984) compared the abilities of gifted and nongifted students to solve quantitative insight problems. An example of such a problem is, "A man has black socks and blue socks in a drawer mixed in a ratio of 4 to 5. It is dark, and so the man cannot see the colors of the socks he removes from the drawer. How many socks need the man remove from the drawer in order to be assured of having a pair of socks of the same color?" The correct answer to the problem is 3.

Davidson and Sternberg tested the hypothesis that the reduced performance of the nongifted students could be traced in part to their failure spontaneously to generate three kinds of insights: (1) *selective encoding*, in which relevant information for problem solution is distinguished from irrelevant information; (2) *selective combination*, in which relevant information is combined in a meaningful way so as to allow problem solutions; and (3) *selective comparison*, in which new information in the problem is related to old information that one had stored in long-term memory.

In order to test this hypothesis, problems such as the socks problem were presented in either of two fashions. In one fashion, the problems were presented in the standard way. The students would see the problem and have to solve it. In the second fashion, students were given an insight of one of the three kinds in order to facilitate their problem solution. For example, selective encoding insights were provided by underlining in each given problem only that information relevant to problem solution. In the socks problem, for instance, the ratio information is irrelevant to the solution of the problem; yet many students attempt to use it in order to solve the problem. Davidson and Sternberg found that providing insights of each of the three kinds significantly facilitated performance in only the nongifted students. The gifted students seemed to generate the insights on their own, and hence providing them with these insights did not facilitate their performance.

The steps involved in representing and solving mathematical problems can become quite complicated, and some investigators have sought to do justice to this degree of complication by constructing computer simulations of students' problem solving processes. For example, Greeno (1978) has written a computer program, PERDIX, that simulates the performance of high school students in solving geometry problems. In fact, Greeno formulated the project on the basis of a fairly extensive study of students' thinking-aloud protocols as provided in the course of their actual solutions of geometry problems. Two important features of this program are its use of a generate-and-test strategy and its use of subgoals. The generate-and-test strategy is used when one knows what kind of information is needed at a given point during problem solution but does not know which particular items of information in the problem are of this kind. In this strategy, one scans the list of possible items that may provide the needed kind of information and tests each one to see if it fits. Resnick and Ford (1981) provide a good example of the generate-and-test strategy. Suppose one needs to find the list of all prime numbers (i.e., numbers whose only factors are themselves and 1) in the range from 1 to 50. Usually, what a person will have to do is to generate the numbers between 1 and 50 one at a time and test each one to see if it has any factors other than itself and 1. Only those numbers that have no other factors are retained in the list of primes.

The use of subgoals is a reflection of the fact that plane geometry theorem proving is usually too complicated for the use of just a single goal. In order to construct a proof, students usually set up a series of subgoals that represent states in the proof that they need to reach along the way toward the final solution of the proof.

In conclusion, mathematical abilities seem to involve a number of information-processing skills. At least some of these skills are hierarchically related. For example, computational skills presuppose counting skills, and problem solving skills presuppose at least some computational skills. Information-processing analyses of ability can tend to obscure the "big picture" as far as quantitative abilities are concerned. Although quantitative abilities can be decomposed into a large number of component information processes, the abilities to use these processes are certainly correlated. Thus, some people seem to be better quantitatively, overall, than are other people. There seems to be a need for theories that combine the best aspects of psychometric and information-processing analysis. Psychometric analysis gives one a good sense of quantitative ability as comprising one factor or, at most, a small number of factors. It does not, however, specify the processing components involved in this factor. Information-processing analysis can specify processing components, but it is often hard to see how they fit together into an overall ability structure. Thus, there is a need for a theory that specifies the information-processing components of quantitative abilities but that also specifies how these components fit together into a higher order ability that distinguishes more quantitatively able people from less quantitatively able ones.

Sources of individual differences in the computational metaphor

Computational approaches tend to stress commonalities among individuals in information processing. However, contemporary work has sought to understand sources of individual differences as well as commonalities in people's performance. Consider two theories of what the major aspects of individual differences in information processing are.

Snow's theory

Snow (1979) has identified four sources of individual differences in information processing: (1) parameter differences (p-variables),

(2) sequence differences (q-variables), (3) route differences (r-variables), and (4) summation or strategic differences (s-variables).

The distinctions between p-, q-, and r-variables can be clarified by imagining two flow charts that characterize the performance of two different individuals on some task; p-variables would refer to differences between the individuals on particular steps or components (e.g., capacity of STM, time needed for stimulus encoding, etc.); g-variables would be shown by the two flow charts taking the same steps, but in different sequences (e.g., early vs. late work on some subgoal); r-variables would be indicated by the inclusion of qualitatively different steps in the two flow charts (e.g., visual image rotation, or double checking, used in one chart and not in the other). (Snow, 1979, p. 110)

Sternberg's theory

Sternberg (1977) has proposed six primary sources of individual differences in information processing. These sources of differences are as follows:

1. *Components.* Some individuals use more components, fewer components, or different components from those used by other individuals. For example, one individual might solve a problem using components, *a, b,* and *c.* Another individual might solve the same problem using components *b, d,* and *e.*
2. *Combination rule for components.* Some individuals combine components according to one rule, whereas others combine them according to a different rule. For example, one individual might combine components additively: $a + b + c$. Another individual might combine them multiplicatively: $a \times b \times c$.
3. *Order of component processing.* Some individuals order components in one sequence, others in a different sequence. For example, one individual might order components so that *c* follows *b,* which follows *a.* Another subject might order them in the reverse order or in some other permutation.
4. *Mode of component processing.* Some individuals might process particular components in one mode, others in another mode. For example, one individual might process components *a, b,* and *c* in self-terminating mode: He or she will cease execution of a given component process as soon as possible. A second individual might process these same components in exhaustive mode: He or she will execute the processes to completion, even if a solution to the problem presents itself before process execution has been completed. Exhaustive information processing is not necessarily a waste of time, because it is more likely, in many cases, to lead to correct answers

than is self-terminating information processing (Sternberg, 1977; Sternberg & Rifkin, 1979).

5. *Component time or accuracy*. Some individuals may process particular components more quickly or more accurately than do other individuals, as when one individual may execute a given component process, *a,* in considerably less time than is taken by a second individual.

6. *Mental representation on which components act*. Some individuals may use one particular representation for information, whereas others use a different representation. For example, it has been found that in linear syllogistic reasoning (which involves problems such as "John is taller than Pete. Pete is taller than Dick. Who is tallest?"), some individuals represent information about the problems in a primarily linguistic fashion, whereas others represent information in a primarily spatial fashion.

Conclusion

The computational metaphor and the information-processing theories and methods used to elaborate it have not been without their problems. Consider three of the main ones (Sternberg, 1983, 1985a). First, it is not clear just how similar computer programs and human intelligence are. There are those who would argue that we should be seeking to understand the programmers, not the programs, in our quest to understand intelligence. Of course, people differ from computer programs in a number of ways, not the least of which is their considerably greater complexity and range of mental functioning. In using the computational metaphor, these differences may tend to receive rather short shrift.

Second, and in common with most geographically based theories, it is not clear whether the kinds of laboratory and testlike instruments that have dominated the study of intelligence truly measure psychological constructs that are interesting in and generalizable to the outside world. Everyone knows people who perform well on tests but who seem to perform rather poorly in their everyday lives, and neither the computational nor the geographic metaphor seems to account for just what, if anything, is wrong or missing when these people apply their intelligence to their everyday lives.

Third, the computational metaphor may not take sufficient account of, or specify the differences in, what people mean by intelligence in various parts of the world. An assumption of the computational metaphor has been that we need to discover programs of operation that are intelligent for a given set of tasks. But tasks of life differ from one place and time to another and so, some would argue, does the nature of intelligence.

Finally, computational metaphors are strictly molar. For the most part, they have not been directly related to brain functioning. Yet ultimately, we would seek to understand intelligence in terms of the main organ of the body that is responsible for that intelligence, namely, the brain. In the next chapter, the biological metaphor, which seeks to understand intelligence in terms of brain functioning, is examined.

7

The biological metaphor

The biological metaphor provides a basis for understanding intelligence by studying the brain and the operation of the central nervous system. It is the most reductionist of the various metaphors, in that one seeks understanding of intelligence directly in terms of biological function, rather than indirectly through molar levels of processing. However, I will argue that the inferences that can be made from the biological approach are often as indirect and even, at times, more indirect than the inferences that are made from alternative approaches. Although adherents to the biological metaphor have in common their interest in studying intelligence in terms of the brain and central nervous system, they differ fairly widely in the approaches they take to studying intelligence. I will divide the chapter into three main parts. In the first, I will discuss neuropsychological approaches, which seek to understand intelligence in terms of the size and structure of the brain. In the second, I will discuss electrophysiological and blood flow approaches, which seek understanding of intelligence in terms of either electroencephalographic measurement or in terms of the flow of blood to various portions of the brain during thinking. In the last section of the chapter, I will discuss what the biological metaphor has and has not told us about the nature of intelligence.

Neuropsychological approaches

Neuropsychological approaches to intelligence are often traced back to Hippocrates, who in the fifth century B.C. suggested that the brain might be the basis of human intelligence. In more recent times, the approach traces back to Gall (1825), who suggested correctly that cognition derives from the interaction of the two hemispheres of the brain. Gall, a German anatomist, was probably the first to suggest that the brain is not uniform, but rather that various mental faculties could be localized in different parts of the brain. Today, modular theories of intelligence (e.g., Gardner, 1983) have their basis, curiously enough, in the theorizing of Gall. But Gall also believed that the shape of the skull and the pattern of bumps on the head could give important clues to an individual's intellectual characteristics. This view is rejected today, and was rejected by most scientists even in Gall's time. Gall was dismissed as a fraud, and unfortunately, his good ideas received no more attention than his bad ones.

The theory was wrong, but the basis was set for understanding human intelligence in terms of the structure and functioning of the brain. Since Gall's, other structural theories have been proposed. Some of these theories have been with respect to the brain as a whole, others with respect to its two hemispheres, and still others have combined the two types of theorizing. I will consider each of these three types of theories in turn.

Global theories of brain function

One of the earlier general theories of brain function was proposed by Halstead (1951). He suggested four biologically based abilities: (1) the integrative field factor (C), (2) the abstraction factor (A), (3) the power factor (P), and (4) the directional factor (D). Halstead attributed all four of these abilities primarily to the cortex of the frontal lobes. Halstead's theory seems not to have had much substantial long-term effect on theorizing about intelligence.

A second theory of interest more for historical reasons than for its contemporary influence is that of Konorski (1967). Konorski's main concern was with learning in the structure of long-term memory. He postulated an associative network constituted as a collection of elements that he called "gnostic units." Konorski viewed short-term memory as that portion of the memory elements that was in a temporary state of excitation at a given time. According to Konorski, gnostic units represent patterns of stimulation. A large number of factors affect the likelihood of whether a gnostic unit will be activated or, earlier on, of whether it will be formed. Konorski used his theory to account for a variety of learning-based phenomena, such as habituation and classical conditioning. Although Konorski was ignored for many years, his work has recently experienced a revival (see Dickinson & Boakes, 1979). Konorski's work has been found to be prescient with respect to contemporary theories of classical conditioning.

Without doubt, one of the most respected and influential theories in psychology during the twentieth century has been Hebb's. Hebb (1949) was very interested in the problem of understanding intelligence neuropsychologically. He proposed that the word "intelligence" has been used in three different ways and that these different meanings are often confused with each other.

Intelligence A is innate potential. It is biologically determined and represents the capacity for development. Hebb describes it, not very informatively, as amounting "to the possession of a good brain and a good neural metabolism" (p. 294). Intelligence B is the functioning of the brain in which development has occurred. It represents an average level of performance by a person who is partially grown. Although some inference is necessary in determining either intelligence, Hebb suggests that inferences about intelligence A are far less direct than inferences about intelligence B. Hebb argues that most disagreements about intelligence are over intelligence A, or innate potential, rather than intelligence B, which is the estimated level of functioning at varying degrees of maturity. Hebb has also distinguished an intelligence C, which would be the score one obtains on an intelligence test. It is the basis for inferring either of the other intelligences.

Hebb's main interest was in intelligence A, and his theory, the neuropsychological theory of the organization of behavior, can be seen in large part as an attempt to understand what intelligence A is. The core of Hebb's theory is in terms of the concept of the *cell assembly*. Hebb proposed that repeated stimulation of specific receptors slowly leads to the formation of an assembly of cells in the association area of the brain. These cells can act briefly as a closed system after stimulation has stopped. Hebb assumes that the growth process accompanying synaptic activity makes the synapse more readily traversed. As he states it, "When an axon of cell A is near enough to excite a cell B and repeatedly or persistently takes part in firing it, some growth process or metabolic change takes place in one or both cells such that A's efficiency, as one of the cells firing B, is increased" (p. 62).

So, according to Hebb, any two cells or systems of cells that repeatedly are active at the same time tend to become associated. As collections of cells tend to become associated, they form cell assemblies. An individual cell or other unit of transmission may enter into more than one assembly at different times. Moreover, over time, it may enter into new cell assemblies or drop out of old ones. The cell assembly acts on an all-or-none basis. In other words, it fires or it does not. Hebb uses the concept of cell assembly to account for many different psychological phenomena, among them, intelligence.

Although Hebb believed in the importance of inheritance for intelligence, he also recognized a role for environment. He believed that IQ could not be trusted as an index of intelligence A unless the social backgrounds of subjects being compared were identical. Because backgrounds are never identical, he stated that "we cannot in any rigorous sense measure subjects' innate endowment" (p. 300). Intelligence A can be estimated, but it cannot be precisely measured.

Hebb's theory is no longer widely accepted as such, because recent neuropsychological evidence is inconsistent with it in some respects. But the theory was tremendously influential because it was the largest-scale attempt to understand the human brain in its relation to cognitive functioning at the time of its publication. Arguably, that statement is still true today.

A theory with great impact on the field of intelligence research is that of the Russian psychologist, Alexander Luria (1973, 1980). Luria believed that the brain is a highly differentiated system whose parts are responsible for different aspects of a unified whole. In other words, separate cortical regions act together to produce thought and action of various kinds. Luria (1980) suggested that the brain comprises three main units. The first, a unit of arousal, includes the brain stem and midbrain structures. Included within this first unit are the medulla, reticular activating system, pons, thalamus, and hypothalamus. The second unit of the brain is a sensori-input unit, which includes the temporal, parietal, and occipital lobes. The third unit includes the frontal cortex, which is involved in organization and planning. It comprises cortical structures anterior to the central sulcus.

The most active research program on Luria's theory has been that of J. P. Das, and indeed, the resulting theory is sometimes referred to as the Luria–Das theory. Das has devoted the major portion of his career to demonstrating that Luria's theory can be validated factor-analytically. Das, Kirby, and Jarman (1979) provide a wealth of evidence that they believe validates the theory. I personally believe that factor-analytic validation of the theory depends upon somewhat careful selection of tests so that they will clump together in the way the theory predicts.

Das and his colleagues have constructed an impressive array of tests that measure all three aspects of functioning in Luria's theory, namely, attention-arousal, planning, and mode of sensori-input and processing.

With respect to the last, Das's tests measure both simultaneous and successive processing. Simultaneous processing refers to the parallel processing of multiple chunks of information at a time. Successive or sequential processing refers to serial processing of chunks of information, one following the other. Tests such as Raven Matrices and Gestalt Closure would measure simultaneous processing, whereas serial recall tests would measure successive processing. Das and Jack Naglieri, the latter of Ohio State University, are currently constructing an individual intelligence test based upon Luria's theory.

Das and Naglieri are not the first to construct a test based on this theory. The first such test was that of Kaufman and Kaufman (1983), the Kaufman Assessment Battery for Children (K–ABC). This test does not measure the attention-arousal and planning functions separately, but it does measure simultaneous and successive processing and provides separate scores for each. I have reviewed this test elsewhere in some detail (Sternberg, 1984b). The K–ABC also has a separate achievement section, which is similar to what one would find on other tests of verbal intelligence, such as the Stanford–Binet.

Clearly, Luria's neuropsychological theory has been fruitful outside as well as inside the area of neuropsychology. It has probably been the single neuropsychological theory that has most affected the measurement of human intelligence.

Theories of hemispheric specialization

The theories described above have in common that their specification of intellectual activities with respect to the brain are based on divisions of the brain other than those between the left and right hemispheres. An exceptionally productive line of research, however, has involved specification of the functions of the two respective hemispheres. Although not all researchers studying hemispheric specialization have been interested in intelligence, per se, their work has many implications for the understanding of intelligence.

An excellent review of work on hemispheric specialization can be found in Springer and Deutsch (1985), upon which the review here is partially based. Springer and Deutsch trace the study of hemispheric specialization in the brain to an obscure country doctor in France, Marc Dax, who in 1836 presented a little-noticed paper to a medical society meeting in Montpellier. Dax had treated a number of patients suffering from loss of speech as a result of brain damage. This condition, known today as aphasia, had been reported even in ancient Greece. But Dax noticed a connection between loss of speech and the side of the brain in which damage had occurred. Indeed, having studied more than 40 patients with aphasia, Dax noticed that in every case, there had been damage to the left hemisphere of the brain. He was not able to find even one case in which damage had occurred to the right hemisphere only. The paper aroused no interest.

One of the next major figures in the study of hemispheric specialization was Paul Broca. At the meeting of the French Society of Anthropology, Broca claimed that a patient of his who was suffering a loss of speech was shown postmortem to have a lesion in the left frontal lobe of the brain. Broca was thereby confirming the view of Gall and of Jean Baptiste Bouillaud that speech is localized in the frontal lobes. No one paid much attention. However, Broca soon became associated with a hot controversy over whether functions, particularly speech, are indeed localized in the brain. The area that Broca identified as involved in speech is today referred to as Broca's area. By 1864, Broca was convinced that the left hemisphere of the brain is critical in the functioning of speech.

Others continued in the tradition of Broca, studying problems such as apraxia – inability to perform purposeful movements upon request – and agnosia – inability to recognize familiar objects, often faces. For example, Penfield and Roberts (1959) were able to map specific functions to particular areas of the brain. They noticed that temporary aphasia could follow stimulation of the speech area of the brain. But the individual most responsible for modern-day theory and research on hemispheric specialization is certainly Roger Sperry.

Sperry (1961) has argued that each hemisphere behaves in many respects like a separate brain. It would be hard to overstate the contribution of Sperry to modern split-brain research, especially because so many of the people working in the area have been graduate students of Sperry or have worked at one time or another in his laboratory. In a classic experiment, Sperry, Myers, and Schrier (1960) showed that visual information presented to one hemisphere in a cat with its corpus callosum severed was not available to the other hemisphere. In other words, severing the tissue connecting the left hemisphere to the right hemisphere resulted in information failing to be transferred from one hemisphere to the other.

Some of the most interesting information about the functioning of the human brain has emerged from studies of individuals whose corpus callosa were cut surgically in order to reduce symptoms of epilepsy. Although such individuals behave normally in many respects, in other respects, their behavior can be somewhat bizarre. For example, instances have been reported of their left hand fighting with their right hand in order to accomplish a task, such as putting on pants. In another instance, such a patient, angry at his wife, reached for her with his left hand while his right hand tried to stop his left one (Gazzaniga, 1970). Some patients have had difficulty learning to associate names with faces (Levy, Trevarthen, & Sperry, 1972), and others have had difficulty with geometric problems.

One of the most active debates in the field has been over whether language is completely localized in the left hemisphere. Zaidel (1975, 1978) has conducted studies in which he has argued for right-hemisphere processing of language. Gazzaniga (1985), on the other hand, has argued that right-hemispheric processing of language is extremely rare and has been found in only a very small number of patients. Gazzaniga argues that normal people do not have any language in their right hemisphere. Gazzaniga believes that to the extent that one ever sees right-hemispheric language processing, it is because of early damage to the left hemisphere, resulting in transfer of language functions to the right hemisphere early in life.

Although there are arguments about whether the right hemisphere can process language, it is generally agreed that visual and spatial functions are primarily localized in the right hemisphere, although even this conclusion has been subject to controversy (Farah, 1988). Gazzaniga and LeDoux (1978), for example, have found that certain preoperative patients who can draw decent three-dimensional representations of cubes with both hands before surgery can draw a reasonable representation of the cube after surgery only with the left hand. The picture drawn by the right hand is not even recognizable as a cube or as being three dimensional. This finding is important because of contralateral association between hands and hemispheres of the brain. In other words, the left hemisphere controls the right hand and the right hemisphere, the left hand.

Franco and Sperry (1977) tested right-handed split-brain patients and normal control subjects in their ability to match unseen objects by touch with geometric shapes presented visually. They discovered that the patients performed consistently better when using the left hand than the right hand, consistent with the notion of right-brain control of the task. Moreover, superiority of the left hand increased as the shapes became more irregular and hence difficult to name. When the objects to be matched were wholly free-form, the right hand performed at a level scarcely above chance. Normal subjects, whose left and right hemispheres were able to communicate with each other, were able to use both hands.

The topic of major interest among those who study hemispheric specialization has been with regard to the differences in information-processing style or preference in the two hemispheres. A leader in this area of research has been Jerre Levy, who has argued that the left hemisphere tends to process information analytically, whereas the right hemisphere tends to process it holistically (Levy, 1974).

Levy is perhaps most well known for her experiments using chimeric faces (Levy et al., 1972). In a typical experiment, the subject is told that a picture will be presented on the screen. The subject is asked to fixate the center of the screen visually. A composite picture is flashed in which one side of the face is of one individual and the other side of the face is of a different individual. The subject is then asked to identify the picture that was seen. Identification may be either verbal or by pointing with one hand or the other. Typically, split-brain patients are unaware that the the stimuli display conflicting information in the two halves of the picture. When asked to give an answer vocally, they choose the picture from the right-field half of the chimeric stimulus. In other words, the left hemisphere controls processing. When asked to point, subjects choose the picture from the left field, indicating right-hemispheric control. In other words, the task that the subjects are asked to perform is crucial in determining what face the subject will believe him or herself to have seen.

Levy (1974) has suggested that two factors determine performance on the task. The first is dominance, the tendency for one hemisphere to control responding. The other is capacity, or the ability of a hemisphere to perform a task as required by an experiment. Joseph Bogen, another pioneer in studying split-brain patients, has suggested that the difference in processing of the two stimuli in the two hemispheres can be characterized in terms of propositional versus appositional information processing (Bogen, 1975). The use of the term *propositional* refers to the left-hemispheric dominance of speaking, writing, and other verbal activities, whereas the use of the term *appositional* emphasizes the nonpropositional processing in the right hemisphere. The right hemisphere understands patterns and relationships that are not susceptible to propositional analysis and that may not even be logical.

Some of Levy's most interesting work is on the relationship between how people hold their pen or pencil in writing and the hemisphere in which language is centered. Levy and Reid (1976) suggest that right-handed individuals normally have their language functions specialized in the left hemisphere of the brain. However, right-handers writing in an inverted position – who hold their pencil such that it is behind rather than in front of the hand and who tend to have a back-leaning slant in their writing – normally will have their language functioning specialized in the right hemisphere. This phenomenon is relatively uncommon. However, the inverted position for holding a pen or a pencil is more common in left-handers. Levy and Reid suggest that the inverted hand position for left-handers indicates centralization of the language functions in the left hemisphere but that the normal writing position indicates centralization of language functioning in the right hemisphere. Thus, whereas right-handers are more likely to have language centralized in the left hemisphere, left-handers are more likely to have it centralized in the right hemisphere.

Another way of studying hemispheric specialization is through the use of lateral eye movements. Day (1964) noted that patients often look consistently either to the left or the right when answering questions. He suggested that the direction of looking might be associated with certain personality characteristics. Whereas some studies have suggested that some people tend to be left-lookers and others, right-lookers, work by Gur, Gur, and Harris (1975) suggests that if artifacts are removed, which way subjects look depends on the type of question posed rather than upon individual difference in preference for looking one way versus the other.

Michael Gazzaniga (1985) has disassociated himself from the position of Sperry and his colleagues, Levy, Bogen, and Trevarthen. He believes that the experiments showing different modes of processing between the two hemispheres are susceptible to alternative interpretations. The fact that subjects favor so-called right-brain stimuli, for example, does not necessarily mean that the right brain is responding more assertively because of a specialized holistic analyzer. It may be that the right hemisphere asserts itself because the left hemisphere loses out in certain tasks to more literal direct interpretation by the right hemisphere. After reviewing alternative explanations, Gazzaniga concludes that it is not at all clear that the conventional interpretations assigned to split-brain studies are correct.

Others have investigated the development of hemispheric specialization. Lenneberg (1967), for example, concluded that lateralization of brain function seems to develop over time but that it is not completed until puberty. Woods and Teuber (1978), however, suggested that hemispheric specialization is already complete very soon after birth. A number of studies were done to try to determine when hemispheric specialization is complete. Although the results are not clear, present evidence suggests earlier rather than later completion of hemispheric specialization (Springer & Deutsch, 1985). This is not to say, however, that even with specialization completed, the two halves of the brain do not develop in different ways such that people may show more specialization in processing as they grow older. Moreover, present data suggest that the brain is especially plastic in young children, so that if there is damage to one of the hemispheres in infancy or early childhood, the possibilities for compensation in the other hemisphere are much greater than if the damage occurs later during development.

Still other investigators have looked at sex differences in information processing (e.g., Coltheart, Hull, & Slater, 1975; Witelson, 1976). The consensus of these studies is that males tend to be more lateralized with respect to the two hemispheres than are females. For example, with respect to verbal and spatial abilities, males would be more clearly dominant in the left hemisphere for verbal processing and dominant in the right hemisphere for spatial processing than would be females, who would be more bilateral in their representation of both types of processing. It has been suggested that the greater lateralization of males may represent an evolutionary adaptation whereby males have needed more to perform spatial functions for survival and hence have needed a greater specialization in order to perform these functions successfully.

Alternative views of hemispheric cooperation and competition

Gazzaniga (1985) argues that the brain is organized modularly. In other words, he believes that it is organized into relatively independent functioning units that work in parallel. His view is in the spirit of present connectionist models of human performance (McClelland & Rumelhart, 1986). There exist many discrete units of the mind, each operating relatively independent of the others. Moreover, many of these modules operate at a level that is not conscious. They operate in

parallel to our conscious thought and contribute to conscious processing in identifiable ways. In particular, the left hemisphere tries to assign
interpretations to the processing of these modules. Thus, the left hemisphere may perceive the individual operating in a way that does not
make any particular sense or that is not particularly understandable,
and its job is to assign some meaning to that behavior. In general, we
resist the interpretation that the behavior is capricious, but rather seek
to try to interpret the behavior in terms of some sensible hypothesis,
even if there is none. Gazzaniga gives the example of attending a
Christmas party where one's beliefs in marital fidelity are seriously
challenged as one finds oneself being attracted to a particular individual. The attraction may be the work of one of the modules of the brain.
But as the left hemisphere perceives what is happening, it starts to
question the value of fidelity, and beliefs thereby change on the basis
of behavior, rather than the other way around.

   Thus, Gazzaniga (1985) believes that brains are organized such that
many mental systems coexist in what might be referred to as a confed-
eration. This view is largely consistent with that of Fodor (1983), who
also believes that information processing is largely determined by independent modules operating in parallel. Although Gazzaniga's view is
not the common one among neuropsychologists, not all neuropsychologists accept the degree of separation between the hemispheres suggested by Sperry and his co-workers. For example, Broadbent (1985)
finds that normal people show surprising amounts of interference between stimuli and responses on one side of the body and those on the
other. He suggests that the two hemispheres therefore should be seen as
performing different parts of an integrated performance rather than totally
separate, parallel functions. In other words, Broadbent sees more integration between the processing of the two hemispheres than do some others.

   Another model of brain functioning has been proposed by Marcel
Kinsbourne (Kinsbourne & Hicks, 1978). Kinsbourne has investigated
what he refers to as "functional cerebral space." He suggests that the
distance between areas of the brain controlling various movements is
reflected in the extent to which there is competition among several
movements attempted simultaneously. For example, two arms are better at cooperating with each other in movement than is the combination
of an arm and a leg. But the two arms are worse at performing competitive tasks.

   Kinsbourne suggests that the area of the brain controlling an arm is
closer to the area of the brain controlling the other arm than it is to the

area of the brain controlling the leg. Kinsbourne's studies have attempted to map functional cerebral space. Typically, his studies have involved subjects vocalizing while doing something else with one of their limbs at the same time. By setting up competitive situations, it becomes possible to determine the functional cerebral distance between areas controlling different movements. For example, in one of his first studies, right-handed subjects were asked to balance a dowel rod on their index finger either in silence or while repeating short sentences. Kinsbourne and Cook (1971) found that when a subject is speaking, the right hand cannot maintain balance as well or for as long as when the subject is silent. This result suggests left hemispheric control of speaking and of the right hand. The same result was not obtained when balancing was done with the left hand. In this case, subjects performed equally well when they were either silent or speaking.

Brain size

Some investigators have looked at brain size and form. Much of this literature is reviewed by Jerison (1982), who has concluded that brain size is highly correlated with intellectual level across but not within species. Geschwind and Levitsky (1968) showed that there are asymmetries in the two hemispheres with respect to regions important for speech. They found that of 100 brains studied postmortem, 65 had longer temporal planes in the left hemisphere than in the right, 11 had longer temporal planes in the right hemisphere than in the left, and 24 showed no difference. On average, the temporal plane was one-third longer in the left than in the right hemisphere. The size of these asymmetries is rather large and suggests that the size of particular areas may develop as a function of use, at least evolutionarily, over many generations.

To conclude, neuropsychological studies have been rather fruitful for understanding some of the bases of human intelligence. At the same time, they obviously have a long way to go. We are nowhere yet near a specific mapping of intellectual functions to exact parts of the brain.

Electrophysiological and blood flow approaches

Electrophysiological approaches to the study of intelligence involve measurement of electrical activity in various portions of the brain as a means to understanding intelligence. Early studies tended to use electroencephalogram (EEG) measurement. The idea was to relate patterns of EEG activity to intelligence or other cognitive functions. For example, Galin and Ornstein (1972) showed a link between amount of EEG activity in each of the hemispheres and the type of tasks performed by a subject. In particular, they found that the ratio of right- to left-hemisphere EEG processing was greater in verbal than in spatial tasks. This pattern of results might seem to be the opposite of what would be expected. However, Galin and Ornstein were measuring alpha activity, which tends to be associated with the brain at rest. Therefore, a higher ratio indicates less active processing by the hemisphere of the brain being measured at a given time.

EEG measurement is highly problematic because it is a hash recording. It involves measurement of many different things at once, so that it is hard to separate out just what wave forms are coming from where. For this reason, investigators have more and more turned to the use of evoked potentials (EP), which are measured by averaging wave forms on successive presentations of a stimulus obtained from EEG recording. In other words, an evoked potential is an average EEG recording in which the error has, to some extent at least, been averaged out.

Some of the most interesting electrophysiological work has been done by Emanuel Donchin and his colleagues at the University of Illinois and elsewhere. Much of this work has utilized the P300 wave form. The label P300 refers to a positive component of evoked potentials that has a latency anywhere from 300 to 900 msec after the presentation of a stimulus. P300 has been linked to processes of stimulus identification and classification (McCarthy & Donchin, 1981). The amplitude of P300 seems to reflect the allocation of cognitive resources to a given task. P300 seems to be stronger the greater the amount of surprise that a subject experiences as a result of the presentation of a stimulus. It is not exactly clear what the psychological correlates of P300 are. Some suggested ones have been orientation, resolution of uncertainty, delivery of task-relevant information, decision making, and updating of context, among others (see Donchin, 1979). It is clear, however, that the magnitude of P300 is related to subjective (as opposed to objective) surprise.

Another evoked potential that has been studied is N400, a negative potential recorded approximately 400 msec after stimulus presentation. N400 is recorded in association with responses to semantically anomalous words. It is not found in response to semantically appropriate endings. In other words, it reflects linguistic surprise in at least some instances rather than the perceptual and decisional surprise characterized by P300.

Schafer (1982) has suggested that the tendency to show a large P300 response to surprising stimuli may be an individual-differences variable. Schafer believes that a functionally efficient brain will use fewer neurons to process a stimulus that is familiar and more to process a stimulus that is novel or unfamiliar. In other words, according to Schafer, more intelligent individuals should show a greater P300 response to novel stimuli than would less intelligent ones. At the same time, more intelligent individuals should show smaller P300 to expected stimuli than would less intelligent ones. Schafer reported a correlation of .82 between an individual-differences measure of evoked potential and IQ. The higher the IQ, the greater the difference in evoked-potential amplitude between expected and unexpected stimuli. This result suggests that more intelligent individuals are more flexible in responding to novel stimuli than are less intelligent individuals. The size of the correlation is enough to scare some people away, as test reliabilities are usually not higher than .8 or .9, and it is hard to believe that evoked-potential difference measures would be any more reliable than psychometric intelligence tests.

Some investigators have chosen to study electrophysiological responses more directly with respect to their relation to intelligence. This work is favorably reviewed by Eysenck and Barrett (1985), although not everyone takes as favorable a view on this research as do Eysenck and his colleagues. Early work in this area was done by Ertl and his colleagues (e.g., Chalke & Ertl, 1965; Ertl, 1966; Ertl & Schafer, 1969). These investigators found consistent correlations between averaged evoked potentials and IQ. Unfortunately, subsequent studies often failed to replicate Ertl's results (see Eysenck, 1986). In recent times, Hendrickson and Hendrickson (1980) have conducted a program of research attempting to link electrophysiological responses to observed intelligence. Their measurements are obtained while the subject is at rest. Their basic theories suggest that errors can occur in the passage of information through the cerebral cortex. These errors, which probably occur at synapses, are alleged to be responsible for variability in evoked potentials. Thus, it would follow that individuals with normal circuitry that conveys information accurately will form correct and accessible memories more quickly than individuals whose circuitry is noisy and hence who make errors in transmission.

Moreover, the Hendricksons have suggested that individuals with low IQs will have noisy channels of information processing, with the result that when evoked potentials are averaged out, they will have a smoother appearance than those produced by individuals with more consistent and less noisy channels. The Hendricksons have published pictures of what they allege to be typical wave forms for subjects with high and low IQ, and indeed, the wave forms for subjects with high IQ are more complex than the wave forms for subjects with low IQ. The Hendricksons used a string to measure the length of the wave forms over a given period of time, on the view that greater string lengths would reflect greater complexity in the wave form and hence higher IQ. Somewhat oddly, given the reliability of the measures, they obtained a correlation of .83 between an evoked-potential measure and scores on the Wechsler Adult Intelligence Scale. A replication of this study has been reported by Blinkhorn and Hendrickson (1982) using Raven's Advanced Progressive Matrices as well as a variety of verbal intelligence tests. In this study, the correlation was .84, corrected for restriction of range. These correlations are so high as to be troubling to some, myself included.

Yet another way of studying the relationship between the brain and intelligence is in terms of cerebral blood flow in different regions of the cerebrum. The idea is that blood goes to portions of the brain that are being used in the processing of a given task. It is possible to use radioactive tracers that are inhaled in order to monitor flow of blood during information processing. Studies by Risberg, Maximilian, and Prohovnik (1977) as well as others have shown the usefulness of these techniques for measuring which portion of the brain is being used in information processing. Probably the leading investigator for the use of these techniques in the study of intelligence is John Horn (1986), who has related blood flow to different regions for tasks requiring crystallized versus fluid abilities.

Conclusion

The biological metaphor has generated a substantial amount of research relating functioning of the brain to cognition, in general, and to intelligence, in particular. As Gazzaniga (1985) points out again and again, interpretation of this research is often by no means straightforward. For example, what does it mean to show a relationship between average evoked potentials and psychometrically derived intelligence test scores? Do the evoked potentials somehow cause intelligent cognition? Or equally plausibly, does intelligent cognition lead to certain patterns of evoked potential? Or do both intelligent information processing and the evoked potentials depend on some aspect of the brain, whether conceived biologically or cognitively? As one reflects on the correlation, one is reminded of the rule one learns in undergraduate school that one cannot infer causation from correlation. Despite the striking magnitude of some of the correlations, we are far from understanding the neural mechanisms that are actually responsible for them. I believe that the evidence suggests a relationship between certain aspects of evoked potentials and psychometrically measured intelligence, but I think we are a long way off from understanding just what this relationship is and why it appears. Until we understand the relationship better, I am unenthusiastic about using evoked potentials as some kind of "culture-free" intelligence test, because the relationship may represent nothing more than that more intelligent subjects are more active in their thinking at rest than are less intelligent subjects. In other words, when given instructions simply to sit and not perform any particular task, the more intelligent subjects may be busy thinking about issues that are on their minds, whereas the less intelligent subjects may be less likely to be thinking in this way, or at all! This difference might generate a spurious correlation. Indeed, the evidence suggests that the correlation goes down as subjects perform more and more complex tasks. In other words, when subjects are actually doing a task given by the experimenter, one no longer easily obtains a correlation between average evoked potentials and scores on that test.

I do not think that the ambiguities of this approach are necessarily any greater than those of any other approach. But sometimes the claims, particularly by certain investigators, are more sweeping and more aggressive than those made by investigators using other approaches. I believe that there is a great need for an integration of neuropsychological, electrophysiological, and cognitive research, an integration that is being attempted by a number of investigators (e.g., Farah, 1988; Kosslyn, 1987). But we have a long way to go in this integration, and it is moving faster in the field of mental imagery, I believe, than it is in the field of intelligence. Nevertheless, I believe that such an integration represents one of the most promising future directions for intelligence research.

8

The epistemological metaphor

The epistemological metaphor draws very heavily upon philosophy, and especially the philosophy of knowledge, for its conceptualization of intelligence. Epistemological theorists, influenced heavily by Jean Piaget, tend to be developmental in the range of issues they consider. I will first consider Piaget's theory, and then the neo-Piagetian theories that followed the theory of Piaget.

Piaget and the theory of genetic epistemology*

Jean Piaget first entered the field of cognitive development when, working in Binet's laboratory, he became intrigued with children's *wrong* answers to Binet's intelligence test items. To understand intelligence, Piaget reasoned, one's investigation must be twofold. First, one must look at the way a person acts upon the environment – at a person's performance. But also, and here is where Piaget began to part company with Binet, one must consider *why* the person performs as she or he does, taking account of the cognitive structures underlying the individual's actions. Through his repeated observation of children's performance and particularly their errors in reasoning, Piaget concluded that there are coherent logical structures underlying children's thought but that these structures are different from those underlying adult thought. In the six decades that followed, Piaget focused his research on delineating what these cognitive structures might be at different stages of development and how they might evolve from one stage to the next.

What is intelligence?

Piaget thought that there were two interrelated aspects of intelligence: its function and its structure. Piaget, a biologist by training, saw

*This section and the next one were written in collaboration with Janet Powell.

the function of intelligence to be no different than the function of other biological activities. This function is adaptation, which includes assimilating the environment to one's own structures (be they physiological or cognitive) and accommodating one's structures (again, either physical or mental) to encompass new aspects of the environment. "A certain continuity exists . . . between intelligence and the purely biological process of morphogenesis and adaptation to the environment" (Piaget, 1952b, p. 1). In Piaget's theory, the function of intelligence – adaptation – provided this continuity with lower biological acts. "Intelligence is thus only a generic term to indicate the superior forms of organization or equilibrium of cognitive structuring. . . . Intelligence . . . is essentially a system of living and acting operations" (Piaget, 1972, p. 7). Piaget rejected the sharp delineation proposed by the Gestaltists and others between intelligent acts, which were proposed to require insight or thought, and nonintelligent acts, such as habits and reflexes. Instead, he preferred to speak of a continuum in which "behavior becomes more intelligent as the pathways between the subject and the objects on which it acts cease to be simple and become progressively more complex" (Piaget, 1972, p. 10).

Piaget further proposed, however, that the internal organizational structures of intelligence and how intelligence will be manifested differ with age. It is obvious that an adult does not deal with the world in the same way as does a neonate. For example, the infant typically acts on his or her environment via sensorimotor structures and, thus, is limited to the apparent, physical world. The adult, in contrast, is capable of abstract thought and, thus, is free to explore the world of possibility. Much of Piaget's research was a logical and philosophical exploration of how knowledge structures might develop from primitive to sophisticated forms. Guided by his interest in epistemology and his observations of children's behavior, Piaget divided the intellectual development of the individual into discrete, qualitative stages. "Each stage is characterized by an overall structure in terms of which the main behavior patterns can be explained" (Piaget & Inhelder, 1969, p. 153). As the child progresses from one stage to the next, the cognitive structures of the preceding stage are reorganized and extended, through the child's own adaptive actions, to form the underlying structures of the equilibrium characterizing the next stage. Piaget wrote, "At each new stage, the mechanisms provided by the factors already in existence make for an equilibrium which is still incomplete, and the balancing process itself leads to the next level" (Piaget, 1972, p. 49). This equilibrium process is repeated as "intelligence tries to embrace the universe" (p. 49).

Piaget's theory described the stages of the development of intelligence from birth to adolescence. Piaget was in agreement with many psychometricians in seeing infant intelligence as set apart from adult intelligence. But Piaget not only saw the infant's intellectual structures as different from those of the adult but also hypothesized still other intellectual structures for childhood. In fact, Piaget (1972) proposed three distinct periods, or stages, of development: the sensorimotor period (which lasts from birth to approximately age 2), the period of preparation for and organization of concrete operations (which is often subdivided into a preoperational and a concrete operational stage, lasting approximately from age 2 to age 12), and the formal operational period (which is begun at approximately age 12 and which continues through adulthood).

Underlying Piaget's description of the child's intellectual development are three core assumptions about the nature of this developmental process. First, in Piaget's view, there are four factors that interact to bring about the development of the child. Three of these factors are the ones usually proposed: maturation, experience of the physical environment, and the influence of the social environment. To these three factors, however, Piaget added a fourth, which coordinates and guides the other three: equilibration, that is, the child's own self-regulatory processes (Piaget, 1970). Thus, Piaget's theory centers on the assertion that the child is a very active participant in the construction of his or her own intelligence. Second, Piaget asserted that this intellectual development results in the appearance of developmental stages and that these stages follow an invariant sequential order, with each succeeding stage incorporating and extending the accomplishments of the preceding stage. Third, although the rate of development may vary across children, the stages themselves and their sequence were considered by Piaget to be universal. In sum, Piaget's theory asserted that there is a single route of intellectual development that *all* humans follow, regardless of individual differences, although their progression along this route may be at different rates and they may stop off somewhere along the way rather than follow the route to completion.

Aside from the equilibration model, proposed to handle structural change at the broadest level of development as well as at the level of performance on a specific task (Piaget, 1977), Piaget spoke very little about actual thought processes or how these processes develop. The primary purpose of his research was to understand and describe the structures underlying the child's thought, and not primarily to investigate how the child actually performs on a given task or set of tasks, or how the components of the child's performance change with age. Thus, except for the fact that Piaget insisted that structure and process are interdependent and evolve together, Piaget's model is vague concerning the "how" of cognitive development. Many researchers, especially information-processing theorists (see the upcoming section, Methodological and theoretical challenges to Piaget's theory of intellectual development), would argue that Piaget is equally vague on the "what."

In general, cross-cultural and other studies support the universal sequence of the appearances of Piaget's major stages, but these same studies contest the invariant sequence of the individual psychological operations within a stage (Dasen, 1977). Training studies, even some done by members of the Genevan camp (e.g., Inhelder, Sinclair, & Bovet, 1974), suggest that there may be more than one developmental route to the acquisition of some constructs. Again, the reader is referred to other sources for a detailed presentation of criticisms of Piaget's theory (e.g., Brown & Desforges, 1979; Siegel & Brainerd, 1978; see also Gelman & Baillargeon, 1983), but the next section deals with some of the major challenges to Piaget's theory.

Equilibration

Piaget (1926, 1928, 1952b, 1972), like many other theorists of intelligence, recognized the importance of adaptation to intelligence. Indeed, he believed adaptation to be its most important principle. In adaptation, the individual learns from the environment and learns to address the changes in the environment. Adjustment consists of two complementary processes: assimilation and accommodation. Assimilation is the process of absorbing new information and fitting it into an already existing cognitive structure about what the world is like. The complementary process, accommodation, involves forming a new cognitive structure in order to understand information. In other words, if no existing cognitive structure seems adequate to understand new information, a new cognitive structure must be formed through the accommodation process.

The complementary processes of assimilation and accommodation, taken together in an interaction, constitute what Piaget refers to as equilibration. Equilibration is the balancing of the two and it is through this balance that people either add to old schemas or form new ones. A schema, for Piaget, is a mental image or action pattern. It is essentially a way of organizing sensory information. For example, we have schemas for going to the bank, riding a bicycle, eating a meal, visiting a doctor's office, and the like. The concept of a schema has been elaborated in information-processing terms by Schank and Abelson (1977), who have relabeled the schema, a *script*. But whatever it is called, it is clear that schemas, or scripts, or mental models are necessary to adaptation to the environment.

Periods of development

According to Piaget, the intelligence of children proceeds through four discrete stages, or periods of development. Each of these periods builds upon the preceding one, so that development is essentially accumulative.

The first period is the sensorimotor one, which occupies birth through roughly 2 years of age. The newborn baby exhibits only innate, preprogrammed reflexes, such as grasping and sucking. Intelligence begins to exhibit itself as the innate reflexes are refined and elaborated. With time, the baby starts to grasp for things, such as toys, and to suck on a nipple or a pacifier. Understanding of the world is only through direct perception. Instrumentality – the discovery of how actions can lead to outcomes – develops through trial and error. Eventually, however, simple plans can be constructed, as, for example, if the infant wants a rattle or a toy and learns that grasping it will result in his obtaining the object. By the end of the sensorimotor period, the infant has started to acquire object permanence, or the realization that objects can exist apart from him or herself. In early infancy, the infant does not ascribe a separate reality to objects. Thus, if a toy is hidden under a pillow or behind a barrier, the infant will not search for the toy because as far as he or she is concerned, it no longer exists when it goes out of sight. By $1^1/2$ to 2 years of age, however, the child understands that objects can exist even when they are not being seen at a given time. He or she knows that a search will lead to finding the object. Similarly, if the infant's mother leaves the room, the infant becomes aware that she still exists and will reappear later on.

The second period is the preoperational one, which takes place roughly in ages 2 through 7. The child is now beginning to represent the world through symbols and images, but the symbols and images are directly dependent upon the immediate perception of the child. The child is still essentially egocentric. He or she sees objects and people from only his or her own point of view. Thus, to the extent that thinking takes place, it is egocentric thinking.

Children begin to acquire a language and show a newfound curiosity about the world. They believe that natural phenomena are actually created by people, and they are likely to be atomistic, assigning properties of animal or human existence to natural objects.

Concrete operations

The third period, that of concrete operations, occupies roughly ages 7 through 11. In this period, the child is able to perform concrete mental operations. Thus, the child can now think through sequences of actions or events that previously had to be enacted physically. The hallmark of concrete operational thought is reversibility. It is now possible for the child to reverse the direction of thought. The child comes to understand subtraction, for example, as a reverse of addition and division as the reverse of multiplication. The child can go to the store and back home again or trace out a route on a map and see the way backward.

The period is labeled one of "concrete" operations because operations are performed for objects that are physically present. In this period, the child develops fairly sophisticated skills of classifying and sequencing. Thus, he or she can distinguish objects on the basis of color, size, shape, or other attributes and can also order objects, for example, from smallest to largest. A major acquisition of the concrete operational period is conservation, which involves a child's recognizing that objects or quantities can remain the same, despite changes in their physical appearance. Suppose, for example, that a child is shown two glasses, one of which is short and fat and the other of which is tall and thin. If a preoperational child watches water poured from the short, fat glass to the tall, thin one, she or he will say that the tall, thin glass has more water then the short, fat one had. Thus, the child does not conserve quantity. But a concrete operational child will recognize that the quantity of water is the same in the new glass as in the old glass, despite the change in physical appearance.

Formal operations

Formal operations begin to evolve at around age 11, and usually would be fairly fully developed by the age of 16, although arguably, some adults never completely develop formal operations. In the period of formal operations, the child comes to be able to think abstractly and hypothetically, not just concretely. The individual can view a problem from multiple points of view and can think much more systematically than in the past. For example, if asked to provide all possible permutations of the numbers 1, 2, 3, and 4, the child can now implement a systematic strategy for listing all of these permutations. In contrast, the concrete operational child would have essentially listed permutations at random, without a systematic strategy for generating all of the possible permutations. The child can now think scientifically and use the hypotheticodeductive method to generate hypotheses and to test them.

Methodological and theoretical challenges to Piaget's theory of intellectual development: a brief overview

Piaget's theory adds a great richness to our conception of intellectual development: Not the least of his contributions are the Piagetian tasks and a vast data base describing the child's performance on these tasks. Spada and Kluwe (1980) describe his impact as follows:

Almost no investigation of cognitive development is made without referring to or basing the work on the theory of Piaget and his Genevan collaborators. The empirical studies by these authors are unsurpassed in richness of detail and findings, and their theory is the only one that claims to explain cognitive development so completely. (p. 2)

However, his theory has also come under fierce attack on both theoretical and methodological grounds. Brown and Desforges (1979) have written an excellent psychological critique of Piaget's theory, and Siegel and Brainerd (1978) edited a collection of papers proposing alternatives to Piagetian theory. The following four challenges to Piaget's theory draw extensively upon these sources.

1. Replicability. Much attention by researchers attempting to replicate Piaget's results has been focused on the tasks that he uses. Interexperimenter variance owing to the flexibility of Piaget's clinical method is a major problem in such replication attempts. At least one researcher, Tuddenham (1971), has attempted to construct a standardized battery of Piaget's tasks to help alleviate this problem. (See Green, Ford, & Flamer, 1971, for an example of the dialogue going on between psychometricians and Piagetians.) But, as Brown and Desforges (1979) note, most of Piaget's critics are not questioning the replicability of his observations per se; instead, their criticisms rest on the validity of the Piagetian methodology and on the interpretation of Piaget's observations of the child's performance.

2. Interpretation: Are apparent failures really failures and successes really successes? At the heart of this controversy is the issue of identifying the ages at which different Piagetian constructs appear. Challenges to Piaget's theory falling in this camp come from two major directions: defining successful performance on a given Piagetian task and ensuring the age and culture appropriateness of a given task.

Much controversy has been created over the criteria used by the investigator to define successful completion of a task. In general, the Genevans (preferring to err in favor of fewer false successes) argue for more stringent criteria with resulting later acquisition ages for the various constructs; other researchers (preferring to err in favor of fewer false negatives) argue for less stringent criteria so that the tasks identify the absolute earliest age at which a psychological construct appears.

Bowers (1967, 1974) and Cornell (1978), for example, have argued that the object-permanence concept appears earlier than proposed by Piaget but that Piaget's performance criteria are too high to recognize the presence of the construct. A similar criterion problem exists in a typical Piagetian conservation task in which the child is asked to judge whether or not two quantities are equal with respect to some empirical factor. In such a task, after affirming the initial equality of the quantities, the child witnesses some transformation of one or both of the quantities and then is again questioned as to whether the quantities are equivalent. In addition, the child is required to justify or explain his or her response, and sometimes (especially in situations where the effects of training are being assessed) the child is expected also to resist the examiner's attempt to dissuade the child from his or her convictions by surreptitiously making additions to or deletions from the quantity under consideration.

In the conservation tasks, much of the debate centers around whether a correct response is sufficient evidence for conservation (judgment-only criterion) or whether the child should also be expected to justify his or her response (judgment-plus-explanation criterion) – the former is, of course, a much less stringent requirement than the latter and, thus, would provide for earlier acquisition ages than the latter. Brainerd (1977) has attempted to resolve the debate by claiming that whether one's criteria err in the direction of including actual nonconservers or excluding actual conservers is irrelevant; instead, one's criteria should be the ones resulting in the lowest error rate, which, he argues, means that judgment alone, without explanation, is the preferred, that is, most accurate, response.

Other critics have further argued not only that the experimenter's criteria are sometimes too high but also that the criteria often result in the experimenter's leading the child to give a wrong answer. Hall and Kaye (1978) have objected to the experimenter's requirement, especially the Genevans' requirement in training studies, that the child, in addition to responding correctly and justifying his or her response, must resist the investigator's attempts to shake the child's conviction. Hall and Kaye suggest that requiring the child to appeal to logical necessity ("But it has to be the same!") in the face of conflicting evidence surreptitiously set up by the experimenter is asking the child to exhibit within the special context of the experiment a behavior that is normally maladaptive for learning and development in general. If one sticks consistently to one's belief regardless of the apparent facts, then, indeed, how can learning or development come to pass at all? Therefore, Hall and Kaye argue that such a logical-necessity criterion should not be employed in the assessment of conservation.

Rose and Blank (1974) have gone even further by arguing that the very way in which the conservation tasks are usually structured (i.e., the use of pre- and posttransformation questions as to equality) requires a response that is unnatural in comparison with what is expected in nonexperimental contexts. These investigators suggest that the fact that the examiner is asking the same question twice implies to the child that the intervening transformation must have involved change on the relevant dimension. Indeed, Rose and Blank found that children do perform better, earlier, on one-question (after-only) tasks and that this improvement carries over to standard, two-question forms of the tasks.

The issue of both age and culture appropriateness of a given task has yielded even more debate between the Genevans and critics. Many of the cross-cultural attempts at validation of Piaget's theory (see, e.g., Dasen, 1977) have found that non-Western children often fail Piagetian tasks if presented in their traditional forms, but when the tasks are translated into content more familiar to the children, then non-Western children's performance more nearly resembles that of Western children. (See also Greenfield, 1969; Price-Williams, Gordon, & Ramirez, 1969.) Familiarity with the materials makes a difference in cross-cultural studies of children's abilities. Therefore, the issue arises: How much should one make allowances for a child's background in designing, administering, and interpreting performance on Piagetian tasks, and how much does making such allowances leave out phenomena of interest?

Researchers investigating the earliest ages at which Piaget's constructs appear – especially those researchers attempting to train young children in developmentally more mature tasks – are concerned with the problem of how one makes a Piagetian task age appropriate. The extensive reliance on language in Piagetian tasks, especially on the child's own verbalizations, is particularly at issue when investigators attempt to use the traditional Piagetian tasks with younger children (Siegel, 1978). Some researchers (e.g., Braine, 1968) have attempted to generate nonverbal tasks for use with preschool-age children. In general, these nonverbal tasks support Piaget's theory of the sequence of development, but they consistently produce evidence for the appearance of Piaget's constructs, especially concrete operations, at earlier ages than do the traditional Piagetian tasks. Piagetians rebut these claims by arguing that the nature of the criterion task has been changed in these nonverbal tasks. S. A. Miller (1976) also warns that in such attempts to modify the traditional Piagetian tasks, great care must be taken to be sure that the alternative versions of the tasks still measure the same constructs as did the original tasks (see also Sigel & Hooper, 1968). But this is a difficult criticism to get around because the tasks are designed to define the operations. In addition, there have been relatively few information-processing analyses of the tasks to see what processes children actually have to use to perform each kind of task. This leads us to the next of the challenges to Piaget's theory to be discussed.

3. Interpretation: What does "failure" or "success" on a given task mean in terms of evaluating a child's intelligence? Two issues arise under this heading of drawing conclusions about a child's intelligence. First is the issue of construct validity: Does the task measure what it is proposed to measure and nothing else? Second, given that an individual operation is found to be or not to be used by a child, can one then go on to conclude that the child is in a given stage of development, possessing the attendant broad cognitive structures proposed by Piaget?

In regard to the first issue, some researchers have questioned whether even the original Piagetian tasks necessarily measure the hypothesized psychological constructs that Piaget intended them to measure. Because of his primary interest in epistemology rather than in psychological processes per se, Piaget did not systematically investigate the strategies and processes children actually use to solve various tasks. Instead, he made process assumptions on the basis of his logicomathematical model of intelligence and concentrated his empirical energies on finding evidence to support his hypothetical constructs. Riley and Trabasso (1974) have noted a problem with this lack of attention to the actual information-processing demands of Piaget's tasks. These researchers reported successfully training preoperational children to solve a transitive-inference task involving a series of sticks of different lengths; this outcome contradicts Piaget's theory, according to which children cannot use transitive inference (i.e., cannot coordinate the members of two premises via a middle term) until the concrete operational period of development. Upon further investigation, however, Riley and Trabasso concluded that these preoperational children were not using transitive inference, as it is usually defined, to solve a problem. Instead, the children were creating a mental spatial array and then answering inferential questions by scanning this internal array.

Riley and Trabasso's results serve as a reminder that one cannot assume that there is only one strategy possible for task solution; some sort of task analysis from the viewpoint of the task's information-processing requirements definitely appears to be needed. As Brown and Desforges assert, "If we wish to establish the absence or presence of a particular operation we need tasks which require the use of that and only that operation and which can be done in no other way" (1979, p. 50). In this regard, information-processing theorists working with Piaget's theory are making some headway (e.g., Case, 1978; Pascual-Leone, 1979, 1980).

Stages, according to Piaget's theory, are characterized by specific underlying cognitive structures that organize the child's thought and other activities. Piaget assumed that, through his tasks, an investigator could tap these cognitive structures and thereby ascertain that child's current stage of development. But is there consistency in performance across the tasks proposed to reflect a given cognitive structure? Existing empirical evidence on consistency of performance is not encouraging for stage theory. As Brown and Desforges (1979) observe, cognitive structures should be content free; yet the content of a task seems to make a great deal of difference for the individual's performance (see Martorano, 1977; Uzgiris, 1968). A number of studies (e.g., Brown & Desforges, 1979; Pascual-Leone, 1970; Sigel & Hooper, 1968) have referred to low correlations between alternative measures of a particular operation.

The lack of a strong relationship between tasks using different content to measure the same construct, or between tasks measuring multiple constructs theoretically proposed to emerge in the same stage of development (because they share a common structure), pose problems for evaluating Piaget's stage theory of intellectual development. In explaining such data, Piagetians point to the existence of transitional stages and of horizontal decalage, in which a cognitive structure is exhibited first in content areas most familiar to the child and later in more abstract and unfamiliar tasks (Lovell, 1971; Piaget, 1972). Flavell (1971) notes that it is not necessary in a stage theory to postulate abrupt all-or-nothing stages of development. (See Beilin, 1980, for a revisionist's view of apparent inconsistencies within a stage.) Yet one wonders whether because so much fuzziness is attached to Piaget's stage theory, it would not be better to abandon, at least for the time being, notions of a coherent underlying structure d'ensemble and to focus instead on the development of individual processes and strategies. And, as Siegel and Brainerd's (1978) book illustrates, alternative explanations of Piaget's observations (i.e., explanations not requiring the postulation of general stages of development) are rampant. Piagetians have done little empirical work designed to eliminate such alternative interpretations, whereas these alternatives are often testable and, when tested, fit Piaget's data quite well. For these reasons, the theory is not faring extremely well today as a psychological theory of intellectual development, despite its many extremely admirable features.

4. Usefulness of the theory. Unfortunately, Piaget's theory has often been used only to attach yet another label to children while telling us little about the child's specific abilities in his or her daily functioning (see, e.g., Green, Ford, & Flamer, 1971). But apart from how the theory has been used is the question of how it could be used. Piaget (1972) noted that his model is a competence model and not a model of the individual's specific performance on a specific task: Performance does not necessarily equal competence, and contextual and content factors often influence how an individual will perform at a given time. Piagetians basically try to determine only whether or not a construct is there, not whether it is ordinarily used or even under what conditions it will be used. Information-processing theorists argue that a much more constructive approach to evaluating a child's intellectual capabilities would be to look first at the child's usual performance – at the cognitive processes and strategies that the child utilizes – and at the nature of the interaction between external and internal determinants of performance.

Piaget's theory is further limited, in that, except for the admission that rate of intellectual development may vary across individuals, it pays insufficient attention to individual differences in children's ability. The theory assumes that the reason individuals differ in their cognitive functioning is that some are further advanced along the route of cognitive development than are others. Level of cognitive development is equated with intelligence, and no mention is made of possible differences between children within a common stage of development or of inherent differences in ability. These criticisms are not necessarily damning of Piaget's theory, in the sense that the existence of individual differences disproves the theory, but rather they point to the limited usefulness of the theory in explaining and predicting many aspects of performance.

In conclusion, it appears that although Piaget's formal theory of development is indeed elegant, the elegance is due to the fact that the theory tends to be derived from epistemological considerations and verified only later by the observation and testing of children. Some aspects of the theory are untestable; other aspects, when tested, prove inadequate as descriptions of, and explanations for, children's development (see Brown & Desforges, 1979; Siegel & Brainerd, 1978). Yet despite these criticisms, it is certainly true that, whether we agree with the theory or not, Piaget has changed the way we think about children's thinking. And, as Beilin (1980), a researcher offering a revisionist view of Piaget's theory, wrote, "Piaget's theory has been with developmental psychology for some 60 years despite almost continuous criticism, but [it] appears in no immediate danger of being superseded" (p. 245).

Robbie Case and neo-Piagetian theory

Basic ideas

Case (1984, 1985, 1987), like Piaget, believes that cognitive development proceeds through four general stages that take place between age 1 month and adulthood. The stages comprise substages, each of which emerges at a characteristic age and each of which builds upon the preceding substage, just as the stages build on each other. But Case, unlike Piaget, attempts to model the processes as well as the structures that develop in children's thinking. Although Case views himself primarily in the rationalist tradition (that of Piaget), he also draws upon two other traditions, namely, the empiricist and the historicocultural one. Case believes that a major shortcoming of Piagetian research was its simultaneous variation of both task structure and content, so that developmental conclusions were inevitably confounded. Case, in contrast, systematically manipulates content within a given task structure presented across age levels, so that the conclusions drawn will be, to the extent possible, unconfounded ones.

Basic assumptions

Case makes four basic assumptions. First, children's mental processes are claimed to be divisible into two categories: those that represent recurrent patterns of stimulation and those that represent ways in which these patterns can be transformed. Case labels the former *figurative schemes* or *state representations,* and the latter *operative schemes or operations.* Second, from birth onward, the activation of any scheme or set of schemes can have either a positive, neutral, or negative affective tone. Third, from birth onward, children can exercise some degree of voluntary control over their own cognitive and affective experiences. Fourth and finally, the structures that permit such control consist of temporally organized sequences of figurative and operative schemes.

Structure

Case's theory draws heavily upon the three-prong control structure for thought, involving a representation of a problem situation, an objective, and a strategy. The representation of the *problem situation,* called the problem space by others, is the individual's representation of the problem. The *objective,* called a goal by others, is the transformation the individual wishes to effect in the problem space. The *strategy* is the means by which the transformation will be effected. For example, in a very simple use of the balance scale – which Case draws upon heavily in his research – an infant might represent a problem situation as one of an interesting object moving out of view in a downward direction; the objective would be to return the pattern of stimulation to its original state. The strategy by which this might be accomplished is to move the head and eyes in a downward (or upward) direction, probably by using peripheral input from the object (which is a block) as a guide. As children grow older, the allowable complexity of the problem situation, objective, and strategy increases, but the basic control structure remains the same. In his earlier work, Case drew heavily on Pascual-Leone's (1970) concept of the M-space for an understanding of the amount of mental processing space that could be allocated to each of the aspects of cognitive structure at different ages. In his more recent writings, however, Case has deemphasized the "M"-construct, although he still believes the amount of short-term storage space available to the individual is critical in determining what resources can be devoted to a given problem.

Processes

Case believes that information processes play a major role in cognition and development. He believes that four processes are especially key. Often, in information processing, it is necessary to activate two schemes either at the same time or in immediate succession. Thus, one or more processes are needed to perform this dual activation. The first of Case's proposed processes is schematic search, by which a second schema is sought for activation while a first schema remains active. This process is basically a nonexecutive one. A second process is schematic evaluation, by which the utility of the combination of the two schemas is evaluated. This process is an executive one. A third process is retagging, which involves relabeling the two schemes into a single paired, or higher order scheme, so that the two schemes can be retrieved in a single operation the next time around. This process is a learning, or knowledge acquisition process. The final process is schematic consolidation, which involves forming a new, smoothly running unit comprising the two formerly separated schemes. This process is also one of learning.

Mechanisms of development

For Case, perhaps the most critical point about development is that a stage of cognition is in short-term storage space, and this space, he believes, increases with age. The growth of this space within each stage is affected by an increase in operational efficiency, which itself is alleged to be dependent upon maturational factors such as neurological myelinization. Case believes, however, that amount of practice matters as well, at least to some extent. Thus, the stage on which cognition performs its acts increases in size over the years. The props on this stage are the executive control structures, which go through four stages: sensorimotor, relational, dimensional, and vectorial. The players who act on these props are the four elementary information processes, schematic search, evaluation, retagging, and consolidation, as described earlier.

Kurt Fischer and skill theory

Basic ideas

Fischer (1980, 1987; Fischer & Pipp, 1984) has proposed a three-tier, or stage theory, with the three tiers comprising 10 separate levels of "skill structures." The levels are generated from the tiers by a system whereby each tier involves four levels, such that the last level of one tier is the first of the next. The levels differ in the number of items that need to be related to one another. These items may be either sensorimotor (first tier), representational (second tier), or abstract (third tier). Whereas Piaget views qualitative (but not necessarily, quantitative) cognitive development as ending at roughly the age of 12, Fischer does not view it as ending until roughly double that age.

Basic assumptions

Fischer assumes that development can be understood primarily in terms of two key concepts, which provide instantiations for the notions of competence and performance as they have been discussed by others. The first concept is that of *optimal level,* which specifies the upper limit on the complexity of skill that an individual can bring to bear upon a problem. The second concept is that of the *skill,* which appears to be a set of processes that can be brought to bear upon problems. Skills differ in complexity, and indeed, the complexity of skills that can be brought to bear upon a problem is a key source of development in Fischer's theory. Development of skills is gradual, but development of optimal levels is sudden. The former is also much more under environmental control than the latter.

Structure

In Fischer's account, there are 13 main structures. The structures differ in terms of the complexity of information and relations they can handle. The 13 main structures are (a) single reflex sets (3–4 weeks), (b) reflex mapping (7–8 weeks), (c) reflex systems (10–11 weeks), (d) systems of reflex systems, which are single sensorimotor sets

(4 months), (e) sensorimotor mappings (7–8 months), (f) sensorimotor systems (11–13 months), (g) systems of sensorimotor systems, which are single representational sets (20–24 months), (h) representational mappings (4–5 years), (i) representational systems (6–7 years), (j) systems of representational systems, which are single abstract sets (10–12 years), (k) abstract mappings (14–16 years), (l) abstract systems (18–20 years), and (m) systems of abstract systems, which are single principles (24–26 years). For detail and a description of each of these structures, see Fischer and Pipp (1984).

Processes

Although Fischer's theory is one of skill development, it is surprisingly difficult to ascertain exactly what its processing claims are. This is because Fischer talks more about skill structures than about skills. So far as I can tell, the processes of Fischer's theory appear to be four-fold. These processes, however, are ultimately sources of structural change. A first involves controlling variations in a single set, as in encoding a stimulus. A second involves combining several sets to produce a new structure. This structure, which Fischer refers to as a mapping, defines a simple relation between two or more sets. The third process involves the integration of several mappings to produce a system, that is, a relation between two or more subsets of two or more sets. The fourth process involves combining several systems to produce a system of systems. Consider an example of each process from Fischer's own work. The first process would be involved in a child's treating a doll as an independent agent, for example, as a doctor or as a child. The second process would be involved in a child's coordinating social roles of two dolls, such as those of doctor and patient. The third process would involve recognizing that the patient of the doctor might be the doctor's daughter, such that the two individuals bear two relations to each other: doctor and patient, and father and daughter. The fourth and highest-level process would involve recognizing that this system of interrelations could apply in other ways and other families as well, for example, if the father of a friend who is that father's daughter is also acting as the lawyer of the friend.

The role of context

Fischer suggests that optimal levels will develop according to a maturational schedule that is minimally, if at all, affected by the environment.

But the environment will be crucial in the development of the cognitive skills that are able to manifest themselves within a given developmental level. Thus, competence is primarily maturational, but performance will be heavily influenced by contextual factors. Fischer differs from Piaget in a key respect: For Piaget, development within as well as between levels is primarily maturational, whereas for Fischer, development between levels is primarily maturational, but development within levels is largely experientially determined.

Mechanisms of development

For Fischer, there are two primary developmental mechanisms, increase in optimal level and development of skills. Fischer believes the former is largely biologically determined and the latter largely determined through the interaction of the organism with the environment. Together, therefore, biology and interaction with the environment determine cognitive development, collectively forming 10 levels of development. Fischer and Farrar (1987) have cited a number of studies of cognitive growth spurts that would presumably reflect passage from one level to another. Although they were initially skeptical of such reports, Fischer's own research has confirmed their apparent existence.

Halford and structure-mapping theory

Basic ideas

Graeme Halford's (1982) structure-mapping theory draws heavily upon concepts of analogy and transfer of training. According to Halford, there are four levels of structure mapping that differ in the complexity of what is mapped. The theory resembles Fischer's in its emphasis upon the number of items that need to be interrelated at various levels of performance. Element mappings, for example, at the lowest level would involve the interrelation of just two items. Relational mappings, in contrast, involve interrelation of two sets of two elements.

Basic assumptions

Halford assumes that what he calls structure mappings (assignment rules) are part of the process by which children understand concepts and that we can account for children's ability to acquire concepts by defining the types of structure mappings they can construct.

Structure

Halford defines the structure as a set of elements. A structure mapping is a rule for assigning elements of one structure to elements of another, such that any functions or relations between elements of the first structure will also be assigned to corresponding functions or relations in the second structure. Halford distinguishes among four levels of mappings.

Element mappings involve simply the mapping of one item to another. There are two types of element mappings. The first involves mapping an object or event to a mental image. The second involves mapping an object or event to a word. Thus, these two kinds of mappings correspond roughly to spatial or imaginal representation, on the one hand, and verbal representation, on the other.

Relational mappings involve seeing the relation connecting two element mappings. For example, one might recognize that a man is taller than a boy and that the Sears Tower is taller than the Empire State Building. No connection is made between the two people, on the one hand, and the two buildings, on the other hand, other than that both involve a relation of *taller than*.

Systems mappings involve elements and relations in one system being mapped consistently into elements and relations in a second system. For example, one might relate *John is taller than Bill* to *Bill is taller than Dave,* thereby linking John and Dave and transitively inferring that John is taller than Dave.

Multiple-system mappings are similar to system mappings, except their binary operations (or ternary relations) are mapped, instead of binary relations. Whereas the closest task analog to a system mapping is transitive inference, the closest task analog to multiple-system mapping is analogical reasoning. Multiple-system mapping is what I have referred to as higher order mapping (Sternberg, 1977), in which a relation is spotted between two relations. For example, spotting the relation between Vietnam and Asia, on the one hand, and El Salvador and Central America, on the other hand, would involve a multiple-system mapping. One mapping is that both have been alleged to be subject to internal revolutions against oppressive governments. An alternative mapping would be that both have been alleged to be initiators for a possible domino effect whereby communism would infiltrate a continent.

Processes

Although Halford uses different names and tasks, the processes in his theory appear to be almost identical to those in Fischer's theory, despite the fact that the two theories were developed independently. Hence, I will not discuss these processes in detail. The processes, respectively, are those of encoding, comparison of two elements, comparison of two relations (as in a transitive inference), and higher order comparison of two relations (as in an analogy). An additional process is that of consistency checking.

Mechanisms of development

Halford, like Case, believes that information-processing capacity increases with age, but unlike Case (and Fischer), he asserts that there is no evidence that increases occur in a discontinuous fashion. To the contrary, he believes that any discontinuities are more likely to reflect task characteristics than actual abrupt changes in cognitive capacity. Halford believes that there is likely to be an upper, maturationally determined limit to cognitive capacity, although he reads the evidence as inconclusive at distinguishing between capacity and processing limitations. He suggests that primary memory is the locus of cognitive processing. Unlike some investigators, he carefully distinguishes primary memory from short-term memory: His distinction is in terms of experimental operations he used to identify each, and it is not clear what the structural psychological difference is, if indeed there is one.

Pascual-Leone and dialectical constructivism

Basic ideas

Pascual-Leone (1970, 1987) has been heavily influenced by Piagetian concepts and by the dialectical ideas of Hegel and his successors. Three laws of dialectics – the principle of transformation of quantity into quality, and vice versa; the principle of interpenetration of opposites; and the principle of the negation of the negation – underlie the ideas of Pascual-Leone. Pascual-Leone is most well known for his introduction of the concept of the M-space, according to which development is characterized largely by an increase in processing space with age. But in its current form (Pascual-Leone, 1987), Pascual-Leone's thinking is heavily influenced by the interaction of the organism with the environment, with the recognition that the form the interaction takes differs substantially as a function of the age of the organism.

Basic assumptions

Pascual-Leone proposes three basic principles, which here would be classified as assumptions, although he might not view them in that way. The first is the principle of the transformation of quantity into quality and vice versa, according to which the amount of attentional capacity/ working memory that an individual brings to bear in a problem determines the pattern of performance in that problem. The second principle, the interpenetration of opposites, applies to problems and situations in which there is irrelevant or misleading information. The principle refers to the interaction, in such problems and situations, of the factors that lead to correct versus incorrect performances. The third principle, that of the negation of the negation, asserts that in a dialectical system (such as development), a process that negates an initial process is often itself negated, in turn, by another process, causing a change toward the initial direction.

Structure

The most critical structural concept in Pascual-Leone's model is the reserve of mental attentional capacity, which Pascual-Leone refers to as *structural M-capacity*. This is the total amount of processing space available to an individual for use in any kind of information processing. An allied concept, *functional M-capacity,* refers to the amount of structural M-capacity that a person actually utilizes in typical tasks and situations. Thus, Pascual-Leone's basic structural mechanism is a quantitative one, in alliance with his principle that qualitative changes can result from quantitative developments.

Processes

Pascual-Leone's theory appears to posit four key mental processes. The first is what Pascual-Leone refers to as an *M-operator*. Pascual-

Leone views this process as a capacity for mental energy, and it appears to be the means by which working-memory space is recruited to problem solving. The second process is the *I-operator*, which is the individual's capacity actively to inhibit or interrupt the activation of task-irrelevant structures. The third process is the *F-operator*, which is the individual's capacity to produce a performance as a single, integrated whole, despite the fact that a number of different structures may have determined the overall performance. The fourth process is the *E-operator*, which comprises the repertoire of executive schemes and structures that monitor the mobilization of the *M*- and *I*-operators. This operator, then, might be conceived of as a set of executive processes that controls the nonexecutive ones.

The role of context

Of all the neo-Piagetian theorists considered so far, Pascual-Leone is the most explicitly contextualist. Somewhat paradoxically, he also seems to be the most rationalist! He describes seven dialectical principles that he believes must be taken into account by theories of cognitive development. The two most relevant ones in the present context are, first, that causal theories of human development apply not only to children (or adults) as growing organisms, but also to the theorists. Theories, including Pascual-Leone's own, show up in historical development as a function of context. Thus, it is no coincidence that so many theories of the 1960s emphasized process, so many of the 1970s emphasized knowledge, and so many of the 1980s have tried to integrate the two. A second dialectical principle is that a theory of development needs to take into account the mediators and tutors who, with their interventions of various kinds, help children to grow. Clearly, the availability and quality of such tutors will be contextually determined.

Mechanisms of development

The main mechanism of cognitive development in Pascual-Leone's theory is *M*-power. Pascual-Leone links levels in Piagetian theory to increases in *M*-power. Essentially, each increase in *M*-power gives the individual an additional processing slot within which mental operations could take place. Although increases in *M*-power are the main mechanism of development, there are others. For example, development results also as a function of the dialectical interaction of the various operators discussed earlier, and especially the *E*- and *I*-operators, which handle cognitive conflict.

Demetriou and experimental structuralism

Basic ideas

Demetriou (Demetriou & Efklides, 1985, 1987) has proposed a theory of experiential structuralism. Demetriou postulates four basic principles of development and six basic cognitive capacities that operate according to these principles. A variety of methodologies, including factor analysis, cross-lag panel analysis, and regression analysis have been used to support experiential structuralism.

Basic assumptions

The assumptions of Demetriou take the form of basic principles underlying the model. The first principle is that of the *domain specificity of capacities*, according to which the cognitive system constructs different functional systems to correspond to different domains of reality. The second principle, that of *formal-procedural specificity of capacities*, asserts that different capacities function as mental models denoting special types of knowledge. Demetriou draws upon Churchman's "five inquiring systems" (described later) – the Leibnizean, Lockean, Kantian, Dialectical/Hegelian, and Singerian – in order to flesh out the second principle. The third principle, that of the *symbolic bias of capacities*, alleges that each capacity is biased toward a particular symbolic system that is particularly conducive to the fulfillment of that capacity – to represent the properties in relations of its own reality domain and to go through the inquisition processes effortlessly and as errorlessly as possible. The fourth principle is that of the *subjective distinctness of capacities*, according to which each capacity is experienced differently and consciously, at least to some extent, by the organism.

Structure

Demetriou draws upon a rather different notion of structure from that of some others, most notably, Case. He posits six structures, or capacity spheres, which have been derived primarily from a basically structural model, namely, that of factor analysis. The six structures are quantitative-relational, qualitative-analytic, imaginal-spatial, causal-experimental, verbal-propositional, and metacognitive-reflecting.

The *quantitative-relational capacity* is concerned with quantifiable reality. The *qualitative-analytic capacity* is concerned primarily with the qualitative properties of reality, such as categorical, matrix, and serial structures. The last of these others might consider quantitative. The *imaginal-spatial capacity* is used to visualize the environment inside one's head. The *causal-experimental capacity* is used to determine causal relations. The *verbal-propositional capacity* is used to represent information in linguistic or propositional form. This last capacity is different from the others described above, in that it is not tied to any one particular domain of observable reality, but rather is a medium for semantic representation. Finally, the *metacognitive-reflecting capacity* is used to represent, process, apprehend, and reflect on the other capacities. Thus, whereas the others capacities act on the environment, this capacity operates instead on the other capacities, and hence, integrates them into a unified whole.

Processes

For Demetriou, information processing appears to be a role assigned to the abilities that are nested under each of the capacities. Quantitative-relational capacity involves three abilities: quantitative specification and representation, construction of dimensions and directions, and coordinating multiple dimensions or directions. Critical to the qualitative-relational capacity are analytical or disembedding abilities, as might be used, say, to disentangle the properties of an apple (that it is a fruit, red, picked from a tree, etc.). Critical abilities involved in the exercise of the imaginal-spatial capacity are addition and subtraction of details, integration, re-formation and/or transformation of images and their parts, rotation of images, and referential coordination between an image and its frame of reference. Critical abilities involved in the exercise of the causal-experimental capacity are combinatorial abilities (as in determining all possible combinations of a set of digits), hypothesis formation abilities (needed to infer causality), experimentation abilities (needed to test hypotheses), and model construction abilities (needed to provide an interpretive framework for one's experimental results). Demetriou does not specify a set of clearly defined verbal abilities underlying the verbal-propositional capacity. Four abilities are involved in the exercise of the metacognitive capacity. Acquaintance estimators consider whether a given task or task environment has been encountered before. Task-capacity affiliation estimators ask whether there is a ready-made procedure available to apply to a given problem. Processing load estimators judge how difficult a problem is with respect to the demands of the problem upon mental resources. Success estimators judge the appropriateness and correctness of a proposed solution.

The role of context

The role of context in Demetriou's theory is emphasized in the name of the model, namely, *experiential* structuralism. Demetriou uses this term to indicate that the cognitive performance is a direct reflection not only of the mind, but of a person's experience. The form this experience will take will depend upon the context of a person's life.

Mechanisms of development

The major source of development in Demetriou's theory appears to be in the creation of mental models through the action of so-called inquiring systems. The inquiring systems, based on Churchman (1971), are Leibnizean, Lockean, Kantian, Dialectical/Hegelian, and Singerian.

The first, the Leibnizean system, is strictly deductive. The Lockean system is an inductive experimental system. The Kantian system takes as input the fact-nets produced by the Leibnizean and Lockean systems and generates alternative integral perspectives for dealing with an issue or problem. Model construction and hypothesis testing are examples of Kantian operations. The Dialectical/Hegelian system constructs completely antithetical representations to those constructed by any of the three preceding systems. Thus, it creates conflict and thereby enhances the opportunities for intellectual growth. Demetriou views propositional capacity as an essentially Hegelian inquirer, although the reasons for this view are less clear to me than to him. The Singerian system is used to study all of the other inquiring systems.

Siegler and the model of strategy choice

Basic ideas

The thinking of Robert Siegler has gone through a number of stages, and I represent here the most recent evolution of that thinking. In his early work Siegler (1978, 1981) was concerned with the development of rule-based thinking in children. By 1984, he was proposing a model of development based on an analogy to evolution (Siegler, 1984). In his most recent work, Siegler (1986, 1987) has been concerned with the issue of strategy choice and its role in development. Siegler's goal in this work is not to propose a full-fledged model of intellectual development, but rather to present a detailed, computer-simulated model of an important aspect of intellectual development, namely, the selection of strategies in cognitive task performance. The model grew out of Siegler's earlier work on rule assessment but is itself different in kind as well as in detail from his earlier modeling of rule implementation. This model addresses not the contents of one or another rule, but rather the issue of how children choose a particular rule or set of rules in the first place. Whereas in his earlier work Siegler was concerned almost exclusively with developmental differences across age levels, in his present work, he is as concerned with individual differences within as across age levels, because he has found such widespread individual differences within age in the strategies that children choose to solve problems that, at first glance, appear to be straightforward and not particularly susceptible to individual differences in strategy for solution.

Basic assumptions

Siegler makes a number of assumptions in his model, although he is somewhat less explicit about them than some of the other theorists. First, he assumes that performance in problem solving is heavily dependent upon prior associations of solutions to a problem. Associative theories, once in vogue in psychology, now have differential acceptance, depending upon whom one asks. Second, he assumes that computer simulation is a valid tool for simulating task performance, in particular, and intellectual development, in general. Many cognitive scientists would not question this assumption, but others would. Finally, Siegler assumes that strategies are essentially a backup for knowledge retrieval. Yet one could plausibly argue that there are instances in which the ordering is reversed – in which one tries to solve a difficult problem in a new and innovative way and resorts to retrieval of tried and tested routines only when one is unable to come up with something new. Anyone who has ever attempted to write a scholarly paper and has ended up with a rehash of an old paper will know what I am talking about.

Structure

Siegler's model is heavily dependent upon the interaction of knowledge with process. Siegler relies heavily upon associative structure in discussing the organization of knowledge. But Siegler's use of association is not the usual one, say, between words and other words or between words and concepts, but rather one between problems and potential solutions to these problems. Each problem is posited to have associated with it a set of solutions, both correct and incorrect. These solutions differ in their associative strength to the problem, and hence form a distribution of associative strengths. Just as the solutions vary in their associative strength with respect to a particular problem, so do the problems differ in their distributions of associations. Some problems may have relatively peaked distributions, in which one answer (right or wrong) may have greater associative strength than others. Other problems may have relatively flat distributions, with little difference in association between various solutions to the problem. Associated with each problem, or kind of problem, is also a confidence criterion. When an individual solves a problem, the probability that a given solution will be retrieved is proportional to its associative strength. If the retrieved solution exceeds the individual's confidence criterion, that solution is selected. But if the solution is not over the criterion, further efforts are made to retrieve a solution that is. Associated with each problem is also a search length. The individual will go on retrieving solutions until a solution exceeds the criterion or until the preset search length is reached. At this point, the individual turns to what Siegler calls "backup strategies." In sum, the speed and accuracy with which the problem is solved will depend critically upon the structure of associations that links a set of possible solutions to a given problem.

Processes

In Siegler's model, the particular processes used in task performance depend largely upon the task being performed. These processes are the elements of the backup strategies that are used when associative solution fails. Siegler somewhat downplays the role of the executive, or at least of metacognitive knowledge, in strategy selection. He suggests that the use of strategies may be much more automatic than we had previously thought. Nevertheless, executive processes may play a more important role in Siegler's own theory than he recognizes. For example, although he does not explicitly acknowledge it, executive processes would seem to play a role in setting the confidence criterion in the length of time one is willing to go on searching for an associative solution before moving on to backup strategies.

Siegler (1984) emphasizes two processes in development: encoding and combination. Children as well as adults encode features of the world and combine subsets of them into conjunctive, disjunctive, prototypic, configural, or other relations. If the rules a person has generate inaccurate predictions, then the person will recombine the features into new relations. Siegler further divides encoding and combination, encoding comprising value monitoring and feature construction and combination comprising feature selection, feature integration, and rule execution processes.

With respect to encoding, *value monitoring* means keeping track of values of features as they are being encoded. *Feature construction* involves generating new features that can be used mentally to represent what is being encoded. With respect to combination, *feature selection* involves choosing which features, from all those encoded, will be incorporated into a rule. *Feature integration* involves selecting among alternative organizations those features to be used in a rule. Finally, *rule execution* involves inserting values of selected features into a chosen organization so as to produce judgments, predictions, and other behaviors.

The role of context

Siegler has never been particularly contextualist in his theorizing. Yet it seems reasonable to suppose that a child's distribution of associations of solutions to problems, to the extent to which a child has associations at all, will be largely contextually determined: Certainly, they are not inborn.

Mechanisms of development

The main mechanisms of development in Siegler's theory of strategy choice appear to be through learning. In Siegler's simulation, every time the cognitive system solves a problem, the association between that answer and the problem increases. The increment in association value is twice as large for correct as for incorrect answers, because, on the average, correct responses are more strongly reinforced than incorrect ones under most circumstances. Thus, at least for the types of familiar problems with which Siegler deals, the development of an associative network would be a key to development. Another source of development would be in the formation and elaboration of backup strategies. Siegler does not explicitly say where these come from, but they, too, presumably develop out of experience rather than through maturation.

General principles

Conclusions and transparadigmatic principles

In my review of alternative epistemological theories, certain prospective loci of intellectual development seem to have emerged in multiple approaches. These loci of development are of particular interest because they suggest the possibility that there may be at least some principles that cross paradigms (Sternberg & Powell, 1983b). Consider what some of these principles might be.

More sophisticated control strategies develop with age

Control strategies, executive functioning, or whatever one chooses to call the homunculus that directs everything else, are an essential element to most of the theories. Piaget described the increased systematization of thought involved in the child's development from sensorimotor modes of interacting with the world to formal-operational reasoning (Inhelder & Piaget, 1958; Piaget, 1972; Piaget & Inhelder, 1969). Not only does the child develop more efficient and more sophisticated schemes as she or he matures – a process that itself suggests the guidance of some sort of metacomponents – but the child also develops a more inclusive and more integrated underlying logical structure that allows for the construction and coordination of these schemes. Thus, Piaget's view of intellectual development can be seen as emphasizing the development of metacomponential processes as much as, if not more than, it emphasizes the development of specific information-processing capabilities. Piaget (1972) defined intellectual development as the movement toward greater flexibility and increased intentionality of thought, and his research program detailed the child's transition from reflex behavior, controlled by heredity and the environment (Piaget, 1952b), to the development of formal operations in which the child has such control over his or her own mental processes that he or she has little need to deal with the concrete world at all but, instead, can use mental representations of reality and possibility (Inhelder & Piaget, 1958). Using a variety of tasks, such as the colored-liquids problem, which requires the child to discover what combination of four liquids produces a specific chemical reaction, Piaget found that, with increasing age, the child is better able to plan beforehand how she or he will attack a problem, carry out this planned investigation systematically, and monitor the results and evaluate various hypotheses until she or he arrives at the best explanation for the phenomena observed (Inhelder & Piaget, 1958; Lovell, 1961). So Piaget and his colleagues have also demonstrated that the child develops more sophisticated planning, regulatory, and evaluative processes, that is, more sophisticated metacomponents, with increasing age.

Case speaks of executive processes in terms of schematic evaluation. Fischer and Farrar (1987) referred to people as controlling sources of variations in their actions, including thoughts, which is clearly executive in nature. In Halford's theory, consistency checking is an executive evaluation process. In Pascual-Leone's theory, the I-operator, or the individual's ability to inhibit or interrupt activation of task-irrelevant structures, is also executive in nature. And most importantly, the E-operator is a repertoire of executive schemes and structures to monitor the mobilization of other operators. Demetriou also makes use of executive processes, such as the processing-load estimators, which judge how difficult a problem is with respect to the demands of the problem on mental resources, and success estimators, which judge the appropriateness and correctness of a solution that one is prepared to propose. Neither Halford nor Siegler directly discusses executive processes, but in Halford's theory, higher structures develop from lower structures by integration, and the integration would presumably involve executive processing in deciding what structures can be integrated. In Siegler's theory, the setting of criteria for going on to backup strategies and the decision as to which backup strategies to use would also be executive in nature. Moreover, deciding on the length of time one is willing to search for an associative solution would also require at least some executive processing.

Information processing becomes more nearly
exhaustive with age

There is a great deal of evidence in Piaget's research to support the claim that information processing becomes more nearly exhaustive with age. Much of this evidence lies in his descriptions of the development of the conservations. In numerous studies, Piaget and his colleagues demonstrated that as the child matures, his or her thought becomes increasingly decentered, that is, as the child develops, she or he learns to use all of the information at hand rather than allow his or her judgments to be inappropriately dominated by only a portion of this input (Elkind, 1961; Piaget, 1952a; Piaget & Inhelder, 1962). This increasing liberation from appearances resulting from more exhaustive processing enables the child to construct the conservations of the object's permanence, mass, weight, volume, and so on through transformations of appearance. Piaget also demonstrated that with age, the child becomes more able to generate all possible combinations of variables, to carry out these combinations systematically, and to compare their results. An older child is less likely to be satisfied with the first explanation of a phenomenon or solution to a problem that she or he happens upon. Instead, he or she is more likely to test thoroughly the solution or explanation for correctness; an older child is also more likely to look for alternative solutions or multiple causes of a phenomenon (Inhelder & Piaget, 1958; Lovell, 1961). The older the child, the more likely he or she is to go beyond his or her solution – classification, seriation, hypothesis, and so on – to account for future events and possibilities, not just present circumstances (Inhelder & Piaget, 1958, 1964; Piaget, 1952a). Thus, the research of Piaget and his colleagues definitely supports the conclusion that with increasing age, the child becomes more capable of exhaustively exploring reality and possibility.

In Case's theory, the representation of a problem situation and the strategy for solving the problem both become more nearly complete as the child grows older. In Fischer's theory, the development of successively more complex structures enables the child to see aspects of a problem that he or she could not see if only simple structures could be brought to bear upon the problem. The same would be true in Halford's theory. In Demetriou's theory, older children are better able to perceive and coordinate multiple dimensions, enabling them to process information more nearly exhaustively as they grow older. In Siegler's theory, with age, children acquire more backup strategies and so are better able to solve a problem if their initial associative attempt fails.

The ability to comprehend relations of successively higher orders develops with age

Piaget has demonstrated how as the child matures he or she becomes better able to comprehend higher order relations. By the middle to the end of the concrete operational period of development, the child has mastered the first-order relations involved in understanding classifications, seriations, causation, and so on (Inhelder & Piaget, 1958, 1964; Piaget, 1952a, 1952b, 1954, 1970, 1972). According to his theory, however, the child is not capable of performing second-order operations on the results of these first-order, concrete operations until she or he attains formal operational thought. Thus, the attainment of formal operational thought marks the attainment of the ability to perceive and construct relations between relations (Inhelder & Piaget, 1958; Piaget, 1972). As the child grows older, he or she is more likely to be able to perceive and to propose more abstract, higher order connections between phenomena. Older children are also more likely to look for higher order relations; Inhelder and Piaget (1958) found that older children are less likely to be content with a situation-specific task solution and are more likely to seek generalizable, abstract rules or principles when presented problems to solve. Thus, Piaget found that an increasing ability to handle higher order relations and more abstract forms of reasoning characterizes the child's development.

Case (1978) suggests that if there exist any periods beyond Piaget's four, then they might stem from the perception of success of the higher order relations. Fischer's successive structures are each of higher orders than the previous ones, and build on the earlier structures, as is the case for Halford's successively more complex mappings. Pascual-Leone's theory is more quantitative than qualitative in its account of development, but the understanding of higher order relations in his theory becomes possible as M-capacity increases. In Demetriou's theory, children are able to engage in more complex combinatorial and hypothesis formation activities with increasing age and to construct more complex mental models. Finally, in Siegler's (1978) theory, rules become successively more complex as children grow older.

Flexibility and use of strategy or information develops with age

Flexibility in strategy or information utilization means that an individual knows when to change strategy or transfer information and when not to do so. One often associates intellectual immaturity with inflexibility in strategy change and information transfer. But changing strategy when it is unnecessary or harmful or transferring information when the information is inappropriate to the use to which one puts it can be just as dangerous as failing to change or transfer. The locus of development, then, is not so much the ability to change as the ability to know when to change.

A major element of Piaget's (1972) definition of intellectual development is the progression toward greater mobility or flexibility of thought. Sensorimotor thought begins with rigid sensorimotor reflexes and gradually is extended through the development of the semiotic function to handle representational thought. As the child matures and constructs concrete operations, thought becomes reversible, and the child becomes capable of integrating these concrete operations into higher order systems providing still greater flexibility of thought. For example, Inhelder and Piaget (1964) found that the child first learns to construct rigid series and classes by trial and error and is unable to extend them to incorporate additional elements until later in development. As the child moves toward the development of formal operational thought, she or he becomes more capable of handling possibility as well as reality. Piaget proposes the development of two complex logical structures, the combinatorial system and the group of four transformations, to explain this ultimate flexibility of thought (Piaget, 1972; Piaget & Inhelder, 1969). Thus, as the child develops, his or her cognitive structures become more flexible and better able to assimilate reality. In task after task, Piaget reports that younger children tend to approach problems with preformed convictions about their solution, and they remain convinced about these stereotyped notions, even in the face of contradictory evidence. Older children are more likely to respond to findings that contradict, or that are not accounted for by, their explanation. Not only are older children more likely to be able to solve a larger variety of Piaget's tasks, but they are also more willing to look for alternative ways of reaching the same result (Inhelder & Piaget, 1958, 1964; Piaget, 1972; Piaget & Inhelder, 1962, 1969).

In Case's theory, greater flexibility results from more complex and varied possible representations of problem situations and strategies for solving problems. In Fischer's theory, increased flexibility is the result of increased numbers of structures and cognitive skills. In Halford's theory, the child becomes more flexible as the level at which she or he can view a problem becomes more complex. Flexibility in Demetriou's theory results from the ability to apply the various inquiring systems – Leibnizean, Lockean, Kantian, Dialectical/Hegelian, and Singerian – to problem situations. Pascual-Leone believes the brain to have considerable adaptive plasticity, and its plasticity increases as control structures develop. Finally, in Siegler's theory, flexibility results as one learns to encode and combine information in a greater variety of ways.

In sum, although Piaget and the neo-Piagetian theorists differ in their theories in some respects, all draw upon the epistemological metaphor, some explicitly, and some implicitly. They agree on some principles of development, such as those suggested here, all of which point to increasingly skillful acquisition and utilization of knowledge as children grow older.

Part IV

Theories of intelligence looking outward

9

The anthropological metaphor

The basic idea of the anthropological metaphor is what Irvine and Berry (1988) refer to as the law of cultural differentiation. It is based on a statement by Ferguson (1954): "Cultural factors prescribe what shall be learned and at what age; consequently different cultural environments lead to the development of different patterns of ability" (p. 121). It should be stated right off that not all psychologists believe in this law, and hence it might be useful to precede the discussion of the anthropological metaphor by a consideration of alternative models of how intelligence can be characterized cross-culturally.

In order to discuss cultural effects on intelligence and in order to understand how the anthropological metaphor functions, we need first to define culture. The definition used here will be that of Kroeber and Kluckhohn (1952), as quoted in Brislin, Lonner, and Thorndike (1973):

Culture consists of patterns, explicit and implicit, of and for behavior acquired and transmitted by symbols, constituting the distinctive achievement of human groups, including their embodiments in artifacts; the essential core of culture consists of traditional (i.e., historically derived and selected) ideas and especially their latest values; culture systems may, on the one hand, be considered as products of action, on the other as conditioning elements of further action. (pp. 4–5)

A framework for characterizing theories of intelligence as applied cross-culturally

Anthropological positions on intelligence could be viewed as falling in a continuum regarding their claims of relativity versus constancy in the nature of intelligence across cultures. However, such a continuum would not fully express the subtlety of the differences, as well as similarities, among positions. Although perhaps no schematic framework

can fully capture these subtleties, the one proposed here is an attempt
to take at least one step in this direction. An interesting and related
framework is proposed by Irvine (1984).

Figure 9.1 shows five different conceptions of how intelligence might
be conceived of cross-culturally. Of the different conceptions – Ia, Ib,
II, III, and IV – the first two are variants of each other, so that there are
really just four basic models. The models differ in two key respects:
whether or not there are cross-cultural differences in the instruments
used to measure intelligence and in the mental organization, or dimen-
sionalization by which performance on these instruments is accomplished. What, exactly, is an instrument and a dimension underlying
performance on the instrument? From the standpoint of the present
abstract framework, this question is left open, because it does not matter. For a psychometrically oriented psychologist, the instrument is
likely to be an ability test, and the dimension is likely to be a factor
(e.g., Irvine, 1979). For a Piagetian, the instrument is likely to be a
Piagetian task used to assess the developmental level of a schema (or
possibly a developmental period, depending upon the orientation being
pursued) and the dimension to be the actual schema or period (e.g.,
Dasen, 1977). For a cognitive psychologist, the instrument is likely
to be a cognitive task and the dimension a cognitive ability, such
as memory (e.g., Cole & Scribner, 1977). For a cultural relativist
who emphasizes the ecology of person–environment interactions, the

Figure 9.1. Four alternative models of the relationship between culture and
intelligence. In Model I*a*, intelligence is viewed as identical in Cultures A
and B. In Model I*b*, the locations of abilities in psychological space are the
same, but the axes for interpreting theses abilities are different. Thus it is the
interpretation of the psychological space of intelligence, rather than the space
itself, that varies across cultures. In Model II, the same abilities are involved
in Cultures A and B, but the locations of these abilities and hence their
interrelations are different in the two cultures. The differences in locations
may be affected by a change in the dimensionality of the space, or merely by
different placements of points in the same number of dimensions. The new
dimensions will almost inevitably have different interpretations from the old
ones. In Model III, the number and interpretation of dimensions are the same
in Cultures A and B, but different abilities enter into intelligence. The
abilities in Culture B may be a subset, overlapping set, or superset of those
in Culture A. In Model IV, both the abilities and the dimensions along which
these abilities fall differ between Cultures A and B. In terms of testing,
Models I and II allow the same tests between cultures (with adjustments for

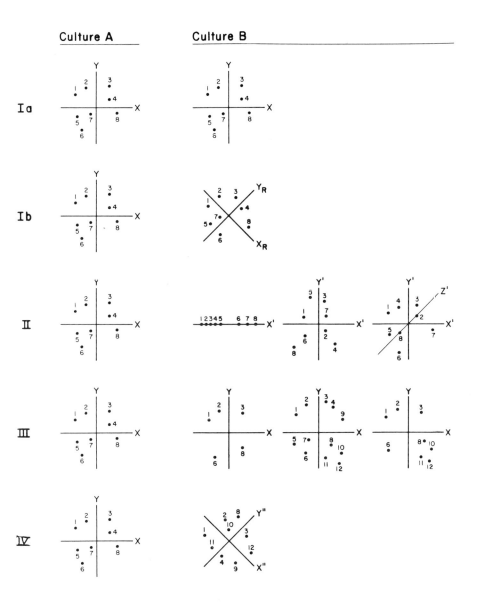

cultural variations), whereas Models III and IV do not. (From Sternberg, A triarchic view of intelligence in cross-cultural perspective; in S. H. Irvine & J. W. Berry, eds. *Human abilities in cultural context*. New York: Cambridge University Press, 1988.)

instrument is likely to be a measure of cognitive style, and the dimension, the style itself (e.g., Berry, 1974, 1976). For a contextualist emphasizing what Irvine (1979) referred to as *extra* hominem variables (rather than *intra* hominem variables, as in the four cases above), the instrument is likely to be a measure of environmental context, and the dimension is likely to be the kind of context being measured or otherwise assessed. For a Vygotskian, whose emphasis is likely to be on what Irvine refers to as *inter* hominem variables, the instrument is likely to be a measure of interpersonal interaction, and the dimension one of the kinds of interaction possible (e.g., Vygotsky, 1962, 1978). The fundamental point to be made is that the basic framework can be applied to a large number of different cross-cultural orientations, regardless of the theory or theories upon which they are based.

The four basic models simply represent the four possible combinations of difference and no difference on the two binary attributes of instrument and dimension. Consider an abstract characterization of each of these four basic models, as well as two examples of each, one psychometrically oriented and the other cognitively oriented.

Models Ia and Ib

In Model Ia, both the instruments and the dimensions into which these instruments are organized are the same across cultures. In Ib, the instruments are the same, and the dimensions are rotational variants of the dimensions in Ia. If one assumes a "Euclidean psychological space," these dimensions are intermappable with the ones in Ia, and what may be taken to represent a genuine difference between cultures instead represents a different way of organizing information on the part of the investigator rather than the investigatees! If one assumes any other metric for psychological space, however, Ib represents a genuine psychological difference in the subjects being studied.

Consider, for example, Model I from a psychometric orientation, such as that of Spearman (1927) or Thurstone (1938). Model Ia would refer to an identity across cultures in the tests and factors used to assess and understand intelligence, respectively. Model Ib would refer to an identity in tests but a set of factors that differ in orientation of axes across cultures. For instance, the same set of tests can yield a solution emphasizing a general factor if left unrotated (along the lines of Spearman's theory) but a solution emphasizing primary mental abilities if rotated to simple structure (along the lines of Thurstone's theory). From the present point of view, the differences in orientations of axes for the same set of tests represents a difference in emphasis rather than in psychological makeup (see Sternberg, 1977, 1984a). Although there might be disagreements as to which are more basic – the general factor or the group factors (a disagreement into which Spearman and Thurstone actually got themselves) – such disagreements seem to be empirically irresoluble, and possibly less than meaningful psychologically as well.

Consider, next, Model I from a cognitive orientation, such as that of Cole, Gay, Glick, and Sharp (1971). In this model, one can carry over the tasks used to assess cognitive abilities in one's own culture (although in translated form, of course, with suitable cultural adjustments). Moreover, it would be argued that the basic structure of the cognitive abilities being studied is the same – that members of other cultures perceive or remember things the same ways that members of one's own culture do. In Conceptualization Ia, one would choose to focus on the complete identity of tests and structures. In Model Ib, one might choose to focus on different aspects of the system, such as levels of processing in memory rather than separate functional memory stores, despite the fact that one could view separate memory stores as generating multiple levels of processing, both within and between memory stores.

The theoretical positions of Jensen (1982) and Eysenck (1982) represent Model-I types of positions. The argument is that the nature of intelligence is precisely the same cross-culturally and that this nature can be assessed identically without regard to culture. For Jensen, the assessment would consist of a measure of choice reaction time using a choice-box apparatus. For Eysenck, the assessment would consist of a rather complex measure of evoked potentials obtained in a resting state on the part of the examinee (see Hendrickson, 1982). Theorists such as Jensen and Eysenck would not hesitate to acknowledge differences in the ways in which intelligence is manifested in different cultures, but they would view any observed differences as ones at a surface structural level, rather than as ones at a more fundamental, deep structural level.

Model II

Model II represents a difference in dimensionality but no difference in instruments. The measures used to assess intelligence are the same across cultures, but the outcomes obtained from using these measures are structurally different as a function of the culture being investigated.

It is thus not possible directly to compare scores on the measures across cultures, because the scores mean different things as a function of the cultures in which they are administered.

Consider, for example, what Model II would look like from a psychometric perspective. The basic tests would be more or less the same across cultures, but the factor structures would be different. As a result, whereas direct comparisons of factor scores are possible under Model I, such comparisons are not possible under Model II. The factors may differ either in number (more or less intellectual differentiation in one culture than in another) or in identities for a given number of factors. In the latter case, the difference across cultures is not in intellectual differentiation, but in the way a given amount of differentiation is expressed mentally.

Model II would look similar from a cognitive point of view. Here, the cognitive tasks used would be essentially the same across cultures, but the results obtained by them would not be. One might find, for example, that the way in which information is organized in long-term memory differs from one culture to another (see, e.g., Wagner, 1978). Or one might find that susceptibility to perceptual illusions is so different between members of two cultures that one would be inclined to view the members of the two cultures as perceiving the objects in different ways, one of which leads to the illusion and the other of which does not (see, e.g., Segall, Campbell, & Herskovits, 1966). Such a conclusion would result not from small quantitative differences in amount of illusory perception, but from substantial qualitative differences, for example, in whether the illusion is even perceived in the first place.

Model III

Whereas in Model II the instruments of measurement are the same, but the dimensions are not, in Model III the dimensions of intellect are the same, but the instruments of measurement are not. On this view, measurement processes must be emic, that is, derived from within the context of the culture being studied, rather than from outside it. A test such as the Raven Progressive Matrices, however appropriate it may be within the context of North American or European culture, might be viewed as inappropriate for measuring general intelligence in certain African cultures, where testing paradigms using abstract geometric forms may be much more nonentrenched than in North American or European cultures.

From a psychometric point of view, Model III would employ different testing instruments as a function of the culture being studied, but the factor structure obtained from the instruments would be the same (within measurement error), regardless of the culture. For example, one might measure reasoning skills by asking individuals to classify objects indigenous to their environment or by asking them to seriate familiar objects. Such tests might measure the same skills as would the Raven Matrices in another culture.

From a cognitive point of view, different tasks might be used to assess the same skills. For example, Wagner (1978) had some individuals remember patterns of Oriental rugs and others remember pictures of everyday objects, such as a rooster and a fish. There was no evidence of a difference in memory structure, but the evidence of a lack of difference depended precisely upon using tests that were appropriate in their content for the individuals being studied. Using the same tests might have resulted in the false appearance of differences that were artifactual.

Model IV

In Model IV, both the instruments of measurement and the ensuing dimensions of intelligence are different as a function of the culture under investigation. This position obviously embraces the radical cultural-relativist position but also less extreme positions: For example, there may be substantial overlap in instruments and dimensions, even though they are nonidentical across cultures.

From a psychometric point of view, Model IV would result in the need to construct separate ability tests that are culturally appropriate. The result of testing would be a different factor space in each culture. From a cognitive point of view as well, different instruments would be needed in each culture, with resultant different models of cognitive functioning across cultures.

Psychologists who believe that the nature of intelligence is wholly or partly determined by what a culture values – that is, who subscribe to either Model II, III, or IV – are often called contextualists. Within this metaphor, at least four positions of varying degrees of extremity can be designated. I will organize the remainder of the chapter around these four positions.

Radical cultural relativism

Radical cultural relativism, proposed by Berry (1974), entails the rejection of assumed psychological universals across cultural systems and requires the generation from within each cultural system (emic approach) of any behavioral concept that is to be applied to it. Specifically, for the concept of *intelligence,* this position requires that indigenous notions of cognitive competence be the sole basis for the generation of cross-culturally valid descriptions and assessments of cognitive capacity.

In this approach, it is essential to understand how context shapes intelligence. In order to achieve this understanding, one first needs to understand just what context is.

Berry and Irvine (1986) have described four levels of context that can affect intelligence and the way it is evaluated. At the highest level is ecological context. This kind of context comprises all of the permanent or almost permanent characteristics that provide the backdrop for human action. It is the natural cultural habitat in which a person lives. The second kind of context is the experiential context, or the pattern of recurrent experiences within the ecological context that provides a basis for learning and development. When cross-cultural psychologists try to determine independent variables that affect behavior in a particular habitat, they are usually dealing with a level of experiential context. The third kind of context is the performance context, which is itself nested under the first two kinds. This context comprises the limited set of environmental circumstances that account for particular behaviors at specific points in space and time. Finally, nested under these three levels of context is the experimental context. This context comprises environmental characteristics manipulated by psychologists and others to elicit particular responses or test scores. Although this context should be nested within the three described above, it often is not, in which case the experimental context will not represent appropriately the conditions under which a given set of subjects lives.

Berry and Irvine suggest that paralleling each of the four contexts are four effects, with each one of the effects corresponding to one of the levels of context. First, achievements refer to complex, long-standing, and developed behavior patterns that constitute adaptive responses to an ecological context. Included within achievements are established and shared patterns of behaviors distributed over a cultural group. Second, behaviors are learned over time within the experiential context. Berry and Irvine include within behaviors abilities, traits, and attitudes that have been developed in particular cultural roles or that are acquired by specific training or education. Third, corresponding to the performance context are responses, which appear as an outcome of immediate stimulation or experience. In contrast to behaviors, they are not a function of long-term training, but rather appear as immediate outcomes of particular experiences. Fourth, corresponding to the experimental context is a set of scores, gleaned from psychological experimentation or testing of various kinds. The scores can be representative of responses, behaviors, and achievements to the extent that the experimental context is nested under the performance, experiential, and ecological ones.

Berry has done a great deal of research within the radical-relativistic approach that he proposes. Much of this research has focused on cognitive styles. For example, Berry (1974) conducted a study of ten subsistence-level groups to test the hypothesis that people in a hunting culture should possess good visual discrimination and spatial skills. Their cultures are expected to support the development of such skills through the presence of many geometric and spatial concepts. To test this hypothesis, Berry ranked cultural groups according to the importance of hunting to their existence and compared these rankings with test scores for perceptual discrimination and other related skills. For example, he used the embedded-figures test, often used as a measure of psychological differentiation. He found, as predicted, that the more central the role of hunting to a culture, the better the psychological test scores. He therefore concluded that "visual skills are developed to a degree predictable from an analysis of the ecological demands facing the group and the cultural aids developed by them" (Berry & Dasen, 1974, p. 140). In another study, Berry (1976) found that cultural groups that show a subsistence pattern of hunting and gathering, who are nomadic in settlement pattern, and who are loose in sociopolitical stratification are different in cognitive style from cultural groups that are agricultural, sedentary, and tight in stratification. Berry's work, therefore, does suggest that cognitive style can be influenced by the sociocultural patterns displayed in the environment.

The Berry–Irvine model of context and Berry's research on cognitive styles both provide interesting insights into how the anthropological metaphor can be effectively exploited in studying intelligence and its relation to context. However, it is debatable whether either the model of context or the research are truly as radically culturally relativistic as Berry seems to believe. Indeed, one could argue that his position is somewhat more flexible than the radical one. For example, the very notions of cognitive style, in general, and of psychological differentiation, in particular, are both ones that originated within the

Western psychological tradition. Witkin, for example, the originator of the notion of psychological differentiation (Witkin, Dyk, Faterson, Goodenough, & Karp, 1962), was himself a North American psychologist. Witkin's (1967) own approach to using cognitive styles for cross-cultural research was based on a theory that had originally been proposed for North Americans. Indeed, it was probably impossible to go into another culture totally freed of one's preconceptions about how the intellect is organized, structurally or functionally.

Another problem with this approach is that even if one accepts the notion of psychological differentiation as an emic one, there is now a strong body of evidence to suggest that psychological differentiation is not clearly distinguishable from spatial ability (MacLeod, Jackson, & Palmer, 1986). Hence, it might be that what was thought to be a construct that is uniquely suitable for the emic study of intelligence in other cultures amounts to nothing more than a reconceptualization in different terms of what in the past has been called spatial ability.

Yet another problem with this approach is that of determining causality. It is possible, of course, that culture gives rise to various cognitive styles. But it is also possible, at least to some extent, that people within various cultures have been selected over the years genetically for different patterns or levels of ability. It is also possible that psychological differentiation or other cognitive styles are really proxies for some other variable that is the one that is truly affected by culture. It is very difficult carefully to control all of the possible correlated variables that might be causally related to effects of context, with the result that what appears to be a causal variable might in fact be only a correlate.

Conditional comparativism

Most cross-cultural psychologists accept the conditional-comparative view of the relation between intelligence and culture. They believe it is possible to do some kind of conditional comparison in which an investigator sees how different cultures have organized experience to deal with a single activity, such as writing, reading, or computing. This comparison is possible, however, only if the investigator is in a position to assert that performance of the task or tasks under investigation is an achievement that is attained in every culture being compared.

This is the view taken by, among others, Michael Cole and his colleagues in the Laboratory of Comparative Human Cognition (1982). Cole and his colleagues assert that the radical cultural-relativists' position does not take into account the fact that cultures interact. They assume that learning is context specific, and that context-specific intellectual achievements are the primary basis for intellectual development. They state specifically that they do not deny the existence of any intercontextual generality of behavior. But they further state that such intercontextual generality is a secondary phenomenon and one in which the cultural organization of experience plays a major role. The idea in this view is that each experience within a cultural context can be linked to a specific task performance. There is no central process or general ability intervening between experiences and behaviors. Learning is viewed as primarily event or context specific. The extent to which learning in one context influences or even controls performance in another depends on just what the person learns in the first context, the similarity between the first context and the second, and exactly what happens in the second context, particularly with regard to the activity of other people in that context.

Cole and his colleagues give as an example of the specific learning model a study by Super (1976). Super found evidence that African infants sit and walk earlier than do their counterparts in the United States and Europe. But Super also found that mothers in the cultures he studied made a self-conscious effort to teach babies to sit and walk as early as possible. He concluded that the African infants are more advanced because they are specifically taught to sit and walk earlier and are encouraged through the provision of opportunities to practice these behaviors. Other motor behaviors were not more advanced. For example, infants found to sit and walk early were actually found to crawl later than did infants in the United States.

Cole and his colleagues attempt to counter suggestions that environments for children in other cultures are somehow deprived, thereby leading to generalized deficits. For example, Vernon (1969) has suggested that retarded practical intelligence may be the result of inadequate psychomotor experience in the absence of constructive play. McFie (1961) suggested that lack of toys and construction games encouraging accurate standards of orientation and imitation might lead to inferior perceptual abilities on the part of African infants.

Serpell (1979) designed a study to distinguish between a generalized perceptual-deficit hypothesis and a more context-specific hypothesis. He selected four perceptual tasks that, by a general-process interpretation, should result in lower performance for Zambian than for English children. A first task required mimicry of the position of an experimenter's hands. A second required drawing two-dimensional figures with pen and paper. A third required molding two-dimensional wire objects with strips of wire. And a fourth involved making copies of three-dimensional objects from clay. Serpell hypothesized that whereas the English children would have more experience with the two-dimensional representations of the pen and paper tasks, Zambian children would have more practice molding wire into two-dimensional objects. Serpell therefore predicted that English children would score higher on the pen-and-paper task but not as high on the wire-shaping task. For the Zambian children, Serpell made the opposite prediction. Serpell's data supported his prediction. The English children did better at the drawing task, but the Zambian children did better on the wire-shaping task. There were no significant differences between groups on the clay-modeling or hand-mimicry tasks.

Another study showing the effects of the kind of training one receives on how one performs was done by Greenfield (Bruner, Olver, & Greenfield, 1966). Greenfield and her colleagues studied children of the Wolof tribe in rural Senegal. Children received sets of pictures mounted on cards. The cards were designed so that within each of the sets, the child could form pairs based on various attributes – color, form, or function. A child was first asked to show the investigator which of the two pictures in a given set were most alike. The child was then asked why they are most alike. Subjects were selected from children in three populations: Bush children who had not attended school, children in school from the same town as the bush children, and school children living in Dakar, the capital of Senegal. Greenfield found that children who had attended school, regardless of where, performed much as American children did. Preference for color decreased sharply with grade, whereas preference for form and function increased. Moreover, an increasing proportion of older children justified their classifications in terms of superordinate categories. Children who had not attended school and lived in the bush responded quite differently. They showed a greater preference for color with increasing age and rarely justified responses in terms of superordinate language structure.

Even when the objects to be dealt with are familiar, the way they are typically used or thought about may influence how people perform with them. When Cole and his colleagues (Cole et al., 1971) asked adult Kpelle tribespeople to sort 20 familiar objects into "groups of things that belong together," their subjects separated the objects into functional groups (a knife with an orange, for example), as children in Western societies do. The researchers had expected to see taxonomic groupings (tools and foods, for example) from these adults, because Western adults typically sort taxonomically. The Kpelle proved to be perfectly capable of taxonomic sorting: When the subjects were asked specifically to sort the objects the way a stupid person would do it, they immediately arranged them into neat piles of tools, foods, clothing, and utensils. Taxonomic sorting of these objects seemed stupid to the Kpelle because it was inconsistent with the way they deal with these objects in everyday life (i.e., functionally). In another classification task, the Kpelle sorted leaves taxonomically (as either "tree" leaves or "vine" leaves) with ease. In this case, the taxonomic approach seemed completely appropriate – as farmers, the Kpelle are frequently called upon to make such discriminations – hence the adoption of this sorting strategy.

The Kpelle seem to view certain kinds of problems holistically, which inhibits the transfer of problem solving skills to other contexts that appear to be dissimilar. Cole et al. (1971) showed that the Kpelle were completely stymied by a problem in inferential combination that utilized an unfamiliar apparatus but successfully solved an analogous problem that involved familiar objects. The American apparatus consisted of a box with three compartments. When a button was pushed on one of the compartment doors, a marble would be released. Pushing a button on a second door resulted in the release of a ball bearing. Insertion of a marble into a hole in the third door led to the release of a piece of candy. Even though the Kpelle learned how to obtain the item from each compartment individually, they were almost always unable to figure out how to start with nothing and end up with a piece of candy (i.e., by pushing the button to get the marble and then inserting the marble into the hole in the other door). The second version of the problem was constructed so as to require the identical steps for its solution. In this case, the candy was in a box locked with a red key. Each of two nearby matchboxes contained a key; one key was red, the other, black. To solve this problem, the red key had to be removed from its matchbox and used to unlock the box containing the candy. After learning what the individual containers held, nearly all the Kpelle subjects solved this problem spontaneously. The lack of transfer to the American version of the problem can be attributed to the subjects' failure to compare the problems on a point-by-point basis. Holistically viewed, the American version seemed to be a totally new and different problem.

Another example of different strategies affecting task performance comes from Kearins's (1981) study of visuospatial memory in aboriginal and Anglo-Australian children. Aboriginals have been shown to remember spatial displays better than Anglo-Australians, an ability sometimes explained as adaptive for the survival of a nomadic people. Kearins sought to identify the behavioral aspects of this ability by examining how the two groups went about remembering – and then reproducing – the arrangement of items in a matrix. During the 30-sec observation period, the Anglo-Australians typically moved around the three-dimensional display, picking up the objects and naming them. The aboriginals, however, chose a single position from which to view the display and then sat motionless before it, apparently trying to "burn" the image of the matrix into their minds. In reproducing the matrix, the Anglo-Australians would replace the first few items very quickly, then proceeded much more slowly, often moving items they had already placed. The aboriginals worked at a more constant pace, deliberating before placing each item and rarely moving one that had been positioned. When asked how they had performed the task, many Anglo-Australians mentioned verbal strategies, whereas the aboriginals showed a reliance on their visual memory, saying they remembered the "look" of the matrix. Clearly, each group tended to use strategies that were appropriate for the tasks most familiar to them: The Anglo-Australians used verbal (school-appropriate) strategies, and the aboriginals used visual (desert nomad-appropriate) strategies.

Cross-cultural studies of classification, categorization, and problem solving behavior illustrate the effects of *selective encoding, selective combination,* and *selective comparison.* Selective encoding is at issue in studies of attribute preference in classification tasks. In these tasks, a subject may be shown a red triangle, a blue triangle, and a red square, and asked which two things belong together. Western literature shows a consistent developmental trend, such that very young children choose color as the decisive (or relevant) stimulus attribute, whereas older children shift their preference to form by about age 5 (see Suchman & Trabasso, 1966). Cross-cultural studies, however, often fail to show this color-to-form shift (Cole et al., 1971). Cole and Scribner (1974) suggest that the preference for form versus color may be linked to the development of literacy (in which alphabetic forms acquire tremendous importance), which differs widely across cultures.

Luria (1976) provides an illustration of selective combination in a categorization task. Shown a hammer, a saw, a log, and a hatchet, an illiterate central Asian peasant was asked which three items were similar. He insisted that all four fit together, even when the interviewer suggested that the concept "tool" could be used for the hammer, saw, and hatchet, but not for the log. The subject in this instance combined the features of the four items that were relevant in terms of his culture and arrived at a functional or situational concept (perhaps one of the "things you need to build a hut"). In his failure to combine the "instrumental" features of the tools selectively into a concept that excluded the log, however, the subject was not performing intelligently – at least, from the perspective of the experimenter's culture.

In many of Luria's studies, the unschooled peasants have great difficulty in solving the problems given them. Often, they appear to be thrown off by an apparent discrepancy between the terms of the problem and what they know to be true. For example, take one of the math problems: "From Shakhimardan to Vuadil it is three hours on foot, while to Fergana it is six hours. How much time does it take to go on foot from Vuadil to Fergana?" The subject's response to this problem was, "No, it's six hours from Vuadil to Shakhimardan. You're wrong . . . it's far and you wouldn't get there in three hours" (Luria, 1976, p. 129). In terms of selective comparison, performance suffered precisely because the subject was comparing incoming data to what he knew about his world, which was irrelevant to the solution of the problem. As Luria put it, the computation could readily have been performed, but the condition of the problem was not accepted.

The attitude toward children taken by the Kaluli of Papua New Guinea is very different from that of middle-class Americans. The Kaluli perceive their infants as "soft" or helpless and without understanding. According to Ochs and Schiefflin (1982), caregivers view their responsibility toward children as one of helping them "harden" into mature members of their society. Because everyday life in Kaluli culture is "overtly focused around verbal interaction" (Ochs & Schiefflin, p. 24), language learning is an important aspect of "hardening." The speech of caregivers around Kaluli infants differs in several ways from American "motherese."

Although Kaluli mothers explicitly teach their children specific forms (through the pointed use of a special word meaning, for example, "Say it like this"), they do not expand upon their children's utterances or guess about their meaning. The Kaluli avoid interpreting the utterances of others, saying, "One cannot know what another thinks or feels" (Ochs & Schiefflin, p. 27). One result of this tendency is that "the responsibility for clear expression is with the speaker" (Ochs & Schiefflin, p. 33), even when the speaker is a child of two. The need for Kaluli children to adapt to their social and verbal environment is demonstrated in this striking departure from earlier (middle-class American) findings about motherese (see Brown & Bellugi, 1964; Cazden, 1965), which emphasized the willingness of mothers to accommodate to their children through "rich interpretation."

The Kaluli children's need to adapt goes beyond making themselves clear; they must extract meaning from the utterances of people who are not simplifying their vocabulary or syntactic forms for the children's sake, another difference between Kaluli and middle-class American motherese. Whereas American mothers typically attempt to enhance their communication with young children by repeating themselves (sometimes with variation) and by using a simplified lexicon, Kaluli mothers believe that doing so would result in the acquisition of a babyish language – clearly a counterproductive move in the effort to "harden" the child (Ochs & Schiefflin, p. 33). From these and other ways of socializing their children emerges a "pattern for fitting (or pushing) the child into the situation rather than changing the situation to meet the interests or abilities of the child" (Ochs & Schiefflin, p. 32). This is dramatic evidence of the extent to which a child may be required to adapt in being socialized into a way of life.

The linguistic socialization of children in Western Samoa bears some resemblances to Kaluli upbringing: Children are initially talked *about*, rather than *to*, the conversation around them tends to involve many people, and they are responsible for expressing themselves clearly to their elders. The underlying belief systems that lead to these surface manifestations are quite different, however. Whereas the Kaluli are an egalitarian people, the Samoans live in a rigidly stratified society: Samoan children are responsible for making themselves clear, not because interpretation is discouraged, but because they are lower ranking members of society. If a high-ranking Samoan says something ambiguous or unintelligible, lower ranking hearers must decide upon the meaning for themselves. Like the Kaluli, the Samoans encourage their children to repeat forms as they are presented by caregivers, but the intent is to teach children memorization skills so that they can begin serving as verbatim messengers (Ochs & Schiefflin, p. 41).

The stratification of Samoan society is reflected in caretaking practices, as well. Normally, a child will be cared for by a number of people of differing social rank, ranging from older siblings through unmarried aunts to parents. Interpretation of the infant's gestures and vocalizations typically filters up through the hierarchy from lowest- to highest-ranking caregiver, with subsequent instructions filtering back down to the lowest-ranking caregiver (as in Western military protocol). This system has two important consequences for language learners: First, if a message, such as "Pesio's hungry again," is repeated by two or three caregivers on its way to the child's mother, Pesio will have been exposed more often to the phrase in a single context and will be likely to learn its meaning quickly, as well as the fact that the meaning is maintained in the words even though the voices are different. Second, children learn the "chain of command" quickly, and soon begin to voice their requests directly to the highest-ranking person present, without necessarily expecting the response to come from that person (Ochs & Schieifflin, p. 39). This knowledge of the appropriate routing of utterances is vital to becoming a viable member of the hierarchical Samoan society. In fact, the stratification of Samoan society, combined with the belief that children are naturally persons of lower rank, encapsulates the Samoan attitude toward childcare and development. In teaching children to fit into the hierarchy and to interact socially with people of various ranks, "the Samoan way is to encourage the child to meet the needs of the situation, i.e., to notice others, listen to them, and adapt one's own speech to their particular status and needs" (Ochs & Schieifflin, p. 41).

Cultural differences in adaptation to the environment certainly apply to domains other than the language socialization emphasized in our ethnographic examples. For example, Berry (1971) has found that individuals from low food-accumulating societies (in particular, the Eskimo) tend to be superior on spatial ability tests and measures of cognitive differentiation to individuals from high food-accumulating societies (in particular, the Temne). People in the former kind of societies typically depend on hunting and fishing for their food and hence need, from an early age, to develop their spatial skills as fully as possible. People in the latter kind of societies are not as dependent on spatial skills and hence have less need to develop them.

Another culture in which the development of spatial skills is highly adaptive is that of the Puluwat, who inhabit the Caroline Islands in the South Pacific. Those individuals who are able to master knowledge domains including wind and weather, ocean currents, and movements of the stars, and to integrate this knowledge with mental maps of the islands, become navigators and are highly respected in their world (Gladwin, 1970).

Cole and Scribner (1974) give many examples of tasks in which people with different cultural upbringings perform the tasks differently. The bottom line is that in order to match a task from one culture to another and thereby make it appropriate in both cultures, the tasks must be made comparable, not only in terms of the content of the objects or the words to be manipulated, but also in terms of the extent to which the coherence of structure of the materials is made manifest to the subjects. Even the situation of testing can have a major effect on test performance.

My goal here is not to review empirical studies conducted under the conditional-comparative approach, but rather to illustrate how comparisons may be possible, if special care is taken to ensure that the task is truly comparable for the members of one culture and another. It is important to realize that there can never be any guarantee of comparability. Hence, comparisons must always be guarded. But the suggestion of work within this tradition is that there are commonalities across cultures in the nature of intelligence. What is hard is to design studies explicitly to find them.

Dualism

A number of psychologists have suggested essentially dualistic models that incorporate, although may not rely exclusively upon, the anthropological metaphor. Theorists such as Keating (1984), Jenkins (1979), Baltes, Dittmann-Kohli, and Dixon (1984), and Charlesworth (1979) have in one way or another attempted to incorporate both cognitive and contextual elements into their models of intelligence. Although they discuss how cognition and context work together, I believe that none of these theorists have fully integrated the two. Neither have I (Sternberg, 1985a). Consider some of the ways in which these psychologists have attempted to take into account both cognition and culture.

In his ethological approach to studying intelligence, Charlesworth has focused on what he refers to as the "other part" of intelligence – intelligent behavior as it occurs in everyday life rather than in test situations – and how these situations may be related to developmental changes (Charlesworth, 1979). Keating (1984), in his research, has studied how intelligence develops through a number of cognitive psychological paradigms but more recently has suggested that these paradigms are more or less vacuous when it comes to understanding how cognition interacts with culture. He suggests that we need to consider contextual as well as cognitive factors. He does not quite show how to integrate them. Baltes (e.g., Dixon & Baltes, 1986) argues that it is necessary to look at both the mechanics and the pragmatics of intelligence. In his early work, he studied how aging affects the mechanics of intelligence and how training can be used to combat aging effects. More recently, he has shifted his focus to studying context. For example, his studies of wisdom (Baltes & Smith, 1990) suggest that wisdom cannot be understood outside the context of the environment in which one develops. However, it is not clear in Baltes's work how the mechanics and pragmatics of intelligence interact. In my own work (e.g., Sternberg, 1985a), I speak of the componential and contextual subtheories of intelligence and suggest that the components of intelligence can be understood only through the context in which they are applied. I suggest that they are applied to various contexts for the purposes of adaptation to, selection of, and shaping of environments. But the theory does not specify what is adaptive where or when, nor does it specify how one knows which components to call up within a given context. Again, there is an attempt to combine elements of a computational theory with elements of an anthropological one, but the combination is not complete.

Universalism

Universalism can take many forms. Its primary tenet is that there are significant commonalities in the nature of intelligence and of the mind in general across cultures. For example, Levi-Strauss (1966) argued that there are no differences between how the mind works in one culture and how it works in another culture, or even how it works from one time to another. Primitive and Western systems of thinking merely represent different ways by which people try to understand nature and make it susceptible to rational inquiry. According to Levi-Strauss, cultures do not differ in their levels of mental development. All seek knowledge about the universe. All seek to order and systematize. What differs across cultures is the content of thought. For example, one culture might differ from another in the attributes used to form classes. Primitive systems of classification are more likely to be based on attributes that are readily perceived or otherwise experienced. Modern scientific classification systems rely on attributes that are inferred from relations in the structures of objects. Thus, structurally there are no differences among cultures. What differs is content.

Levi-Strauss's view may seem tame today, but it rose from a tradition in which many believed that cultures differed in the level of thinking that they obtained. Herbert Spencer (1886), for example, cited by the Laboratory of Comparative Human Cognition (1982), stated:

> During early stages of human progress, the circumstances under which wandering families live, furnish experiences comparatively limited in their numbers and kinds; and consequently there can be no considerable exercise of faculty which takes cognizance of the *general truth* displayed throughout many special truths. . . . In a like manner it is clear that only after there have been received many experiences which differ in their kinds but present some relation in common, can the first step be taken towards the conception of a truth higher in generality than these different experiences themselves. . . . General ideas can arise only as fast as social conditions render experiences more multitudinous and varied. (pp. 521–2)

Cole and his colleagues view this and other positions as suggesting (incorrectly) that cultures vary in their level on an evolutionary scale, that the level of culture reflects the level of development in the mind, and that the thinking of adults evolves out of the thinking of children.

A major figure in the universalistic stance in psychology has been Jean Piaget. Piaget proposed a theory of intellectual development that has been one of the most influential theories in all of psychology. Piaget (1966) has considered the issue of the cross-cultural application of his theory.

Piaget suggested that there are four factors that need to be considered in development and that the main advantage of cross-cultural studies is to allow some understanding of these factors, particularly the association between sociocultural and individual ones. The four factors are biological ones, equilibration ones, social factors of interpersonal coordination, and factors of educational and cultural transmission.

According to Piaget, biological factors owe nothing to society. He believed that the periods of development in his system were biologically determined. He suggested that inversions in the sequence of stages or major modifications in their characteristics would pose a major problem for his theory. Piaget also believed equilibration factors to be general and independent of social environment. Thus, some balance between assimilation and accommodation should be observed in every culture, and the absence of such an observation would again pose a problem for his theory. Piaget was interested in social factors because he believed that equilibration exists not only within the individual but across individuals within the society. Again, then, cross-cultural studies would serve as a basis for verifying his theory. Finally, if differences in education across cultures resulted in differences in stages or in the equilibration process, that, too, would be evidence against Piaget's theory.

Piaget (1966) cites an unpublished study by Mohseni in Teheran that he views as providing support for his theory, but at the same time providing some suggestions as to how intelligence develops differently across cultures. The three main results of the study, done with children ranging in age from 5 to 10 years, were, first, that on the whole, the same stages are found in both city and country children in Teheran as in Geneva; that there is a systematic delay of two to three years for operational tests between country and city children, but that there is no difference between the city children (from Teheran) and children in Europe; and that the delay is greater for performance tests than for operational tests. Piaget (1966) suggests that in numerous cultures, adult thinking may not proceed beyond the level of concrete operations, but in all cultures, the order of development is the same, whether or not the stages are achieved at the same age.

Perhaps the main exponent of Piagetian psychology from a cross-cultural point of view has been Pierre Dasen. For example, Dasen (1974) reports the study of how the four factors discussed by Piaget – biological, equilibration, social, educational – influence the intellectual development of Australian aborigines. He concludes that his research does not enable him definitely to assess the relative importance of any one of these factors. He found that concepts develop through the same periods and subperiods both in Europe and among the aborigines. Hence, he could conclude that biological and equilibration factors are universal to at least some extent. At the same time, he found an extremely slow rate of development among the aborigines, suggesting that social and cultural factors are more important for cognitive development than Piaget had hypothesized. He found that degree of contact with Europeans was an important mediator of development, suggesting the particular importance of Piaget's fourth factor, namely, educational and cultural transmission. At the same time, he suggested that malnutrition may possibly slow down development.

Dasen (1972) reviewed and summarized a wide variety of cross-cultural studies based upon a Piagetian point of view. Other summaries have been done by Goodnow (1969), Jahoda (1970), and LeVine (1970).

According to Dasen, most cross-cultural studies motivated by the work of Piaget have asked whether cognitive development in non-Western cultures follows the same succession of periods as described by Piaget for Western children. A further question has been whether these periods appear at approximately the same ages across cultures.

Some studies have been done on sensorimotor intelligence. For example, Paraskevopoulos and Hunt (1971) studied the development of infants in Athens, Teheran, and Israel using the Uzgriris and Hunt (1966) scales. Some studies have also been done on formal operations. Goodnow (1962), for example, found that for tasks using combinations and permutations, Chinese children with English schooling performed as well as or better than Europeans, whereas children with Chinese schooling or of very low income families did somewhat worse than did European children. Were (1968) administered verbal and logical tests of formal operations to children of ages 14 to 16 in Guinea. He failed to find any signs of formal thought among the children in these age groups. But most of the studies that have been done cross-culturally have looked at children who are concrete operational. The major question has dealt with the passage from the preoperational to the concrete operational.

All of these studies have reported that concrete operations are attained by children in all cultures. The question of interest is the extent to which these operations are attained and the age at which they are attained. Dasen suggests that there are four possible relations between the concrete operational attainments of children in Western cultures versus those in other cultures. A first possibility is that children in other cultures develop at the same rate and to the same asymptote as children in European cultures. A second possibility is that children in other cultures develop the same operations, but earlier. A third possibility is that the children in other cultures develop the same operations, but more slowly. And a fourth possibility is that children in other cultures develop operations more slowly and also never reach the same asymptote as do children in Western cultures. There is evidence to support each of these positions, with the evidence depending upon the investigator, the tasks used, and the culture in which the studies have been done.

For example, Price-Williams (1961) found no difference between the Tiv children of central Nigeria and European children in the ages at which they acquired conservation of both continuous and discontinuous quantities. Tuddenham (1968, 1970) found that Asian-American children in California were superior to white children on a set of concrete operational tests.

Perhaps the most typical finding has been that children in other cultures attain the same level of performance as children in Western European culture, but more slowly. For example, the Tiv children tested by Price-Williams (1962) lagged slightly behind European children in classification. Bovet (1968, 1971) found that illiterate Algerian children were slower to achieve conservation of liquid, speed, and time than were typical Western subjects. Vernon (1969) found that Kampala boys in Uganda scored lower than English ones on a variety of types of Piagetian items. The biggest difference was in conservation tasks. Vernon also found that Eskimo and Canadian Indians were weak relative to English children on a variety of conservation tasks.

A few studies have found that in some cultures, even older children do not seem fully to reach concrete operational performance. For example, Prince (1968, 1969) found that some New Guinean children never achieved all kinds of conservation. Bovet (1973) found that even some adults seem to have difficulty differentiating speed and time. Peluffo (1967) found only 20 percent of adults in Sardinia conserved volume. Of course, it is difficult in these studies to know whether the problem was in the subjects or in the testing procedures, so that any conclusions to be drawn have to be very tentative ones.

Conclusion

Use of the anthropological metaphor has prevented theory and research on intelligence from being wholly ethnocentric with respect to North American and Western European cultural groups. In this chapter, I have summarized a small sample of the theory and research that shows different theoretical approaches that are possible within the general anthropological metaphor. There is a tendency for many people to believe that members of all other cultures end up doing what members of Western cultures do, only not as well. It is important to remember that this is not always the case. It has been found, for example, that African infants show superior early sensorimotor development relative to Western infants (E. E. Werner, 1972), at least with respect to some aspects of sensorimotor functioning. Gerber (1956, 1960) found that Baganda neonates are superior to Western ones in sensorimotor skills, and this finding has been replicated and extended by Ainsworth (1967) and by Kilbride, Robbins, and Kilbride (1970). In the Kilbride et al. study, 75 percent of the sample scored at least one standard deviation above the average on the Bayley scales. Although the immediacy of this superiority at birth suggests at least some genetic component to the difference, there appears also to be an environmental component that may derive from high levels of stimulation and low levels of stress among Baganda mothers during pregnancy and from high levels of activity and stimulation for the infants upon birth (Munroe & Munroe, 1957; see also Segall, 1979).

Schooling appears to make a large difference in the pattern of developed abilities. Goodnow and Bethon (1966), for example, found that unschooled 11-year-old Chinese boys performed as well as American children of average IQ on all tasks except those requiring mental transformations (in the case of this study, combinatorial reasoning). Schooling appears to develop this skill in a possibly unique way, leaving those without schooling behind in this skill.

In order to understand the interaction between adaptation and cultural context, one must go beyond strictly cognitive indices and observe the way other, noncognitive aspects of a culture operate. An interesting analysis of this kind has been performed by Sinha (1983) for Indian populations. Consider just a subset of the factors that Sinha suggests may penalize Indians exposed to standard Western tests of intelligence.

1. *Response set.* Western culture emphasizes decisiveness and making up one's mind. If a Westerner were to be given the choice "I'm not sure" or "I can't decide," he or she would know that this would not be an answer that generates points, at least for most cognitive item types. But Indians are much more drawn to such responses than are others. Obviously, indecisiveness will not benefit one on a standard intelligence test. There may be times in anyone's life, however, when an indecisive response may be more adaptive than an incorrect or hastily conceived decision.

2. *Courtesy.* Indians will often show a "courtesy effect" (Doob, 1968; Sinha, 1977), giving an interviewer or tester the responses that the subject thinks are desired. In the United States, retarded children often show this same tendency (Zigler, 1971) (which is perhaps a sad commentary on the role of courtesy in U.S. culture!).

3. *Cultural gap.* In some rural areas, subjects may be suspicious or evasive, and inhibited in responding. This tendency, like the tendency toward courtesy, directs attention away from the cognitive demands of the task and toward task-irrelevant thought and action that is likely to reduce a subject's score.

4. *Communication failures.* The examiner may simply not understand or misunderstand the response the examinee is trying to convey. Most often, failure in communication puts the examinee at a disadvantage, because it is natural for the examiner to attribute blame for the breakdown in communication to a lack of cognitive skill in the examinee rather than in him or herself. One has only to look at the way North Americans treat foreigners whose first language is not English to see where the attribution of blame is directed. People in the United States, in particular, are wont to believe that foreigners are stupid because of their inability to communicate effectively (in English, of course). The Americans can rarely speak the language of the visitor, or if they do, speak it more poorly than the visitor speaks the English language.

Sinha's work, as well as that of many others, makes clear that there is a substantial gap between intelligence as it is manifested in one's culture and intelligence as it is manifested in a testing situation. Adaptive intelligence is naturally exhibited in Berry's (1983) ecological and experiential contexts. The gap between these contexts and the experimental one will be differentially large for individuals with differing backgrounds and will be greatest for those for whom the experimental context is most foreign. Predictably, such individuals will be ones whose cultures differ most from those of the experimenters coming into a given culture to do research. Yet test scores take little or no account of the differential gap for different groups of people.

Recent anthropologically oriented work within the United States shows how tenuous conclusions about cultural differences can be. For example, Lave (1988) has found that housewives who can easily perform calculations at the supermarket to determine which of two products is a better buy may have difficulty when taking arithmetical computation tests in pencil-and-paper format, even if these computation tests require the same operations as the housewives would perform at the supermarket. Ceci and Liker (1986) have found that adults who can make complex calculations at a race track in order to decide which of several horses would be the best bet may have very low IQs and perform dismally on standardized tests, despite their superior performance quantitatively at the race track. Scribner (1984) has found that workers in a milk-packing plant can devise complex schemes to make their jobs easier, despite the fact that they are in low entry-level jobs that would be viewed from the outside as not requiring much intelligence. Ceci and Bronfenbrenner (1985) have found that the way children monitor time in determining when to take cupcakes out of the oven can be totally different in a home versus an experimental laboratory setting. The general point is that any conclusions we draw must take into account Irvine and Berry's (1988) admonition that an experimental context may not be embedded in the normal context of human functioning. Thus, the anthropological metaphor is a valuable one, but we must remember that the conclusions from studies conducted under it must be subject to careful scrutiny.

10

The sociological metaphor

The sociological metaphor differs only subtly from the anthropological one. Whereas the anthropological metaphor deals with the effects of enculturation, the sociological metaphor deals with the effects of socialization. Adherents to the anthropological metaphor concern themselves primarily with how culture affects intelligence. They deal with the question of whether intelligence is the same thing across cultures and, if it is not, how it is different. Adherents to the sociological metaphor care about cultural effects but tend to be less interested in the question of how intelligence differs from one culture to another than in the question of how socialization within any culture affects the development of intelligence. Although they may look at socialization across cultures, their main interest is in the socialization process itself, and especially how it is similar across cultures even though the content of the socialization may vary quite substantially across cultures (or subcultures). In other words, socialization may affect children in various cultures through quite comparable mechanisms (the main concern of the sociological metaphor), even though the content of the socialization may differ quite radically from one culture or subculture to another (the main concern of the anthropological metaphor).

In this chapter, I will consider the sociological view, and especially the work of three major scholars. The first, Lev Vygotsky, a Russian psychologist (now deceased), might be viewed as the father of the sociological approach. The second, Reuven Feuerstein, an Israeli psychologist, developed views very similar to some of Vygotsky's, although independently. Moreover, his theory is substantially more detailed than Vygotsky's. The third scholar is an ethnographer, Shirley Brice Heath. Heath is not usually thought of as a theorist of intelligence. In fact, I doubt that she has ever been thought of this way. But I believe that she has done some of the most important work on the development of intelligence under the sociological metaphor and hence I will discuss her views.

Lev Vygotsky and the theory of internalization

Lev Semyonovitch Vygotsky lived only 38 years. Yet he is arguably the greatest Russian psychologist of all time and one of the greatest psychologists of any country. I believe that Vygotsky made three signal contributions to the theory of intelligence: the theory of internalization, the theory of the convergence of speech and practical activity, and the zone of potential development.

The theory of internalization

In his theory of internalization, Vygotsky turned the views of Piaget on their head. Although Piaget and Vygotsky were both interactionists, they were ones who believed that individual intelligence started at essentially opposite points. Piaget believed that intelligence matured from the inside and directed itself outward. Vygotsky, in contrast, believed that intelligence begins in the social environment and directs itself inward. The process of the direction of intelligence from the outside to the inside is what Vygotsky refers to as *internalization*.

Internalization is the internal reconstruction of an external operation. The basic notion is that we observe those in the social environment around us acting in certain ways and we internalize their actions so that they become a part of ourselves. For example, we might learn how to teach young children by watching how our parents teach us, or we might learn how to speak or ride a bicycle or even read a book by watching how others do it. Vygotsky (1978) gives as an example of internalization the development of pointing. He suggests that initially, pointing is nothing more than an unsuccessful attempt to grasp something. The child attempts to grasp an object beyond his reach and, initially, is likely to fail. When the mother sees the child attempting to grasp an object, she comes to his aid and is likely to point to the object. He thereby learns to do the same. Thus, the child's unsuccessful attempt engenders a reaction from the mother or some other individual, which leads to his being able to perform that action. Note that it is the social mediation, rather than the object itself, that provides the basis for the child's learning to point.

Vygotsky suggests that the process of internalization consists of three stages, or transformations:

1. "An operation that initially represents an external activity is reconstructed and begins to occur internally" (Vygotsky, 1978, pp. 56–57).

Thus, the child acts in a way that imitates the person in the social environment, often the mother, and thereby begins to be able to do what she can do.

2. "An interpersonal process is transformed into an intrapersonal one" (p. 57). What starts on the social level is transferred to the individual level. In other words, what happens inside the person first happens between people. Thus, intelligence begins not inside the head, but in the relations between people.

3. "The transformation of an interpersonal process into an intrapersonal one is the result of a long series of developmental events" (p. 57). Internalization does not occur, for the most part, simply as the result of mimicry of a single action. Rather, it is a process that continues over time. At first, the action may be imperfectly imitated or its meaning not quite understood. Moreover, even after an action is internalized, its linkage to other internalized acts may take quite some time. Some functions are never internalized: They remain forever as external signs. According to Vygotsky, the internalization of socially based and historically developed activities is what distinguishes humans from animals. It is the qualitative difference between human and animal intelligence.

The convergence of speech and practical activity

Vygotsky observed that the study of tool use has taken place, for the most part, in isolation from the study of sign use. Similarly, the origin and development of speech is often treated as independent of the organization of a child's practical activities. Psychologists, according to Vygotsky, preferred to study the use of signs (such as language) as an example of pure intellect, and not as an example of practical activity. But Vygotsky suggested that "the most significant moment in the course of intellectual development, which gives birth to the purely human forms of practical and abstract intelligence, occurs when speech and practical activity, two previously completely independent lines of development, converge" (p. 24).

For Vygotsky, then, children's intelligence is somewhat similar to that of animals, and especially apes, right up to the point that speech and practical activity come together. And it is when they come together that children undergo a qualitative leap and begin truly to achieve mastery of the symbolic as well as the actual environment. To Vygotsky, a child's speech is as important as action in attaining goals. As children develop, speech and action become part of one and the same complex psychological function, with the goal of solving problems that the child confronts. The more complex the solution required by the problem, the more important, in general, speech will be.

The zone of potential development

Probably Vygotsky's most exciting contribution to the psychology of intelligence is his notion of the zone of potential (or proximal) development. Consider a situation posed by Vygotsky.

Vygotsky asked the reader to consider the investigation of two children whose chronological age is 10 years and whose mental age is 8 years. He asks the question of whether one can characterize them as being of the same age mentally. He responds to his own question, "Of course." But he asks the reader to consider what this answer means. It means that both children can deal with tasks up to the degree of difficulty characteristic of 8-year-olds. One could say that the actual developmental level of the two children is the same. Stated in another way, they have completed the same amount of mental development. But, Vygotsky asks, can one thereby ascertain that the subsequent course of their mental development and their school learning will be the same, because both depend on their intellect? Naturally, there are nonintellectual factors that may influence their school learning or their mental development. But for the time being, consider these nonintellectual factors as being comparable for the two children. Most people would assume that one could make comparable predictions about each of the children, and indeed, the whole predictive use of intelligence testing in the United States is based on this assumption. Vygotsky argues that this view is incorrect.

Suppose that a teacher-examiner provides guided assistance to each of the two children in order to help them solve a given problem. It turns out that with this guided assistance, the first child can deal with problems up to the level of a 12-year-old, whereas the second child can only deal with problems up to the level of a 9-year-old. Would we still want to conclude the two children are mentally the same? Vygotsky suggests that we would not, for the first child has been shown to be better able to profit from instruction than the second child. Hence, it is reasonable to suppose that with regard to future as opposed to past development, the first child is superior to the second child and has a better prognosis. The difference between mental age 12 and mental age 8, for the first child, or between mental age 9 and mental age 8, for the second child, is what Vygotsky refers to as the zone of potential (or proximal) development. "It is the distance between the actual developmental level as determined by independent problem solving and the level of potential development as determined through problem solving under adult guidance or in collaboration with more capable peers" (Vygotsky, 1978, p. 86).

Vygotsky suggests, therefore, that we need to be prospective as well as retrospective in our understanding and assessment of intelligence. But conventional views have been only retrospective, looking at where a child has come from rather than to where a child is going:

The zone of proximal development defines those functions that have not yet matured but are in the process of maturation, functions that will mature tomorrow but are currently in an embryonic state. These functions could be termed the "buds" or "flowers" of development rather than the "fruits" of development. The actual developmental level characterizes mental development retrospectively, while the zone of proximal development characterizes mental development prospectively. (p. 86–87)

Brown and French (1979) give a fairly detailed example of how the zone of potential development can be measured, and Ferrara, Brown, and Campione (1986) illustrate the use of the zone of potential development in considerable detail.

Although I initially had some doubts as to whether the zone of potential development measures what it is supposed to measure, the results of Brown and her colleagues are very encouraging. I remain concerned, however, that the operationalization of the zone of potential development may not sufficiently take into account individual differences in abilities and styles of learning. The instruction that works well for one child might work only poorly for another child, with the result that the first child might appear to have a larger zone of potential development than the second. In order for the measure to be fair, we would have to make sure that the form of instruction used was equally suitable for all children receiving that instruction, and it is unlikely that any form of instruction will be equally suitable for all. Hence, I believe that we do have to be careful in our interpretation of results of tests that measure the zone of potential development. Moreover, we need to recognize that there may be zones of potential development that are domain-specific rather than domain-general and that may differ not only as a function of domain but as a function of how learning takes place. For example, some children might learn quite well with the kind of direct instruction given in tests of the zone of potential development, whereas other children might learn better on their own. In short, we need to be as careful about overgeneralization of results on these tests as we do for results on any other tests. These concerns notwithstanding, the concept of a zone of potential development is one of the more exciting in the psychology of intelligence, because it gives us a way of addressing the question of what will happen in the future, not based just upon retrospective measurement, but based upon simulations of prospective processing of information.

Feuerstein and the theory of mediated learning experience

The nature of mediated learning experience

In order to understand any of Reuven Feuerstein's thinking, one needs to understand his basic premise – that intelligence is modifiable, and quite drastically so. Feuerstein has made good on this assumption: He has taken retarded performers and effected quite substantial increases in their level of functioning. Feuerstein uses the term *retarded performer* rather than *retarded person*. Feuerstein believes that it is the performance, not the person, who is retarded and hence that the retardation can be mitigated by improving the performance. But he is not a behaviorist. He believes that structural changes are possible in the organism through interventions such as his own program of Instrumental Enrichment.

The key concept in Feuerstein's conception of intelligence and its development is mediated learning experience (MLE). Mediated learning experience is

the way in which stimuli emitted by the environment are transformed by a "mediating" agent, usually a parent, sibling, or other caregiver. This mediating agent, guided by his intentions, culture, and emotional investment, selects and organizes the world of stimuli for the child. The mediator selects stimuli that are most appropriate and then frames, filters, and schedules them; he determines the appearance or disappearance of certain stimuli and ignores others. Through this process of mediation, the cognitive structure of the child is affected. The child acquires behavior patterns and learning sets, which in turn become important ingredients of his capacity to become modified through direct exposure to stimuli. (Feuerstein, 1980, p. 16)

Feuerstein believes that the two main ways to attain modification of cognitive structure are direct exposure to stimuli and MLE, but that it is MLE that will enable the individual effectively to use direct exposure to stimulation. Thus, in mediating the environment for the child, the parent or teacher not only teaches the child important knowledge and skills, but develops in that child the capacity to profit from the environment without mediation. To Feuerstein, therefore, MLE is the critical ingredient in cognitive development and in differentiating people who perform better or worse in cognitive tasks. Clearly, Feuerstein's notion of MLE is similar to Vygotsky's concept of internalization, although Feuerstein emphasizes less the social environment as a whole and more the influence of one-on-one interaction, especially of the mother with a child. The difference, however, is one of degree rather than one of kind.

Feuerstein believed that MLE has several components. First is the selection of stimuli. The caregiver selects those stimuli that she believes will profit the child. Second is scheduling of stimuli. It is not enough just to pick out the right stimuli. The caregiver needs to schedule the presentation of stimuli so that the child will be able to learn from them in an optimal way. Third is anticipation. The child needs to be taught to anticipate certain outcomes as a result of certain actions. A fourth component is imitation. One of the most powerful tools of MLE is the provision of models that the child can imitate. A fifth component is the provision of specific stimuli. Feuerstein notes that such stimuli are usually culturally determined and that the child's attention is consistently directed toward the stimuli. A sixth component is repetition and variation. Feuerstein, like Vygotsky, recognizes that children do not internalize what they observe right away. Repetition and variation are necessary for full internalization to take place. A seventh component is the transmission of the past and the representation of the future. The child learns what has been true in the past and what he or she can expect of the future. And the last component is comparative behavior, by which the child learns to see how things are similar and different.

Feuerstein believes that MLE can occur either through the intervention of a particular individual, such as the parent, or through general cultural transmission. Children who are culturally deprived – who have inadequate exposure to their own culture – will tend to receive inadequate MLE. Note that, for Feuerstein, cultural deprivation is not in terms of a mainstream or host culture, but in terms of the culture of the child and his family.

Feuerstein has suggested that there are two main sources of lack of MLE: the nature of the individual's environment and the condition of an individual at a given point in his or her development. With respect to environmental determinants, Feuerstein suggests several that can lead to lack of MLE: breakdown in cultural transmission, poverty, ideology, inadequate parent–child relationship, and pathological conditions of parents. With respect to conditions of the child, he notes as well several sources of lack of absorption of MLE: autism, constitutional factors (such as hyperactivity), and emotional disturbance.

Deficient cognitive functions

Feuerstein proposes a number of deficient cognitive functions that can result from a lack of MLE, as well as other sources. He does not claim completeness for his list, but merely that the functions he lists are ones that he has found deficient time and again. The functions he describes fit into four categories: impairments in cognition at the input phase, impairments in cognition at the elaborational phase, impairments in cognition at the output phase, and affective motivational factors. I will not attempt to list all of the functions Feuerstein describes but, rather, some representative ones.

Impairments affecting the input phase include unplanned, impulsive, and unsystematic exploratory behavior; lack of, or impaired, receptive verbal tools and concepts affecting discrimination; lack of, or impaired, spatial orientation, including the lack of stable systems of reference that impair the organization of space; and lack of, or impaired, capacity for considering two sources of information at once, reflected in dealing with data in a piecemeal fashion rather than as a unit of organized facts. Examples of impaired cognitive functions affecting the elaborational phase include inadequacy in experiencing the existence of an actual problem and subsequently in defining it; inability to select relevant, as opposed to irrelevant, cues in defining a problem; narrowness of the mental field; and lack of, or impaired, strategies for hypothesis testing. Examples of impaired cognitive functions affecting the output phase include egocentric communicational modalities; trial-and-error responses; lack of, or impaired, verbal tools for communicating adequately elaborated responses; and impulsive acting-out behavior, affecting the nature of the communication process. Feuerstein does not actually list the affective and motivational factors that can adversely affect cognitive processes; he merely states that they exist.

The cognitive map

Feuerstein suggests that mental acts can be analyzed, categorized, and ordered via a cognitive map involving seven parameters. In this respect, one is reminded of the geographic metaphors and particularly of Guttman's (1965) approach to understanding intelligence in terms of facets. The parameters of the cognitive map are content, operations, modality (e.g., figurative, numerical, verbal), phase (input, elaboration, output), level of complexity, level of abstraction, and level of efficiency. The idea of the cognitive map, again, is to fit mental performances into some unified framework.

To conclude, Feuerstein, like Vygotsky, believes in the importance of socialization for intelligence and its development. The key construct of Feuerstein's theory, MLE, may be viewed as the process by which Vygotsky's internalization takes place. The two theories are thus largely compatible, although quite different in their orientation from the other theories we have considered to this point, with the possible exception of the anthropological ones.

Heath and the ethnographic approach to socialization

Shirley Brice Heath, an ethnographer at Stanford University, does not, strictly speaking, have a theory of intelligence. But her approach to understanding language development (Heath, 1983) can tell us perhaps as much about the socialization of intelligence as can any of the approaches we have considered so far. Hence, I include her work because I find it so informative with respect to direct observation of how socialization affects the intelligence of children.

Heath's work is especially of interest to those who care about education. Heath's work shows the potential similarities and differences between a community's view of intelligence and a "school's-eye view of intelligence" (Sternberg, 1987b). Ultimately, it is the school's-eye view of intelligence that will determine what is rewarded and what is punished in school, and to some extent, in society. To the extent that the views of the parents in the community regarding the nature of

intelligence differ from the views of the school, children may be socialized into a form of intelligence that works in the community or in the
home, but not in the school.

Heath studied language development in three communities in the
Piedmont Carolinas: Trackton (lower-class black), Roadville (lower-
class white), and Gateway (middle-class white). It is possible to present here only a fraction of the observations she has made on the effects
of match and mismatch between what constitutes intelligent behavior
from the point of view of the school and from the point of view of the
community in which a given child was raised.

Children in Trackton start off on the wrong foot by not being able to
answer even so simple a question as whether they are present in the
class. They have grown up with nicknames different from those on their
birth certificates and often do not know the name on their birth certificate – hence, their failure to respond when asked their name. Moreover, even having found out this name, they object to being called by
it and are reluctant to answer to it. Teachers, however, protest using
names like "Frog" and "Red Girl" and hence often insist on using the
formal name.

Moreover, in Trackton, questions for which the questioner has or
expects the specific information needed for an answer are rare. A
question such as, "What's my name?" or "What's your name?" is not
expected to yield a literal answer, but rather, recognition of a social
relationship. The name given will depend on who asks it and on why
the question is asked. In even so simple a situation as responding to
one's name, therefore, the Trackton children appear stupid because of
their unwillingness or inability to respond appropriately.

Roadville children also confront a problem in naming, although a
very different kind of problem. In Roadville, a very small number of
first names – such as Robert, Betty, and Elizabeth – tend to be favored
for children. The result is that there will be many children of the same
age with the same name. In school, as a result, multiple Roadville
children may respond to a given name. The obvious solution, to use
additional initials (such as the middle or last ones), is resisted by the
children, causing frustration for both teachers and students alike.

The problem of Trackton children goes beyond mere naming. Trackton children do not expect adults to ask them questions, in general,
because in Trackton, children are not seen as information givers or as
question answerers. As a result, the very act of being asked a question
is strange to them. When Heath asked Trackton children to do tasks she

gave them or to do jobs she assigned them, the children often protested, seeing no reason why they should do these tasks. Trackton children particularly have trouble dealing with indirect requests, such as "It's time to put our paints away now," because such unfamiliar kinds of statements may not even be perceived as requests. These children have particular difficulty with "Why?" questions, because adults in Trackton do not engage children in conversations in which such questions are asked, in stark contrast to typical middle-class upbringing.

In Roadville, as in Gateway, the situation young children confront is very different. Adults see themselves as teachers, and thus ask and answer questions, including "Why?" questions. By the time they go to school, these children have had considerable experience with both direct and indirect requests. Unfortunately, parents in Roadville do not persist in this attitude. Once their children start school, they more or less abdicate their role as teachers, leaving it to the school to do the job. From their point of view, their days as teachers are now over.

Heath suggests that there is an implicit conflict in means of resource allocation across the three communities she has studied. One of the ways American schools prepare children for a schedule-dominated adulthood is through the expectation that the schools' fairly strict schedules will be observed. Place constraints are equally important. Things are expected to go in their proper place at the proper time. In Trackton, the flow of time is casual. There are no timed tasks at home and few tasks that are even time linked. For example, people eat when they are hungry, and there are few constraints on which parts of the meal come before or after which other parts. There are few scheduled activities, and routines, such as going to bed, may happen at very different times on different days. The children are used to a flow of time in which their wants and needs are met as a function of whether there is someone there to meet them and whether the provisions needed are available. It is thus odd for the Trackton child to adhere to a schedule that appears to the child as essentially arbitrary and capricious. Timed tests, of course, seem even stranger than do school schedules: Before entering school, the child may have had literally no experience with being timed in the performance of a cognitive task. In Trackton, things get done, basically, when they get done!

The Trackton child has similar difficulties with space allocation. Being told to put things in a certain place has little or no meaning to the Trackton child. He or she is used to putting things down when done, but the place may vary from time to time. The child has so few possessions that it will generally not be a problem finding the object later. The Trackton child's relatively poor handling of time and space becomes a basis for teachers' unfavorable judgments almost from the start of school.

Children from Roadville and Gateway have a very different sense of time and place. Roadville parents want their children to grow up with a very strict sense of everything having its time and place. In Roadville, even the stories maintain a strict chronological order, emphasizing sequences of events. In Gateway, life is strictly scheduled, and even babies are expected to adhere to this scheduling. Things have a time and a place, and children are expected to learn what these are, just as they will later be expected to do so in school.

Trackton children are at a disadvantage, when they start school, from the standpoint of understanding similarities and differences between objects, a skill that is important in school and critical on typical intelligence tests. Trackton children never spontaneously volunteer to list the attributes of two objects that are similar to or different from each other. Instead, they seem to view objects holistically, comparing the objects as wholes rather than attribute by attribute. Although they may be sensitive to shape, color, size, and so on, they do not use these attributes to make judgments as to how the two objects are similar or different. This unfamiliarity with abstraction and the children's viewing of things in holistic contexts impede progress in reading as well as in reasoning. The Trackton child experiences a holistic coherence with respect to printed words such that if the print style, type font, or even the context of a given word changes, the child notices the change and may become upset. At the same time, the child fails to realize the symbolic equivalence of the print under these transformations, which, although relevant to the child, are irrelevant to the meaning of the printed word. Each new appearance of a word in a new context results in a perception of a different word.

The holistic perceptual and conceptual style of the Trackton child also interferes with the child's progress in mathematics, in which one object plus one object may be perceived as yielding one object, in that the two objects are viewed as a new whole rather than as composed of two discrete parts resulting from the summation. Rather than carrying rules over from one problem to another, children may see each problem as a distinct whole, needing new rules rather than transferring old ones.

The situation is quite different in Roadville. Adults encourage children to label things, and they talk to the children about the attributes of these things. A primary goal in adults' play with children is to encourage them to define the attributes of the play stimuli, and the toys the adults give the children encourage them to match attributes such as color, shape, size, and so on. Gateway parents, too, give their children educational toys from an early age. Children are encouraged to note points of similarity and difference between objects and to label these differences as they are encountered. Gateway parents talk to children about names of things in books as well as in the world, discussing matters of size, shape, and color as they arise.

Trackton children are disadvantaged in reading as much by attitudes toward reading as they are by their perception of the reading material. In Trackton, reading is strictly a group affair. An individual who chooses to read on his or her own is viewed as antisocial. Solitary reading is for those who are unable to make it in the Trackton social milieu. Moreover, there are few magazines, books, or other reading material in Trackton, so that children have little opportunity to practice reading or to be read to. Whereas Roadville parents frequently read to their children, especially at night, such a practice would be most unusual in Trackton.

McDermott (1974) has noted that reading is an act that aligns the black child with the wrong forces in the universe of socialization. Whereas reading is a part of the teacher's agenda and a game the teacher wishes the students to play, it is not a part of the black students' agenda and the games they wish to play. Not reading is accepting the peer group's games over the teachers' games, and Trackton children are likely to make just this choice.

Attitudes toward reading are different in Roadville and Gateway from those in Trackton, but the attitudes of these two communities also differ between themselves. Once children start school, parents in Roadville generally stop reading to their children, expecting the school to take on this task. Adults encourage children to watch Sesame Street, one means for the children to pick up reading, but the adults themselves scarcely set examples to model. Heath notes that the two outstanding features of reading habits in Roadville are, first, that everyone talks about it but that few people do it, and second, that few take any follow-up action on the reading they do. Unlike in Trackton, Roadville homes do have reading matter, such as magazines. But the magazines usually pile up unread and are then thrown away in periodic cleanings of the house.

Attitudes toward reading are different, yet again, in Gateway. There, children are coached before they enter school in both reading and listening behaviors. Children are encouraged to read, to learn the structures of stories, and to use what they learn in their lives.

A major difference between communities is in preferred mode of communication. In Trackton, there is a heavy emphasis upon nonverbal, as opposed to verbal, forms of transmission of knowledge. Adults pay little or no attention to a baby's words. Even sounds that are clearly linked to objects are ignored. In contrast, adults pay careful attention to babies' nonverbal responses and praise responses such as coos and smiles that seem appropriate to a situation. People talk about babies, but rarely to them. During the first 6 months to a year of life, babies are not even directly addressed verbally by adults. Signs of aggressive play in children are acknowledged and generally encouraged. Babies sit in the laps of mothers and other adults frequently during the first year. During that time, a child literally feels the nonverbal interaction of the conversationalist. Children are expected to pay close attention to nonverbal signals about the consequences of their actions and to act accordingly. When older children show younger children how to do things, they do not generally describe the required actions in words. Rather, they exhibit the behavior and simply tell the younger child to do it in the way she or he is seeing it be done. Watching and feeling how to do things are viewed as more important than talking about how to do them.

In Roadville, there is much more stress on verbal interaction and development. When babies respond to stimuli verbally, adults notice these responses and ask questions and make statements in response that are directed at the baby. When the children start to combine words, usually between 18 and 22 months, adults respond with expansions of these combinations. Children are encouraged to label things and, as importantly, to communicate their needs and desires verbally.

Habits of verbal learning in Roadville, despite these desirable features, do not very closely match up with what will later be expected in school. Home teaching and learning are modeled not upon modes of knowledge transmission in the schools, but rather upon modes of knowledge transmission in the church. Children are expected to answer questions with prescribed routines. The measure of a child's understanding of things is his or her ability to recite back knowledge verbatim. The style of learning is passive: One listens, repeats back, and thereby is expected to learn. The sign of learning is memorization, not understanding. Even in their play, Roadville children use language in the same way as in more serious endeavors: They tell stories in strict chronological order and do not embellish them with either evaluations or creative fictions.

In Gateway, modes of learning are different, yet again. As in Roadville, early language use is encouraged and reinforced. Mothers talk to babies and assume that the babies are listening to them and will want to respond. Parents believe that a child's success in school will depend, in part, upon the amount of verbal communication directed to the child and received from the child. But whereas Roadville parents discourage fantasy, Gateway parents encourage it and praise children's imaginary tales. When children ask questions, adults answer at some length and probe the children's knowledge in order to assess just what is known and what needs to be known. The goal is to encourage understanding rather than verbatim recall.

When the goal of learning is verbatim recall, however, the techniques used by Roadville mothers are extremely effective. In Islamic cultures, for example, memorization of lengthy passages from the Koran is a goal unto itself. According to Cole and Scribner (1974), Nigerian children in Koranic schools are trained to memorize the Koran in Arabic, a language they do not speak or understand. In Nigeria, as in Roadville, the mode of learning is geared to what is to be learned; the result is perfectly acceptable in its immediate context but may not be ideal in other situations.

In school and in later life, children will encounter many novel situations. A measure of their intelligence will be their ability to cope with these novelties. Children in all three environments – Trackton, Roadville, and Gateway – learn to deal with novelties, but novelties of very different kinds.

Children in Trackton need to acquire flexibility from an early age. Indeed, flexibility is a key element of success in Trackton. As their first year of life comes to an end, Trackton children learn to play out roles on a community stage, and it is crucial for them to learn to gauge audience reactions to their actions. They have to interpret cues, know what to say when, and adjust their behavior as needed. As boy toddlers become a part of the Trackton milieu, they are teased and challenged, both verbally and nonverbally. Clever put-downs win praise, and successful responses to these kinds of challenges are taken as a sign of intelligence. Heath notes that by the age of 4, a child is usually able to come up with the right level and content of ridicule in one-liner responses to aggressive challenges. Use of insult, and especially rhyming insult, is strongly reinforced by peers right through early adolescence.

Because preschoolers are physically unable to meet aggressive challenges of new and varied kinds, they must learn to outwit their aggressors, dealing with novel challenges as they go along. Later on, they will be very quick at besting teachers in verbal combat, but this skill in coming up with novel and quick retorts will probably not elicit the same admiration from the teachers that it does from their peers and even from elders in Trackton. In sum, the Trackton child acquires considerable flexibility and ability to deal with novelty, but in a domain that will be nonreinforced, or punished, in later schooling.

Children in Trackton engage in other forms of novelty as well. Storytelling is an important aspect of Trackton life. A good story is one that is creatively fictionalized in a way that expands upon real events. The story may be fictionalized to the extent that the outcome has little resemblance to what actually happened. All that is required is that the story have some seminal basis in fact. The best stories are "junk," which consists of highly exaggerated and fictionalized narrative. Stories are not intended to convey actual events, but to promote social interaction and to enhance the reputation of the storyteller. Stories emphasize one's accomplishments, victories over adversity, cleverness, and personal power. The audience gladly accepts the fictive characteristics of the stories and the expansions upon reality in the stories without any need for acknowledgment of what actually happened or of what was embellished. Unfortunately, the audience of the teacher in school does not react the same way at all. Accounts of Trackton children that would be accepted in Trackton may well be perceived as deliberate lies and as attempts to deceive the teacher or other school authorities. Again, the creative abilities that are developed in Trackton do not provide the Trackton student with a needed edge in school, because of the very thin line that is drawn between truth and fiction.

The situation in Roadville is entirely different. Stories are intended to recount actual events as they actually happened. There are rigid rules of chronicity and factuality in stories, and children are thus discouraged from exercising creativity in invention of narrative or from exploring alternative ways of creating stories. Children are not expected to evaluate the actions of characters, nor to elaborate on the inner emotions of characters. It is considered inappropriate for children to introduce fictive characters or fancy into their stories.

As a result, by the time they enter nursery school, Roadville children have had little or no experience with creative storytelling. When the children are asked to tell stories, they do not create or repeat fictional or fanciful stories. In order for Roadville children to accept such stories, a distinct frame of mind must be created in which departures from reality are to be allowed. Even when such departures are allowed, the Roadville child's fictional stories often fail to set the scene, to introduce characters, or even to have any particular point. The child is simply unable to form coherent stories of the kind that the school expects. This situation is scarcely surprising, as the stories that are requested in schools would be received at home as lies and would be likely to bring upon the children immediate punishment.

The attitude of Roadville children toward stories also emerges in their play. Although these children are very conscientious about following rules, they have trouble following rules when the play turns from realistic play to fantasy play. These children simply do not know how to engage in fantasy play. Eventually, Roadville children were observed to stop playing in those areas of the classroom where they could not bring to bear their play habits from home. The schools do not follow the norms of Roadville any more than they follow the norms of Trackton. Whereas a child from Trackton may easily be perceived as a liar, a child from Roadville may easily be perceived as utterly lacking in spontaneous creativity. Thus, the encouragement of creativity in Trackton and the discouragement of it in Roadville both lead to unfortunate ends when the child from either community enters school.

The situation in Gateway is quite different from that in either Trackton or Roadville. Children's imaginary tales are acknowledged and praised, so long as they take the form of fantasy and are clearly introduced with the signals appropriate for fictional stories. Children are encouraged to mix fact and fiction, but only so long as it is clear to both child and listener which is which. Children learn the difference between expository and fictional accounts and later will be able to generate each with relative ease. Stories by Gateway children do not have the exaggerated characteristics of the stories by Trackton children, but neither do they have the extremely literal and formulaic character of stories by Roadville children. Gateway children learn to balance their synthetic and creative abilities with their analytic and critical ones in a way that will later be praised and rewarded in the schools.

In sum, Heath's research in Trackton, Roadville, and Gateway is exemplary of how we can use ethnography to understand the socialization of intelligence. Clearly, children receive very different socialization in each of the three environments, and the result is that their intellectual performance seems quite different in school and, particularly, on tests. We could not understand these differences unless we understood the environment of socialization and, in Feuerstein's terms, the MLE that gave rise to the kinds of intellectual abilities that children have. Thus, the sociological metaphor is useful in focusing upon experiences that other metaphors shed little or no light on and, for the most part, ignore.

Part V

Theories of intelligence looking
inward and outward

11

The systems metaphor

The systems metaphor is an attempt to bring together various other metaphors by viewing intelligence in terms of a complex interaction of various cognitive and other systems. Although systems theory has been around for some time, it is only recently that it has been applied, in a modified way, to understanding intelligence. The three major attempts to understand intelligence in terms of interacting systems are those of Howard Gardner, in his theory of multiple intelligences, of Robert Sternberg, in his triarchic theory of human intelligence, and of Stephen Ceci, in his bioecological theory of intelligence.

Howard Gardner and the theory of multiple intelligences

Fundamental principles

Howard Gardner's (1983) theory of multiple intelligences may be viewed as having three fundamental principles. First, intelligence is not a single thing, whether viewed unitarily or as comprising multiple abilities. Rather, there exist multiple intelligences, each distinct from the others. The multiple intelligences Gardner proposes in his 1983 book are linguistic, logical-mathematical, spatial, musical, bodily-kinesthetic, interpersonal, and intrapersonal. In some ways, the distinction between positing one intelligence comprising multiple abilities and positing multiple intelligences, each distinct from the others, is subtle. But the positing of multiple intelligences emphasizes the separateness of each set of skills and also emphasizes Gardner's view that each intelligence is a system in its own right, rather than merely one aspect of a larger system, namely, what we traditionally call "intelligence." The second fundamental principle is that these intelligences are independent of each other. In other words, a person's abilities as assessed under one intelligence should, in theory, be unpredictive of that person's abilities as assessed under another intelligence. Obviously, the claim of independence is a strong one, but Gardner believes that it is justified by what we know about the mind. The third fundamental principle is that the intelligences interact. Although they are distinct from each other, no one could ever get anything done if their distinctness and independence meant that they couldn't work together. In such an instance, a mathematical word problem requiring, say, the application of both linguistic and logical-mathematical intelligences would be insoluble. Rather, on Gardner's view, the two intelligences work together to produce a solution to the problem. Gardner defines an intelligence as "an ability or set of abilities that permits an individual to solve problems or fashion products that are of consequence in a particular cultural setting" (Walters & Gardner, 1986, p. 165).

Prerequisites of an intelligence

How do we know what constitutes an intelligence? In other words, what criteria can one use to identify the multiple intelligences in Gardner's theory or other possible intelligences that have not yet been identified? Gardner proposes eight criteria for distinguishing an independent intelligence.

1. *Potential isolation by brain damage.* Occasionally, natural or man-made interventions result in lesions in certain parts of the brain or in parts of the brain literally being destroyed. Neuropsychologists are particularly interested in patients with brain lesions, because such patients can be helpful to these psychologists in isolating portions of the brain that are responsible for particular mental functions. The logic is that if a portion of the brain is hypothesized to be responsible for a certain function, then an individual lacking that portion of the brain should be unable to perform the function. Gardner believes that each intelligence resides in a separate portion of the brain and hence that a given intelligence should be isolable by studying brain-damaged patients.

2. *The existence of idiots savants, prodigies, and other exceptional individuals.* Idiots savants and prodigies both seem to have some rather specific area of intellectual functioning that is exceptionally highly developed relative to other areas of functioning. Under the assumption that this high level of development represents growth in a particular portion of the brain, the existence of idiots savants and prodigies within the domain of a given intelligence would provide

increased evidence for the existence of that intelligence. Contrariwise, the near absence of an intelligence in children with a specific learning disability or possibly in certain austistic children would also provide a confirmation of an intelligence, as seen from a complementary point of view.

3. *An identifiable core operation or set of operations.* Because each of the intelligences is independent, each should have its own distinctive set of operations that is used in the exercise of that intelligence. The identification of the complete set of operations or of some core operation would further enhance the plausibility of the existence of one of the intelligences.

4. *A distinctive developmental history, along with a definable set of expert "end-state" performances.* One way of separating a given intelligence from any other is to show a pattern of development that is distinctive with respect to that intelligence. Each intelligence should show a clear developmental trajectory, which might, though not necessarily, be distinctive for a given intelligence. Furthermore, there should be a set of stages of expertise that is recognizable for each of the intelligences.

5. *An evolutionary history and evolutionary plausibility.* The origins of each of the intelligences go back millions of years. The plausibility of a specific intelligence is enhanced by the demonstration of its evolutionary antecedents and course of development. Thus, bird song might plausibly be a forerunner of musical intelligence, and primate social organization might plausibly be a forerunner of interpersonal intelligence.

6. *Support from experimental psychological investigations.* Experimental psychological investigations showing the distinctness of one ability or set of processes from another provide an additional way to isolate intelligences. Especially useful are studies that show patterns of interference. Such patterns can lead to the conclusion that the tasks that interfere with each other tap a single intelligence, whereas tasks that do not interfere with each other are more likely to tap separate intelligences. The additive-factor method might also be used to investigate patterns of additivity and interaction, with additivity indicating the effects of separate intelligences and interactivity indicating effects of a single intelligence.

7. *Support from psychometric findings.* Patterns of intercorrelations and factor analysis provide yet another way of supporting the theory of multiple intelligences. To the extent that the patterns of test interrelations do not support the theory, the theory is undermined. However, Gardner points out that intelligence tests do not always test what they are claimed to test, that many tests involve the use of more than the

targeted ability, and that stress on paper-and-pencil methods often precludes meaningful measurement of the various intelligences.

8. *Susceptibility to encoding in a symbol system.* Each of the intelligences should have its own distinctive symbol system. For linguistic intelligence, for example, the symbol system is language, for musical intelligence it is notes, and for logical-mathematical intelligence it is logical or mathematical notations. From Gardner's point of view, symbol systems have developed as a response to the need to manifest each of the separate intelligences.

The seven intelligences

Linguistic intelligence. This intelligence includes the skills involved in reading and writing, listening and talking. Walters and Gardner (1986) note that a specific area of the brain, Broca's area, is responsible for the production of grammatical sentences and that people with damage to this area can understand sentences but have difficulty in producing them. They note that even among the deaf, children who do not learn sign language will often invent their own.

Logical-mathematical intelligence. Logical-mathematical intelligence is involved in numerical computation, deriving proofs, solving logical puzzles, and most scientific thinking. It is involved, together with linguistic intelligence, in the solution of mathematical word problems. And, of course, it is used in everyday life, as when a shopper decides which of two differently sized containers is a better buy.

Spatial intelligence. Spatial intelligence is used in marine navigation, as well as in piloting a plane or even driving a car. It is used to figure out how to get from one location to another and to figure out one's orientation in space, especially if one is in a chamber, such as an airplane, that is not level with respect to the ground. Spatial intelligence is important in the visual arts, and even in playing chess, in which many players imagine what the board will look like in subsequent moves. According to Walters and Gardner (1986), damage to the right posterior region of the brain leads to reduction in certain aspects of spatial intelligence, such as the ability to find one's way around a site and to recognize faces or scenes.

Musical intelligence. This intelligence is involved in singing, playing an instrument, conducting an orchestra, composing, and, to some extent, in appreciating music. The skills involved in musical intelligence appear to be located in the right hemisphere of the brain, although musical skill is not as clearly localized as is language skill. Available evidence suggests that musical intelligence is universal, applying to people in all cultures.

Bodily-kinesthetic intelligence. This intelligence involves the ability to use one's whole body or various portions of it in the solution of problems or in the construction of products or displays. It is involved in dancing, athletics, acting, surgery, and the like. This intelligence is largely localized in the motor cortex, with each of the two hemispheres controlling bodily movements of the contralateral side.

Interpersonal intelligence. This intelligence is involved in understanding and acting upon one's understanding of others. It involves the capacity to notice distinctions among others and to discern their moods, temperaments, and intentions. It permits us to read others even when they seek to conceal what they are thinking or feeling and to understand a person's needs at a given time and place. The skill is particularly important in occupations that involve extensive dealings with others, such as politics, sales, psychotherapy, and teaching. It can express itself through both verbal and nonverbal means, as when a person reads between the lines of what others are saying to interpret what they really mean on the basis of their gestures and facial expressions.

Intrapersonal intelligence. This intelligence involves the ability to understand oneself – to know how one feels about things, to understand one's range of emotions, to have insights about why one acts the way one does, and to behave in ways that are appropriate to one's needs, goals, and abilities. Gardner believes that intrapersonal intelligence is symbolized in the world of dreams, but even at the conscious level, one frequently finds oneself thinking about why one is acting as one is.

Gardner's analysis of critiques of multiple intelligences theory

All new theories of intelligence, or in this case of intelligences, come under criticism, and the present theory is no exception. Walters and Gardner (1986) have listed some of the main critiques that they have heard and their responses to them. Consider some of these critiques and their responses.

A first criticism has been that what Gardner calls multiple intelligences are not intelligences at all, but rather talents. On this view, multiple intelligences theory is nothing more than new wine in old bottles, as lists similar to Gardner's have been presented before under the rubric of talents (e.g., Marland, 1972).

One might elaborate this criticism by suggesting that what Gardner calls "bodily-kinesthetic intelligence" is a good example of something that is truly a talent and not an intelligence. After all, people who lack bodily-kinesthetic intelligence due to paralysis, disease (e.g., multiple sclerosis), or accidents are not normally referred to as mentally retarded, nor is it clear that we would want to refer to them as mentally retarded. For example, Helen Keller is not usually thought of as having been mentally retarded. People with physical disabilities may lack a skill or set of skills, but it is not clear that they lack an intelligence.

Gardner replies by noting that there is nothing magical about the word "intelligence." He has chosen it in order to emphasize his point that abilities not typically considered as intelligences by Western culture, such as the bodily-kinesthetic ones, should be placed on an equal footing with the abilities more conventionally viewed as intelligence, especially linguistic and logical-mathematical abilities. Hence, he sees part of his mission as taking these latter two abilities off the pedestal that they seem uniquely to occupy, so as to encourage people to give more credence to and recognition of other abilities that tend to be ignored.

A second criticism considered by Walters and Gardner (1986) is the criticism that multiple intelligences theory is not really a theory. It merely lists intelligences without making clear what exactly is involved in them or what their boundaries are. The presentation of the theory seems to select data that support the theory and, at the same time, to ignore data that tend to refute it. For example, factor-analytic evidence overwhelmingly suggests that abilities are not independent, as claimed by Gardner, and many people (e.g., Jensen, 1972) interpret the factor-analytic evidence as supporting the notion of g, or general intelligence.

Gardner replies that it is impossible to consider all evidence because there are so many data available. He describes what he has done as based on "subjective factor analysis" (Walters & Gardner, 1986, p. 176), which seeks to discover natural kinds of abilities. He suggests that there are a number of ways in which the theory could be disconfirmed, and also that the evidence just is not all in yet. For example, factor analysis can only be as good as the tests to which it is applied, and Gardner believes that many, if not most, of the tests are fairly trivial measures of the kinds of intelligences about which he speaks. Moreover, he does not deny the existence of g, but rather questions its explanatory importance outside of the environment of formal schooling. There may well be a g for conventional tests of intelligence, but these tests are so narrow that it is unlikely the g will be of much importance outside the narrow domains in which the tests apply. Moreover, he suggests that many of the correlations between tests can be attributed to the requirement of all the tests that one be test-wise, that is, have sophisticated test-taking skills. Gardner further argues that the intelligences, although more simply conceived of as independent, may at times overlap. He views his concept of independence as nothing more than "a good working hypothesis."

A third criticism considered by Walters and Gardner is that the number of intelligences posited could expand indefinitely, resulting in a number much greater than seven. In fact, since the publication of his book, Gardner has suggested in informal conversations that there are more than seven intelligences. He never claimed in the book or elsewhere that the "true" number of intelligences is seven. Rather, he applied the criteria he suggested for distinguishing an intelligence and came up with seven as a working hypothesis. He admits that there are likely to be subunits under each intelligence: He makes no claim that they are undifferentiated. Moreover, he is not uncomfortable with a notion of the number of intelligences being greater than seven. But he views seven as a good working number and one that is large enough to express diversity and yet small enough to be manageable.

Finally, one might argue that the advantage of conventional theories is that they are more susceptible to measurement operations. After all, we have intelligence tests based on psychometric theories, whereas the kinds of intelligences of which Gardner speaks seem less susceptible, at least in some cases, to measurement. Gardner replies, however, that the intelligences he proposes are measurable, although perhaps not with the same kind of measurements used by conventional intelligence tests. However, he has little interest in such measurements but prefers, instead, measurements that are closer to the kinds of activities in which children engage in their everyday lives in school (Gardner & Feldman, 1985). For example, one can look at children's compositions in school, their choices of activities, their performance in athletic events, and so on.

In my view, Gardner's theory is overinclusive and too vague to assess any details. From the standpoint of this book, however, the main issue with respect to Gardner's theory is not whether it is correct in all its details but whether it represents a new contribution in terms of synthesizing metaphors for understanding the mind. In my opinion, the theory does represent a substantial step forward in this direction. In viewing multiple intelligences in terms of an interlocking system, we gain elements of different metaphors. For example, Gardner draws upon theories and empirical evidence from the geographic, computational, anthropological, and biological streams of thought. In attempting to meld together these different approaches, he has gone beyond viewing intelligence in terms of just a single one of those conventional metaphors, which I believe to be a contribution indeed.

Robert Sternberg and the triarchic theory of human intelligence

The triarchic theory of human intelligence (Sternberg, 1985a, 1988) seeks to explain in an integrative way the relationship between (1) intelligence and the internal world of the individual, or the mental mechanisms that underlie intelligent behavior; (2) intelligence and the external world of the individual, or the use of these mental mechanisms in everyday life in order to attain an intelligent fit to the environment; and (3) intelligence and experience, or the mediating role of one's passage through life between the internal and external worlds of the individual. Consider some of the basic tenets of the theory.

Intelligence and the internal world of the individual

Psychometricians, Piagetians, and information-processing psychologists have all recognized the importance of understanding what mental states or processes underlie intelligent thought. In the triarchic theory, this understanding is sought through the identification and understanding of three basic kinds of information-processing components, which are referred to as metacomponents, performance components, and knowledge acquisition components.

Metacomponents. Metacomponents are higher order, executive processes used to plan what one is going to do, to monitor it while one is doing it, and to evaluate it after it is done. These metacomponents include (1) recognizing the existence of a problem, (2) deciding upon the nature of the problem confronting one, (3) selecting a set of lower order processes to solve the problem, (4) selecting a strategy into which to combine these components, (5) selecting a mental representation upon which the components and strategy can act, (6) allocating one's mental resources, (7) monitoring one's problem solving as it is happening, and (8) evaluating one's problem solving after it is done. Consider some examples of some of these higher order processes.

Deciding upon the nature of a problem plays a prominent role in intelligence. For example, with young children as well as older adults, their difficulty in problem solving often lies not in actually solving a given problem, but in figuring out just what the problem is that needs to be solved (see, e.g., Flavell, 1977; Sternberg & Rifkin, 1979). A major feature distinguishing retarded from normal persons is the retardates' need to be instructed explicitly and completely as to the nature of the particular task they are solving and how it should be performed (Butterfield, Wambold, & Belmont, 1973; Campione & Brown, 1979). The importance of figuring out the nature of the problem is not limited to retarded persons. Resnick and Glaser (1976) have argued that intelligence is the ability to learn from incomplete instruction.

Selection of a strategy for combining lower order components is also a critical aspect of intelligence. In early information-processing research on intelligence, including my own (e.g., Sternberg, 1977), the primary emphasis was simply on figuring out what subjects do when confronted with a problem. What components do subjects use and into what strategies do they combine these components?

Soon, information-processing researchers began to ask the question of why subjects use the strategies they choose. For example, Cooper (1982) reported that in solving spatial problems, and especially mental-rotation problems, some subjects seem to use a holistic strategy of comparison whereas others use an analytic strategy. She has sought to figure out what leads subjects to the choice of one strategy over another. Siegler (1986) has proposed a model of strategy selection in arithmetic computation problems that links strategy choice to both the rules and mental associations one has stored in long-term memory. MacLeod, Hunt, and Mathews (1978) found that high-spatial subjects tend to use a spatial strategy in solving sentence–picture comparison problems, whereas high-verbal subjects are more likely to use a linguistic strategy. In my own work, I have found that subjects tend to prefer certain strategies for analogical reasoning over others because they place fewer demands upon working memory (Sternberg & Ketron, 1982). Similarly, subjects choose different strategies in linear-syllogistic reasoning (spatial, linguistic, mixed spatial-linguistic), but in this task, they do not always capitalize upon their ability patterns so as to choose the strategy most suitable to their respective levels of spatial and verbal abilities (Sternberg & Weil, 1980). In sum, the selection of a strategy seems to be at least as important for understanding intelligent task performance as is the efficacy with which the chosen strategy is implemented.

Intimately tied up with the selection of a strategy is the selection of a mental representation for information. In the early literature on mental representations, the emphasis seemed to be upon understanding how information is represented. For example, can individuals use imagery as a form of mental representation (Kosslyn, 1980)? In more recent research, investigators have realized that people are quite flexible in their representations of information. The most appropriate question to ask seems to be not how information is represented, but which representations are used in what circumstances. For example, Sternberg (1977) found that analogy problems using animal names can draw upon either spatial or clustering representations of the animal names. In the studies of strategy choice mentioned above, it was found that subjects can use either linguistic or spatial representations in solving sentence–picture comparisons (MacLeod et al., 1978) or linear syllogisms (Sternberg & Weil, 1980). Sternberg and Rifkin (1979) found that the mental representation of certain kinds of analogies can be either more or less holistic, depending upon the ages of the subjects.

As important as any other metacomponent is one's ability to allocate one's mental resources. Different investigators have studied resource allocation in different ways. Hunt and Lansman (1982), for example, have concentrated upon the use of secondary tasks in assessing information processing and have proposed a model of attention allocation in the solution of problems that involves both a primary and a secondary task. In my work, I have found that better problem solvers tend to spend relatively more time in global strategy planning (Sternberg, 1981a). Similarly, in solving analogies, better analogical reasoners seem to spend relatively more time encoding the terms of the problem than do poorer reasoners, but to spend relatively less time in operating upon these encodings (Sternberg, 1977; Sternberg & Rifkin, 1979). In reading as well, the superior readers are better able than poorer readers to allocate their time across reading passages as a function of the difficulty of the passages to be read and the purpose for which the passages are being read (see Brown, Bransford, Ferrara, & Campione, 1983; Wagner & Sternberg, 1987).

Finally, monitoring one's solution processes is a key aspect of intelligence (see also Brown, 1978). Consider, for example, the Missionaries and Cannibals problem, in which the subjects must "transport" a set of missionaries and cannibals across a river in a small boat without allowing the cannibals an opportunity to eat the missionaries, an event that can transpire only if the cannibals are allowed to outnumber the missionaries on either side of the river bank. The main kinds of errors that can be made are either to return to an earlier state in the problem space for solution or to make an impermissible move (Simon & Reed, 1976; see also Sternberg, 1982b). Neither of these errors would result if a given subject closely monitored his or her solution processes. For young children learning to count, a major source of errors in counting objects is to count a given object twice, an error that, again, can result from a failure in solution monitoring (Gelman & Gallistel, 1978). The effects of solution monitoring are not limited, of course, to any one kind of problem. One's ability to use the strategy of means–ends analysis (Newell & Simon, 1972) – that is, reduction of differences between where one is in solving a problem and where one wishes to get in solving that problem – depends upon one's ability to monitor just where one is in problem solution.

Performance components. Performance components are lower order processes that execute the instructions of the metacomponents. These lower order components solve the problems according to the plans laid out by the metacomponents. Whereas the number of metacomponents used in the performance of various tasks is relatively limited, the number of performance components is probably quite large. Many of these performance components are relatively specific to narrow ranges of tasks (Sternberg, 1979, 1983, 1985a).

One of the most interesting classes of performance components is that found in inductive reasoning of the kind measured by tests such as matrices, analogies, series completions, and classifications. These components are important because of the importance of the tasks into which they enter: Induction problems of these kinds show the highest loadings on the so-called *g,* or general intelligence factor (Jensen, 1980; Snow & Lohman, 1984; Sternberg & Gardner, 1982). Thus, identifying these performance components can give us some insight into the nature of the general factor. In saying this, I am not arguing for any one factorial model of intelligence (i.e., one with a general factor) over others: To the contrary, I believe that most factor models are mutually compatible, differing only in the form of rotation that has been applied to a given factor space (Sternberg, 1977). The rotation one uses is a matter of theoretical or practical convenience, not of truth or falsity.

The main performance components of inductive reasoning are encoding, inference, mapping, application, comparison, justification, and response. They can be illustrated with reference to an analogy problem, such as LAWYER : CLIENT :: DOCTOR : (a) PATIENT, (b) MEDICINE. In encoding, the subject retrieves from semantic memory semantic attributes that are potentially relevant for analogy solution. In inference, the subject discovers the relation between the first two terms of the analogy, here, LAWYER and CLIENT. In mapping, the subject discovers the higher order relation that links the first half of the analogy, headed by LAWYER, to the second half of the analogy, headed by DOCTOR. In application, the subject carries over the relation inferred in the first half of the analogy to the second half of the analogy, generating a possible completion for the analogy. In comparison, the subject compares each of the answer options to the mentally generated completion, deciding which, if any, is correct. In justification, used optionally if none of the answer options matches the mentally generated solution, the subject decides which, if any, of the options is close enough to constitute an acceptable solution to the examiner. In response, the subject indicates an option, whether by means of pressing a button, making a mark on a piece of paper, or whatever.

Two fundamental issues have arisen regarding the nature of performance components as a fundamental construct in human intelligence. The first, mentioned briefly above, is whether their number simply keeps expanding indefinitely. Neisser (1982), for example, has suggested that it does. As a result, he views the construct as of little use. But this expansion results only if one considers seriously those components that are specific to small classes of problems or to single problems. If one limits one's attention to the more important, general components of performance, the problem simply does not arise, as shown, for example, in Sternberg and Gardner's (1982) analysis of inductive reasoning or in Pellegrino and Kail's (1982) analysis of spatial ability. The second issue is one of the level at which performance components should be studied. In so-called cognitive correlates research (Pellegrino & Glaser, 1979), theorists emphasize components at relatively low levels of information processing (Hunt, 1978, 1980; Jensen, 1982). In so-called cognitive components research (Pellegrino & Glaser, 1979), theorists emphasize components at relatively high levels of information processing (e.g., Mulholland et al., 1980; Snow, 1980; Sternberg, 1977). Because of the interactive nature of human information processing, it would appear that there is no right or wrong level of analysis. Rather, all levels of information processing contribute to both task and subject variance in intelligent performance. The most expeditious level of analysis depends upon the task and subject population: Lower level performance components might be more important, for example, in studying more basic information-processing tasks, such as choice reaction time, or in studying higher level tasks in children who have not yet automatized the lower order processes that contribute to performance on these tasks.

Knowledge acquisition components. Knowledge acquisition components are used to *learn how to do* what the metacomponents and performance components eventually do. Three knowledge acquisition components appear to be central in intellectual functioning: (1) selective encoding, (2) selective combination, and (3) selective comparison.

Selective encoding involves sifting out relevant from irrelevant information. When new information is presented in natural contexts, relevant information for one's given purpose is embedded in the midst of large amounts of purpose-irrelevant information. A critical task for the learner is that of sifting the "wheat from the chaff", recognizing just what among all the pieces of information is relevant for one's purposes (see Schank, 1980).

Selective combination involves combining selectively encoded information in such a way as to form an integrated, plausible whole. Simply sifting out relevant from irrelevant information is not enough to generate a new knowledge structure. One must know how to combine the pieces of information into an internally connected whole (see Mayer & Greeno, 1972).

My emphasis upon components of knowledge acquisition differs somewhat from the focus of some contemporary theorists in cognitive psychology, who emphasize what is already known and the structure of this knowledge (e.g., Chase & Simon, 1973; Chi, 1978; Keil, 1984). I should point out, again, therefore, that these various emphases are complementary. If one is interested in understanding, for example, differences in performance between experts and novices, clearly one would wish to look at the amount and structure of their respective knowledge bases. But if one wishes to understand how these differences came to be, merely looking at developed knowledge would not be enough. Rather, one would have to look as well at differences in the ways in which the knowledge bases were acquired. It is here that understanding of knowledge acquisition components will prove to be most relevant.

We have studied knowledge acquisition components in the domain of vocabulary acquisition (e.g., Sternberg, 1987a; Sternberg & Powell, 1983a). Difficulty in learning new words can be traced, at least in part, to the application of components of knowledge acquisition to context cues stored in long-term memory. Individuals with higher vocabularies tend to be those who are better able to apply the knowledge acquisition components to vocabulary-learning situations. Given the importance of vocabulary for overall intelligence, almost without respect to the theory or test one uses, utilization of knowledge acquisition components in vocabulary-learning situations would appear to be critically important for the development of intelligence. Effective use of knowledge acquisition components is trainable. I have found, for example, that just 45 minutes of training in the use of these components in vocabulary learning can significantly and fairly substantially improve the ability of adults to learn vocabulary from natural-language contexts (Sternberg, 1987a).

To summarize, then, the components of intelligence are an important part of the intelligence of the individual. The various kinds of components work together. Metacomponents activate performance and knowledge acquisition components. These latter kinds of components in turn provide feedback to the metacomponents. Although one can isolate various kinds of information-processing components from task performance using experimental means, in practice, the components function together in highly interactive, and not easily isolable, ways. Thus, diagnoses as well as instructional interventions need to consider all three types of components in interaction, rather than any one kind of component in isolation. But understanding the nature of the components of intelligence is not, in itself, sufficient to understand the nature of intelligence, because there is more to intelligence than a set of information-processing components. One could scarcely understand all of what it is that makes one person more intelligent than another by understanding the components of processing on, say, an intelligence test. The other aspects of the triarchic theory address some of the other aspects of intelligence that contribute to individual differences in observed performance, outside of testing situations as well as within them.

Intelligence and experience

Components of information processing are always applied to tasks and situations with which one has some level of prior experience (including the null level). Hence, these internal mechanisms are closely tied to one's experience. According to the experiential subtheory, the components are not equally good measures of intelligence at all levels of experience. Assessing intelligence requires one to consider not only components, but the level of experience at which they are applied.

During recent years, there has been a tendency in cognitive science to study script-based behavior (e.g., Schank & Abelson, 1977), whether under the name of "script" or under some other name, such as "schema" or "frame." There is no longer any question that much of our behavior is scripted, in some sense. However, from the standpoint of the present subtheory, such behavior is nonoptimal for understanding intelligence. Typically, one's actions when one goes to a restaurant, doctor's office, or movie theater do not provide good measures of intelligence, even though they do provide good measures of scripted behavior. What, then, is the relation between intelligence and experience?

According to the experiential subtheory, intelligence is best measured at those regions of the experiential continuum that involve tasks or situations that are either relatively novel, on the one hand, or in the process of becoming automatized, on the other. As Raaheim (1974) pointed out, totally novel tasks and situations provide poor measures of intelligence: One would not want to administer, say, trigonometry problems to a first-grader of roughly 6 years of age. But one might wish to administer problems that are just at the limits of the child's understanding, in order to test how far this understanding extends. Related is Vygotsky's (1978) concept of the zone of proximal development, in which one examines a child's ability to profit from instruction to facilitate his or her solution of novel problems. In order to measure automatization skill, one might wish to present a series of problems – mathematical or otherwise – to see how long it takes for solution of them to become automatic, and to see how automatized performance becomes. Thus, both slope and asymptote (if any) of automatization are of interest.

Ability to deal with novelty. Several sources of evidence converge upon the notion that the ability to deal with relative novelty is a good way of measuring intelligence. Consider three such sources of evidence. First, we have conducted several studies on the nature of insight, both in children and in adults (Davidson & Sternberg, 1984; Sternberg & Davidson, 1982). In the studies with children (Davidson & Sternberg, 1984), we separated three kinds of insights: insights of selective encoding, insights of selective combination, and insights of selective comparison. Use of these knowledge acquisition components is referred to as insightful when they are applied in the absence of existing scripts, plans, frames, or whatever. In other words, one must decide what information is relevant, decide how to put the information together, or decide how new information relates to old in the absence of any obvious cues on the basis of which to make these judgments. A problem is insightfully solved at the individual level when a given individual lacks such cues. A problem is insightfully solved at the societal level when no one else has these cues either. In our studies, we found that children who are intellectually gifted are so in part by virtue of their insight abilities, which represent an important part of the ability to deal with novelty.

The critical finding was that providing insights to the children significantly benefited the nongifted, but not the gifted children. (None of the children performed anywhere near ceiling, so that the interaction was not due to ceiling effects.) In other words, the gifted children spontaneously had the insights and hence did not benefit from being given these insights. The nongifted children did not have the insights spontaneously and hence did benefit. Thus, the gifted children were better able spontaneously to deal with novelty.

Another source of evidence for the proposed hypothesis relating coping with novelty to intelligence derives from the large literature on fluid intelligence, which is in part a kind of intelligence that involves dealing with novelty (see R. B. Cattell, 1971). Snow and Lohman (1984; see also Snow et al., 1984) have multidimensionally scaled a variety of such tests and found the dimensional loadings to follow a radex structure. In particular, tests with higher loadings on *g*, or general intelligence, fall closer to the center of the spatial diagram. The critical thing to note is that those tests that best measure the ability to deal with novelty fall closer to the center, and tests tend to be more removed from the center as their assessment of the ability to deal with novelty becomes more remote. In sum, evidence from the laboratories of others as well as myself supports the idea that the various components of intelligence that are involved in dealing with novelty, as measured in particular tasks and situations, provide particularly apt measures of intellectual ability.

Ability to automatize information processing. There are several converging lines of evidence in the literature to support the claim that automatization ability is a key aspect of intelligence. For example, Sternberg (1977) found that the correlation between People-Piece (schematic-picture) analogy performance and measures of general intelligence increased with practice, as performance on these items became increasingly automatized. Skilled reading is heavily dependent upon automatization of bottom-up functions, and the ability to read well is an essential part of crystallized ability, whether as viewed from the standpoint of theories such as R. B. Cattell's (1971) or Vernon's (1971), or from the standpoint of tests of crystallized ability, such as the verbal portion of the Scholastic Aptitude Test. Poor comprehenders often are those who have not automatized the elementary, bottom-up processes of reading and hence who do not have sufficient attentional resources to allocate to top-down comprehension processes. Ackerman (1987; Kanfer & Ackerman, 1989) has provided a three-stage model of automatization in which the first stage is related to intelligence although the later two appear not to be.

Theorists such as Jensen (1982) and Hunt (1978) have attributed the correlation between tasks such as choice reaction time and letter matching to the relation between speed of information processing and intelligence. Indeed, there is almost certainly some relation, although I believe it is much more complex than these theorists seem to allow for. But a plausible alternative hypothesis is that at least some of that correlation is due to the effects of automatization of processing: Because of the simplicity of these tasks, they probably become at least partially automatized fairly rapidly and hence can measure both rate and asymptote of automatization of performance. In sum, then, although the evidence is far from complete, there is at least some support for the notion that rate and level of automatization are related to intellectual skill.

The ability to deal with novelty and the ability to automatize information processing are interrelated, as shown in the example of reading from this section. If one is well able to automatize, one has more resources left over for dealing with novelty. Similarly, if one is well able to deal with novelty, one has more resources left over for automatization. Thus, performance at the various levels of the experiential continuum are related to one another.

These abilities should not be viewed in a vacuum with respect to the componential subtheory. The components of intelligence are applied to tasks and situations at various levels of experience: The ability to deal with novelty can be understood in part in terms of the metacomponents, performance components, and knowledge acquisition components involved in it. Automatization refers to the way these components are executed. Hence, the two subtheories considered so far are closely intertwined. We need now to consider the application of these subtheories to everyday tasks, in addition to laboratory ones.

Intelligence and the external world of the individual

According to the contextual subtheory, intelligent thought is directed toward one or more of three behavioral goals: *adaptation to an environment, shaping of an environment,* or *selection of an environment.* These three goals may be viewed as the functions toward which intelligence is directed: Intelligence is not aimless or random mental activity that happens to involve certain components of information processing at certain levels of experience. Rather, it is purposefully directed toward the pursuit of these three global goals, all of which have more specific and concrete instantiations in people's lives.

Adaptation. Most intelligent thought is directed toward the attempt to adapt to one's environment. The requirements for adaptation can differ radically from one environment to another – whether environments are defined in terms of families, jobs, subcultures, cultures, or whatever. Hence, although the components of intelligence required in these various contexts may be the same or quite similar and although all of them may involve, at one time or another, dealing with novelty and automatization of information processing, the concrete instantiations that these processes and levels of experience take may differ substantially across contexts. This fact has an important implication for our understanding of the nature of intelligence. According to the triarchic theory, in general, and the contextual subtheory, in particular, the processes and experiential facets and functions of intelligence remain essentially the same across contexts, but the particular instantiations of these processes, facets, and functions can differ radically. Thus, the content of intelligent thought and its manifestations in behavior will bear no necessary resemblance across contexts. As a result, although the mental elements that an intelligence test should measure do not differ across contexts, the vehicle for measurement may have to differ. A test that measures a set of processes, experiential facets, or intelligent functions in one context may not provide equally adequate measurement in another context. To the contrary, what is intelligent in one culture may be viewed as unintelligent in another.

Different contextual milieus may result in the development of different mental abilities. For example, as noted in Chapter 9, Puluwat navigators must develop their large-scale spatial abilities for dealing with cognitive maps to a degree that far exceeds the adaptive requirements of contemporary Western societies (Gladwin, 1970). Similarly, Kearins (1981) found that aboriginal children probably develop their visuospatial memories to a greater degree than do Anglo-Australian children, who are more likely to apply verbal strategies to spatial memory tasks than are the aborigines, who employ spatial strategies. In contrast, participants in Western societies probably develop their abilities for thinking abstractly to a greater degree than do societies in which concepts are rarely dealt with outside their concrete manifestations in the objects of the everyday environment.

One of the most interesting differences among cultures and subcultures in the development of patterns of adaptation is in the matter of time allocation, a metacomponential function. In Western cultures, in general, careful allocation of one's time to various activities is a prized commodity. Our lives are largely governed by careful scheduling at home, school, work, and so on. There are fixed hours for certain activities and fixed lengths of time within which these activities are expected to be completed. Indeed, the intelligence tests we use show our prizing of time allocation to the fullest. Almost all of them are timed in such a way as to make completion of the tests a nontrivial challenge. A slow or very cautious worker is at a distinct disadvantage.

Not all cultures and subcultures view time in the same way that we do. For example, among the Kipsigi, schedules are much more flexible, and hence these individuals have difficulty understanding and dealing with Western notions of the time pressure under which people are expected to live (Super & Harkness, 1982). In Hispanic cultures, such as Venezuela, my own personal experience indicates that the press of time is taken with much less seriousness than it is in typical North

American cultural settings. Even within the continental United States, though, there can be major differences in the importance of time alloca-tion (Heath, 1983).

The point of these examples has been to illustrate how differences in environmental press and people's conceptions of what constitutes an intelligent response to it can influence just what counts as adaptive behavior. To understand intelligence, one must understand it, not only in relation to its internal manifestations in terms of mental processes and its experiential manifestations in terms of facets of the experiential continuum, but also in terms of how thought is intelligently translated into action in a variety of different contextual settings. The differences in what is considered adaptive and intelligent can extend even to differ-ent occupations within a given cultural milieu. For example, Sternberg (1985b) has found that individuals in different fields of endeavor (art, business, philosophy, physics) view intelligence in slightly different ways that reflect the demands of their respective fields.

Shaping. Shaping of the environment is often used as a backup strategy when adaptation fails. If one is unable to change oneself so as to fit the environment, one may attempt to change the environment so as to fit oneself. For example, repeated attempts to adjust to the demands of one's romantic partner may eventually lead to attempts to get the part-ner to adjust to oneself. But shaping is not always used in lieu of adaptation. In some cases, shaping may be used before adaptation is ever tried, as in the case of the individual who attempts to shape a romantic partner with little or no effort to shape him or herself so as better to suit the partner's wants or needs.

In the laboratory, examples of shaping behavior can be seen in strategy selection situations where one essentially molds the task to fit one's preferred style of dealing with tasks. For example, in comparing sentence statements to pictures that either do or do not accurately rep-resent these statements, individuals may select either a verbal or a spatial strategy, depending upon their pattern of verbal and spatial abil-ities (MacLeod, et al., 1978). The task is "made over" in conformity to what one does best.

In some respects, shaping may be seen as the quintessence of intelli-gent thought and behavior. One essentially makes over the environ-ment rather than allowing the environment to make over oneself. Perhaps it is this skill that has enabled humankind to reach its current level of scientific, technological, and cultural advancement (for better or for worse). In science, the greatest scientists are those who set the paradigms (shaping), rather than those who merely follow them (adaptation). Similarly, in art and in literature, the individuals who achieve greatest distinction are often those who create new modes and styles of expression, rather than merely following existing ones. It is not their use of shaping alone that distinguishes them intellectually, but rather a combination of their willingness to do it with their skill in doing it.

Selection. Selection involves renunciation of one environment in favor of another. In terms of the rough hierarchy established so far, selection is sometimes used when both adaptation and shaping fail. After attempting to both adapt to and shape a marriage, one may decide to deal with one's failure in these activities by "deselecting" the marriage and choosing the environment of the newly single. Failure to adjust to the demands of work environments, or to change the demands placed upon one so as to make them a reasonable fit to one's interests, values, expectations, or abilities, may result in the decision to seek another job altogether. But selection is not always used as a last resort. Sometimes one attempts to shape an environment only after attempts to leave it have failed. Other times, one may decide almost instantly that an environment is simply wrong for oneself and feel that one need not or should not even try to fit into or to change it. For example, we get, every now and then, a new graduate student who realizes almost immediately that he or she came to graduate school for the wrong reason or who finds that graduate school is nothing at all like the continuation of undergraduate school she or he expected. In such cases, the intelligent thing to do may be to leave the environment as soon as possible, in order to pursue activities more in line with one's goals in life.

Environmental selection is not usually directly studied in the laboratory, although it may have relevance for certain experimental settings. Perhaps no research example of its relevance has been more salient than the experimental paradigm created by Milgram (1974), who, in a long series of studies, asked subjects to "shock" other subjects (who were actually confederates and who were not actually shocked). The finding of critical interest was how few subjects either shaped the environment by refusing to shock their victims or employed the device of selection by simply refusing to continue with the experiment and walking out of it. Milgram has drawn an analogy to the situation in Nazi Germany, where obedience to authority created an environment whose horrors continue to amaze us to this day, and always will. This example is a good one in showing how close matters of intelligence can come to matters of personality. In fact, many Jews refused to leave Nazi-occupied territories for fear of losing their property, peers, and so on. Their refusal may have been due to personality factors, but for many of them, their decision to stay was in some respects the supreme act of unintelligence, as it resulted in their death, not through choice, but later through having no choice at all in the matter.

To conclude, adaptation, shaping, and selection are functions of intelligent thought as it operates in context. They may, although they need not, be employed hierarchically, with one path followed when another one fails. It is through adaptation, shaping, and selection that the components of intelligence, as employed at various levels of experience, become actualized in the real world. In this section, it has become clear that the modes of actualization can differ widely across individuals and groups, so that intelligence cannot be understood independently of the ways in which it is manifested.

Conclusions and implications

The triarchic theory consists of three interrelated subtheories that attempt to account for the bases and manifestations of intelligent thought. The componential subtheory relates intelligence to the internal world of the individual. The experiential subtheory relates intelligence to the experience of the individual with tasks and situations. The contextual subtheory relates intelligence to the external world of the individual.

The elements of the three subtheories are interrelated: The components of intelligence are manifested at different levels of experience with tasks and in situations of varying degrees of contextual relevance to a person's life. The components of intelligence are posited to be universal to intelligence: Thus, the components that contribute to intelligent performance in one culture do so in all other cultures as well. Moreover, the importance of dealing with novelty and automatization of information processing to intelligence are posited to be universal. But the manifestations of these components in experience are posited to be relative to cultural contexts. What constitutes adaptive thought or behavior in one culture is not necessarily adaptive in another culture. Moreover, thoughts and actions that would shape behavior in appropriate ways in one context might not shape them in appropriate ways in another context. Finally, the environment one selects will depend largely upon the environments available to one and the fit of one's cognitive abilities, motivations, values, and affects to the available alternatives.

Stephen Ceci and the bioecological theory of intelligence

The most recent systems theory of human intelligence has been proposed by Ceci (in press). His theory is somewhat less elaborated at this point than is Gardner's or Sternberg's theory and hence is explained in less detail. Ceci's bioecological theory is based upon three key proposals. First, in accordance with Gardner (1983), Ceci argues that there does not exist any one cognitive potential or g, but rather multiple potentials. Second, the role of context is critical both in the development of cognitive potentials and in their display through test performance. Ceci defines context broadly, including within its purview motivational forces, social and physical aspects of a setting or task, and the knowledge domain in which the task is embedded. Third, Ceci suggests that knowledge and aptitude are fundamentally inseparable: Cognitive potentials continually access the knowledge base and, in turn, alter the contents of the structure of the knowledge base.

Ceci provides evidence to support each of these propositions. Moreover, he attempts to discredit evidence that is inconsistent with his beliefs. For example, he notes that although g is well understood as a statistical concept, it is only poorly understood as a psychological concept. Whatever g results from intelligence tests could be a function of environmental variables, biological variables, metacognitive variables, or motivational variables. Indeed, g may have no psychological reality at all and be merely a conglomeration of these or other factors.

At present, the bioecological framework is not fully developed, and so it is not clear exactly where it will go or what it will be capable of explaining or predicting. But the theory represents another attempt to integrate cognition and context, taking into account what happens both inside and outside the head.

12

Implications of the metaphorical
approach

In this book, I have described some of the major metaphors that underlie our thinking about intelligence and the kinds of theories they generate. I have also discussed some of the implicit theories that lie behind
explicit theories of intelligence. One obvious question arises with
respect to the metaphorical approach: Why should we care what metaphors generate or guide our theories of intelligence? In this chapter, I
will consider first theoretical implications and then practical implications for society and how the metaphorical approach can help enlighten
our thinking about human intellect.

Theoretical implications

The main theoretical implication of the metaphorical point of view is
that in the study of human intelligence (as well as other phenomena),
we pay too much attention to answers at the expense of paying enough
attention to questions. As a result, we often see theories as competing,
when in fact they are not: They are different answers to different questions, not different answers to the same question. Even when we recognize that two theories address different questions, we may still try to
compare them on some illusory basis that prejudices the outcome of our
comparison in favor of one theory or the other.

We can, of course, try to address the issue of how fundamental
various questions are. For example, we could decide that the relation of
intelligence to the mind of the individual is somehow the most fundamental question, with other questions relegated to inferior status. The
problem with this approach, of course, is that various investigators will
disagree among themselves as to how fundamental each question is.

A more fruitful approach, I believe, is to ask how fundamental a
question is for a given purpose. If one's goal is a complete theory of
intelligence, then one will need somehow to address the questions

raised by all or certainly most of the metaphors considered in this book. If one's goal is the more realistic one of addressing only some of the questions addressed by the various metaphors, then the important decision is to choose one or more of the metaphors that are appropriate for the questions one wishes to address. For example, the computational metaphor will address questions of process but will generally beg questions of socialization effects on intelligence, which would be better addressed by the sociological metaphor.

One of the problems the field of intelligence faces is the parochialism of those who work within it. We tend to view as important the questions that we happen to address and to view as much less important or even trivial the questions other people address. Of course, we do not view this tendency as one of parochialism, but rather as one of good taste in problems, which of course we all believe we have. The arguments for one metaphor over another tend to reduce to one's own preferred metaphor being better.

People who try to be broad and even to combine metaphors in their individual approach to intelligence risk being accepted by none of the existing camps of theorists. Those who do not wish to be confined to the questions addressed by a single approach, rather than being applauded, are likely to be labeled "grandiose" or "unfocused."

I believe this labeling phenomenon is a serious impediment to progress in the field of intelligence, because comprehensive theories of the future will almost inevitably have to blend, rather than merely juxtapose, metaphors. These theories will have to address a broader set of questions than have been addressed by typical theories of the past. My concern is that investigators will shun rather than believe such integrative effects, which they are likely to perceive as the work of upstarts encroaching upon their turf. I hope I am wrong.

The metaphorical approach is useful in helping us apprehend just what questions our theories are – and are not – addressing. To the extent that the approach succeeds in making us more self-aware, it has the potential for helping us understand what we can and cannot accomplish through any chosen metaphor.

Practical implications

Consider now some practical implications of the metaphorical approach. Because the book has emphasized the theoretical at the expense of the practical, I will devote more emphasis in this chapter to the latter.

I will consider four issues: (a) testing of intelligence, (b) teaching of intelligence, (c) group differences and heritability of intelligence, and (d) extreme levels of intelligence.

Testing of intelligence

Intelligence testing has been dominated almost exclusively by a single metaphor, namely, the geographic one. Indeed, intelligence testing and the main methodology through which the geographic metaphor has been operationalized – factor analysis – grew up hand and hand. Not only is it difficult to separate testing from the geographic metaphor, but for many if not most of the people who do testing, there is no other way. The goal of testing, for these people, is to yield one or more scores corresponding to levels of ability with respect to each of the regions of the mind posited by a given theory, whether it is just a single region or multiple regions. Even those who do not subscribe to the geographic metaphor often end up using tests generated under the geographic metaphor as the criterion by which the validity of their tests will be judged. For example, users of information-processing tests, generated under the computational metaphor, have frequently ended up employing psychometric tests as the basis for evaluating the validity of their instruments (e.g., Hunt et al., 1973; Sternberg, 1977). Similarly, Piagetian tests have been validated against psychometric ones generated by the geographic metaphor (see Tuddenham, 1970). A review of the literature leaves no doubt that conventional tests serve as the standard against which other tests are evaluated. The evaluation can be something of a "Catch-22": If the new tests are highly correlated with the psychometric ones, then an argument can be made that the new tests are not needed and that they merely repeat the function of tests that already exist; but if the new tests are poorly correlated with the psychometric tests, the argument can be made that whatever it is that the new tests measure, it is not intelligence. Can there, then, be any doubt that we are now locked into the geographic metaphor, at least with respect to the testing of intelligence?

I would argue that there are good reasons for having tests based on metaphors other than the geographic one. First, it is not clear that the tests generated under the geographic metaphor really should serve as the standard against which other tests are measured. The fact that such tests have been in existence for a number of years does not in itself make them a viable standard. To the extent that external criteria have been used in the development of conventional tests, the validation criteria have generally been performance in school as measured by indices such as school grades and teachers' evaluations. But clearly, these indices provide only one kind of criterion against which to evaluate tests or theories. Certainly, school grades are not an adequate measure of success in life. And after people graduate from school, they are of essentially no importance at all. One could argue that the present tests are quite narrow in what they measure (e.g., Gardner, 1983; Sternberg, 1985a), so that if a new test did correlate highly with the old ones, it would indicate that the new test is just as narrow as the old ones. In effect, it is an historical accident that the intelligence-testing business got its main start when Binet was asked to distinguish groups of students in a school. Had he or someone else been asked to do the same for performance at work, or in some other domain, the tests that resulted might have been quite different, and possibly different in kind.

Second, new tests might provide an operational basis for expanding our conception of intelligence. To the extent that the tests do not correlate highly with conventional ones, we need at least to be open to the possibility that the new tests are measuring an aspect of intelligence that the old ones do not measure.

Third, new tests can give us kinds of information that are not yielded by conventional psychometric tests, regardless of the correlation of the new tests with the conventional ones. They cannot only give us new information, but can help us conceive of individual people's intelligence in new ways. Consider the various metaphors and the kinds of tests they have generated.

Psychometric tests, of course, give an IQ or comparable measurement. Some of them give multiple IQs or multiple ability scores based on logical or empirical analysis. The idea behind such tests is to evaluate the quality of each of the regions of the mind.

Computationally based tests, regardless of their correlation with the geographically based ones, give completely different kinds of information. They can tell, for an individual examinee, the processes used to solve problems; the strategy or strategies into which these processes are combined; the amount of time spent on each process; in some cases, the susceptibility of each process to error; and also, in some cases, the form of representation of information in the mind. Thus, we potentially learn quite a bit about a person's mode and quality of information processing. Geographically based tests do not give us these kinds of information, except perhaps in confounded fashion. Indeed, psychometric factors are often a combination of process and content that makes it difficult to separate the effects of the two.

Biologically based tests provide very different kinds of information. Such tests may indicate specific neuropsychological deficits, patterns of hemispheric specialization, performances of different regions of the brain, or in the case of evoked-potential measurement, patterns of brain waves. The interpretability of this information, as in the case of any test information, will depend upon the quality of theory upon which the test is based. But biologically based tests are, for the most part, the only ones that really map onto brain functioning, whether directly or indirectly.

Tests based upon the epistemological metaphor reveal specific competencies and may be useful from a criterion-referenced point of view. For example, such tests can help us discover whether a particular child conserves and in what domains he or she conserves. They can tell us a child's ability to take alternative perspectives or to reverse operations. Using Siegler's (1978) approach, we can learn the levels of rules children are employing for different information-processing tasks, or using Pascual-Leone's (1983) approach, we can learn the amount of working-memory space, or M-power, available to the individual.

All of the tests considered above are based on a view that intelligence is primarily something internal to the individual. It is, at least metaphorically, inside the head. But tests need not make this assumption. Tests based upon the anthropological metaphor will need to be tailored, not just translated or adjusted, to the culture in which the testing is taking place. Tests based upon the internally oriented metaphors have been used with almost no modification across cultures, under the assumption that what they measure should be universal. But this is a big assumption, and as shown in Chapter 9, changing the content vehicles and the format of a test, and even the location in which it is given, can have a major effect upon test scores. Thus, children who might look quite stupid on tests based upon metaphors that view intelligence as inside the head might look quite smart on tests based on metaphors that are oriented toward the outside. What is of greatest interest is that adherents to the anthropological metaphor, who make a living of studying intelligence across cultures, will almost all believe that mere translation or minor modifications do not adequately control for cultural differences in intelligence testing, whereas adherents to the geographic metaphor, most of whom do not specialize in cross-cultural work, are happy just to translate or make minor modifications of their tests. So the metaphor under which one works can have profound implications for how intelligent a person will appear when tested, because the metaphor determines what will be tested and how the testing will be done.

Adherents to the sociological metaphor emphasize the importance of socialization experiences in understanding intelligence, and their testing reflects their beliefs. For example, two of the main exponents of this approach, Vygotsky and Feuerstein, independently came up with very similar ideas, which Vygotsky labeled the zone of potential development and Feuerstein labeled learning potential. In both cases, the examiner guides the examinee while the testing is taking place, rather than the examiner keeping distance and going out of his or her way not to give any clues as to how test items should be performed. Thus, the role of the examiner is virtually the opposite of the conventional one. The examiner is involved in helping the child, as opposed to making sure that she or he does not inadvertently help the child and thereby distort the score. In this approach, the emphasis in testing is on learning at time of test, rather than on learning that took place in the past. Feuerstein (1979), who compared the psychometric to the dynamic approach, has found substantial differences in how people perform in the one kind of test versus the other.

Finally, in the systems approaches, the actual testing that is done will depend on the way the system of the mind is conceived. But again, individuals may perform quite differently from the way they do on standard tests. Sternberg (in press) is currently developing a test based upon his triarchic theory of intelligence, which will provide processing scores for componential skills, coping with novelty skills, automatization skills, and practical intellectual skills. Only the first of these, componential skills, are really dealt with at all on conventional tests. Similarly, Howard Gardner and David Feldman, in their project Spectrum, are developing tests based on Gardner's (1983) theory of multiple intelligences. These tests, unlike the conventional ones, and unlike Sternberg's, are not paper-and-pencil at all, but rather measure children's thinking skills in an enriched classroom environment where children are performing criterion activities.

In sum, intelligence testing involves radically different forms and contents as a function of the metaphor under which the test is generated. Simply assuming that the tests generated under one metaphor give a "correct" score is not only unjustified, but unfair to the persons being tested. People may go along thinking that the test provides some measure of their "true intelligence," whereas in fact it only provides an approximate measure under one metaphor. Their score under another metaphor might be quite different.

Teaching of intelligence

Just as testing has borne a different face under each of the metaphors, so has the teaching of intelligence, as have views regarding whether intelligence can be taught in the first place. Believers in the geographic metaphor have, for the most part, been skeptical about the teachability of intelligence. And if one looks at the way they study intelligence, one can see why. One of the major criteria for the quality of a test is test–retest or alternate-forms reliability. The higher the reliability, supposedly, the better the test. But training can reduce the reliability of a test, as it may change the rank order of individual differences. Moreover, testers have staked much of their reputation on the notion that test scores, such as IQ, should remain relatively constant in value over long periods of time. Thus, they may feel that they have a vested interest in the stability of scores. Indeed, most testing organizations do not look fondly on courses designed to raise scores on their tests. Presumably, they would not look fondly even on (hypothetical) courses to lower test scores, because their goal is not to send scores down or up, but to keep them constant.

The psychometric approach is also not very fruitful in terms of its implications for how intelligence would be taught (Wagner & Sternberg, 1984). Because the psychometric model is a static one, it is not clear what one would do to change the way people perform in a dynamic situation. Indeed, to the extent that there has been training at all under the psychometric approach, it has been largely by giving practice on the kinds of items that IQ tests contain. Such practice, based on our own experience, is not likely to result in very substantial gains in test scores (Sternberg, 1987c). The training courses that are successful are ones that get away from the static geographic metaphor and either teach processes of problem solving for item types on the test or teach test-taking strategies. The Stanley Kaplan course would be an example of a course that concentrates on the former; the Princeton Review course is an example of one that concentrates on the latter.

The computational metaphor is much richer in its implications for teaching intelligence, because it suggests the processes, strategies, and mental representations that people do or, in some cases, should use in order to think intelligently and to perform well on tests of various kinds. Whereas the early literature on teaching intelligence was not extremely promising (Detterman & Sternberg, 1982; Jensen, 1969), training based on a computational metaphor has shown considerable promise (Baron & Sternberg, 1987; Detterman & Sternberg, 1982; Nickerson, Perkins, & Smith, 1985). Adherents to the information-processing view do not have the same vested interest in unchanging scores, and indeed, my experience is that most of them are not even quite sure of what psychometric reliability is! One almost never sees references to test–retest or alternate-forms reliability in articles or books based upon the computational metaphor. Indeed, one of the ways of testing information-processing theories has been through training experiments (e.g., Belmont & Butterfield, 1971; Brown & Campione, 1977). Thus, information-processing researchers, especially those who use training methods to validate theories, have, if anything, a vested interest in gains, and indeed, gains are what they have, for the most part, found. Again, the metaphor has fairly drastic implications for how the data come out. Although scientists like to think that data from scientific experiments are immune to the personal biases of the investigator, the very conceptualization of the experiments they do is strongly affected and, in some cases, even determined by the metaphor, so that the results can be very different as a function of the metaphor that is used.

The biological approach has not been terribly suggestive of ways of teaching intelligence, at least to date. It is not clear, for the most part, how we can change biological functioning, although it might be possible to change evoked potentials or EEG patterns by instructing people to think actively or in particular ways while measurements are taking place. To the extent that neuropsychologists have been involved in teaching intelligence, it has been, for the most part, with respect to helping patients with brain lesions regain lost functioning. But instruction of this kind tends not to be based on any particular theory, but rather to be pragmatically based, with the goal of simply improving function in whatever way is possible.

Piaget was himself skeptical about the teaching of intelligence, and indeed, as mentioned earlier, believed Americans were too concerned with accelerating intellectual performance. Because he believed that functions tend to emerge at certain ages, to some extent, his theory would have been undermined if teaching of the competencies in his theory were too successful. Neo-Piagetians, and especially Case and Siegler, have been very interested in training and have shown that at least some training effects can be obtained. The whole difference is in the variant of epistemology being used. Piaget's was that knowledge is acquired at a fixed age or at least in a fixed sequence, whereas Siegler and Case have been more flexible in their points of view, although they too have posited sequences whose order is more or less fixed.

Believers in the anthropological approach have not been much interested in teaching to intelligence tests, because they believe the content of these tests, or at least the conventional ones, is so culturally bound. It is not clear to them why one would want to teach, say, members of an African tribe how to perform well on tests that were made by and for North Americans. As it happens, the best way to increase scores on these tests seems to be through education of the North American variety. Indeed, when this sort of education is introduced to members of other cultures, unsurprisingly, their scores on our tests go up. Were they the creators of intelligence tests, requiring, say, navigation of ships based only on positions of stars or skill in hunting animals whose tracks are difficult or impossible for us in North America to follow, we would probably improve our scores only if we received the kind of education that their children received. Thus, for the anthropologically oriented investigator, before teaching intelligence, one would have to ask which intelligence and why it should be taught. Arguably, teaching North American skills and values can result in the discontinuation or even destruction of the indigenous culture, and therefore may be perceived as a negative thing. Indeed, members of many cultures around the world are trying in the present day to preserve their culture, which often means achieving some degree of immunity from Western values.

Believers in the sociological metaphor are those who are most enthusiastic about the teaching of intelligence. Again, their enthusiasm is understandable in terms of their metaphor, because the sociological metaphor emphasizes how intelligence is taught through environmental socialization. For the sociological theorist, intelligence is being taught all the time. Feuerstein (1980), for example, emphasizes how mediated learning experience is the means through which much of intelligence is acquired, and it is an integral part of the social environment. It is not a part of some particular course for teaching intelligence, unless the course is a remedial one for children who have had inadequate mediated learning experiences. So important is teaching and learning to the sociological theorist that teaching is even an integral part of the testing, and indeed, the testing cannot be done without teaching in the testing context. To the sociological theorist, intelligence is, in large part, the ability to learn from teaching in a testing or other environment. For this theorist, teaching and testing cannot well be separated. Obviously, this view is in substantial contrast to the beliefs of adherents of most other points of view.

Finally, adherents of the systems metaphor are likely to believe that intelligence is eminently teachable if they believe, as indeed they do, that interventions are possible within the intellectual system. They may differ in the locus at which they believe interventions are possible, but both Gardner and Sternberg, for example, have been actively involved in attempts to teach intelligence, Sternberg through his Intelligence Applied Course (Sternberg, 1986) and Gardner through his Project Propel. Most people believe that systems are modifiable in at least some degree. If systems were not modifiable, they would tend to degenerate through stagnation or decay, whether they are intellectual systems, organizational systems, relationship systems, or whatever. Hence, again, the metaphor guides the thinking.

To conclude, metaphors have a powerful effect upon people's thinking about the teachability of intelligence. For the most part, people's views on whether intelligence can be taught, and how well it can be taught, can be predicted from the metaphor to which they adhere.

Group differences

Views on group differences, like views on practically everything else that is intelligence related, are largely a function of the metaphor to which a person subscribes. We again find high predictability of people's points of view on the basis of the metaphor they use in their theorizing.

Geographic theorists have been avid investigators of group differences. It is hardly surprising that they would be, because the entire approach has been based on understanding individual differences in scores, and so it is only a small step to taking averages and looking at differences between and among groups. The whole idea of norm referencing – scaling scores by comparing the performances of people to each other – invites individual and group comparisons. For the most part, geographic theorists have argued that differences are not in the mental maps, but in what we might call the "quality of life" in each region. In other words, these theorists believe in differences in scores more than in mental structures. Indeed, differences in structures would be dangerous, because they would suggest that no one psychometric theory works across cultures. None of the psychometric theorists has been eager to say that his or her theory of intelligence is one that applies only, say, to North Americans or to the British.

Geographic theorists differ in their attributions of the origins of group differences. Most of them assign a considerable hereditary component to intelligence, although they admit to at least some environmental components (see, for commentaries, Loehlin, Lindzey, & Spuhler, 1975; Plomin, 1988; Scarr & Carter-Saltzman, 1982). All of these studies of group differences, of course, are predicated on psychometric tests, and unfortunately, the estimates of group differences and heritability can be no better than the tests are. So even when group differences are found, we need to be at least somewhat skeptical of the results, because their very existence is predicated on the basis of the geographic metaphor and, in particular, its instantiation through conventional psychometric tests.

Computational theorists, who earlier were mentioned as generally having less interest in individual differences than do the geographic theorists, have also shown less interest in group differences. There have been few studies of groups differences in information processing, at least with respect to racial, ethnic, and socioeconomic groups. Such studies could be done: Computational theorists just have not expressed much interest in them. Their interest has been in a different kind of group difference, namely, that between experts and novices. The reason for this interest is that they have hoped to trace the development of expertise and to understand what it is that distinguishes expert from novice performance. But in testing experts versus novices, the presupposition of studying group differences is very different from that of studying different ethnic groups: In studying experts versus novices, one expects differences and is generally disappointed when they do not occur. In studying different ethnic groups, there is or at least should be no prior expectation of group differences, or at least so many people believe. When differences occur, they have to be accounted for. When studying experts versus novices, the absence of group differences can be an embarrassment because of the suggestion that the test distinguishing experts from novices is not sufficiently sensitive or is inappropriate for measuring the differences of interest.

Biological theorists have studied group differences, but generally the groups that are compared are patients with various syndromes, or patients with a given syndrome versus normals. Again, the nature of the group differences studied is fairly predictable from the metaphor, because biological theorizing is so often based on use of patients. Thus, again, the metaphor generates the research and even the research questions. Few people seriously believe that brain structure is different from one culture to another, which may be why it has not been studied cross-culturally. In earlier times, however, members of other cultures were certainly considered to have brains more resembling those of the primates (see Gould, 1981). My impression is that at least some measurers of evoked potentials are closet psychometricians, and so it would not surprise me if before too long they got serious about measuring cultural group differences in EEG. But at present, we know almost nothing about group differences in brain wave measures.

Epistemologists study knowledge and its acquisition, and hence it makes sense that the major group differences that have been studied by epistemologically oriented theorists have been developmental differences, with the idea being to compare knowledge, structures of knowledge, and acquisition of knowledge across age levels. Cross-cultural studies have been done and have shown that rate of development may differ somewhat across cultures.

Because anthropologists investigate cross-cultural similarities and differences, one might expect them to be most energetic in studying group differences in intelligence. But in some respects, they are the people who are the most cautious about studying such differences. Their caution results from their realization of just how difficult it is to compare groups across cultures. Most of the people who are serious in this field have paid attention to the question of how groups can be compared (see, e.g., Berry & Irvine, 1986; Cole & Means, 1981). Some anthropologically oriented investigators take a so-called etic point of view, which argues for the cross-cultural applicability of a framework. But those who take an "emic" point of view believe that the framework for comparison must be indigenous to each culture itself, and hence comparisons become extremely hard. Thus anthropologists, by virtue of their metaphor, are both those most interested in group differences and those most sensitive to how very difficult it is to study them.

Sociological theorists, like anthropological ones, study environmental variables, although they are less involved in cross-cultural comparisons than are anthropologists. Nevertheless, they have been quite sensitive to group differences and have sought to elaborate group differences through a variety of means of investigation (see, e.g., Heath, 1983). Adherents to the sociological view are likely to look at socialization differences across cultures, as has Feuerstein (1980). He has been aware of how differences in socialization across groups can result in radically different performances on tests. Thus, intervention in learning and compensation for socialization that may not have adequately prepared people to meet the demands of their own society can be a useful way of studying group differences. Again, the sociological theorist tends to combine training with study and is likely to study the group differences through an intervention experiment.

The systems theories of intelligence are relatively new, and so there just has not been much time yet to study group differences. Certainly, the approaches lend themselves to such study, and when it is done, it is likely to be in terms of how groups differ in the systems they bring to bear upon problems. That, at least, has been the direction of what speculation has been done so far (e.g., Sternberg & Suben, 1986).

Extreme levels of intelligence

The most energetic investigators of extremes in intelligence are those who have been around the longest, namely, the geographic theorists. Dating back to the Terman study, giftedness has been a major topic of research among psychometricians, as has mental retardation. Perhaps unsurprisingly, giftedness has tended to mean very high scores on intelligence tests, whereas mental retardation has tended to mean very low scores on intelligence tests. Indeed, for many years, labels have existed defining different levels of mental retardation or different levels of giftedness. For example, we used to speak of idiots, imbeciles, and morons, and now speak of profoundly retarded, moderately retarded, and mildly retarded, but the labels are still there, even though in euphemistic form.

Investigators have occasionally tried other forms of measurement to use in classification. For example, the American Association for Mental Deficiency has defined retardation in terms of social competence as well as cognitive criteria. But theorists as well as practitioners seem to keep reverting to IQ-based measurement (Zigler, Balla, & Hodapp, 1984). Sometimes, the additional criteria used for classification are other psychometric tests that, although not called intelligence tests, are fairly similar to them. But among geographic theorists, the extremes are generally defined in terms of the measurements that are used.

Computational theorists are much newer to the measurement of extremes, although there now exists a growing literature on both giftedness (e.g., Horowitz & O'Brien, 1985; Sternberg & Davidson, 1986) and on mental retardation (see, e.g., Sternberg & Spear, 1985). Unsurprisingly, followers of the computational metaphor tend to view both extremes in terms of qualitative and quantitative differences in information processing between people in the middle of the spectrum and those at each of the extremes. They are what Zigler et al. (1984) refer to as "difference" theorists, because they look at information-processing differences between the extreme and typical groups. Such differences have been found. The advantage of the computational approach is that it gives some level of understanding of how the extremes differ from the typicals, not just in terms of a score, but in terms of the way or speed with which people process information.

Biological theorists have dealt a great deal with the organic as opposed to the familial side of mental retardation. Some of their patients retain fairly high levels of IQ, despite severe localized deficits in processing. Of course, because so many people are wedded to the geographical view, they may end up believing that the typical IQ, despite the severe deficits in processing, indicates that intelligence has not been affected. In fact, what may remain constant is only that part of intelligence that the psychometric tests measure. There is not, at least yet, a substantial literature on the biology of giftedness.

Adherents to the epistemological metaphor have been less interested in extremes than adherents to some other metaphors, perhaps because they believe that most children do progress along a certain trajectory of development, sooner or later. For them, the biggest difference may be in developmental rate rather than in a value judgment about what is better or worse. On this view, retarded individuals are ones who develop slowly mentally. Indeed, Brown (Ferrara et al., 1986) has noted the phenomenon of "academic retardation," that is, mental retardation that seems to apply only in the school setting. Many of the children who are labeled as mentally retarded in school do just fine in their lives after school ends. So they may be slow to develop, but they reach a point at which they can function effectively. However, from a developmental standpoint, it is reasonable to suppose that not every individual reaches the same asymptote in terms of his or her level of intellectual development.

Anthropological theorists are likely to see both retardation and giftedness as embedded in a cultural context. What is retarded or gifted in one culture may be typical in another, or what is retarded in one culture may even be gifted in another, and vice versa. It all depends on what abilities are valued and how these abilities are measured. Indeed, if one considers the difference between who will succeed as a hunter and who will succeed, say, as an accountant, it is clear that differing values could lead to different conceptions of who is smart or stupid. The anthropological view makes clear just how fragile our conceptions of the extremes are, because our conceptions are so culturally dependent. People who are at an extreme are so only with respect to the cultural context in which they live. Internally oriented views simply fail to take this fact into account.

At least one sociologically based theorist, Feuerstein, has been very interested in the lower extreme of the intellectual spectrum. Indeed, much of his work has been devoted to demonstrating that retarded performers can be brought up to a level that approximates the performance of children who function normally. As noted earlier, Feuerstein does not even accept the notion of a "retarded individual," preferring to refer to "retarded performers." In other words, it is the performance rather than the person that is retarded. In the sociological metaphor, retardation is seen as, at least in part, an externally based phenomenon, that is, one due to inadequate socialization. Indeed, Feuerstein refers to children as culturally deprived if they receive inadequate experiencing of their own culture, whatever that culture may be. Again, the metaphor is determinative of the way in which intelligence-related phenomena are perceived. Similarly, gifted children are often children who receive superior socialization, and indeed, we know that scores on various kinds of tests and performances of various kinds are highly related to socioeconomic status. Although a number of variables may be confounded with socioeconomic status, it is clear that children who have more resources available to them perform better on most tests of intellectual skills.

Systems theorists view extremes of intelligence in terms of the performance of a system. I have analyzed (Sternberg, 1985a) both retardation and giftedness in terms of various aspects of his triarchic theory. For example, a retarded individual tends to have inadequate metacomponential (executive) functioning, whereas a gifted individual seems often to be exceptional, not only in metacomponential performance, but in use of knowledge acquisition components when applied insightfully (Sternberg & Davidson, 1983; see also Davidson, 1986). I have also emphasized the importance in giftedness of how well one uses the system one has. I describe intelligence in terms of capitalizing on strengths and compensating for weaknesses. In other words, gifted individuals, especially practically gifted ones, are almost always people who figure out what it is they are good at and what it is they are not so good at, and then find ways to make the most of their strengths and to get around their weaknesses. This view is a very different one from the conventional psychometric one. Gifted individuals may not be good at many things. But they find something that they are really good at, and then find ways of exploiting that strength.

I view giftedness as being of multiple kinds, as would be retardation. Componential, experiential, and contextual strengths and weaknesses can all lead to different patterns of giftedness or retardation, and hence, for me, giftedness and retardation are in no way unitary phenomena. The same would be true for Gardner (1983). Gifted individuals could excel in any one or more of the seven intelligences. An exceptionally gifted pianist, for example, would excel in musical intelligence, whereas a gifted accountant might excel in logical-mathematical intelligence. There is no need in these conceptions to have a high IQ. Rather, one can be gifted simply because of an excellence in one area of the system. But a weakness in one area of the system or one intelligence can also lead to the label of retardation. For example, in Gardner's theory, a child who is exceptionally weak in linguistic intelligence will probably be labeled as retarded, regardless of his strengths in other areas. That child will come out with a low IQ, and thereby be labeled, even if she or he is exceptionally strong in other areas.

To conclude, I have taken four different practical issues that arise from the theory of intelligence and attempted to show how the metaphor to which one subscribes both directly and indirectly affects the views one is likely to have with regard to each of these issues. In understanding a theorist's or practitioner's point of view on a given practical problem, it is important to understand the metaphor from which the individual is working, because this individual's point of view is likely to be shaped by that metaphor. We really cannot understand the practice as well as the theory behind the technology of intelligence unless we understand the metaphors on which each technology is based. To understand the field and to understand intelligence, we must understand the underlying metaphors.

References

Ackerman, P. L. (1987). Individual differences in skill learning: An integration of psychometric and information processing perspectives. *Psychological Bulletin, 102*, 3–27.

Ainsworth, M. D. S. (1967). *Infancy in Uganda*. Baltimore, MD: Johns Hopkins University Press.

Anderson, J. E. (1940). The prediction of terminal intelligence from infant and preschool tests. In G. M. Whipple (Ed.), *Intelligence: Its nature and nurture*. Bloomington, IL: Public School Publishing.

Anderson, J. R. (1983). *The architecture of cognition*. Cambridge, MA: Harvard University Press.

Anderson, J. R. (1986). Knowledge compilation: The general learning mechanism. In R. S. Michalski, J. G. Carbonell, & T. M. Mitchell (Eds.), *Machine learning: An artificial intelligence approach* (Vol. 2, pp. 289–310). Los Altos, CA: Kaufmann.

Anderson, J. R., & Freebody, P. (1979). *Vocabulary knowledge* (Tech. Rep. No. 136). Champaign: Center for the Study of Reading, University of Illinois.

Asch, S. (1936). A study of change in mental organization. *Archives of Psychology*, Whole No. 195.

Atwood, M. E., & Polson, P. G. (1976). A process model for water jug problems. *Cognitive Psychology, 8,* 191–216.

Baltes, P. B., Dittmann-Kohli, F., & Dixon, R. A. (1984). New perspectives on the development of intelligence in adulthood: Toward a dual-process conception and a model of selective optimization with compensation. In P. B. Baltes & O. G. Brim, Jr. (Eds.), *Life-span development and behavior* (Vol. 6, pp. 33–76). New York: Academic Press.

Baltes, P. B., & Schaie, K. W. (1976). On the plasticity of intelligence in adulthood and old age: Where Horn and Donaldson fail. *American Psychologist, 31,* 720–5.

Baltes, P. B., & Smith, J. (1990). Toward a psychology of wisdom and its ontogenesis. In R. J. Sternberg (Ed.), *Wisdom: Its nature, origins, and development* (pp. 87–120). Cambridge University Press.

Baron, J. (1985). *Rationality and intelligence*. Cambridge University Press.

Baron, J. B., & Sternberg, R. J. (Eds.) (1987). *Teaching thinking skills: Theory and practice.* New York: Freeman.

Bayley, N. (1933). Mental growth during the first three years. A developmental study of 61 children by repeated tests. *Genetic Psychology Monographs, 14,* 1–92.

Bayley, N. (1943). Mental growth during the first three years. In R. G. Barker, J. S. Kounin, & H. F. Wright (Eds.), *Child behavior and development* (pp. 87–105). New York: McGraw-Hill.

Bayley, N. (1949). Consistency and variability in the growth of intelligence from birth to eighteen years. *Journal of Genetic Psychology, 75,* 165–96.

Bayley, N. (1951). Development and maturation. In H. Helson (Ed.), *Theoretical foundations of psychology* (pp. 145–99). New York: Van Nostrand.

Bayley, N. (1955). On the growth of intelligence. *American Psychologist, 10,* 805–18.

Bayley, N. (1966). Learning in adulthood: The role of intelligence. In H. J. Klausmeier & C. W. Harris (Eds.), *Analysis of concept learning* (pp. 117–38). New York: Academic Press.

Bayley, N. (1968). Behavioral correlates of mental growth: Birth to thirty-six years. *American Psychologist, 23,* 1–17.

Bayley, N. (1970). Development of mental abilities. In P. H. Mussen (Ed.), *Carmichael's manual of child psychology* (Vol. 1, 3rd ed., pp. 1163–209). New York: Wiley.

Bayley, N., & Oden, M. H. (1955). The maintenance of intellectual ability in gifted adults. *Journal of Gerontology, 10,* 91–107.

Beilin, H. (1980). Piaget's theory: Refinement, revision, or rejection? In R. H. Kluwe & H. Spada (Eds.), *Developmental models of thinking* (pp. 245–61). New York: Academic Press.

Belmont, J. M., & Butterfield, E. C. (1971). Learning strategies as determinants of memory deficiencies. *Cognitive Psychology, 2,* 411–20.

Belmont, J. M., Butterfield, E. C., & Ferretti, R. (1982). To secure transfer of training, instruct self-management skills. In D. K. Detterman & R. J. Sternberg (Eds.), *How and how much can intelligence be increased?* (pp. 147–54). Norwood, NJ: Ablex.

Berg, C. A., & Sternberg, R. J. (1985). Response to novelty: Continuity versus discontinuity in the developmental course of intelligence. In H. Reese (Ed.), *Advances in child development and behavior* (Vol. 19, pp. 2–47). New York: Academic Press.

Berry, J. W. (1971). Ecological and cultural factors in spatial perceptual development. *Canadian Journal of Behavioral Science, 3,* 324–36.

Berry, J. W. (1974). Radical cultural relativism and the concept of intelligence. In J. W. Berry & P. R. Dasen (Eds.), *Culture and cognition: Readings in cross-cultural psychology* (pp. 225–9). London: Methuen.

Berry, J. W. (1976). *Human ecology and cognitive style: Comparative studies in cultural and psychological adaptation.* New York: Sage-Halsted.

Berry, J. W. (1983). Textured contexts: Systems and situations in cross-cultural psychology. In S. H. Irvine & J. W. Berry (Eds.), *Human assessment and cultural factors* (pp. 117–25). New York: Plenum.

Berry, J. W. (1984). Towards a universal psychology of cognitive competence. In P. S. Fry (Ed.), *Changing conceptions of intelligence and intellectual functioning* (pp. 35–61). Amsterdam: North-Holland.

Berry, J. W., & Dasen, P. R. (Eds.) (1974). *Culture and cognition: Readings in cross-cultural psychology.* London: Methuen.

Berry, J. W., & Irvine, S. H. (1986). Bricolage: Savages do it daily. In R. J. Sternberg & R. K. Wagner (Eds.), *Practical intelligence: Nature and origins of competence in the everyday world* (pp. 271–306). Cambridge University Press.

Binet, A., & Simon, T. (1916a). *The development of intelligence in children* (E. S. Kite, Trans.). Baltimore, MD: Williams & Wilkins.

Binet, A., & Simon, T. (1916b). *The intelligence of the feeble-minded* (E. S. Kite, Trans.). Baltimore, MD: Williams & Wilkins.

Birkhill, W. R., & Schaie, K. W. (1975). The effect of differential reinforcement of cautiousness in intellectual performance among the elderly. *Journal of Gerontology, 30,* 578–82.

Bisanz, G. L., & Voss, J. F. (1981). Sources of knowledge in reading comprehension: Cognitive development and expertise in a content domain. In A. Lesgold & C. A. Perfetti (Eds.), *Interactive processes in reading* (pp. 215–39). Hillsdale, NJ: Erlbaum.

Blinkhorn, S. F., & Hendrickson, D. E. (1982). Averaged evoked responses and psychometric intelligence. *Nature, 295,* 596–7.

Bobrow, D. G. (1968). Natural language input for a computer problem solving system. In M. Minsky (Ed.), *Semantic information processing* (pp. 146–226). Cambridge, MA: MIT Press.

Bogen, J. E., 1975). Some educational aspects of hemispheric specialization. *UCLA Educator, 17,* 24–32.

Boring, E. G. (1923, June 6). Intelligence as the tests test it. *New Republic,* 35–37.

Boring, E. G. (1950). *A history of experimental psychology.* New York: Appleton-Century-Crofts.

Borkowski, J. G., & Wanschura, P. B. (1974). Mediational processes in the retarded. In N. R. Ellis (Ed.), *International review of research in mental retardation* (Vol. 7). New York: Academic Press.

Botwinick, J. (1977). Intellectual abilities. In J. E. Birren & K. W. Schaie (Eds.), *Handbook of the psychology of aging* (pp. 580–605). New York: Van Nostrand.

Bovet, M. C. (1968). Etudes interculturelles de développement intellectuel et processus d'apprentissage. *Revue Suisse de Psychologie Pure et Appliquée, 27,* 190–9.

Bovet, M. C. (1971). *Etude interculturelle des processus du raisonnement. Notions de quantités physiques et relations spatio-temporelles chez des enfants et des adultes non-scolarises.* Unpublished doctoral dissertation, University of Geneva.

Bovet, M. C. (1973). Cognitive processes among illiterate children and adults. In J. W. Berry & P. R. Dasen (Eds.), *Culture and cognition: Readings in cross-cultural psychology* (pp. 311–34). London: Methuen.

Bower, T. G. R. (1967). The development of object-permanence: Some studies of existence constancy. *Perception and Psychophysics, 2,* 411–18.

Bower, T. G. R. (1974). *Development in infancy.* New York: Freeman.

Braine, M. D. S. (1968). The ontogeny of certain logical operations: Piaget's formulation examined by nonverbal methods. In I. E. Sigel & F. H. Hopper (Eds.), *Logical thinking in children: Research based on Piaget's theory* (pp. 164–206). New York: Holt, Rinehart, & Winston.

Brainerd, C. J. (1977). Response criteria in concept development research. *Child Development, 48,* 360–6.

Bransford, J. D., Barclay, J. R., & Franks, J. J. (1972). Sentence memory: A constructive versus interpretive approach. *Cognitive Psychology, 3,* 193–209.

Brislin, R. W., Lonner, W. J., & Thorndike, R. M. (Eds.) (1973). *Cross-cultural research methods.* New York: Wiley.

Broadbent, D. E. (1975). Division of function and integration of behavior. In B. Milner (Ed.), *Hemispheric specialization and interaction* (pp. 31–41). Cambridge, MA: MIT Press.

Broman, S. H., Nichols, P. L., & Kennedy, W. A. (1975). *Preschool IQ: Prenatal and early developmental correlates.* Hillsdale, NJ: Erlbaum.

Brown, A. L. (1978). Knowing when, where, and how to remember: A problem of metacognition. In R. Glaser (Ed.), *Advances in instructional psychology* (Vol. 1, pp. 77–165). Hillsdale, NJ: Erlbaum.

Brown, A. L., Bransford, J., Ferrara, R., & Campione, J. (1983). Learning, remembering, and understanding. In P. H. Mussen (Series Ed.) & J. Flavell & E. Markman (Vol. Eds.), *Handbook of child psychology* (Vol. 3, 4th ed., pp. 77–166). New York: Wiley.

Brown, A. L., & Campione, J. (1977). Training strategic study time apportionment in educable retarded children. *Intelligence, 1,* 94–107.

Brown, A. L., & Campione, J. C. (1978). Permissible inferences from cognitive training studies in developmental research. In W. S. Hall & M. Cole (Eds.), *Quarterly newsletter of the Institute for Comparative Human Behavior, 2,* 46–53.

Brown, A. L., & DeLoache, J. S. (1978). Skills, plans, and self-regulation. In R. Siegler (Ed.), *Children's thinking: What develops?* (pp. 3–35). Hillsdale, NJ: Erlbaum.

Brown, A. L., & French, A. L. (1979). The zone of potential development: Implications for intelligence testing in the year 2000. In R. J. Sternberg & D. K. Detterman (Eds.), *Human intelligence: Perspectives on its theory and measurement* (pp. 217–35). Norwood, NJ: Ablex.

Brown, G., & Desforges, C. (1979). *Piaget's theory: A psychological critique*. Boston: Routledge & Kegan Paul.

Brown, J. S., & Burton, R. R. (1978). Diagnostic models for procedural bugs in basic mathematical skills. *Cognitive Science, 2,* 155–92.

Brown, R., & Bellugi, U. (1964). Three processes in the child's acquisition of syntax. *Harvard Educational Review, 34,* 133–51.

Bruner, J. S., Olver, R. R., & Greenfield, P. M. (1966). *Studies in cognitive growth*. New York: Wiley.

Bruner, J. S., Shapiro, D., & Tagiuri, R. (1958). The meaning of traits in isolation and in combination. In R. Tagiuri & L. Petrollo (Eds.), *Person perception and interpersonal behavior* (pp. 277–88). Stanford, CA: Stanford University Press.

Burt, C. (1940). *The factors of the mind*. London: University of London Press.

Burt, C. (1949). Alternative methods of factor analysis and their relations to Pearson's method of "principal axes." *British Journal of Psychology, Statistical Section, 2,* 98–121.

Burt, C. (1955). The evidence for the concept of intelligence. *British Journal of Educational Psychology, 25,* 158–77.

Butterfield, E. C., & Belmont, J. M. (1977). Assessing and improving the executive cognitive functions of mentally retarded people. In I. Bialer & M. Sternlicht (Eds.), *The psychology of mental retardation: Issues and approaches* (pp. 277–320). New York: Psychological Dimensions.

Butterfield, E. C., Wambold, C., & Belmont, J. M. (1973). On the theory and practice of improving short-term memory. *American Journal of Mental Deficiency, 77,* 654–69.

Campione, J. C., & Brown, A. L. (1978). Toward a theory of intelligence: Contributions from research with retarded children. *Intelligence, 2,* 279–304.

Campione, J. C., & Brown, A. L. (1979). Toward a theory of intelligence: Contributions from research with retarded children. In R. J. Sternberg & D. K. Detterman (Eds.), *Human intelligence: Perspectives on its theory and measurement* (pp. 139–64). Norwood, NJ: Ablex.

Campione, J. C., Brown, A. L., & Ferrara, R. (1982). Mental retardation and intelligence. In R. J. Sternberg (Ed.), *Handbook of human intelligence* (pp. 392–490). Cambridge University Press.

Cantor, N. (1978). *Prototypicality and personality judgments.* Unpublished doctoral dissertation, Department of Psychology, Stanford University, Stanford, CA.

Carbonell, J. G. (1979). *Subjective understanding: Computer models of belief systems.* Unpublished doctoral dissertation (Computer Science Research Report No. 150), Yale University, New Haven, CT.

Carroll, J. B. (1976). Psychometric tests as cognitive tasks: A new "structure of intellect." In L. B. Resnick (Ed.), *The nature of intelligence* (pp. 27–56). Hillsdale, NJ: Erlbaum.

Carroll, J. B. (1981). Ability and task difficulty in cognitive psychology. *Educational Researcher, 10,* 11–21.

Carroll, J. B. (1988). *Human cognitive abilities.* Unpublished manuscript.

Case, R. (1978). Intellectual development from birth to adulthood: A neo-Piagetian interpretation. In R. Siegler (Ed.), *Children's thinking: What develops?* (pp. 37–71). Hillsdale, NJ: Erlbaum.

Case, R. (1984). The process of stage transition: A neo-Piagetian view. In R. J. Sternberg (Ed.), *Mechanisms of cognitive development* (pp. 20–44). New York: Freeman.

Case, R. (1985). *Intellectual development: Birth to adulthood.* New York: Academic Press.

Case, R. (1987). The structure and process of intellectual development. *International Journal of Psychology, 22,* 571–607.

Cattell, J. M. (1890). Mental tests and measurements. *Mind, 15,* 373–80.

Cattell, R. B. (1971). *Abilities: Their structure, growth, and action.* Boston: Houghton Mifflin.

Cattell, R. B., & Cattell, A. K. (1963). *Test of g: Culture fair, Scale 3.* Champaign, IL: Institute for Personality and Ability Testing.

Cazden, C. (1965). *Environmental assistance to the child's acquisition of grammar.* Unpublished doctoral dissertation, Harvard University, Cambridge, MA.

Ceci, S. J. (in press). *On intelligence . . . More or less.* Englewood Cliffs, NJ: Prentice-Hall.

Ceci, S. J., & Bronfenbrenner, U. (1985). "Don't forget to take the cupcakes out of the oven": Prospective memory, strategic time-monitoring, and context. *Child Development, 56,* 152–64.

Ceci, S. J., & Liker, J. (1986). Academic and nonacademic intelligence: An experimental separation. In R. J. Sternberg & R. K. Wagner (Eds.), *Practical intelligence: Nature and origins of competence in the everyday world* (pp. 119–42). Cambridge University Press.

Chalke, F., & Ertl, J. (1965). Evoked potentials and intelligence. *Life Sciences, 4,* 1319–22.

Chapman, A. J., & Jones, D. M. (Eds.) (1980). *Models of man.* Leicester: British Psychological Society.

Charlesworth, W. R. A. (1979). An ethological approach to studying intelligence. *Human Development, 22,* 212–16.

Chase, W. G., & Simon, H. A. (1973).The mind's eye in chess. In W. G. Chase (Ed.), *Visual information processing* (pp. 215–81). New York: Academic Press.

Chi, M. T. H. (1978). Knowledge structure and memory development. In R. S. Siegler (Ed.), *Children's thinking: What develops?* (pp. 73–96). Hillsdale, NJ: Erlbaum.

Chi, M. T. H., Feltovich, P., & Glaser, R. (1981). Categorization and representation of physics problems by experts and novices. *Cognitive Science, 5,* 121–52.

Chi, M. T. H., Glaser, R., & Rees, E. (1982). Expertise in problem solving. In R. J. Sternberg (Ed.), *Advances in the psychology of human intelligence* (Vol. 1, pp. 7–75). Hillsdale, NJ: Erlbaum.

Chiesi, H. L., Spilich, G. J., & Voss, J. F. (1979). Acquisition of domain-related information in relation to high and low domain knowledge. *Journal of Verbal Learning and Verbal Behavior, 18,* 257–73.

Churchman, C. W. (1971). *The design of inquiring systems. Basic concepts of systems and organizations.* New York: Basic.

Clark, M. P. (1944). Changes in primary mental abilities with age. *Archives of Psychology, 291,* 30.

Cleary, T. A., Humphreys, L. G., Kendrick, S. A., & Wesman, A. (1975). Educational uses of tests with disadvantaged students. *American Psychologist, 30,* 15–41.

Cole, M., Gay, J., Glick, J., & Sharp, D. W. (1971). *The cultural context of learning and thinking.* New York: Basic.

Cole, M., & Means, B. (1981). *Comparative studies of how people think.* Cambridge, MA: Harvard University Press.

Cole, M., & Scribner, S. (1974). *Culture and thought.* New York: Wiley.

Cole, M., & Scribner, S. (1977). Cross-cultural studies of memory and cognition. In R. V. Kail, Jr., & J. W. Hagen (Eds.), *Perspectives on the development of memory and cognition* (pp. 239–71). Hillsdale, NJ: Erlbaum.

Coltheart, M., Hull, E., & Slater, D. (1975). Sex differences in imagery and reading. *Nature, 253,* 438–40.

Cooper, L. A. (1982). Strategies for visual comparison and representation: Individual differences. In R. J. Sternberg (Ed.), *Advances in the psychology of human intelligence* (Vol. 1, pp. 77–124). Hillsdale, NJ: Erlbaum.

Cornell, E. H. (1978). Learning to find things: A reinterpretation of object permanence studies. In L. S. Siegel & C. J. Brainerd (Eds.), *Alternatives to Piaget: Critical essays on the theory.* New York: Academic Press.

Cronbach, L. J. (1957). The two disciplines of scientific psychology. *American Psychologist, 12,* 671–84.

Cullingford, R. E. (1978). *Script application: Computer understanding of newspaper stories.* Unpublished doctoral dissertation (Computer Science Report No. 116). Yale University, New Haven, CT.

Darwin, C. (1859). *Origin of species.* London: John Murray.

Das, J. P., Kirby, J. R., Jarman, R. F. (1979). *Simultaneous and successive cognitive processes.* New York: Academic Press.

Dasen, P. R. (1972). Cross-cultural Piagetian research: A summary. *Journal of Cross-Cultural Psychology, 3,* 23–40.

Dasen, P. R. (1974). The influence of ecology, culture and European contact on cognitive development in Australian Aborigines. In J. W. Berry & P. R. Dasen (Eds.), *Culture and cognition: Readings in cross-cultural psychology* (pp. 381–408). London: Methuen.

Dasen, P. R. (1977). *Piagetian psychology: Cross-cultural contributions.* New York: Gardner.

Davidson, J. E. (1986). The role of insight in giftedness. In R. J. Sternberg & J. E. Davidson (Eds.), *Conceptions of giftedness* (pp. 201–22). Cambridge University Press.

Davidson, J. E., & Sternberg, R. J. (1984). The role of insight in intellectual giftedness. *Gifted Child Quarterly, 28,* 58–64.

Day, M. E. (1964). An eye movement phenomenon relating to attention, thought, and anxiety. *Perceptual and Motor Skills, 19,* 443–6.

Dearborn, W. R., & Rothney, J. W. M. (1941). *Predicting the child's development.* Cambridge, MA: Science-Art Publishing.

Dearborn, W. R., Rothney, J. W. M., & Shuttleworth, F. K. (1938). Data on the growth of public-school children (from the materials of the Harvard Growth Study). *Monographs of the Society for Research in Child Development, 3,* 1 (Serial No. 14).

DeGroot, A. D. (1965). *Thought and choice in chess.* The Hague: Mouton.

Dehn, N., & Schank, R. C. (1982). Artificial and human intelligence. In R. J. Sternberg (Ed.), *Handbook of human intelligence* (pp. 352–91). Cambridge University Press.

Demetriou, A., & Efklides, A. (1985). Towards a determination of the dimensions of domains of individual differences in cognitive development. In E. deCorte, H. Lodewijks, R. Parmentier, & P. Span (Eds.), *Learning and instruction.* Oxford: Pergamon Press.

Detterman, D. K., & Sternberg, R. J. (Eds.) (1982). *How and how much can intelligence be increased.* Norwood, NJ: Ablex.

Dickinson, A., & Boakes, R. A. (Eds.) (1979). *Mechanisms of learning and memory.* Hillsdale, NJ: Erlbaum.

Dixon, R. A., & Baltes, P. B. (1986). Toward life-span research on the functions and pragmatics of intelligence. In R. J. Sternberg & R. K. Wagner

(Eds.), *Practical intelligence: Nature and origins of competence in the everyday world* (pp. 203–35). Cambridge University Press.

Donchin, E. (1979). Event-related brain potentials: A tool in the study of human information processing. In H. Begleiter (Ed.), *Evoked potentials and behavior* (pp. 13–75). New York: Plenum.

Doob, L. (1968). Just a few of the presumptions and perplexities confronting social psychological research in developing countries. *Journal of Social Issues, 24*, 71–81.

Duda, R. O., Gaschnig, J. G., & Hart, P. E. (1979). Model design in the PROSPECTOR consultant system for mineral exploration. In D. Michie (Ed.), *Expert systems in the micro-electronic age* (pp. 153–67). Edinburgh University Press.

Dweck, C. S., & Elliott, E. S. (1983). Achievement motivation. In P. H. Mussen (Series Ed.) & E. M. Hetherington (Vol. Ed.), *Handbook of child psychology* (Vol. 4, 4th ed., pp. 643–91). New York: Wiley.

Egan, D. E. (1976). *Accuracy and latency scores as measures of spatial information processing* (Research Report No. 1224). Pensacola, FL: Naval Aerospace Medical Research Laboratories.

Egan, D. E. & Greeno, J. G. (1973). Acquiring cognitive structure by discovery and rule learning. *Journal of Educational Psychology, 64*, 85–97.

Elkind, D. (1961). Children's discovery of the conservation of mass, weight, and volume: Piaget replication study II. *Journal of Genetic Psychology, 98*, 219–27.

Erman, L. D., Hayes-Roth, F., Lesser, V., & Reddy, D. (1980). The HEARSAY-II speech-understanding system: Integrating knowledge to resolve uncertainty. *Computer Surveys, 12*, 213–53.

Ertl, J. (1966). Evoked potentials and intelligence. *Revue de l'Université d'Ottawa, 30*, 599–607.

Ertl, J., & Schafer, E. (1969). Brain response correlates of psychometric intelligence. *Nature, 223*, 421–2.

Estes, W. K. (1982). Learning, memory, and intelligence. In R. J. Sternberg (Ed.), *Handbook of human intelligence* (pp. 170–224). Cambridge University Press.

Eysenck, H. J. (1982). *A model for intelligence*. Berlin: Springer.

Eysenck, H. J. (1986). The theory of intelligence and the psychophysiology of cognition. In R. J. Sternberg (Ed.), *Advances in the psychology of human intellegence* (Vol. 3, pp. 1–34). Hillsdale, NJ: Erlbaum.

Eysenck, H. J., & Barrett, P. (1985). Psychophysiology and the measurement of intelligence. In C. R. Reynolds & V. Wilson (Eds.), *Methodological and statistical advances in the study of individual differences* (pp. 1–49). New York: Plenum.

Farah, M. J. (1988). Is visual imagery really visual? Overlooked evidence from neuropsychology. *Psychological Review, 95*, 307–17.

Feigenbaum, E. A., Buchanan, B. G., & Lederberg, J. (1971). On generality and problem solving: A case study using the DENDRAL program. In B. Meltzer & D. Michie (Eds.), *Machine intelligence* (Vol. 6, pp. 165–90). Edinburgh University Press.

Feldman, J. A., & Ballard, D. H. (1982). Connectionist models and their properties. *Cognitive Science, 6,* 205–54.

Ferguson, G. A. (1954). On learning and human ability. *Canadian Journal of Psychology, 8,* 95–112.

Ferrara, R. A., Brown, A. L., & Campione, J. C. (1986). Children's learning and transfer of inductive reasoning rules: Studies of proximal development, *Child Development, 57,* 1087–99.

Feuerstein, R. (1979). *The dynamic assessment of retarded performers: The learning potential assessment device, theory, instruments, and techniques.* Baltimore, MD: University Park.

Feuerstein, R. (1980). *Instrumental enrichment: An intervention program for cognitive modifiability.* Baltimore, MD: University Park.

Fischer, K. W. (1980). A theory of cognitive development: The control and construction of hierarchies of skills. *Psychological Review, 87,* 477–31.

Fischer, K. W. (1987). Relations between brain and cognitive development. *Child Development, 57,* 623–32.

Fischer, K. W., & Farrar, M. J. (1987). Generalizations about generalization: How a theory of skill development explains both generality and specificity. *International Journal of Psychology, 22,* 643–77.

Fischer, K. W., & Pipp, S. L. (1984). Processes of cognitive development: Optimal level and skill acquisition. In R. J. Sternberg (Ed.), *Mechanisms of cognitive development* (pp. 45–75). New York: Freeman.

Flavell, J. H. (1971). Stage related properties of cognitive development. *Cognitive Psychology, 2,* 421–53.

Flavell, J. H. (1977). *Cognitive development.* Englewood Cliffs, NJ: Prentice-Hall.

Flavell, J. H. (1981). Cognitive monitoring. In W. P. Dickson (Ed.), *Children's oral communication skills* (pp. 35–60). New York: Academic Press.

Flavell, J. H., Wellman, H. M. (1977). Metamemory. In R. V. Kail, Jr., & J. W. Hagen (Eds.), *Perspectives on the development of memory and cognition* (pp. 3–33). Hillsdale, NJ: Erlbaum.

Fodor, J. A. (1983). *The modularity of mind.* Cambridge, MA: MIT Press.

Franco, L., & Sperry, R. W. (1977). Hemisphere lateralization for cognitive processing of geometry. *Neuropsychologia, 15,* 107–14.

Frederiksen, J. R. (1980). Component skills in reading: Measurement of individual differences through chronometric analysis. In R. E. Snow, P.-A. Federico, & W. E. Montague (Eds.), *Aptitude, learning, and instruction: Cognitive process analyses of aptitude* (Vol. 1, pp. 105–38). Hillsdale, NJ: Erlbaum.

Fry, P. S. (1984). Teachers' conceptions of students' intelligence and intelligent functioning: A cross-sectional study of elementary, secondary and tertiary level teachers. In P. S. Fry (Ed.), *Changing conceptions of intelligence and intellectual functioning: Current theory and research* (pp. 157–74). New York: North-Holland.

Galin, D., & Ornstein, R. (1972). Lateral specialization of cognitive mode: An EEG study. *Psychophysiology, 9*, 412–18.

Gall, F. J. (1825). *Sur les fonctions du cerveau et sur cells de ses parties* (six volumes). Paris: Bailhere.

Galton, F. (1883). *Inquiry into human faculty and its development*. London: Macmillan Press.

Gardner, H. (1983). *Frames of mind: The theory of multiple intelligences*. New York: Basic.

Gardner, H., & Feldman, D. (1985). *Project Spectrum*. Annual Report submitted to the Spencer Foundation. Unpublished.

Garrett, H. E. (1938). Differentiable mental traits. *Psychological Record, 2*, 259–98.

Garrett, H. E. (1946). A developmental theory of intelligence. *American Psychologist, 1*, 372–78.

Garrett, H. E., Bryan, A. I., & Perl, R. (1935). The age factor in mental organization. *Archives of Psychology, 176*, 1–31.

Gazzaniga, M. S. (1970). *The bisected brain*. East Norwalk, CT: Appleton-Century-Crofts.

Gazzaniga, M. S. (1985). *The social brain: Discovering the networks of the mind*. New York: Basic.

Gazzaniga, M. S., & LeDoux, J. E. (1978). *The integrated mind*. New York: Plenum.

Gelman, R., & Baillargeon, R. (1983). A review of some Piagetian concepts. In P. H. Mussen (Series Ed.) & J. Flavell & E. Markman (Vol. Eds.), *Handbook of child psychology: Cognitive development* (Vol. 3, 4th ed., pp. 167–230). New York: Wiley.

Gelman, R., & Gallistel, C. R. (1978). *The child's understanding of number*. Cambridge, MA: Harvard University Press.

Gentner, D., & Grudin, J. (1985). The evolution of mental metaphors in psychology: A 90-year retrospective. *American Psychologist, 40*, 181–92.

Gerber, M. (1956). Le développement psychomoteur de l'enfant africain. *Courrier, 6*, 17–28.

Gerber, M. (1960). Problèmes posés par le développement du jeune enfant africain en fonction de son milieu social. *Travail Humain, 23*, 97–111.

Geschwind, N., & Levitsky, W. (1968). Human brain: Left–right asymmetries in temporal speech region. *Science, 161*, 186–9.

Gill, R., & Keats, D. M. (1980). Elements of intellectual competence: Judgments by Australian and Malay university students. *Journal of Cross-Cultural Psychology, 11,* 233–43.

Ginsburg, H. (1977). *Children's arithmetic.* New York: Nostrand.

Gladwin, T. (1970). *East is a big bird.* Cambridge, MA: Harvard University Press.

Goldstein, I. P., & Papert, S. A. (1976). *Artificial intelligence, language, and the study of knowledge.* Artificial Intelligence Memo No. 337. Cambridge, MA: MIT Press.

Goodnow, J. J. (1962). A test of milieu effects with some of Piaget's tasks. *Psychological Monographs, 76,* Whole No. 555.

Goodnow, J. J. (1969). Cultural variations in cognition skills. In D. R. Price-Williams (Ed.), *Cross-cultural studies* (pp. 246–64). Harmondsworth: Penguin Books.

Goodnow, J. J., & Bethon, G. (1966). Piaget's tasks: The effects of schooling and intelligence. *Child Development, 37,* 573–82.

Gould, S. J. (1981). *The mismeasure of man.* New York: Norton.

Great Books of the Western World (1987). Chicago: Encyclopedia Britannica.

Green, D. R., Ford, M. P., & Flamer, G. B. (1971). *Measurement and Piaget.* New York: McGraw-Hill.

Greenfield, P. M. (1969). On culture and conservation. In D. R. Price-Williams (Ed.), *Cross-cultural studies.* Harmondsworth: Penguin Books.

Greeno, J. G. (1978). A study of problem solving. In R. Glaser (Ed.), *Advances in instructional psychology* (Vol. 1, pp. 13–75). Hillsdale, NJ: Erlbaum.

Groen, G. J., & Parkman, J. M. (1972). A chronometric analysis of simple addition. *Psychological Review, 79,* 329–43.

Guilford, J. P. (1956). The structure of intellect. *Psychological Bulletin, 53,* 267–93.

Guilford, J. P. (1957). *A revised structure of intellect* (Reprint No. 19). Los Angeles: University of Southern California, Psychological Laboratory.

Guilford, J. P. (1967). *The nature of human intelligence.* New York: McGraw-Hill.

Guilford, J. P. (1982). Cognitive psychology's ambiguities: Some suggested remedies. *Psychological Review, 89,* 48–59.

Guilford, J. P., & Hoepfner, R. (1971). *The analysis of intelligence.* New York: McGraw-Hill.

Gur, R. E., Gur, R. C., & Harris, L. J. (1975). Cerebral activation, as measured by subjects' lateral eye movements, is influenced by experimenter location. *Neuropsychologia, 13,* 35–44.

Gustafsson, J. E. (1984). A unifying model for the structure of intellectual abilities. *Intelligence, 8,* 179–203.

Guttman, L. (1954). A new approach to factor analysis: The radex. In P. F. Lazarsfeld (Ed.), *Mathematical thinking in the social sciences* (pp. 258–348). New York: Free Press.

Guttman, L. (1965). A faceted definition of intelligence. In R. R. Eiferman (Ed.), *Scripta Hierosolymitana* (Vol. 14). Jerusalem: Magnes Press.

Guyote, M. J., & Sternberg, R. J. (1981). A transitive-chain theory of syllogistic reasoning. *Cognitive Psychology, 13,* 461–525.

Halford, G. S. (1982). *The development of thought.* Hillsdale, NJ: Erlbaum.

Hall, V. C., & Kaye, D. B. (1978). The necessity of logical necessity in Piaget's theory. In L. S. Siegel & C. J. Brainerd (Eds.), *Alternatives to Piaget: Critical essays on the theory.* New York: Academic Press.

Halstead, W. C. (1951). Biological intelligence. *Journal of Personality, 20,* 118–30.

Hayes, J. R. (1981). *The complete problem solver.* Philadelphia, PA: Franklin Institute Press.

Hayes-Roth, F., Waterman, D. A., & Lenat, D. B. (1983). An overview of expert systems. In F. Hayes-Roth, D. A. Waterman, & D. B. Lenat (Eds.), *Building expert systems* (pp. 3–29), Reading, MA: Addison-Wesley.

Heath, S. B. (1983). *Ways with words.* Cambridge University Press.

Hebb, D. O. (1949). *The organization of behavior.* New York: Wiley.

Heim, A. (1970). *Intelligence and personality: Their assessment and relationship.* Harmondsworth: Penguin Books.

Hendrickson, A. E. (1982). The biological basis of intelligence Part I: Theory. In H. J. Eysenck (Ed.), *A model for intelligence* (pp. 151–96). Berlin: Springer.

Hendrickson, A. E., & Hendrickson, D. E. (1980). The biological basis for individual differences in intelligence. *Personality and Individual Differences, 1,* 3–33.

Hofstaetter, P. R. (1954). The changing composition of intelligence: A study of the t-technique. *Journal of Genetic Psychology, 85,* 159–64.

Hogaboam, T. W., & Pellegrino, J. W. (1978). Hunting for individual differences: Verbal ability and semantic processing of pictures and words. *Memory and Cognition, 6,* 189–93.

Holzinger, K. J. (1938). Relationships between three multiple orthogonal factors and four bifactors. *Journal of Educational Psychology, 29,* 513–19.

Holzman, T. G., Glaser, R., & Pellegrino, J. W. (1976). Process training derived from a computer simulation theory. *Memory and Cognition, 4,* 349–56.

Honzik, M. P. (1938). The constancy of mental test performance during the preschool period. *Journal of Genetic Psychology, 52,* 285–302.

Horn, J. L. (1968). Organization of abilities and the development of intelligence. *Psychological Review, 75,* 242–59.

Horn, J. L. (1970). Organization of data on life-span development of human abilities. In L. R. Goulet & P. B. Baltes (Eds.), *Life-span developmental psychology: Research and theory* (pp. 423–66). New York: Academic Press.

Horn, J. L. (1986). Intellectual ability concepts. In R. J. Sternberg (Ed.), *Advances in the psychology of human intelligence* (Vol. 3, pp. 35–77). Hillsdale, NJ: Erlbaum.

Horn, J. L., & Cattell, R. B. (1966). Refinement and test of the theory of fluid and crystallized ability intelligences. *Journal of Educational Psychology, 57,* 253–70.

Horn, J. L., & Donaldson, G. (1976). On the myth of intellectual decline in adulthood. *American Psychologist, 31,* 701–19.

Horn, J. L., & Knapp, J. R. (1973). On the subjective character of the empirical base of Guilford's structure-of-intellect model. *Psychological Bulletin, 80,* 33–43.

Horowitz, F. D., & O'Brien, M. (Eds.) (1985). *The gifted and talented: Developmental perspectives.* Washington, DC: American Psychological Association.

Hunt, E. B. (1978). Mechanics of verbal ability. *Psychological Review, 85,* 109–30.

Hunt, E. B. (1980). Intelligence as an information-processing concept. *British Journal of Psychology, 71,* 449–74.

Hunt, E. B., Frost, N., & Lunneborg, C. (1973). Individual differences in cognition: A new approach to intelligence. In G. Bower (Ed.), *The psychology of learning and motivation* (Vol. 7, pp. 87–122). New York: Academic Press.

Hunt, E. B., & Lansman, M. (1982). Individual differences in attention. In R. J. Sternberg (Ed.), *Advances in the psychology of human intelligence* (Vol. 1, pp. 207–54). Hillsdale, NJ: Erlbaum.

Hunt, E. B., Lunneborg, C., & Lewis, J. (1975). What does it mean to be high verbal? *Cognitive Psychology, 7,* 194–227.

Inhelder, B., & Piaget, J. (1958). *The growth of logical thinking from childhood to adolescence.* New York: Basic.

Inhelder, B., & Piaget, J. (1964). *The early growth of logic in the child: Classification and seriation.* New York: Norton.

Inhelder, B., Sinclair, H., & Bovet, M. (1974). *Learning and the development of cognition.* Cambridge, MA: Harvard University Press.

Irvine, S. H. (1966). Towards a rationale for testing attainments and abilities in Africa. *British Journal of Educational Psychology, 36,* 24–32.

Irvine, S. H. (1969). The factor analysis of African abilities and attainments: Constructs across cultures. *Psychological Bulletin, 71,* 20–32.

Irvine, S. H. (1970). Affect and construct – a cross-cultural check on theories of intelligence. *Journal of Social Psychology, 80,* 23–30.

Irvine, S. H. (1979). The place of factor analysis in cross-cultural methodology and its contribution to cognitive theory. In L. Eckensberger, W. Lonner, & Y. Poortinga (Eds.), *Cross-cultural contributions to psychology*. Amsterdam, The Netherlands: Swets & Zietlinger.

Irvine, S. H. (1984). The contexts of triarchic theory. *Behavioral and Brain Sciences, 7,* 293–4.

Irvine, S. H., & Berry, J. W. (1988). The abilities of mankind: A revaluation. In S. H. Irvine & J. W. Berry (Eds.), *Human abilities in cultural context* (pp. 3–59). Cambridge University Press.

Jackson, M. D., & McClelland, J. L. (1979). Processing determinants of reading speed. *Journal of Experimental Psychology: General, 108,* 151–81.

Jahoda, G. (1970). A cross-cultural perspective in psychology. *The Advancement of Science, 27,* 1–14.

Jarvik, L. F., Eisdorfer, C., & Blum, J. E. (1973). *Intellectual functioning in adults*. New York: Springer.

Jenkins, J. J. (1979). Four points to remember: A tetrahedral model of memory experiments. In L. S. Cermak & F. I. M. Craik (Eds.), *Levels of processing in human memory* (pp. 429–46). Hillsdale, NJ: Erlbaum.

Jensen, A. R. (1969). How much can we boost IQ and scholastic achievement? *Harvard Educational Review, 39,* 1–123.

Jensen, A. R. (1970). Hierarchical theories of mental ability. In W. B. Dockrell (Ed.), *On intelligence* (pp. 119–90). Toronto: Ontario Institute for Studies in Education.

Jensen, A. R. (1972). *Genetics and education*. London: Methuen.

Jensen, A. R. (1979). *g:* Outmoded theory or unconquered frontier? *Creative Science and Technology, 2,* 16–29.

Jensen, A. R. (1980). *Bias in mental testing*. New York: Free Press.

Jensen, A. R. (1982). The chronometry of intelligence. In R. J. Sternberg (Ed.), *Advances in the psychology of human intelligence* (Vol. 1, pp. 255–310). Hillsdale, NJ: Erlbaum.

Jerison, H. J. (1982). The evolution of biological intelligence. In R. J. Sternberg (Ed.), *Handbook of human intelligence* (pp. 723–91). Cambridge University Press.

Jones, H. E. (1954). The environment and mental development. In L. Carmichael (Ed.), *Manual of child psychology* (2nd ed., pp. 631–96). New York: Wiley.

Jones, H. E., & Conrad, H. S. (1933). The growth and decline of intelligence: A study of a homogeneous group between the ages of ten and sixty. *Genetic Psychology Monographs, 13,* 223–98.

Jöreskog, K. G., & Sörbom, D. (1978). *LISREL IV: Estimation of linear structural equation systems by maximum likelihood methods*. Chicago: National Educational Resources.

Kagan, J. (1971). *Change and continuity in infancy.* New York: Wiley.

Kalmar, D. A., & Sternberg, R. J. (1988). Theory knitting: An integrative approach to theory development. *Philosophical Psychology, 1,* 153–70.

Kanfer, R., & Ackerman, P. L. (1989). Dynamics of skill acquisition: Building a bridge between intelligence and motivation. In R. J. Sternberg (Ed.), *Advances in the psychology of human intelligence* (Vol. 5, pp. 83–134). Hillsdale, NJ: Erlbaum.

Kaufman, A. S., & Kaufman, N. L. (1983). *Kaufman Assessment Battery for Children (K-ABC).* Circle Pines, MN: American Guidance Service.

Kearins, J. M. (1981). Visual spatial memory in Australian Aboriginal children of desert regions. *Cognitive Psychology, 13,* 434–60.

Keating, D. P. (1984). The emperor's new clothes: The "new look" in intelligence research. In R. J. Sternberg (Ed.), *Advances in the psychology of human intelligence* (Vol. 2, pp. 1–45). Hillsdale, NJ: Erlbaum.

Keating, D. P., & Bobbitt, B. L. (1978). Individual and developmental differences in cognitive-processing components of mental ability. *Child Development, 49,* 155–67.

Keats, D. M. (1982). Cultural bases of concepts of intelligence: A Chinese versus Australian comparison. *Proceedings: Second Asian Workshop on Child and Adolescent Development,* 67–75.

Keil, F. C. (1984). Transition mechanisms in cognitive development and the structure of knowledge. In R. J. Sternberg (Ed.), *Mechanisms of cognitive development* (pp. 81–99). New York: Freeman.

Kilbride, J. E., Robbins, M. C., & Kilbride, P. L. (1970). The comparative motor development of Baganda, American White, and American Black infants. *American Anthropologist, 72,* 1422–9.

Kinsbourne, M., & Cook, J. (1971). Generalized and lateralized effects of concurrent verbalization on a unimanual skill. *Quarterly Journal of Experimental Psychology, 23,* 341–5.

Kinsbourne, M., & Hicks, R. E. (1978). Mapping cerebral functional space: Competition and collaboration in human performance. In M. Kinsbourne (Ed.), *Asymmetrical function of the brain* (pp. 267–73). Cambridge University Press.

Kintsch, W., & Van Dijk, T. A. (1978). Toward a model of text comprehension and production. *Psychological Review, 85,* 363–94.

Konorski, J. (1967). *Integrative activity of the brain: An interdisciplinary approach.* Chicago: University of Chicago Press.

Kosslyn, S. M. (1980). *Image and mind.* Cambridge, MA: Harvard University Press.

Kosslyn, S. M. (1987). Seeing and imagining in the cerebral hemispheres: A computational approach. *Psychological Review, 94,* 148–75.

Kroeber, A. L., & Kluckhohn, C. (1952). *Culture: A critical review of concepts and definitions.* Cambridge, MA: Peabody Museum.

Kuhn, T. S. (1970). *The structure of scientific revolutions* (2nd ed.). Chicago: University of Chicago Press.

Laboratory of Comparative Human Cognition (1982). Culture and intelligence. In R. J. Sternberg (Ed.), *Handbook of human intelligence* (pp. 642–719). Cambridge University Press.

Langley, P., & Simon, H. A. (1981). The central role of learning in cognition. In J. R. Anderson (Ed.), *Cognitive skills and their acquisition* (pp. 361–80). Hillsdale, NJ: Erlbaum.

Larkin, J. H., McDermott, J., Simon, D. P., & Simon, H. A. (1980a). Expert and novice performance in solving physics problems. *Science, 208,* 1335–42.

Larkin, J. H., McDermott, J., Simon, D. P., & Simon, H. A. (1980b). Models of competence in solving physics problems. *Cognitive Science, 4,* 317–45.

Lave, J. (1988). *Cognition in practice.* Cambridge University Press.

Lenneberg, E. H. (1967). *Biological foundations of language.* New York: Wiley.

LeVine, R. A. (1970) Cross-cultural study in child psychology. In P. H. Mussen (Ed.), *Carmichael's manual of child psychology* (Vol. 2, pp. 559–612). New York: Wiley.

Lévi-Strauss, C. (1966). *The savage mind.* Chicago: University of Chicago Press.

Levy, J. (1974). Psychobiological implications of bilateral asymmetry. In S. Dimond & S. Beaumont (Eds.), *Hemispheric function in the human brain* (pp. 121–83). New York: Halsted.

Levy, J., & Reid, M. (1976). Variations in writing posture and cerebral organization. *Science, 194,* 337.

Levy, J., Trevarthen, C., & Sperry, R. W. (1972). Perception of bilateral chimeric figures following hemispheric disconnection. *Brain, 95,* 61–78.

Lewis, C. (1978). *Production system models of practice effects.* Unpublished doctoral dissertation, Department of Psychology, University of Michigan, Ann Arbor.

Linn, M. C. (1973). The role of intelligence in children's responses to instruction. *Psychology in the Schools, 10,* 67–75.

Loehlin, J. C., Lindzey, G., & Spuhler, J. N. (1975). *Race differences in intelligence.* New York: Freeman.

Lovell, K. (1961). A follow-up study of Inhelder and Piaget's 'The growth of logical thinking.' *British Journal of Psychology, 52,* 143–53.

Lovell, K. (1971). Some problems associated with formal thought and its assessment. In D. R. Green, M. P. Ford, & G. B. Flamer (Eds.), *Measurement and Piaget* (pp. 81–102). New York: McGraw-Hill.

Luria, A. R. (1973). *The working brain.* New York: Basic.

Luria, A. R. (1976). *Cognitive development: Its cultural and social founda-tions.* Cambridge, MA: Harvard University Press.

Luria, A. R. (1980). *Higher cortical functions in man* (2nd ed., rev. & expanded). New York: Basic.

MacLeod, C. M., Hunt, E. B., & Mathews, N. N. (1978). Individual differences in the verification of sentence–picture relationships. *Journal of Verbal Learning and Verbal Behavior, 17,* 493–507.

MacLeod, C. M., Jackson, R. A., & Palmer, J. (1986). On the relation between spatial ability and field dependence. *Intelligence, 10,* 141–51.

Markman, E. M. (1981). Comprehension monitoring. In W. P. Dickson (Ed.), *Children's oral communication skills* (pp. 61–84). New York: Academic Press.

Marland, S. P. (1972). *Education of the gifted and talented: Report to the Congress of the United States by the U.S. Commissioner of Education.* Washington, DC: U.S. Government Printing Office.

Marshalek, B. (1981). *Trait and process aspects of vocabulary knowledge and verbal ability* (NR 154-376 ONR Tech. Rep. No. 15). Stanford, CA: School of Education, Stanford University.

Martorano, S. C. (1977). A developmental analysis of performance on Pia-get's formal operations tasks. *Developmental Psychology, 13,* 666–72.

Mayer, R. E. (1982). Memory for algebra story problems. *Journal of Educa-tional Psychology, 74,* 199–216.

Mayer, R. E. (1983). *Thinking, problem solving, and cognition.* New York: Freeman.

Mayer, R. E., & Greeno, J. G. (1972). Structural differences between learn-ing outcomes produced by different instructional methods. *Journal of Educational Psychology, 63,* 165–73.

McCall, R. B., Eichorn, D. J., & Hogarty, P. S. (1977). Transitions in early mental development. *Monograph of the Society for Research in Child Development, 42*(3), No. 171.

McCall, R. B., Hogarty, P. S., & Hurlburt, N. (1972). Transitions in infant sensori-motor development and the prediction of childhood IQ. *Ameri-can Psychologist, 27,* 728–48.

McCarthy, G., & Donchin, E. (1981). A metric for thought: A comparison of P300 latency and reaction time. *Science, 211,* 77–9.

McClelland, J. L., & Rumelhart, D. E. (1986). A distributed model of human learning and memory. In J. L. McClelland, D. E. Rumelhart, & The PDP Research Group, *Parallel distributed processing. Explorations in the microstructure of cognition* (Vol. 2, pp. 170–215). Cambridge, MA: MIT Press.

McClelland, J. L., Rumelhart, D. E., & The PDP Research Group. (1986). *Parallel distributed processing. Explorations in the microstructure of cognition. Vol. 2: Psychological and biological models.* Cambridge, MA: MIT Press.

McDermott, R. P. (1974). Achieving school failure: An anthropological approach to illiteracy and social stratification. In G. Spindler (Ed.), *Education and the cultural process.* New York: Holt, Rinehart, & Winston.

McFie, J. (1961). The effects of education on African performance on a group of intellectual tests. *British Journal of Educational Psychology, 31,* 232–40.

McNemar, Q. (1942). *The revision of the Stanford–Binet Scale: An analysis of the standardization data.* Boston: Houghton Mifflin.

McNemar, Q. (1964). Lost. Our intelligence? Why? *American Psychologist, 19,* 871–82.

Miles, T. R. (1957). On defining intelligence. *British Journal of Educational Psychology, 27,* 153–65.

Milgram, S. (1974). *Obedience to authority.* New York: Harper & Row.

Miller, S. A. (1976). Nonverbal assessment of Piagetian concepts. *Psychological Bulletin, 83,* 405–30.

Minsky, M. (1975). A framework for representing knowledge. In P. H. Winston (Ed.), *The psychology of computer vision* (pp. 211–80). New York: McGraw-Hill.

Minsky, M., & Papert, S. (1969). *Perceptrons.* Cambridge, MA: MIT Press.

Mulholland, T. M., Pellegrino, J. W., & Glaser, R. (1980). Components of geometric analogy solution. *Cognitive Psychology, 12,* 252–84.

Munroe, R. L., & Munroe, R. H. (1975). *Cross-cultural human development.* Monterey, CA: Brooks/Cole.

Neches, R., Langley, P., & Klahr, D. (1987). Learning, development, and production systems. In D. Klahr, P. Langley, & R. Neches (Eds.), *Production system models of learning and development* (pp. 1–54). Cambridge, MA: MIT Press.

Neisser, U. (1979). The concept of intelligence. In R. J. Sternberg & D. K. Detterman (Eds.), *Human intelligence: Perspectives on its theory and measurement* (pp. 179–89). Norwood, NJ: Ablex.

Neisser, U. (1982). *Memory observed.* New York: Freeman.

Newell, A., Shaw, J. C., & Simon, H. A. (1958). Elements of a theory of human problem solving. *Psychological Review, 65,* 151–66.

Newell, A., & Simon, H. A. (1961). GPS, a program that simulates human thought. In E. A. Feigenbaum & J. Feldman (Eds.), *Computers and thought* (pp. 279–96). New York: McGraw-Hill. (Reprinted from H. Billing [Ed.], *Lernende Automaten.* Munich: Oldenbourg.)

Newell, A., & Simon, H. A. (1972). *Human problem solving.* Englewood Cliffs, NJ: Prentice-Hall.

Nickerson, R. S., Perkins, D. N., & Smith, E. E. (1985). *Teaching thinking.* Hillsdale, NJ: Erlbaum.

Norman, D. A. (1987). Reflections of cognition and parallel distributed processing. In J. L. McClelland, D. E. Rumelhart, & The PDP Research Group, *Parallel distributed processing. Explorations in the microstructure of cognition. Vol. 2: Psychological and biological models* (pp. 531–46). Cambridge, MA: MIT Press.

Ochs, E., & Schiefflin, B. B. (1982). Language acquisition and socialization: Three developmental stories and their implications. *Sociolinguistic Working Paper, 105,* Austin TX: Southwest Educational Development Laboratory.

Owens, W. A., Jr. (1953). Age and mental abilities: A longitudinal study. *Genetic Psychology Monographs, 48,* 3–54.

Paraskevopoulos, J., & Hunt, J. McV. (1971). Object construction and imitation under differing conditions of rearing. *Journal of Genetic Psychology, 119,* 301–21.

Pascual-Leone, J. (1970). A mathematical model for the transition rule in Piaget's development stages. *Acta Psychologica, 32,* 301–45.

Pascual-Leone, J. (1979). Intelligence and experience: A neo-Piagetian approach. *Instructional Science, 8,* 301–67.

Pascual-Leone, J. (1980). Constructive problems for constructive theories: The current relevance of Piaget's work and a critique of information-processing simulation psychology. In R. H. Kluwe & H. Spada (Eds.), *Developmental models of thinking* (pp. 263–96). New York: Academic Press.

Pascual-Leone, J. (1983). Growing into human maturity: Toward a meta-subjective theory of adulthood stages. In P. B. Baltes & O. G. Brim (Eds.), *Life-span development and behavior* (Vol. 5, pp. 118–56). New York: Academic Press.

Pascual-Leone, J. (1987). Organismic processes for neo-Piagetian theories: A dialectical causal account of cognitive development. *International Journal of Psychology, 22,* 531–70.

Pellegrino, J. W., & Glaser, R. (1979). Cognitive correlates and components in the analysis of individual differences. In R. J. Sternberg & D. K. Detterman (Eds.), *Human intelligence: Perspectives on its theory and measurement* (pp. 61–88). Norwood, NJ: Ablex.

Pellegrino, J. W., & Glaser, R. (1980). Components of inductive reasoning. In R. E. Snow, P. -A. Federico, & W. E. Montague (Eds.), *Aptitude, learning, and instruction: Cognitive process analyses of aptitude* (Vol. 1, pp. 177–217). Hillsdale, NJ: Erlbaum.

Pellegrino, J. W., & Kail, R. (1982). Process analyses of spatial aptitude. In R. J. Sternberg (Ed.), *Advances in the psychology of human intelligence* (Vol. 1, pp. 311–65). Hillsdale, NJ: Erlbaum.

Peluffo, N. (1967). Culture and cognitive problems. *International Journal of Psychology, 2*, 187–98.

Penfield, W., & Roberts, L. (1959). *Speech and brain mechanisms.* Princeton, NJ: Princeton University Press.

Perfetti, C. A., & Lesgold, A. M. (1977). Discourse comprehension and sources of individual differences. In M. Just & P. Carpenter (Eds.), *Cognitive processes in comprehension: The 12th annual Carnegie Symposium on cognition* (pp. 141–83). Hillsdale, NJ: Erlbaum.

Piaget, J. (1926). *The language and thought of the child* (M. Gabain, Trans.). London: Routledge & Kegan Paul; New York: Harcourt Brace.

Piaget, J. (1928). *Judgment and reasoning in the child.* London: Routledge & Kegen Paul.

Piaget, J. (1952a). *The child's conception of number.* New York: Norton.

Piaget, J. (1952b). *The origins of intelligence in children.* New York: International Universities Press.

Piaget, J. (1954). *The construction of reality in the child.* New York: Basic.

Piaget, J. (1966). Necessité et signification des recherches comparatives en psychologie genetique. *Journal International de Psychologie, 1*, 3–13.

Piaget, J. (1970). Piaget's theory. In P. H. Mussen (Ed.), *Carmichuel's manual of child psychology* (Vol. 1, 3rd ed., pp. 703–32). New York: Wiley.

Piaget, J. (1972). *The psychology of intelligence.* Totowa, NJ: Littlefield Adams.

Piaget, J. (1977). *The development of thought: Equilibration of cognitive structures* (Arnold Rosin, Trans.). New York: Viking.

Piaget, J., & Inhelder, B. (1962). *Le développement des quantités physiques chez l'enfant: Conservation et atomisme* (2nd ed.). Neuchatel, Switzerland: Delachaux et Niestle.

Piaget, J., & Inhelder, B. (1969). *The psychology of the child.* New York: Basic.

Plomin, R. (1988). The nature and nurture of cognitive abilities. In R. J. Sternberg (Ed.), *Advances in the psychology of human intelligence* (Vol. 4, pp. 1–33). Hillsdale, NJ: Erlbaum.

Polya, G. (1957). *How to solve it.* New York: Doubleday Anchor.

Posner, M. I., & Mitchell, R. F. (1967). Chronometric analysis of classification. *Psychological Review, 74*, 392–409.

Price-Williams, D. R. (1961). A study concerning concepts of conservation of quantities among primitive children. *Acta Psychologia, 18*, 297–305.

Price-Williams, D. R. (1962). Abstract and concrete modes of classification in a primitive society. *British Journal of Educational Psychology, 32*, 50–61.

Price-Williams, D. R., Gordon, W., & Ramirez, W. G. (1969). Skill and conservation: A study of pottery-making children. *Developmental Psychology, 1*, 769.

Prince, J. R. (1968). Science concepts among school children. *South Pacific Bulletin, 18,* 21–8.

Prince, J. R. (1969). *Science concepts in Pacific culture.* Sydney: Angus & Robertson.

Quinlan, J. R. (1979). Discovering rules from large collections of examples: A case study. In D. Michie (Ed.), *Expert systems in the micro-electronic age* (pp. 168–201). Edinburgh University Press.

Raaheim, K. (1974). *Problem solving and intelligence.* Oslo: Universitetsforlaget.

Raaheim, K. (1984). *Why intelligence is not enough.* Bergen, Norway: Sigma Forlag.

Reitman, J. S. (1976). Skilled perception in Go: Deducing memory structures from inter-response times. *Cognitive Psychology, 8,* 336–56.

Reitman, W. (1965). *Cognition and thought.* New York: Wiley.

Resnick, L. B., & Ford, W. W. (1981). *The psychology of mathematics for instruction.* Hillsdale, NJ: Erlbaum.

Resnick, L. B., & Glaser, R. (1976). Problem solving and intelligence. In L. B. Resnick (Ed.), *The nature of intelligence* (pp.205–30). Hillsdale, NJ: Erlbaum.

Riegel, K. F., & Riegel, R. M. (1972). Development, drop, and death. *Developmental Psychology, 6,* 306–19.

Rieger, C. (1975). Conceptual memory and inference. In R. C. Schank (Ed.), *Conceptual information processing* (pp. 157–288). Amsterdam: North Holland.

Riley, C. A., & Trabasso, T. (1974). Comparatives, logical structures, and encoding in a transitive inference task. *Journal of Experimental Child Psychology, 17,* 187–203.

Risberg, J., Maximilian, V. A., & Prohovnik, I. (1977). Changes of cortical activity patterns during habituation to a reasoning task. A study with the ^{133}XE inhalation technique for measurement of regional cerebral blood flow. *Neuropsychologia, 15,* 793–8.

Roediger, H. (1980). Memory metaphors in cognitive psychology. *Memory and Cognition, 8,* 231–46

Rose, S. A., & Blank, M. (1974). The potency of context in children's cognition: An illustration through conservation. *Child Development, 45,* 499–502.

Rosenblatt, F. (1958). The Perceptron: A probabilistic model for information storage and organization in the brain. *Psychological Review, 65,* 386–407.

Royer, F. L. (1971). Information processing of visual figures in the digit symbol substitution task. *Journal of Experimental Psychology, 87,* 335–42.

Rumelhart, D. E. (1980). Schemata: The building blocks of cognition. In R. J. Spiro, B. C. Bruce, & W. F. Brewer (Eds.), *Theoretical issues in reading comprehension: Perspectives from cognitive psychology, linguistics, artificial intelligence, and education* (pp. 33–58). Hillsdale, NJ: Erlbaum.

Rumelhart, D. E., Hinton, G. E., & McClelland, J. L. (1986). A general framework for parallel distributed processing. In D. E. Rumelhart, J. L. McClelland, & The PDP Research Group, *Parallel distributed processing. Explorations in the microstructure of cognition. Vol. 1: Foundations* (pp. 45–76). Cambridge, MA: MIT Press.

Rumelhart, D. E., & McClelland, J. L. (1986). PDP models and general issues in cognitive science. In D. E. Rumelhart, J. L. McClelland, & the PDP Research Group, *Parallel distributed processing. Explorations in the microstructure of cognition. Vol. 1: Foundations* (pp. 110–46). Cambridge, MA: MIT Press.

Rumelhart, D. E., McClelland, J. L., & The PDP Research Group. (1986). *Parallel distributed processing. Explorations in the microstructure of cognition. Vol. 1: Foundations* (pp. 110–146). Cambridge, MA: MIT Press.

Rumelhart, D. E., Smolensky, P., McClelland, J. L., & Hinton, G. E. (1986). Schemata and sequential thought processes in PDP models. In J. L. McClelland, D. E. Rumelhart, & The PDP Research Group, *Parallel distributed processing. Explorations in the microstructure of cognition. Vol. 2: Psychological and biological models* (pp. 7–57). Cambridge, MA: MIT Press.

Samuel, A. L. (1959). Some studies in machine learning using the game of checkers. *IBM Journal of Research and Development, 3*, 211–29.

Samuel, A. L. (1963). Some studies in machine learning using the game of checkers. In E. A. Feigenbaum & J. Feldman (Eds.), *Computers and thought* (pp. 71–108). New York: McGraw-Hill.

Scarr, S., & Carter-Saltzman, L. (1982). Intelligence and behavior genetics. In R. J. Sternberg (Ed.), *Handbook of human intelligence* (pp. 792–896). Cambridge University Press.

Schafer, E. W. P. (1982). Neural adaptability: A biological determinant of behavioral intelligence. *International Journal of Neuroscience, 17*, 183–91.

Schaie, K. W. (1965). A general model for the study of developmental problems. *Psychological Bulletin, 64*, 92–107.

Schaie, K. W. (1973). Developmental processes and aging. In C. Eisdorfer & M. P. Lawton (Eds.), *The psychology of adult development and aging* (pp. 151–219). Washington, DC: American Psychological Association.

Schaie, K. W. (1974). Translations in gerontology – from lab to life. *American Psychologist, 29*, 802–7.

Schaie, K. W., & Baltes, P. B. (1977). Some faith helps to see the forest: A final comment on the Horn and Donaldson myth of the Baltes–Schaie position on adult intelligence. *American Psychologist, 32*, 1118–20.

Schank, R. C. (1972). Conceptual dependency: A theory of natural language understanding. *Cognitive Psychology, 3*, 552–631.

Schank, R. C. (1975). *Conceptual information processing.* Amsterdam: North Holland.

Schank, R. C. (1978). *Interestingness: Controlling inferences* (Computer Science Research Report No. 145). New Haven, CT: Yale University.

Schank, R. C. (1980). How much intelligence is there in artificial intelligence? *Intelligence, 4,* 1–14.

Schank, R. C. (1984). *The explanation game* (Computer Science Research Report No. 307). New Haven, CT: Yale University.

Schank, R. C., & Abelson, R. P. (1977). *Scripts, plans, goals, and understanding.* Hillsdale, NJ: Erlbaum.

Schank, R. C., Lebowitz, M., & Birnbaum, L. A. (1978). *Integrated partial parsing* (Computer Science Research Report No. 143). New Haven, CT: Yale University.

Schiller, B. (1934). Verbal, numerical and spatial abilities of young children. *Archives of Psychology, 161,* 1–69.

Schneck, M. R. (1929). The measurement of verbal and numerical abilities. *Archives of Psychology, 107,* 1–49.

Schneider, W. (1985). Toward a model of attention and the development of automatic processing. In M. I. Posner & O. S. M. Marin (Eds.), *Attention and performance II* (pp. 474–92). Hillsdale, NJ: Erlbaum.

Schneider, W., & Shiffrin, R. M. (1977). Controlled and automatic human information processing: 1. Detection, search, and attention. *Psychological Review, 84,* 1–66.

Schustack, M. W., & Sternberg, R. J. (1981). Evaluation of evidence in causal inference. *Journal of Experimental Psychology: General, 110,* 101–20.

Scribner, S. (1984). Studying working intelligence. In B. Rogoff & J. Lave (Eds.), *Everyday cognition* (pp. 9–40). Cambridge, MA: Harvard University Press.

Segall, M. H. (1979). *Cross-cultural psychology.* Monterey, CA: Brooks/Cole.

Segall, M., Campbell, D. T., & Herskovits, M. J. (1966). *The influence of culture on visual perception.* Indianapolis, IN: Bobbs-Merrill.

Selfridge, O. G., & Neisser, U. (1960). Pattern recognition by machine. *Scientific American, 203,* 60–8.

Serpell, R. (1974). Aspects of intelligence in a developing country. *African Social Research,* No. 17, 576–96.

Serpell, R. (1976). *Culture's influence on behaviour.* London: Methuen.

Serpell, R. (1979). How specific are perceptual skills? A cross-cultural study of pattern reproduction. *British Journal of Psychology, 70,* 365–80.

Sharp, S. E. (1899). Individual psychology: A study in psychological method. *American Journal of Psychology, 10,* 329–91.

Shepard, R. N., & Metzler, J. (1971). Mental rotation of three-dimensional objects. *Science, 171,* 701–3.

Shiffrin, R. M., & Schneider, W. (1977). Controlled and automatic human information processing: 2. Perceptual learning, automatic attending, and a general theory. *Psychological Review, 84,* 127–90.

Shortliffe, E. H. (1976). *Computer-based medical consultation:* MYCIN. New York: Elsevier.

Siegel, L. S. (1978). The relationship of language and thought in the preoperational child: A reconsideration of nonverbal alternatives to Piagetian tasks. In L. S. Siegel & C. J. Brainerd (Eds.), *Alternatives to Piaget: Critical essays on the theory.* New York: Academic Press.

Siegel, L. S., & Brainerd, C. J. (Eds.) (1978). *Alternatives to Piaget: Critical essays on the theory.* New York: Academic Press.

Siegler, R. S. (1976). Three aspects of cognitive development. *Cognitive Psychology, 8,* 481–520.

Siegler, R. S. (1978). The origins of scientific reasoning. In R. S. Siegler (Ed.), *Children's thinking: What develops?* (pp. 109–49). Hillsdale, NJ: Erlbaum.

Siegler, R. S. (1981). Developmental sequences within and between concepts. *Monographs of the Society for Research in Child Development, 46* (Serial No. 189).

Siegler, R. S. (1984). Mechanisms of cognitive growth: Variation and selection. In R. J. Sternberg (Ed.), *Mechanisms of cognitive development* (pp. 141–62). New York: Freeman.

Siegler, R. S. (1986). Unities across domains in children's strategy choices. In M. Perlmutter (Ed.), *Perspectives on intellectual development: The Minnesota Symposia on child psychology* (Vol. 19, pp. 1–48). Hillsdale, NJ: Erlbaum.

Siegler, R. S. (1987). The perils of averaging data over strategies: An example from children's addition. *Journal of Experimental Psychology: General, 116,* 250–64.

Siegler, R. S., & Richards, D. D. (1982). The development of intelligence. In R. J. Sternberg (Ed.), *Handbook of human intelligence* (pp. 897–971). Cambridge University Press.

Sigel, I. E., & Hooper, F. H. (1968). *Logical thinking in children: Research based on Piaget's theory.* New York: Holt, Rinehart, & Winston.

Simon, D. P., & Simon, H. A. (1978). Individual differences in solving physics problems. In R. S. Siegler (Ed.), *Children's thinking: What develops?* (pp. 325–48). Hillsdale, NJ: Erlbaum.

Simon, H. A, & Kotovsky, K. (1963). Human acquisition of concepts for sequential patterns. *Psychological Review, 70,* 534–46.

Simon, H. A., & Reed, S. K. (1976). Modeling strategy shifts in a problem-solving task. *Cognitive Psychology, 8,* 86–97.

Sincoff, J. B., & Sternberg, R. J. (1987). Two faces of verbal ability. *Intelligence, 11,* 263–76.

Sinha, D. (1977). Orientation and attitude of social psychologists in a developing country: The Indian case. *International Review of Applied Psychology, 26*, 1–10.

Sinha, D. (1983). Human assessment in the Indian context. In S. H. Irvine & J. W. Berry (Eds.), *Human assessment and cultural factors* (pp. 17–34). New York: Plenum.

Snow, R. E. (1979). Theory and method for research on aptitude processes. In R. J. Sternberg & D. K. Detterman (Eds.), *Human intelligence: Perspectives on its theory and measurement* (pp. 105–37). Norwood, NJ: Ablex.

Snow, R. E. (1980). Aptitude processes. In R. E. Snow, P. -A. Federico, & W. E. Montague (Eds.), *Aptitude, learning, and instruction: Cognitive process analyses of aptitude* (Vol. 1, pp. 27–63). Hillsdale, NJ: Erlbaum.

Snow, R. E., Kyllonen, P. C., & Marshalek, B. (1984). The topography of ability and learning correlations. In R. J. Sternberg (Ed.), *Advances in the psychology of human intelligence* (Vol. 2, pp. 47–103). Hillsdale, NJ: Erlbaum.

Snow, R. E., & Lohman, D. F. (1984). Toward a theory of cognitive aptitude for learning from instruction. *Journal of Educational Psychology, 76*, 347–76.

Soloway, E., Lochhead, J., & Clement, J. (1982). Does computer programming enhance problem solving ability? Some positive evidence of algebra word problems. In R. J. Seidel, R. E. Anderson, & B. Hunter (Eds.), *Computer literacy.* New York: Academic Press.

Sontag, L. W., Baker, C. T., & Nelson, V. L. (1958). Mental growth and personality development: A longitudinal study. *Monographs of the Society for Research in Child Development, 23* (2, Whole No. 68).

Spada, H., & Kluwe, R. H. (1980). Two models of intellectual development and their reference to the theory of Piaget. In R. H. Kluwe & H. Spada (Eds.), *Developmental models of thinking* (pp. 1-31). New York: Academic Press.

Spearman, C. (1904). General intelligence, objectively determined and measured. *American Journal of Psychology, 15*, 201–93.

Spearman, C. (1923). *The nature of 'intelligence' and the principles of cognition.* London: Macmillan.

Spearman, C. (1927). *The abilities of man.* New York: Macmillan.

Spencer, H. (1886). *The principles of psychology* (Vol. 5). New York: Appleton.

Sperry, R. W. (1961). Cerebral organization and behavior. *Science, 133*, 1749–57.

Sperry, R. W., Myers, R. E., & Schrier, A. M. (1960). Perceptual capacity of the isolated visual cortex in the cat. *Quarterly Journal of Experimental Psychology, 12*, 65–71.

Springer, S. P., & Deutsch, G. (1985). *Left brain, right brain* (2nd ed.). New York: Freeman.

Stefik, M., Aikins, J., Balzer, R., Benoit, J., Birnbaum, L., Hayes-Roth, F., & Sacerdoti, E. (1983). Basic concepts for building expert systems. In F. Hayes-Roth, D. A. Waterman, & D. B. Lenat (Eds.), *Building expert systems* (pp. 59–86). Reading, MA: Addison Wesley.

Sternberg, R. J. (1977). *Intelligence, information processing, and analogical reasoning: The componential analysis of human abilities*. Hillsdale, NJ: Erlbaum.

Sternberg, R. J. (1979). The nature of mental abilities. *American Psychologist, 34,* 214–30.

Sternberg, R. J. (1980a). Representation and process in linear syllogistic reasoning. *Journal of Experimental Psychology: General, 109,* 119–59.

Sternberg, R. J. (1980b). Sketch of a componential subtheory of human intelligence. *Behavioral and Brain Sciences, 3,* 573–84.

Sternberg, R. J. (1981a). Intelligence and nonentrenchment. *Journal of Educational Psychology, 73,* 1–16.

Sternberg, R. J. (1981b). The nature of intelligence. *New York University Quarterly Review of Education, 12,* 10 17.

Sternberg, R. J. (1981c). Testing and cognitive psychology. *American Psychologist, 36,* 1181–9.

Sternberg, R. J. (Ed.) (1982a). *Handbook of human intelligence.* Cambridge University Press.

Sternberg, R. J. (1982b). Reasoning, problem solving, and intelligence. In R. J. Sternberg (Ed.), *Handbook of human intelligence* (pp. 225–307). Cambridge University Press.

Sternberg, R. J. (1983). Components of human intelligence. *Cognition, 15,* 1–48.

Sternberg, R. J. (Ed.) (1984a). *Human abilities: An information-processing approach.* New York: Freeman.

Sternberg, R. J. (1984b). The Kaufman Assessment Battery for Children: An information-processing analysis and critique. *Journal of Special Education, 18,* 269–79.

Sternberg, R. J. (1985a). *Beyond IQ: A triarchic theory of human intelligence.* Cambridge University Press.

Sternberg, R. J. (1985b). Implicit theories of intelligence, creativity, and wisdom. *Journal of Personality and Social Psychology, 49,* 607–27.

Sternberg, R. J. (1986). *Intelligence applied: Understanding and increasing your intellectual skills.* San Diego: Harcourt Brace Jovanovich.

Sternberg, R. J. (1987a). Most vocabulary is learned from context. In M. McKeown (Ed.), *The nature of vocabulary acquisition* (pp. 89–105). Hillsdale, NJ: Erlbaum.

Sternberg, R. J. (1987b). Second game: A school's-eye view of intelligence. In J. A. Langer (Ed.), *Language, literacy, and culture: Issues of society and schooling* (pp. 23–48). Norwood, NJ: Ablex.

Sternberg, R. J. (1987c). Teaching intelligence: The application of cognitive psychology to the improvement of intellectual skills. In J. B. Baron & R. J. Sternberg (Eds.), *Teaching thinking skills: Theory and practice* (pp. 182–218). New York: Freeman.

Sternberg, R. J. (1988). *The triarchic mind: A new theory of human intelligence*. New York: Viking.

Sternberg, R. J. (in press). *Sternberg Triarchic Abilities Test*. San Antonio, TX: The Psychological Corporation.

Sternberg, R. J., Conway, B. E., Ketron, J. L., & Bernstein, M. (1981). People's conceptions of intelligence. *Journal of Personality and Social Psychology, 41,* 37–55.

Sternberg, R. J., & Davidson, J. E. (1982, June). The mind of the puzzler. *Psychology Today, 16,* 37–44.

Sternberg, R. J., & Davidson, J. E. (1983). Insight in the gifted. *Educational Psychologist, 18,* 51–7.

Sternberg, R. J., & Davidson, (Eds.) (1986). *Conceptions of giftedness.* Cambridge University Press.

Sternberg, R. J., & Detterman, D. K. (Eds.) (1986). *What is intelligence? Contemporary viewpoints on its nature and definition.* Norwood, NJ: Ablex.

Sternberg, R. J., & Gardner, M. K. (1982). A componential interpretation of the general factor in human intelligence. In H. J. Eysenck (Ed.), *A model for intelligence* (pp. 231–54). Berlin: Springer.

Sternberg, R. J., & Ketron, J. L. (1982). Selection and implementation of strategies in reasoning by analogy. *Journal of Educational Psychology, 74,* 399–413.

Sternberg, R. J., & Powell, J. S. (1983a). Comprehending verbal comprehension. *American Psychologist, 38,* 878–93.

Sternberg, R. J., & Powell, J. S. (1983b). The development of intelligence. In P. H. Mussen (Series Ed.) & J. Flavell & E. Markman (Vol. Eds.), *Handbook of child psychology* (Vol. 3, 4th ed., pp. 341–419). New York: Wiley.

Sternberg, R. J., & Rifkin, B. (1979). The development of analogical reasoning processes. *Journal of Experimental Child Psychology, 27,* 195–232.

Sternberg, R. J., & Spear, L. C. (1985). A triarchic theory of mental retardation. In N. Ellis & N. Bray (Eds.), *International review of research in mental retardation* (Vol. 13, pp. 301–26). New York: Academic Press.

Sternberg, R. J., & Suben, J. (1986). The socialization of intelligence. In M. Perlmutter (Ed.), *Perspectives on intellectual development: Minnesota symposia on child psychology* (Vol. 19, pp. 201–35). Hillsdale, NJ: Erlbaum.

Sternberg, R. J., & Weil, E. M. (1980). An aptitude-strategy interaction in linear syllogistic reasoning. *Journal of Educational Psychology, 72,* 226–34.

Sternberg, S. (1969). Memory-scanning. Mental processes revealed by reaction-time experiments. *American Scientist, 4,* 421–57.

Stott, L. H., & Ball, R. S. (1965). Infant and preschool mental tests. *Monographs of the Society for Research in Child Development, 30,* (3, Whole No. 101).

Suchmann, R. G., & Trabasso, T. (1966). Color and form preference in young children. *Journal of Experimental Child Psychology, 3,* 177–87.

Super, C. M. (1976). Environmental effects on motor development: The case of African infant precocity. *Developmental Medicine and Child Neurology, 18,* 561–7.

Super, C. M. (1983). Cultural variation in the meaning and uses of children's "intelligence." In J. B. Deregowski, S. Dziurawiec, & R. C. Annis (Eds.), *Expiscations in cross-cultural psychology* (pp. 199–212). Lisse: Swets & Zeitlinger.

Super, C. M., & Harkness, S. (1982). The infants' niche in rural Kenya and metropolitan America. In L. L. Adler (Ed.), *Cross-cultural research at issue* (pp. 47–55). New York: Academic Press.

Sutton, R. S., & Barto, A. G. (1981). Toward a modern theory of adaptive networks: Expectation and prediction. *Psychological Review, 88,* 135–70.

Terman, L. M. (1925). *Genetic studies of genius: Mental and physical traits of a thousand gifted children* (Vol. 1). Stanford, CA: Stanford University Press.

Terman, L. M., & Merrill, M. A. (1937). *Measuring intelligence.* Boston: Houghton Mifflin.

Terman, L. M., & Merrill, M. A. (1973). *Stanford–Binet intelligence scale: Manual for the third revision.* Boston: Houghton Mifflin.

Terman, L. M., & Oden, M. H. (1959). *Genetic studies of genius (Vol. 4): The gifted group at midlife.* Stanford, CA: Stanford University Press.

Thagard, P. R. (1984). Frames, knowledge, and inference. *Synthese, 61,* 233–59.

Thagard, P. R. (1986). Parallel computation and the mind–body problem. *Cognitive Science, 10,* 301–18.

Thompson, G. H. (1939). *The factorial analysis of human ability.* London: University of London Press.

Thorndike, E. L. (1924). The measurement of intelligence: Present status. *Psychological Review, 31,* 219–52.

Thorndike, E. L., Bregman, E. D., Cobb, M. V., & Woodyard, E. I. (1926). *The measurement of intelligence.* New York: Teachers College.

Thorndyke, P. W. (1976). The role of inferences in discourse comprehension. *Journal of Verbal Learning and Verbal Behavior, 15,* 437–46.

Thurstone, L. L. (1924). *The nature of intelligence.* New York: Harcourt Brace.

Thurstone, L. L. (1938). *Primary mental abilities*. Chicago: University of Chicago Press.

Thurstone, L. L. (1947). *Multiple factor analysis*. Chicago: University of Chicago Press.

Thurstone, L. L., & Thurstone, T. G. (1941). *Factorial studies of intelligence*. Chicago: University of Chicago Press.

Toklas, A. B. (1963). *What is remembered?* New York: Holt.

Tuddenham, R. D. (1968). *Psychometricizing Piaget's methode clinique.* Paper presented at the American Educational Research Association Convention, Chicago.

Tuddenham, R. D. (1970). A "Piagetian" test of cognitive development. In W. B. Dockrell (Ed.), *On intelligence* (pp. 49–70). Toronto: Ontario Institute for Studies in Education.

Tuddenham, R. D. (1971). Theoretical regularities and individual idiosyncrasies. In D. R. Green, M. P. Ford, & G. B. Flamer (Eds.), *Measurement and Piaget* (pp. 64–80). New York: McGraw-Hill.

Uzgiris, I. C. (1968). Situational generality of conservation. In I. E. Sigel & F. H. Hooper (Eds.), *Logical thinking in children: Research based on Piaget's theory* (pp. 40–52). New York: Holt, Rinehart, & Winston.

Uzgiris, I. C., & Hunt, J. McV. (1966). *An instrument for assessing infant psychological development* (Rev. provisional form). Urbana: Dept. of Psychology, University of Illinois.

Vernon, P. E. (1969). *Intelligence and cultural environment*. London: Methuen.

Vernon, P. E. (1971). *The structure of human abilities*. London: Methuen.

Vygotsky, L. S. (1962). *Thought and language*. Cambridge, MA: MIT Press.

Vygotsky, L. S. (1978). *Mind in society: The development of higher psychological processes*. Cambridge, MA: Harvard University Press.

Wagner, D. A. (1978). Memories of Morocco: The influence of age, schooling and environment on memory. *Cognitive Psychology, 10,* 1–28.

Wagner, R. K., & Sternberg, R. J. (1984). Alternative conceptions of intelligence and their implications for education. *Review of Educational Research, 54,* 197–224.

Wagner, R. K. & Sternberg, R. J. (1987). Executive control in reading comprehension. In B. K. Britton & S. M. Glynn (Eds.), *Executive control processes in reading* (pp. 1–21). Hillsdale, NJ: Erlbaum.

Wallach, M. A., & Kogan, N. (1961). Aspects of judgment and decision-making: Interrelationships and changes with age. *Behavioral Science, 6,* 23–36.

Walters, J. M., & Gardner, H. (1986). The theory of multiple intelligences: Some issues and answers. In R. J. Sternberg & R. K. Wagner (Eds.), *Practical intelligence: Nature and origins of competence in the everyday world* (pp. 163–82). Cambridge University Press.

Wechsler, D. (1939). *The measurement of adult intelligence.* Baltimore, MD: Williams & Wilkins.

Wechsler, D. (1958). *The measurement and appraisal of adult intelligence (5th ed.).* Baltimore, MD: Williams & Wilkins.

Wechsler, D. (1974). *Manual for the Wechsler Intelligence Scale for Children* (rev.). New York: Psychological Corporation.

Were, K. (1968). *A survey of the thought processes of New Guinean secondary students.* Unpublished M.Ed. thesis; University of Adelaide.

Werner, E. E. (1972). Infants around the world: Cross-cultural studies of psychomotor development from birth to two years. *Journal of Cross-Cultural Psychology, 3,* 111–34.

Werner, H. (1948). *Comparative psychology of mental development* (rev. ed.). New York: International Universities Press.

Werner, H., & Kaplan, E. (1952). The acquisition of word meanings: A developmental study. *Monographs of the Society for Research in Child Development* (No. 51).

Whitely, S. E. (1980). Latent trait models in the study of intelligence. *Intelligence, 4,* 97–132.

Winston, P. H. (1975). Learning structural descriptions from examples. In P. H. Winston (Ed.), *The psychology of computer vision* (pp. 157–209). New York: McGraw-Hill.

Wissler, C. (1901). The correlation of mental and physical tests. *Psychological Review, Monograph Supplement, 3,* No. 6.

Witelson, S. F. (1976). Sex and the single hemisphere: Specialization of the right hemisphere for spatial processing. *Science, 193,* 425–7.

Witkin, H. A. (1967). Cognitive styles across cultures: A cognitive style approach to cross-cultural research. *International Journal of Psychology, 2,* 233–50.

Witkin, H. A., Dyk, R. B., Faterson, H. F., Goodenough, D. R., & Karp, S. A. (1962). *Psychological differentiation.* New York: Wiley.

Wober, M. (1974). Towards an understanding of the Kiganda concept of intelligence. In J. W. Berry & P. R. Dasen (Eds.), *Culture and cognition: Readings in cross-cultural psychology* (pp. 261–80). London: Methuen.

Wolman, B. B. (Ed.) (1985). *Handbook of intelligence: Theories, measurements, and applications.* New York: Wiley.

Woods, B. T., & Teuber, H. L. (1978). Changing patterns of childhood aphasia. *Annals of Neurology, 3,* 273–80.

Woods, S. S., Resnick, L. B., & Groen, G. J. (1975). An experimental test of five process models for subtraction. *Journal of Educational Psychology, 67,* 17–21.

Yussen, S. R., & Kane, P. (1985). Children's concept of intelligence. In S. R. Yussen (Ed.), *The growth of reflection in children* (pp. 207–41). New York: Academic Press.

Zaidel, E. (1975). A technique for presenting lateralized visual input with prolonged exposure. *Vision Research, 15,* 283–9.

Zaidel, E. (1978). Auditory language comprehension in the right hemisphere following cerebral commissurotomy and hemispherectomy: A comparison with child language and aphasia. In A. Caramazza & E. Zurif (Eds.), *Language acquisition and language breakdown.* Baltimore, MD: Johns Hopkins University Press.

Zigler, E. (1971). The retarded child as a whole person. In H. E. Adams & W. K. Boardman III (Eds.), *Advances in Experimental Clinical Psychology* (Vol. 1). Elmford, NY: Pergamon.

Zigler, E., Balla, D., & Hodapp, R. (1984). On the definition and classification of mental retardation. *American Journal of Mental Deficiency, 89,* 215–30.

Name index

Subject index

abilities: crystallized vs. fluid, 95, 107–9; increase in number of, 100–1; level I and II, 95; primary mental, 92–4; verbal vs. spatial, 94
ability to learn, 24
accommodation, *see* equilibration
adaptation, 75–6; to environment, 223, 225–6, 231–2, 238, 278–9; and functioning in society, 48, 178–9
age: chronological, 79; mental, 79–80
agencies, 95
algorithms, 130–2
anti-intellectualism, 25–6
apprehension, *see* principles of cognition, qualitative
architecture of systems: PDP models and, 144; and problem types, 138–9
artificial intelligence, 45, 130–3; *see also* cognitive science
assimilation, *see* equilibration
associations, 89–90
attention arousal, 165–6
attributes of intelligence, 33–35; comparison of, in 1921 and 1986 Symposia, 50–3; loci of, 36–49
attribution of intelligence, 46
automatization, 123, 277–8

behavior and intelligence: academic, 40; practical, 41; social, 40

beliefs as knowledge structures, 136
Berkeley Growth Study: and absolute increases in intelligence, 107; factor analysis of, 101–3, 105; 5-stage model of, 105, 108
bifactor theory, 94
biology as basis of intelligence, 45
bonds, 88–9; vs. connections, 89–90
brain: right vs. left, 28 (*see also* hemispheric specialization); size, 173
brain damage: and study of multiple intelligences, 262–3; types of, 166–9
brain functioning, 163–6; blood flow studies of, 12, 176; and cell assemblies, 164–5; differentiation of, 165–6; electrophysiological studies of, 173–6; and evoked potentials, 174–5; and functional cerebral space, 172–3; and gnostic units, 163; and hemispheric specialization, 166–73; and intelligence B, 164; modular, 172–3; and novelty, 175; theories of, 163–6

capacities as intelligence, 46, 95
capacity, *see* memory, capacity and processing limitations
cell assembly, 164–5
circumplex, *see* radex
cognitive map, 249, *see also* Mediated Learning Experience